Essays and Reviews

A Selection of Books by Bernard Williams

Morality: An Introduction to Ethics
Utilitarianism: For and Against (with J.J.C. Smart)
Descartes: The Project of Pure Enquiry
Moral Luck
Ethics and the Limits of Philosophy
Shame and Necessity
Plato: The Invention of Philosophy
Truth and Truthfulness: An Essay in Genealogy

   ...

Collections of Essays Published Posthumously

On Opera
*In the Beginning Was the Deed: Realism and Moralism
   in Political Argument*
The Sense of the Past: Essays in the History of Philosophy

Essays and Reviews

1959–2002

Bernard Williams

Foreword by Michael Wood

PRINCETON UNIVERSITY PRESS

Princeton and Oxford

Published by Princeton University Press, 41 William Street,
  Princeton, New Jersey 08540
In the United Kingdom: Princeton University Press, 6 Oxford Street,
  Woodstock, Oxfordshire OX20 1TW

press.princeton.edu

LIBRARY OF CONGRESS CATALOGING-IN-PUBLICATION DATA

Williams, Bernard, 1929-2003.
    Essays and reviews, 1959-2002 / Bernard Williams ; foreword by Michael
    Wood.
        pages cm
    Includes bibliographical references and index.
    ISBN 978-0-691-15985-0 (hardcover : alk. paper)
    1. Philosophy, English—20th century.
    2. Philosophy, British—20th century. I. Title.
    B1674.W49451 2014
    192—dc23   2013022385

British Library Cataloging-in-Publication Data is available

This book has been composed in Sabon and Ideal Sans

Printed on acid-free paper ∞

Printed in the United States of America

10 9 8 7 6 5 4 3 2 1

CONTENTS

In the first of the reviews reprinted in the present volume, Bernard Williams recalls and dismisses what he trusts is an outdated estimation of Plato, sharply expressing his ironic surprise that anyone should ever have offered or accepted it. Far from seeing the *Republic* as "one of the noblest monuments of Western liberalism and enlightenment," Williams finds in it only an "extraordinary tissue of historical falsehood and philosophical misunderstanding," and support for a "political system . . . based on oligarchic deceit and a contempt for much legitimate aspiration and human diversity." Plato represents "as a system of consent what must actually be, on his own premises, a system of coercion." This is fine, fiery writing and leaves us in no doubt about Williams's own political and moral position. Or about his interest in the chances and importance of independence of mind. The same review includes a characteristic use and definition of the word "provocative." The book under consideration, a reissue of *Plato Today*, by Richard Crossman, a Member of Parliament and distinguished Labour Party intellectual, is said to be "provocative in the best sense—provocative of thought."

Williams had a distinguished career as an academic philosopher—he won a prize fellowship at All Souls, Oxford as soon as he had finished his first degree, and was appointed to a chair of philosophy in London at the age of thirty-four. Later he held chairs in Cambridge, Oxford, and Berkeley, and from 1979 to 1987 he was provost of King's College, Cambridge. He chaired a government Committee on Obscenity and Film Censorship; he commented frequently and lucidly on many public issues, ranging from religion and law to science and abortion and the future of universities. Much of this work is reflected in this volume, but the essays themselves suggest an intellectual scope and a variety that go beyond even these diverse activities, a life of the mind that only an adventurous mind could live.

Although he was not explicitly or exclusively addressing his professional colleagues in the pieces collected here, Williams always wrote *as a philosopher* in his own ample sense, insisting that philosophy is doing its job wherever curiosity and thinking come together in any serious or cogent way. Such a position allowed him to pay handsome tribute to the disciplines in which he was trained, both classics and philosophy. Analytical philosophy, he said, offers "certain virtues of civilized thought: because it gives reasons and sets out arguments in a way that can be explicitly followed and considered; and because it makes questions clearer and sorts out what is muddled." At the same time Williams was concerned that English (and to some extent American) philosophy had become far too pleased with its aloofness from French and German schools of thought, to the point of regarding them not as philosophical traditions at all but as a form of intellectual circus.

> While the influence of Hegel radically changed the rest of European thought, and continues to work in it, the sceptical caution of British philosophy left it spectacularly immune to it—splendidly, but to its undoubted loss.

Spectacularly, splendidly. The note of tribute remains, but the charge of complacency could hardly be clearer. There is a point, we may think, where "sceptical caution" threatens to outlaw curiosity, and even the notion of inquiry. The point was identified long ago by Descartes, and before him by Montaigne, and Williams comments very astutely on the former's philosophical irony, the "dry joke" that opens the *Discourse on Method*. "Good sense is of all things in the world the most equally distributed," Descartes says, "Le bon sens est la chose du monde la mieux partagée." We think of ourselves as "so abundantly provided with it, that even those most difficult to please in all other matters do not commonly desire more of it than they already possess." This stealthy (and very funny) proposition allows for all kinds of readings, including the contradictory claims that good sense may be indistinguishable from self-congratulation and that even sensible people don't want to be more sensible than they have to be. It certainly implies, in our context, that it is difficult for us to see the good sense of others when it doesn't look like ours.

Williams's style develops in all kinds of ways over the years, but its energy and clarity never fade, and his central concerns, even across a very wide range of topics, are remarkably consistent. The conjunction of history and philosophy in the remarks on Plato is significant too, and the same pairing appears all the way through these essays and reviews, from the early praise of Stuart Hampshire's *Thought and Action* ("he regards historical understanding as essential to grasping all but the absolutely basic characteristics of the human mind") right to the very latest entry, entitled "Why Philosophy Needs History," an essay closely related to Williams's work for his edition of *The Gay Science* (2001) and to his final book, *Truth and Truthfulness* (2002).

Williams cites Nietzsche on the "lack of a historical sense" as the "hereditary defect of philosophers," and goes on to say that the claim, made in 1878, may seem even truer in the first years of the twenty-first century: "a lot of philosophy is more blankly non-historical now than it has ever been." However, the point is not that philosophers should become historians of philosophy:

What matters more is their neglect of another history—the history of the concepts which philosophy is trying to understand. The starting point of philosophy is that we do not understand ourselves well enough. We do not understand ourselves well enough ethically (how or why we should be concerned, positively or negatively, with some human dispositions and practices rather than others); we do not fully understand our political ideals; and we do not understand how we come to have ideas and experiences . . . Philosophy's methods of helping us to understand ourselves involve reflecting on the concepts we use, the modes in which we think about these various things; and sometimes it proposes better ways of doing this.

The "historical falsehood" named in the Plato review arises from a refusal to consult the available record, and the "philosophical misunderstanding" stems from shabby or sentimental logic. Ignoring realities and misconstruing them, not attending or attending badly: these are our favorite, hallowed methods for error, into which we all fall some of the time.

In such modes we fail variously to "get it right," to borrow a phrase Williams uses repeatedly in these pieces. It's worth saying that there is nothing narrowly positivist or hairsplitting about this demand for a capacious set of accuracies. Williams does not dismiss perspectivism along with relativism, and the suggestion that Alasdair MacIntyre for example, should be more "realistic" does not imply that the philosopher should lower his expectations of anyone's paying heed to his brilliant but nostalgic reconstructions of moral history. It implies that he should think more about the way things are and not as they are colored by anyone's desire and dream. Of one book under review here Williams remarks that it is "sometimes inattentive to everyday truths, and it cannot afford to be: no inquiry that is going to help us understand ourselves can do without that kind of truthfulness, an acute and wary sense of the ordinary." "The ordinary," we note, and not the so-often mystified "ordinary language." When we see the way things are, as Wittgenstein remarked in another context, there is a good deal that we shall not say.

Williams believes then, as many philosophers do not, at least when they are doing philosophy, in concrete historical context, what words and actions mean in their place and time—according to "some actual authority in some actual social circumstances," as he says at one point in this book. "All our ways of thinking about the world are conditioned by a given historical context of conventions, manners, and interests." For this reason (among others) he recommends the practice of what he calls "partial scepticism."

The overall sceptical argument that we know nothing at all about other people's minds, for instance, is painless, because it is totally theoretical; it is more disturbing to consider that perhaps we know something about other people, but a lot less than we suppose.

This is to say that a great deal of our knowledge and ignorance is not "totally theoretical," or indeed theoretical at all, and the idea of "painless" skepticism recalls Williams's remark elsewhere about Bertrand Russell's "costless heroics." We might assert, as Henry James did of what he called the real, that the way things are is what we cannot *not* know. We might, but then we would need also to remember that not knowing what we know is one of our favorite forms of evasion and self-protection.

Williams is also unusual among analytic philosophers in (at least) two other ways: he believes in style, and he thinks it is sometimes worth trying to say what can't be said. He describes Descartes, whom we have already seen in action, as "a philosophical stylist of genius." But then "Moore's famous care and precision," Williams says, are virtues to which "he raised an ugly monument in his grinding style," developing "a kind of emphatic vagueness which curiously co-exists with the marks of solicitor-like caution." Heidegger's style is marked by "its lack of light and its dire assertiveness," and his thought cannot escape this marking. Style indeed for Williams is an aspect of thought, a convergence literary historians are as likely to miss or refuse as philosophers are. To their serious disadvantage:

> for how is one to chart the misunderstandings [of a philosopher], without philosophical understanding of what the philosopher really meant? . . . philosophical insight is not something separate from the *literary* understanding of philosophical writing, because it is not separate from understanding philosophical writing at all.

Williams also uses the word "style" more broadly to signify a way of doing philosophy. Thus he can suggest that Nietzsche, in his inflammatory way, was aiming for his own version of accuracy and truthfulness, and that indeed Nietzsche's writing offers a valuable general lesson in this respect: "that there is no one style in philosophy that displays the need to get it right."

Williams has no time for murky or casual thought. "Contradictions in themselves do not make life more abundant. They do not even, much of the time, make it more interesting." Chomsky, we learn, "moves with dangerous speed and simplicity between his theoretical preoccupations and the political ideals for which he has so conspicuously stood up." There is real regret in Williams's noting of a distinguished senior colleague that "there is probably a truth lurking in what Ryle says, but his considerations do not bring it to light."

Yet Williams is allowing for a probability of truth even in this case, and he repeatedly shows what must be seen as a form of wisdom or kindness of thought in relation to human need. We might say of many things, as Williams says of religion, that "it will be hard to give it up even if it is an illusion." He also reminds us that "it is only if religion is true that the most interesting question about it is its truth. If it is false, the most interesting question about it is . . . the content of what it actually tells us about humanity." Williams finds even much of the most original and thoughtful work in modern philosophy—that of John Rawls and Derek Parfit, for example—just a little airless, not quite attentive enough to the "violent and enthusiastic unreasonableness" out there in the historical world.

There is one form of alluring falsehood that tests Williams's kindness to its limits. This is the fancy skepticism found in some deconstructive writing, especially in literary criticism and theory, and sometimes in the arguments of Richard Rorty, which holds that words are all there is or all we can talk about. The rest is silence, or ought to be—a dizzy, literary exacerbation of the last sentence of Wittgenstein's *Tractatus*. As Williams says more than once in this book, citing a colleague at Berkeley, "Tell that to the Veterans of Foreign Texts." The glance—I've heard this saying too from members of the Berkeley community—is toward a notorious sentence in Paul de Man's *Blindness and Insight*: "the bases for historical knowledge are not empirical facts but written texts, even if these texts masquerade in the guise of wars and revolutions." If this sentence means, as de Man may well have thought it did, that wars are nothing but texts, then it is heartless as well as untrue. But is this what it means?

Williams's own generosity of mind helps us to see what is happening. We can ask what needs such claims are supposed to meet, what they tell us about ourselves and others. Manifestly there are many critics and others who have loved the idea of the world as text, to the exclusion of all fleshly pain and sorrow. Equally clearly there are others, and perhaps this set contains even more than the first, who wish to see all talk of text and interpretation as mere obfuscation of the facts we all know. But then we wonder why we or anyone would cherish these simplified, totalizing visions, and our curiosity must wait perhaps on another question, a version of the one Williams takes from Nietzsche and uses to close his eloquent introduction to *The Gay Science*: "it is a question which he wanted his readers to ask themselves not just at the end of this book, but throughout it and indeed throughout all his books—'Is that what you *want*?'"

Reviewing a book on intellectuals, Williams asked and answered in a short space the difficult question the author, Paul Johnson, had spent over three hundred easy pages avoiding. Although the author's argument seemed to be that intellectuals are merely celebrated scoundrels, Williams charitably supposed that Johnson really had a better doubt in mind, namely, "why should the intellectuals have any authority? Why should anyone take any notice of them"—especially if they show no evidence of greater "moral reliability or good judgment" than anyone else? Williams's answer was that if a philosopher like Sartre was respected, it was not because he told some "luminous truth about humanity," in Johnson's sneering phrase, but because he understood

> that politics necessarily involves ideas, and particularly so when it denies this; that political ideas need the surroundings, the criticism, and the life provided by other ideas; and that some people are able to bring those ideas imaginatively into the thoughts of those who are going to live under that politics.

The last words of this review take us back to Williams's early thoughts on Plato's illiberal, coercive vision: "the authority of the intellectual . . . depends on the uncommanded response of those it affects."

A great deal of Williams's thought comes together in these lines: the life of ideas, even when it is unrecognized, the need for imagination in relation to this life—Williams said of Margaret Thatcher and her supporters, "It is not that they have no ideas, but that they lack imagination"—and the sense that the best we can do for others in realms of the mind is think with them rather than for them. We can't command them, and we shouldn't try to improve them. One of Williams's most withering remarks concerns his fear that a book under review "is trying to do a dreadful thing: to lead philosophy back to an aspiration from which the work of this century has done so much to release it, the aspiration to be edifying."

But we can help without seeking to edify—without even seeking to help—and Williams offers a strong suggestion that is invaluable for all serious thinking about thought. Here even Plato gets a kindly nod: at least he went in for provocation.

> As Plato knew, the road to something helpful is not only hard, but unpredictable, and the motives that keep people moving down it don't necessarily have to do with the desire to help. They include that other motive of philosophy, curiosity. In fact, the two motives cannot really be taken apart; the philosophy that is concerned to be helpful cannot be separated from philosophy that aims to help us to understand.

This is a very intricate claim. Philosophy often wants to help—"the starting point of philosophy is that we do not understand ourselves well enough," as I have already quoted Williams as saying—but philosophers themselves may have nothing in mind but their own puzzlement. They may be none the less helpful for that, just as those who advertise their eagerness to help us—think of all those manuals on how to improve our thinking—may do nothing but dump us deeper into our preferred confusion. This is the complex power of Williams's suggestion. The road is hard and unpredictable, but it is a road. It is our road. We are better off for sharing it, and much worse off whenever we pretend it's soft or smooth or give up the idea of help altogether.

Michael Wood

Essays and Reviews

1

Plato Today, by R.H.S. Crossman

Twenty-five years ago Plato's *Republic* was generally viewed as one of the noblest monuments of Western liberalism and enlightenment. Together with the funeral speech which Thucydides in his history put into the mouth of Pericles, it was thought to represent the summit of Greek political wisdom and moral aspiration, and thus to be a primer and inspiration for the rulers and chief administrators who drew their education from the classics. This view of Plato's politics has not entirely disappeared, and no doubt still gets an occasional airing at public-school speech days; but effectively it has gone, shown up for the extraordinary tissue of historical falsehood and philosophical misunderstanding that it always was. Its disappearance from serious discussion is in this country chiefly associated with Professor Popper's massive engine of destruction, *The Open Society and Its Enemies*; but already in 1937 it had suffered a good deal of damage from the lighter, but still telling, weapons which Mr. Crossman deployed in his *Plato Today*.[1] This ingenious and stimulating book has now happily been re-issued, with a few changes and a brief new introduction in which Crossman disarmingly gives his reasons for not changing more.

The oddest thing about the once popular view of Plato is that anyone should have believed it. It needed less knowledge of Greek history than was possessed by Plato's admirers to realise that Platonic political theory represents not the finest philosophical expression of Athenian ideals, but a violent reaction against Athenian democracy and Pericles. Moreover, it needed only a reading of the *Republic* itself, or so one would have thought, to recognise the political system recommended there as a sclerotic monstrosity, high-principled in intent, but ultimately—and explicitly—based on oligarchic deceit and a contempt for much legitimate aspiration and human diversity. That well-informed and humane persons should have mistaken this either for an ideal embodiment of the principles of the Periclean Funeral Speech, or for a decent form of human life, is surprising.

The first, historical, mistake is chiefly explained, as Crossman remarks, by the refusal to think historically about Plato's political ideas at all. Part of Crossman's book is concerned with filling in the historical background, particularly of Plato's life. It is vividly done; scholarly eyebrows will be raised over some of it, but the main points are firmly made, and one comes out with a genuine understanding of Greek politics. More general doubts may be felt about Crossman's treatment of Socrates. He anticipates the line taken by Popper: that Socrates, unlike Plato, was a genuine 'democrat', an anti-authoritarian questioner who was executed for making a nuisance of himself to the tyrannically complacent. This may be true, but it is harder to prove historically than Crossman or Popper allows. We know that Socrates was associated with an anti-democratic clique, and that his execution was connected with this. Admitting as much, Crossman argues both that Socrates was a democrat and, indeed, a saint, and that the democratic faction which executed him was *politically justified* in doing so. This curious piece of jugglery seems indicative of more than merely historical uncertainty.

On the question of Plato's political reputation—why his system should have been thought admirable by people who ought to have known better—Crossman has interesting things to say, both directly and indirectly. Directly, he suggests that a lot of people shrugged off Plato's more repellent proposals by saying that they were the solutions of an idealist who did not consider the weaknesses of human nature; whereas, as Crossman admirably shows, Plato was obsessively aware of the weaknesses of human nature, and devised his rigid hierarchical structure precisely because he thought there was no other way of disciplining them. Crossman does not underestimate the power and subtlety of Plato's pessimistic vision. It would have been interesting if he had gone on to discuss Plato's theory of human nature, and to say something about the complex ways in which this theory allows Plato to represent as a system of consent what must actually be, on his own premises, a system of coercion.

Indirectly, Crossman points to other roots of the traditional admiration for the *Republic* when, in the non-historical part of his book, he imaginatively presents Plato's views on such subjects as British democracy and British education, and suggests that these institutions are more Platonic in inspiration than may appear on the surface. He might profitably have added a Platonic estimate of Britain's mission in the colonies. These parts of the book, in which 'Plato' is made to comment on twentieth-century problems, have lost little of their sparkle in twenty years. Some of it is fairly brittle, and Crossman is inclined to subscribe to what might be called the *Gallic fallacy*, of supposing that political institutions do not stand up to 'rigorous logic', when all that has been shown is that they do not stand up to rigorous logic proceeding from inadequate premises. But it is all provocative in the best sense—provocative of thought.

The book ends with an epilogue in which Crossman gives his own views on the Platonic issues of democracy and authority. It is brief and ultimately elusive; it combines in a dizzying way a virtually anarchical radicalism with a fascinated respect for the facts of power. There is an unresolved tension here—the same, surely, as broke out in the convoluted estimate of Socrates' death. One wonders whether this book, which has in no way dated, shows us not only Plato, but Crossman today.[2]

Notes

1. *Plato Today*, by R.H.S. Crossman, MP, rev. ed. (Allen and Unwin, 1959).

2. This review originally appeared as "Disbanding the Republic," *Spectator*, July 31, 1959.

Richard Crossman was a prominent British Labour Party politician, writer, and editor who served in Harold Wilson's government from 1968 to 1970.

2

English Philosophy since 1900, by G. J. Warnock

It is only in its title that this notably unpretentious book promises more than it gives.[1] It is not a general account of English philosophy since 1900, as it omits moral and political philosophy altogether, and in other fields deals with the work of comparatively few philosophers, and that selectively. These limitations, however, are clearly stated by Mr. Warnock, who explains that his aim has been "to make as clear as possible the general character of the philosophical landscape", and that he has deliberately given brief treatment to subjects, such as Logical Atomism, which have been studied recently in other works. The result of these various restrictions is a spare, elegant little book, admirably clear and very well written.

Its simplicity and clarity, however, are not the products only of restricted concerns and expository skill. It has the basic straightforwardness of a moral tale. At the start we are presented with the macabre picture of British Idealism, intellectually corrupt, fraudulent, staggering to its end in delusions of grandeur. Coming from foreign places, its rule was never more than the tyranny of occupation; and the rise of the hero, Moore, to drive it out is an affirmation not only of the light against the dark but of the native against the exotic. In the ensuing struggles, Moore has his allies, not always reliable: Russell, brave but unsteady; Positivism, secretly in love with the metaphysical enemy. The epic of Wittgenstein is also told, not without a slight sense of strain at having to take so extravagant a figure so seriously. With Ryle, victorious peace is almost achieved; and the story ends with Common Sense again on the throne, and the citizens of Oxford, calm but not idle, earning the unambitious rewards of honest toil.

It should be said that Mr. Warnock's account is not quite as simple as this, and certainly the main divergences between the philosophers he considers are sharply observed and clearly set down. Yet, as he warns us, his preferences are not concealed; it is Moore, and Moore as the defender of Common Sense, who emerges as the most original and important contributor to recent philosophy, and it is in terms of this judgment that the whole account is given. The presuppositions behind this judgment also emerge very distinctly, and it is perhaps the nature of these, and the frankness with which they are revealed, that give the book its undoubted interest and, in a sense, appeal.

The basic presupposition is that metaphysical theses, and even metaphysical perplexity, are always the products, direct or indirect, of theorists, either philosophical or scientific. In a natural state, unharried by theorists, we all hold the "Common Sense view of the world", which is (as Mr. Warnock says Moore found it to be) "perfectly unsurprising, undistressing, quite certainly true" (p. 55). Indeed, it seems that even the activities of theorists can never more than momentarily upset this view of the world: "It appears to me most evidently true that, in its simple foundations, our ordinary 'way of seeing' the world is absolutely stable and obstinately unshakeable . . . It is doubtful how far even Berkeley was able to retain the full sense of his vision for more than an occasional moment; one cannot so easily shake off what is natural to one's species" (p. 142). One result of this is that persons who claim seriously to be metaphysically disturbed are likely to be either in an unbalanced state or, quite possibly, insincere; those who are not will be relieved to learn that "to practise philosophy in the manner of Moore, it is not necessary to have (as most of us doubtless have not) nor to pretend to have (as some at least would be unwilling to do) large-scale metaphysical anxieties" (p. 55). This view of the origin and nature of metaphysical disturbance is a parallel—one might almost say, a recurrence—of a Rousseauesque view of the natural man corrupted by the machinations of priests and kings.

Now one might admit that in the matter of metaphysical scepticism about such things as the existence of the external world, there is something in the Moorean claim that no sane person seriously doubts the truth of "common-sense" beliefs. But even in this sort of case, it is most implausible to suggest that the origin of metaphysical doubts lies in the activities of theorists. For instance, Mr. Warnock considers the metaphysical view of the mind (closely related to scepticism about the external world) as a "man inside". He mentions, and rejects, the idea that the roots of this view lie already in the structure of our ordinary language about the mind, and finds a ready diagnosis of the trouble in a misunderstanding of the findings of neurophysiology and a tendency to assimilate the workings of the nervous system to the familiar workings of a telephone exchange. This diagnosis is absurd. For "the man inside" is already there with Descartes, and (though he was not worried by solipsism) as good as there with Plato—neither of whom—not even Descartes—was driven to the picture by reflections on neurophysiology, nor, one supposes, the telephone exchange. Of course, both were "theorists"; but the naturalness of such a picture for Plato, and the apparent cogency of Descartes' meditations, might suggest that "the man inside" is something which they found as theorists rather than invented. It is surely not irrelevant in this connection that the belief in some sort of human soul, possibly separable from the body, seems to be about as old as the human race, and so, presumably, not younger than "common sense". The idea, however, that there is naturally a problem about consciousness, and that "the man inside" is a picture naturally associated with this problem and lurking even in common sense, is not sympathetic to Mr. Warnock.

It is not clear how far Mr. Warnock confines the "priests and kings" thesis to such matters as the existence of the external world. At some points he seems to suggest that any form of "large-scale metaphysical anxiety" is gratuitous; elsewhere he admits that there are periods when at least some forms of metaphysical anxiety would be at least not patently insincere. The present time, however, is not one of them. In a chapter where he considers and seeks to justify a lack of metaphysical disturbance among present Oxford-style philosophers, he mentions the previous associations of metaphysics and religion, and goes on to say: "(metaphysics) could be expected to show some decline when very many people neither have, nor appear to be much oppressed by the want of, any serious religious convictions . . . Metaphysics, like religion, ought not to be manufactured in deference to any supposed requirements of intellectual decorum, or in the pursuit of some once genuine fervour which, in present conditions, would be synthetic or simulated" (p. 145). These are honourable remarks, inasmuch as, if there is nothing to be worried about, it is certainly dishonourable to simulate worry. Their suggestion, however, seems to be that there is at present nothing to be metaphysically worried about: if this were not the suggestion, the statement that many people are not worried would be merely irrelevant, and no justification of metaphysical inactivity would have been given. And this suggestion is downright astonishing. In fact the whole underlying thesis of this book is astonishing; all the more so for the air with which Mr. Warnock presents it, as one soberly recognizing obvious truths which incomprehensibly escape the notice of others.

It is unhappily probable that some readers, particularly among the un-professional audience for whom the book is chiefly intended, may be tempted, in their puzzlement at this attitude, to diagnose it merely as a certain parochial and academic complacency. This uncharitable reaction would be over-hasty: the sensitivity with which the book is written, the acuteness of its reasoning, and its moral overtones, all demand some deeper characterization of its implausibility. Such a characterization really awaits a proper study of the concept of "common sense" and of the peculiar role it plays in some contemporary philosophy. However, one might say in general that what the attitude of Mr. Warnock's book is most like is that of a work of metaphysics; there is much the same difference between this attitude and complacency as there is between Leibniz and Pangloss. As in some works of metaphysics, notable intelligence is deployed in distorting the facts of human experience to fit an extremely simple view of human nature, science, and philosophy. It would be unfair not to add that, like such works, the present book derives from this activity a genuine unity and even a certain fascination.[2]

Notes

1. *English Philosophy since 1900*, by G. J. Warnock (Oxford University Press, 1958).

2. Originally published in *Philosophy*, 1959, © Cambridge University Press. Reprinted with permission.

3

Thought and Action, by Stuart Hampshire

The chief and persistent influence on British philosophical thought about the human mind has been Descartes. To say this may seem a paradox, since there is no more hallowed contrast in the history of philosophy than that between on the one hand the rationalism of Descartes, with its far-reaching trust in the powers of pure theoretical reason to discover the ultimate structure of reality, and on the other hand the profound empiricist strain of British thought, which has again and again returned to the view that nothing substantial can be learned about the world save through the laborious, tentative, and always corrigible process of generalising from sense-experience and empirical observation.

Nor is this hallowed contrast confined to abstract philosophical opinions about the nature of science. It is equally a platitude—though a much vaguer one—to contrast a certain abstract and theoretical spirit more generally present in French thought with the more cautious, down-to-earth, and perhaps pedestrian temper of English intellectual activities. These contrasts are of course very rough and ready, and, in their more general form, a great deal of rubbish has been talked about them by both the contrasted parties. For all that, there is something in this platitudinous distinction; how then can it be that the prevailing influence on British philosophy of mind is nevertheless Descartes?

There are three main ways, I think, in which it is so. First, British philosophers have constantly returned to Descartes' fundamental belief, that the mind is in some fundamental sense distinct from the body, and that knowledge of the mind, its contents and activities, is more direct than, and is not reached through, our knowledge of the "external" world, where included in the external world are our bodies. This belief, in different forms, is to be found in the three pillars of British empiricism, Locke, Berkeley, and Hume, and once more in the logical positivism famously expounded in A. J. Ayer's *Language, Truth, and Logic*. It is only recently that this belief has been fundamentally challenged, in, for instance, Gilbert Ryle's *Concept of Mind* and the later work of Wittgenstein.

The second point of contact between the British tradition and Descartes is rather different. It lies in their common neglect of, indeed contempt for, *history* as a form of human knowledge, and of historical understanding as a vital part of man's understanding of his world. Although the British tradition differed from Descartes about the nature and methods of natural science, it shared his belief that natural science was the paradigm of human knowledge. Natural science seeks, and seems able to attain, knowledge of universal truths about the world, which hold irrespective of time and place; compared with this, historical study, immersed in the unsystematically particular, may seem a poor thing.

The third point of contact is to be found in a comparable neglect of æsthetics. For Descartes, our experience of art could scarcely appear as a form of knowledge or rational activity at all, and he accordingly has nothing to say of it. The poverty of British æsthetics, at least among philosophers, is notorious. This point is certainly connected with the last, and it is significant that the two British thinkers who are outstanding

exceptions to the prevailing neglect of history—Burke and Collingwood—
are exceptional also in having serious views about the nature of art. Of
course, there is an important difference between the neglect of these
things by Descartes, and their continuing neglect by the British tradition:
the latter needs explanation, while the former scarcely does. Descartes,
a scientist and mathematician in the 17th century, was almost bound to
take such a view; what is odd is that in Britain it should persist so indomi-
tably to the present day. I suspect that the explanation constitutes a rather
engaging paradox of the history of ideas: it is precisely the empirical and
cautious temper of British philosophers that has left them in this curious, perhaps not entirely recognised, alliance with the rationalist Descartes. The elevation of historical understanding and æsthetic experience
to central places in the picture of man's consciousness took place, after
all, amid the deep metaphysical thunder of 19th-century Germany, above
all in Hegel. While the influence of Hegel radically changed the rest of
European thought, and continues to work in it, the sceptical caution of
British philosophy left it spectacularly immune to it—splendidly, but to
its undoubted loss.

It is necessary, I think, to bear in mind these continuing Cartesian characteristics of the British philosophy of mind to appreciate fully the
originality of Stuart Hampshire's book.[1] It is not just that he adopts an
anti-Cartesian view of mind and body: this has been seen recently, in the
work of Wittgenstein and elsewhere (although Hampshire's own views
take an importantly different direction from most of what has appeared).
More immediately remarkable, at least, is the way in which his book
runs against the other two traditions. Throughout the book Hampshire
shows that he regards historical understanding as essential to grasping
all but the absolutely basic characteristics of the human mind. There are
some features of human thought that are basic and essential, those that
follow from man's nature as a bodily creature in a world of solid objects,
who can move and act in this world, and communicate with others of his
kind with whom he lives in society. Beyond this minimum, however (and
one of Hampshire's chief concerns is to determine what this minimum
is), the forms that human thought takes, the structure of language, the
content of morality, the styles of art, are to be understood historically.
All our ways of thinking about the world are conditioned by a given
historical context of conventions, manners, and interests; hence also they
inevitably change. Thus in anything that concerns human thought and
achievement, there are, if any, very few final truths. Hampshire is prepared, indeed, to take the step, not common with philosophers, of applying this conclusion to his own theories: all "determinations of the powers
of the mind," any theoretical picture of the nature and interdependence

of human capabilities and characteristics, must be provisional, his own not excepted.

This concern for the historical dimension runs, though not always obviously, all through the book. His concern for æsthetics is equally deep, but shows itself only towards the end of the book, where he makes it clear that in his view no philosophical theory of mind can be complete unless it gives some account of the universal human desire to produce and appreciate works of art.

Thought and Action covers a large range of topics, from the nature of language and linguistic reference, via the nature of intention and intentional action, to the freedom of the will and morality. In this, too, it is distinguished from much contemporary British work. Hampshire writes in his introduction:

> It has been the discipline of this time to answer separable questions separately, to analyse complex difficulties into elementary difficulties. The rewards of this discipline have been very great: accuracy, clarity, and sometimes even conclusiveness. But it is possible that there are purposes and interests which require that accurate and step-by-step analysis should not always be preferred to a more general survey and more tentative opinions, even in philosophy.

Such a general survey he attempts, and the result is a book of extraordinary sweep, often sketchy and tentative in the connections of its argument, but rich in the variety and novelty of the considerations it assembles.

The free and diverse moment of its thought makes this an exciting and stimulating book; it does not, however, make a book notably easy to digest or summarise. Nor is it made any easier in these respects by the way in which the exposition is put together. The style is extremely graceful, but its literary merits go with a refusal to use the more ponderous devices of footnote and reference which, like metal spikes in mountain-climbing, may be inelegant but do help one over the steep places. In the first chapter, for instance, a number of pages are devoted to arguments which are in fact objections to views held about perception by the logical positivists and similar thinkers, but there is nothing in the text to tell one this. It would also have been helpful, I think, to get us to see the direction of his views, had Hampshire made references to writers whose opinions on various topics he either shares or has been interestingly influenced by. Some of what he says about action and self-knowledge, for instance, bears important relations to some French writing which has not previously had much effect in this country: to Sartre and, in particular, Merleau-Ponty, among contemporaries, and to an earlier tradition going back to Maine de Biran.

Hampshire's austerity in such matters extends also to the devices of cross-reference, sub-heading, and so on; the book is a painting rather than a blue-print, a plant and not an engine. The argument grows, winds, doubles back; and, like a tendril, it tends to proceed spirally, returning to a side of the question it has visited before, but now a little further on. Its direction is not always easily followed, but it has a direction.

The general direction is, very roughly put, something like this. Hampshire starts from the question of what it is for us to be able to talk about the world, and finds as necessary for this our ability to pick out and refer to enduring objects in our environment. What sorts of distinctions we make, and what sorts of similarities we perceive, between features of the environment will to a great extent be a product of society, convention, and history; but that we do identify and refer to enduring objects is a necessary part of our having a language at all. In all these opening sections in particular, Hampshire's argument can be seen as revolving round the old distinction between what is "natural" and what is "conventional"; the possibility of language has a natural basis in the activity of *pointing*, but so long as this basic pointing function is preserved, the forms of a particular language will be conventional.

Hampshire then goes on to argue, in a number of interestingly different ways, that the possibility of language, and so of any conscious thought, presupposes that the beings who use the language should be able to move and act in the world. Here he rejects an important Cartesian idea, that we could image a conscious being whose experience was purely passive, who was a mere recipient of experiences. Such a being, for Hampshire, could not think about or have any concept of his experiences, for mere experiences could not satisfy the conditions of reference and identification necessary for conscious thought. (Here it is that Hampshire argues against the logical positivists; some of his arguments are similar to later views of Wittgenstein.[2]) In order to be able to identify and refer, we must be able to perceive enduring objects distinct from ourselves; the notion of perceiving presupposes that of being able to perceive things from different points of view—for it is precisely this that distinguishes genuine perception from illusion. The notion of perceiving things from different points of view presupposes, in turn, the idea that I can move about in the world, and orientate myself, as a bodily object, in relation to other objects.

The idea of moving myself is then taken up and connected with the notions of action and intention. These notions are, in Hampshire's view—here again a radical departure from Cartesianism—connected with my ability to have direct knowledge of what I am doing or trying to do: "it is essential to the idea of an action," he writes, "that a person's knowledge that an action of his is his own action is not the conclusion of an inference." This knowledge that I have of what I am doing, though in certain cases it may indeed be minimal, is always with me when I am conscious. If someone is conscious, then there is always an answer to the question "what is he doing?"; and a man's own knowledge of what he is doing, not merely in some instantaneous sense, but in the sense of a project in which he is engaged which reaches out beyond the present moment, is the foundation of a man's consciousness of his own identity. (Here Hampshire comes particularly close to phenomenological thinkers such as Merleau-Ponty.)

From this point, two lines of thought in particular are taken up. First, some connections are explored between the idea of action and that of thinking or more generally having conscious psychological experiences. So far from the latter being contrasted with action, as it always has been in the Cartesian tradition, Hampshire finds the two to be intimately connected. So far from an emotion, for instance, being a merely passive experience which may, as a matter of fact, lead to or cause overt action, it is rather, according to Hampshire, a kind of inhibited action; the emotion of anger, for instance, is to be understood as a by-product of the activity, itself rather sophisticated, of stopping myself lashing out or something similar. Similarly, the "psychological state" of belief is to be understood as a kind of inhibited assertion. (These somewhat paradoxical statements may be an oversimplification of Hampshire's view. I suspect, however, that the view as it stands is in any case rather paradoxical.)

The second line of thought pursued from here is an exploration of the notion of "practical knowledge" and its connections with intention. Hampshire holds, if I understand him, that there are two sorts of such knowledge. One is a certain "non-propositional" knowledge, which a man has when he knows what he is going to do or, more particularly, how he is going to do something, but has no words in which he could describe this. Thus an actor, for instance, may know how he means to play his part in the sense that he can show you how he does it, and can recognise if it has failed to come off, but could not *describe* how he was going to do it. The other sort is propositional: a man can tell you what he is going to do, in the form of a definite statement of intention.

Statements of intention are contrasted with predictions of what a man will do, and it is argued that there is a sense in which the two cannot be combined: a man cannot *intend* to do a certain thing if he knows on independent grounds, say some considerations of psychology, that he is going to do the thing anyway. This consideration introduces a doctrine of freedom. I am free, roughly speaking, in so far as my actual actions match my genuine intentions and projects. In particular, the neurotic is not free, since he is constantly frustrated in what he is consciously trying to bring about. In his case, this is because there is something else which in a rather different, subconscious sense, he is trying to do; the way to liberation is through an increased self-consciousness which it is the aim of psycho-analysis to bring about. Here Hampshire (like Spinoza, on whom he earlier wrote a book[3]) connects the idea of freedom with that of self-knowledge, and, by connecting this notion with the doctrines of Freud, tries to give an interpretation of free and responsible action which will avoid the difficulties and obscurities of the bare notion of the freedom of the *will*, as it has been inherited from Kant and the Christian tradition.

Finally, these notions of freedom and responsibility are applied, rather briefly, to an account of morality and the relations of morality and art. In Hampshire's view, the central notion of morality is not, for instance, that of obligation or duty, but that of a good man. He shares with Aristotle the idea that to say of a man that he is good is to say that he is perfect, fully-developed, as a man; almost, that he is an excellent specimen of the type "man." Every morality, accordingly, must contain as its central notion an idea of what a man should be, some doctrine of what is essentially human excellence. Such a notion Hampshire himself seeks to develop in outline from what he has said about the nature of man; in particular, the perfect man must be one who is to the fullest extent free, whose projects are based on a rational understanding of his own dispositions and capabilities, and which accordingly are not destroyed or frustrated by features of himself for which he has not allowed.

Merely from this summary (and I have left a lot out) it will be seen that the book contains a multitude of ideas variously and suggestively connected together. There is a good deal in the book that will certainly provoke doubt and disagreement. In particular, it is unclear that Hampshire has made his case about pointing as the natural foundation of linguistic reference; it may well be that pointing itself, in the sense that is required, is something that presupposes a linguistic context. On the relation between different sorts of intention, again, Hampshire's thesis is obscure, both in respect of the "non-propositional" sort of knowledge of my intentions, and in the relations between the doctrine that to act intentionally involves having a certain sort of knowledge of what I am doing, and the assertion, which Hampshire thinks appropriate to neurotic behaviour, that a man may act in ignorance of his real intentions. The account of morality, further, is markedly schematic and incomplete, and some well-known difficulties in the Aristotelian notion that to be a good man is, roughly, to be good at being a man, are not really answered. More general criticism of the chapter on morality will also occur to the reader; whether, for instance, the rough picture of the good life (remarkably like

Spinoza's in its tone of anti-romantic heroism) could serve for other than a rather special sort of life attainable only in favourable circumstances, and whether allowance has been made for the somewhat unsympathetic consequences of this; and whether Hampshire has not incorporated into the notion of morality itself considerations that unduly narrow the concept, so that certain sorts of morality—religious morality, for instance—become on his view well-nigh incomprehensible.

It will be a long, and fruitful, task for anyone interested in human thought and morality to discuss the difficulties of Hampshire's book. I should like to end by raising just one, more general, sort of criticism. It is my impression that Hampshire's account pays insufficient attention to the applications of natural science to human behaviour, and that some of his distinctions and conclusions may well be called in question when one considers the possible advances in these sciences or even, in some cases, their present state. Now Hampshire certainly denies this, and part of his purpose, like that of Spinoza, is indeed to give an account of human action and freedom compatible with scientific enquiry into the mind. His success in this purpose, however, seems much less striking when the scientific advances for which his position is prepared turn out to be those of psycho-analysis—"the new positive science of human conduct", as he optimistically terms it. To say that a view of human freedom is compatible with scientific advance because it is compatible with developments in psycho-analysis is much like saying that a material is uninflammable because it doesn't burst into flames when one shines an electric torch light on it. This is all the more so in Hampshire's case because he takes a markedly non-deterministic interpretation of psycho-analysis, considering it in effect as a theory of freedom. This is certainly a possible interpretation of psycho-analysis, and it may well be the most illuminating. However, it is only dubiously compatible with a good deal of what Freud, at least, says, and perhaps makes it even less clear than before, if this is possible, in what sense psycho-analysis is a positive science at all.

The really effective enemy against which theories of freedom should be prepared is not psycho-analysis but the neuro-physiology of the brain, and of this Hampshire has nothing to say. It may well be that a good number of his reflections on freedom would withstand any advance in this science as well; I think it is so. But the real enemy should be faced. It may be that Hampshire in fact thinks that neuro-physiology could not possibly advance to the point where it could yield substantial predictions of human behaviour. If so, arguments should be produced—it is a risky sort of claim.

There is another branch of natural science, too, to which Hampshire might have given more consideration. This is zoology; here the point is not that he should have made room for advances in science, but that consideration of its findings might well have modified the rigidity of some of his distinctions. For Hampshire, human action seems to be radically distinct from any other animal behaviour. Now this is in a sense true, in so far as the human possession of language and self-consciousness (which Hampshire rightly connects together) constitutes an enormous conceptual difference in our views of human and of other animal behaviour. But it does not follow from this that the behaviour of other animals is really mechanical, while ours is not; nor that the interpretation of animal behaviour as purposive consists only in reading into a stimulus-response system a pattern merely analogous to a pattern familiar in human action.

It is unclear how far Hampshire accepts this kind of conclusion, but he seems to me tempted to it. Thus, while admitting that animal behaviour is purposive in some sense or other, he certainly denies that we can attribute intentions to animals. Here I suspect Hampshire goes wrong in his concept of intention. It is true that we cannot ascribe sensibly to an animal an intention to do something in the future, which it has not yet embarked on. This is because it makes no sense to think of an animal using temporal ideas, save perhaps in the most rudimentary behavioural contexts. It does not follow from this, however, as Hampshire's concept of intention leads him to infer, that it makes no sense to apply to an animal the concept of its intention *in* doing what it is doing. We can distinguish in the case of an animal, as we can with human beings, between what it is really doing, in the sense of what it is primarily up to, and the things that are merely concomitants of what it is doing. Thus what the dog may be really doing is digging for a bone, or digging a hole: not, in the same primary sense, turning over so many stones or making a scratching noise, though it is *also* doing these things. Of course the evidences for this will be different from those available in a comparable case of a human being, whom we can ask what he is doing. But to say that therefore the concept of intention *in doing* such-and-such therefore does not apply to animals suggests to me an excessively anthropocentric concept of intention; we can and must in the case of complex animal behaviour draw the distinction between what is really being done and what is concomitant, and this seems to me one firm ground of the concept of intention.

This is a highly complex question, and no simple view can be had on it. Yet I feel that as a matter of attitude, to put it no stronger, that had Hampshire had more vividly in mind the astonishing complexities of animal behaviour, and the marked continuities, not only of reaction, but of patterns of purposive action between the other animals and man, he would have allowed concepts of action and intention not so totally restricted to human activities.

Descartes, it will be remembered, thought that animals were machines; perhaps Hampshire's view of animal behaviour constitutes the last Cartesian element in this profound and original anti-Cartesian book.

Notes

1. *Thought and Action*, by Stuart Hampshire (Chatto & Windus, 1959).
2. Cf. "Ludwig Wittgenstein," by Eric Heller, *Encounter*, Sept. 1959.
3. *Spinoza*, by Stuart Hampshire (Penguin, 1951).

4

The Theological Appearance of the Church of England: An External View

My disqualifications for writing about this subject are many; I must start by declaring some. I am not a member of the Church of England, and thus may be suspected of being biassed against it, or at least lacking in sympathy with it. The fact that I am not a member of any other church, either, may do something to alleviate the first suspicion, but may, on the other hand, only tend to aggravate the second, since it may be thought that only Christians are likely to show much understanding in questions of Christian theology. To a certain extent, this must of course be admitted: a theology is not something that can just be "got up", or completely understood from the outside. Nevertheless, it surely cannot be that unbelief is a complete bar to discussion, if the Church is to speak, not only with itself, but with those outside—which is surely what the Church must hope to do. So I hope that some unpolemical remarks from someone outside will not necessarily and completely lack point.

Since I belong to no church, it will be seen that my reasons for unbelief do not consist merely of objections to Anglicanism, but are more general than that. It is not my aim here, however, to raise these general difficulties. I shall merely try to discuss some features of the Anglican position today, as I understand it. Here I shall make the last of my introductory apologies: that I have no doubt that I understand it very imperfectly. Perhaps some of the things I say will be merely misunderstandings. I do hope, though, that if they are misunderstandings, they are not merely personal misunderstandings, but misunderstandings shared with others outside the Church who take an interest in it. If so—and discussions I have had with others suggest that it is so—perhaps I can hope that even my mistakes will have some symptomatic kind of interest.

I have spoken of "the Anglican position". But one immediate and notorious difficulty is that of identifying *an* Anglican position at all. *Quot Anglicani, tot sententiae* would be an unfair exaggeration, but the despairing enquirer has been known to think it. The variation of Anglican opinion is a familiar, but not a trivial, difficulty. There are those who do not find it a difficulty, but rather a recommendation, indicative of a wide freedom of conscience. It seems to me, however, that it undoubtedly is a difficulty, even if not an insuperable one; because the Anglican Church does offer itself to those outside *as a church*, and it is as a church that they are invited to join it. It would not be a church if it were only a kind of federation of beliefs, a label that could be worn without bad conscience by anyone from a Roman Catholic minus Papal infallibility to a Methodist plus bishops. The Anglican Church is not, of course, merely this, but it sometimes seems so; and its seeming so is the reason why its great variation of belief is indeed a difficulty.

It is a platitude to contrast the Church of England in this respect with the Church of Rome. It is important, however, what the point of this contrast is. It is not that the Church of Rome presents in all places uniformly the same appearance; it obviously does not. The point is that with the Church of Rome there is in the end a more or less determinate procedure for discovering what are the central and essential beliefs, and what are local variations, and with the Anglican Church there is not—or, at least, there does not seem to be. It may be objected that Rome earns these advantages by the devices of dogmatic pronouncement and excommunication, repugnant to the Anglican position. This may well be true, but it misses the present point. For it is not being suggested that the Church of England should have the same body of essential belief as Rome, or any as elaborate; but only that there should be *some* central body of beliefs common to all. If it is now suggested that devices of excommunication, etc., are necessary to preserve even that minimum uniformity in the Anglican Church, the questioner will surely be justified in thinking that the *raison d'être* of the Anglican Church as a distinct entity is hard to find.

It will be said that such a minimum uniformity of belief indeed exists. But it is not always easy to believe this; for while the same *words* can be heard more or less from all, the sense that is attached to these words is certainly various. This is a point I shall come back to. Even if there is a central core, however, it should still be made clearer what is the central core, and what the individual variations. When I say that this should be made clearer, I mean among other things that one should be able to discover this by asking those in orders. Here one touches on another notorious contrast with the Church of Rome, that, very broadly speaking, the average Roman Catholic priest seems to be more thoroughly theologically educated (if I may use the expression) than the average clergyman. This is a very well-known point, which raises questions of the training for the priesthood beyond my scope; I only want to make the point, if it needs making, that this difference undoubtedly affects the status of the Anglican Church in the eyes of the intelligent enquirer.

The point needs making, I think, if only because there seem to be many Anglicans, and some in orders, who find an emphasis on theology irrelevant. These will tend, if questioned about the Church, to point primarily to its social work and moral influence. Now there is no doubt that the Church must show itself socially, and in the broader sense politically, concerned; because—to put the point only in crudely tactical terms—it still undeniably has an unfortunate "class image" to live down. It is no accident that both Roman Catholicism and Nonconformism have such powerful roots among working people. But, obviously, there is no point in this social work without a Christian significance, and there will be no Christian significance without a theology. It is only if behind social and moral action there is a belief, and a belief which to some extent can be explained, that the unbeliever will not be justified in merely replying that he prefers his social work without fancy dress.

This may seem quite platitudinous. I hope it is; I would be more convinced that it was if one did not quite often encounter Anglicans—again, unhappily, some in orders—whose views on the relation between their belief and their social or personal morality were quite inadequate. There are those whose religion turns out just to be their morality, whose religious outlook really can be described as "morality tinged with emotion". Others go beyond this, only to introduce God as the crudest kind of sanction for morality. I have myself been addressed by a R.A.F. chaplain who told us that, after all, one wouldn't steal if somebody were watching, and the thing about God is that he is watching one all the time . . . It was unclear whether this curious consideration was supposed to mean that because God exists, one shouldn't steal, or that because one knows that one shouldn't steal, one can see that God exists. I got the impression that the chaplain didn't mind which he meant.

One would have to be very uncharitable to hold such individual idiocies against the Church as a whole. But they do not help it, and steps should be taken to see that no clergyman goes out to represent the Church without a deeper and sounder moral theology. This merely reverts to the training question. There are at least two points, however, on which I have the impression that the Church as a whole needs deeper thought about its moral theology. One concerns the relation between such things in this life as the improvement of living conditions, and the hope of eternal salvation which is said to be the end of the Christian life. It seems possible that these two should conflict: so far as those whose lot is to be bettered are concerned, it is certainly not self-evident that material betterment will improve their chances of living the kind of life which, we are told, is likely to lead to salvation. Some of the darker reactionaries in such places as the Spanish Roman Church notoriously see this point, and holding that their task is to lead souls to salvation and that this life is only a drop in eternity, oppose a good deal of social reform. Some Christians dismiss this view too lightly—it has a kind of savage consistency. If they are to reject this view, as all Anglicans presumably will, they must put something in its place. One simple way is to say that it is a known Christian duty to aid others less fortunate than oneself, and in performing this duty, one pursues one's own way to salvation. But put just like that, this sounds too self-regarding, as though one were making others the instruments of one's own salvation. If it is replied that this is a superficial objection, because the duty in question is precisely not to be self-regarding, but to love others as oneself, a difficulty still remains: for the duty is presumably not to love them and aid them merely as temporal human beings with material wants, but as children of God destined, in his Grace, to salvation. The question then remains, whether the right way of expressing love to men in this character is in all cases to work for their social betterment. Nor will it resolve the difficulty to warn the doubter against the presumption of considering the salvation of others, and to urge him to leave that to them and God, and concern himself with his own; for the doubt will remain, whether pursuing these policies of social betterment is the way for him to concern himself with his own salvation.

This is a practical problem, and a deep problem of the relations, for a Christian, of time and eternity. Many Anglicans seem not to have given enough thought to it.

The second point about moral theology is a yet more general one. Unbelievers often say in a truculent tone that the lives of Christians don't seem all that different from the lives of others. This may just be the relatively superficial point that they don't seem to be much better men; about this the Christian has things, sufficiently familiar, to say. But when those things have been said, a deeper point remains. For even if one granted what the Christian has to say of original sin and the ways in which things become harder if one is a Christian rather than easier, there remains the feeling that there should be a distinctively Christian way of thinking about moral problems, what might be called, for want of a better phrase, a Christian style of moral thought. Now there is such a thing; or, rather, there is more than one. There is, on the one side, what has come to be called "the Nonconformist conscience". Admirable though its possessors often are, the doubter in the modern world, corrupted, perhaps, by complexity, knows that he cannot commit himself whole to its simplifications. On the other hand, there is a highly complex style of Roman Catholic moral thought. The heart of this style is casuistry—not in the pejorative sense, but in the strict sense of a method of moral argument that seeks to bring every action and character that is to be decided or judged under certain fixed categories of virtue or good deed, vice or sin. Here again the doubter must hesitate: surely he *knows* that things cannot be so fixed, that the categories must be open to revision, criticism, extension?

Between is the Church of England. But where? Here, it seems to me, it has both a lack and an opportunity. A lack, because as things are, it scarcely seems to have an individual style of moral thought. Exhortations to the *imitatio Christi* are not, by themselves, enough; up to a point, even the unbeliever can agree to do likewise, and beyond that point, there is need of precisely the kind of moral thinking in essentially Christian terms that is lacking. It has, however, also an opportunity, to find a style of thought more apposite to our complexities than the rigidities, respectively simple and complex, of its neighbours.

Moral theology is, of course, not self-sufficient. Behind it there must be a Christology; and this raises, in the first place, the questions of historicity. Christianity is said by all to be an historical religion, based not only on the facts of Christ's life and crucifixion but on the Resurrection. It is also, I suppose, an historical religion in a rather different sense: it is a religion concerned, like its relatives Judaism and Islam, with its own history, and in particular concerned with the continuity of belief from its beginnings. Now the intelligent unbeliever knows this as well as the Christian does, and will not be impressed by attempts to duck the consequences of it. In particular, he probably recalls that S. Paul said, "If Christ be not risen, then is our faith vain", and will tend very firmly to think that the moment Christians start shuffling on the historical claims for the Resurrection, they might as well shut up shop.

I should not have thought it necessary to say anything so obvious, had I not heard a very distinguished Anglican theologian being questioned closely for about twenty minutes on his belief in the Resurrection, at the end of which it was still not clear whether he thought that as a matter of historical fact Christ rose from the grave or not. There was a good deal of talk about "analogical sense", "surviving spirit"; a theologian might have found in this a sad confusion between the events of Easter Sunday and those of Pentecost, but in brusquer terms, it was just a piece of unconscionable double-talk.

This raises again the question mentioned before, of the unity of belief. This theologian was quite prepared to *say* that Christ rose—the difficulties came when he was asked to say what he meant by it. This is a particularly striking case, of course, because in the case of the Resurrection there is no doubt at all about what the words, in their natural interpretation, do mean. It is not so with many theological doctrines. There are two quite different ways in which theological assertions may cause difficulty to the enquirer: they may be *incredible*, or they may be *incomprehensible*. The doctrine of the Resurrection, if it presents a difficulty, does so only by being incredible: it is perfectly clear what one is required to believe, only it is not easy to believe it. With such doctrines, if they are certainly part of the faith, it is no part of the theologian's task to try to find a new meaning for the terms that express them. If he does so, he is certainly abandoning the religion. With doctrines such as the Incarnation and the Trinity, the situation is different, for the difficulty of these is their incomprehensibility: it is hard, not so much to believe them, as to take the preliminary step of recognising what has to be believed in order to believe them. It is of course essential that anything that is to be called Christianity contains these doctrines, and contains them moreover in a transcendental form, that is, in such a form that what is being asserted by them is not merely something, however "spiritual", about the temporal life and personality of Christ. I have occasionally seen Anglican clergymen slipping nervously in what looked suspiciously like that direction, though it might be unfair to suppose that there was any such dilutionary tendency in Anglican thought as a whole.

Last one comes to the question of God's existence, and of the arguments that can be given for it. It seems to me essential that there should be some arguments, and it has certainly been the tradition of the Church of England to give some. It is essential that there should be such arguments, not so much to persuade unbelievers—not many can have been converted by purely theological considerations—but in order to give some basis to what otherwise might be an utterly subjective feeling, and also to give content to the belief itself: the nature of the arguments itself gives clues to the nature of the God, the existence of whom they purport to prove. Thus the argument from the first cause illustrates God's nature as Creator, the argument from moral experience his goodness and concern with mankind, etc.

In the matter of such arguments, the Church of England is in a peculiarly difficult historical position. It has been its traditional role, and one of its most English features, to rely on those arguments for God's existence that have most empirical content, which appeal most to the observed nature of the world. Chief among these was the so-called Argument from Design, the argument from the evident purposiveness and fitness of natural things, to the existence of the Great Artificer. Such arguments (as Kant observed) are more satisfying, seem to have more real content, than the more abstract proofs from contingency, the nature of being, and so on, on which the Church of Rome has characteristically most relied. This is true, but there is a corresponding disadvantage. Empirical content is like income: the larger it is, the nicer, but also the more tax it attracts, the tax in the case of arguments being the likelihood of empirical refutation.

The tax-collector arrived in the form of the theory of evolution by natural selection; and it was because the Church of England was so attached to the Argument from Design that it experienced a convulsion over Darwinism of a sort that Rome (whose own crisis had come over Galileo) largely managed to avoid. Paley's Watch had been the Church's timepiece, and suddenly it stopped.

It is important to see what the difficulty is. It is not that Darwinism disproves the existence of God. The truth of Darwinism is not incompatible with the existence of God, even if it makes his choice of means seem even more mysterious than before. The difficulty for the Church was not that Darwin disproved their conclusion, but that he removed what was apparently the strongest argument they had for it. That argument depended essentially on pointing to something in the world which, it was alleged, could not be explained except on theological principles; Darwin did explain it on non-theological principles (or, to be fairer, his successors are progressively doing so); and this certainly removes the force from the Argument from Design.

The question "is science incompatible with religion?" is now generally seen to be too vague to admit of an answer. What is true is that there are certain arguments for religion, depending essentially on an appeal to the inexplicable, which do collapse under the advance of scientific explanation; and the Church of England seems to show an eery compulsion to embrace just such arguments. This compulsion still continues. Some Anglicans appeal to the emergence of life from the non-living, and so give hostages to bio-chemistry. Others appeal to the start of the universe, and give hostages to cosmology, which may show that there is no necessity to postulate any start to the universe at all. Others—and it is essentially the same sort of argument—appeal to the existence of religious experience, and so put themselves in the hands of psychological advance; for here again, while it would be quite possible to reconcile any psychological explanation of such experience with the existence of God, if we knew on other grounds that God existed, there is a very poor prognosis for a belief in God which is itself mainly based on the psychological inexplicability of those experiences.

Granted all this, there is of course always one question left, which one knows *a priori* could not be answered by any scientific advance: the question, sufficiently broadly taken, of why the universe exists at all. Since all scientific explanation depends essentially on explaining one part of the universe by reference to another, it cannot in principle explain the existence of the universe as a whole. The trouble is that when the question is taken as broadly as that, its meaning and compulsiveness may seem depressingly to evaporate. We have certainly moved a long way from the impressive workings, to be seen on every side, of Archbishop Paley's Watch.

Here, clearly, the unbeliever can have nothing to say. Since he believes there to be no arguments which will prove this conclusion, he could not, if he dared, suggest where to look for them. But perhaps he may suggest that the Church of England make a more violent effort to detach itself from the *damnosa hereditas* of its addiction to the scientifically refutable, and find something else which will be more solid and enduring, and yet in keeping with its tradition of eschewing the more abstract and rarefied forms of argument in favour of the more familiar and compelling. If it can.

5

The Four Loves, by C. S. Lewis

The Four Loves are Affection, Friendship, Eros and Charity. In this brief book Professor Lewis discusses each; its difficulties, dangers and rewards.[1] He starts off with an introductory chapter in which he principally distinguishes between what he calls Gift-loves and Need-loves—a distinction of some importance to his later thoughts, although he rightly admits its limitations, since there are many whose need it is to make a gift of their love. He also has a chapter on, as he puts it, our 'liking and loves for the sub-human,' and there speaks of such things as patriotism and the love for animals. On his title-page are the words of Donne: 'that our affections kill us not, nor dye'; his aim is to show us a life full of, but not torn apart by, love, something only possible in his view if the love that crowns it is the love of God.

Perhaps we should not say that the author of this book is *Professor* Lewis. This is a work of the C. S. Lewis who wrote *The Screwtape Letters*, and it is appropriate (even if only a publisher's convention) that the list of the author's works on the fly-leaf does not include the history of sixteenth-century English literature, nor *The Allegory of Love*. It is not just that in books like this Lewis writes without professorial solemnity — that, indeed, is true of his critical works as well. It is rather that in approaching his present subject he jettisons that state of mind in which alone one could hope to learn from the literature of love, a state of mind that involves the suspension of assertion and a readiness for any degree of complexity. He starts afresh, with lots of good sense and a genuine humility, to put together some thoughts about his own and the general experience. This gives his work a first-handness not to be despised: it is not derivative or 'literary' in the bad sense.

Yet the price is high. By banishing from his mind that less general experience, those warnings of complexity, that the literature of love offers he hands himself over to his own particular demon — a kind of clubman's crassness which can be heard over and over again in these pages striking a false note. Sometimes he merely expresses himself in a way that makes it hard to believe he can enjoy good writing: 'If we were short of matter on this theme we could turn on the tap by opening the works of the Stoics and it would run till we had a bathful.' Sometimes, particularly in religious matters, he uses some jarringly hearty analogy. Sometimes he throws up the discussion of a serious question with what seems almost a willed superficiality. Having raised the question of the connections, if any, between male friendship and what he calls 'abnormal Eros,' he ends a brief and combative discussion: '. . . and all those hairy old toughs of centurions in Tacitus, clinging to one another and begging for last kisses when the legion was broken up — all pansies? If you can believe that you can believe anything.'

These outbreaks of padre talk make for painful reading. The odd thing about the book, however, is that this is obviously not a padre talking. Now and again, a deeper insight and a freer sensibility are allowed to emerge. There are one or two memorable images: '. . . we picture lovers face to face but Friends side by side; their eyes look ahead.' In this book Lewis is rather like a porpoise; we see its jolly sportings on the surface, and when it goes deeper it disappears from view, but we know that it does have a submarine life.

What is obscure is why Lewis behaves like a porpoise. Partly, perhaps, from a fear of what he sees as spiritual or emotional pretentiousness;

partly, I think, with the aim of popularisation. Wishing to put before a wide public his own way to God, he seizes on the robustly commonplace as that in which most may share. Because he is free of contempt for the robustly commonplace, this is in no way dishonest or condescending; but because there is something in him that sees below it, it is quite often uncomfortable. This uncomfortableness, moreover, must tend to defeat his purpose, since on love, of all subjects, writing can carry conviction only if it is born of everything that a man has in him to say about it.[2]

Notes

1. *The Four Loves*, by C. S. Lewis (Bles, 1960).
2. This review originally appeared as " 'That Our Affections Kill Us Not,' " *Spectator*, April 1, 1960.

6

Discourse on Method, by René Descartes

The fame of Descartes has at least three separate and very firm foundations. In philosophy, it was he who made into the starting point of the philosopher's inquiry the question, 'Of what can I be certain,' and by so doing turned Western philosophy on to a path which in good part it has followed ever since. By asking this question, and by finding as the first and basic answer to it the famous *cogito ergo sum* — 'I am thinking, therefore I exist' — he did something virtually unthinkable to his predecessors: he made the first certainties of philosophy the immediate data of the individual consciousness, and the main problem of philosophy the sceptical difficulty of how I can ever know that anything except these immediate data exists. Earlier philosophers had taken as the first certainties God, or the world, or some other realm of being outside the individual, and asked how the individual was related to them; Descartes took first the experiences of the individual, and asked how he could go beyond them to knowledge of anything 'outside.'

The consequences of this revolution have involved, perhaps, as much darkness as light, and many have now come to doubt whether Descartes did ask the right question after all. Nevertheless, it was a step that thought had to take, and a great depth of insight has been gained from seeing where it leads. One extraordinary feature of Descartes' revolution is that it does seem to have been essentially an individual achievement. Although many elements of his thought are of course less original than he supposed, its central idea seems to have been his alone. Many have supposed themselves to be changing, unaided, the face of philosophy: Descartes really did it.

Second, in mathematics, Descartes has his fame as the founder of analytical geometry. Here his achievement is less startlingly individual. The groundwork was being pursued by his immediate predecessors, and the subject in its present form is said to owe more to the researches, unpublished for many years, of his great contemporary, Fermat. Nevertheless it was he who first clearly brought together algebra and geometry, in a form to produce results of the greatest significance and power.

His third claim to fame is less fundamental but of large historical importance. When in 1637, at the age of forty-one, he produced his first published work, the *Discourse on Method*, he wrote it in French, in order to reach over the heads of the scholarly readers who expected their philosophy in Latin, and to reach a wider public of men of good sense who, he hoped, would be more open to the voice of pure reason than were the fusty pedants of the Schools. He wrote it in a French which, in the elegance and simplicity it gives to abstract thought, is a wonderful literary achievement. By so doing, he made himself the model for an enduring tradition devoted to the values of a rigorous yet unpedantic clarity. This tradition often collapses into a mythology, and Descartes would no doubt pale at the rationalistic idiocies often praised as examples of *l'esprit cartésien*; yet the tradition has great achievements to its credit, and not solely in France.

Thus Descartes, literary as well as philosophical and mathematical innovator, has every right to a proud place in any series of Classics. The present selection gives us, besides the *Discourse on Method*, the *Meditations* of 1641 and one further text.[1] It is a pity, perhaps, that the selection is not rather larger; some extracts from the psychological writings, for instance, would have given a wider view of Descartes' system. A greater pity, however, is what has happened in this version to Descartes' style. Descartes should carry one along; here one stumbles over an uneven terrain, tripping over obscurities, omissions, and occasional downright mistranslations. Enough remains for this to be a passable introduction to Descartes' thought: enough has gone to make at least his third claim to fame, as a philosophical stylist of genius, look rather puzzling.[2]

Notes

1. *Discourse on Method*, by René Descartes, translated by Arthur Wollaston (Penguin Classics, 1960).
2. This review originally appeared as "Certainties," *Spectator*, August 26, 1960.

7

The Individual Reason: L'esprit laïc

No era in the history of scientific ideas is more celebrated than the seventeenth century, the century that contains the work of Kepler, of Galileo, of Descartes, and culminates in the publication, in 1687, of Newton's *Principia*. The celebration of this great century is just, from more than one point of view. The mere intellectual achievements, individual and cumulative, are gigantic. More than that, the century saw a decisive shift in men's general outlook, and the firm establishment of what is, to all intents and purposes, the modern attitude towards the physical universe. Besides this, again, the history of these developments, particularly in the first half of the century, is of the greatest dramatic and personal interest, and it is not surprising that the outstanding example of this element, the life of Galileo, should be a recurrent theme of drama and literature, as well as of the history of ideas.

A Conflict over Freedom of Thought?

If we ask what it is about these events that makes them dramatic, we should naturally say that it was a conflict—a conflict between the new science and traditional authority. This conflict tends to present itself as a straightforward conflict over freedom of thought—a fight between those who claimed the right to discover and publish new truths, and those who claimed the right to suppress and silence them. This simple and recognizable picture of the situation we owe, in good part, to the propagandists of the Enlightenment; those who, a century later and in pursuit of definite political and ideological ends, presented the history of these years, as indeed they saw it, in the light of truth versus obscurantism, freedom against power.

There is some truth in this picture. But it is, of course, grossly over-simplified, and its over-simplifications tend to diminish rather than to enhance the dramatic and historical interest of the conflicts of ideas in the seventeenth century. It is only when one looks rather more closely at the kinds of authority that were being rejected, and the kinds of truth, or of ways of truth, that seventeenth-century thinkers sought to put in their place, that one can see the real importance of the century for the history of ideas. The celebrated conflicts were more than a campaign in the struggle for freedom of thought; they concerned the nature of scientific inquiry itself. They raised, in particular, two vital issues. First, what is the relation of scientific inquiry to traditional authority? To this question the century returned a fairly unambiguous answer. Second, what is the relation of scientific inquiry to the common understanding, to the methods of thought of the ordinary inexpert man? To this question it returned a variety of answers, mostly ambiguous and none entirely satisfactory. This latter problem is still essentially with us. It is these two questions— and they are not unrelated to each other—that I should like to pick out from the seventeenth-century picture. In doing this, I shall concentrate mostly on two thinkers, very different in temperament, both from the first half of the century: Galileo and Descartes.

New Approach to the Idea of Authority

First, what about authority? Here we naturally and immediately think of the authority of the Church, both in the sense of power of the Church, its Inquisition and its censorship, and in the sense of theological authority— the claim of the Church, or of certain of its dignitaries, to lay down on supposedly theological grounds what might and might not be believed in natural science. The conflict of the new ideas with this sort of authority is placed firmly in the centre of the historical scene by the case of Galileo. Yet we must not be misled by this case into thinking that the rejection of authority that went with the new ideas was a rejection peculiarly of ecclesiastical authority—this was only one instance of something more general and, from the point of view of the ideas themselves, more important: a new approach to the whole idea of authority in scientific matters. Nor must we suppose that the authority of the Church in general was being called in question: the most that came into question, in relation to scientific ideas, was the use of theological authority to buttress particular cosmological and mechanical theories. Indeed, the general line of the scientists was to say that there was, strictly speaking, no conflict between any of the new scientific ideas and the doctrines of the Church; what was happening was that certain officers of the Church, through malice or confusion, were involving the Church in matters on which it was not theologically required to pronounce.

This line was in some part dictated by prudence; yet it is interesting that Galileo, radical and even provocative though he is in many respects, seems to stick to it. His attitude is well brought out by a note added in his copy of his *Dialogues Concerning the Two Chief World Systems*, the marvellous book that precipitated his condemnation: 'Take note, theologians, that in your drive to make matters of faith out of propositions relating to the fixity of sun and earth you run the risk of eventually having to condemn as heretics those who would declare the earth to stand still and the sun to move—at such a time as it might be physically or logically proved that the earth moves and the sun stands still'. In such passages, Galileo's thought seems to be that when you see that the authority of religion is merely irrelevant to the demonstration of scientific views, you will have the true measure of both religion and science.

Vast Untidy Cocoon

With Descartes, the situation is more complex. Far more cautious than Galileo—'it is not my temperament', he once said, 'to set sail against the wind'—he wraps his true thoughts about the Church in a vast untidy cocoon of concession, deference, and theological argument. Yet it is certain that his Catholic belief was itself genuine, and further, that he did not think, as Galileo seems to have thought, that theology was actually irrelevant to science. On the contrary, in his *Principles of Philosophy* he himself seeks to derive the basic laws of motion from the properties of God. The derivation is extremely feeble, and the laws in good part mistaken: yet there it is, and something he thought worth doing. But behind this peculiar metaphysical enterprise, so alien to the naturalistic style of Galileo's argument, there is a deeper similarity between the two. For Descartes' supposed derivation is a derivation from first principles, from properties of God supposedly self-evident to the reflective mind: it is not a derivation resting on texts, received authorities, or the accumulated interpretations of the ages. This is their great similarity, and the guiding thread through the conflicts with authority: for neither of these two, nor for the other seventeenth-century makers of the new science, was it relevant to a scientific argument to cite or rely on the inherited authority of texts, or the views of distinguished and admired thinkers of the past: you had to look, and think, for yourself. The fact that those who deployed the received texts and appealed to authority were doing so for the most part in an ecclesiastical interest is largely beside the point; the important thing is that it was the method that was wrong, in whatever interest it was being used.

The point is made over and over again, in different connexions: the point that what was said in the past is relevant to scientific inquiry only if it can stand the tests of rigorous inquiry in the present. Thus Descartes in the earliest of his philosophical works, the *Rules for the Direction of Understanding*, advocates a method for discovering the truth, and characteristically remarks by the way: 'Neither, though we have mastered all the arguments of Plato and Aristotle, if yet we have not the capacity for passing a solid judgment on these matters, shall we become philosophers; we should have acquired the knowledge, not of a science, but of history'. And in Galileo's *Dialogues*, when the scholastic anti-Galilean speaker — characteristically christened by him 'Simplicio' — cites the authority of Aristotle for some supposed scientific law or experimental result, he is always brought up with the same objection: the authority of Aristotle is only that of any other brilliant and observant man, and the question is, 'is the law in fact true?'; 'can the experiments be repeated?'

If, then, a scientific inquiry did not rely, as an historical inquiry must, on the authority of texts; and if the powers of the mind involved in scientific inquiry were not directly those involved in the exegesis of texts, the weighing of authorities, and so on, what were the powers of the mind involved? And who possessed them? What was the seventeenth-century scientists' picture of the scientist himself?

To these questions there is no simple answer. But one recurrent strain that can be found is the tendency of these thinkers, confronted with prejudice and non-comprehension on the part of the academic vested interests, to turn to ordinary educated men of good sense for an audience and a following. In this respect Galileo and Descartes are alike. Both wrote important works in their native language, instead of the Latin that was still the vehicle of learned communication; both seeking by this to go over the heads of monks and professors to men of good sense in the world of non-academic pursuits. Both of them despised the academic hierarchies, and preferred, on the whole, the company of practical men of affairs, who knew what they were talking about in their own fields. Descartes explains, in the *Discourse on Method*, how in his youth he took up travelling and moved in the world of courts and armies: 'It seemed to me that I might meet with much more truth in the reasonings that each man makes on the matters that specially concern him, and the issue of which might very soon punish him if he made a wrong judgment, than in the case of those made by a man of letters in his study touching speculations which lead to no result'. It is notable how many of Descartes' friends were ambassadors or other men of affairs; indeed it was such men who intervened to help him when he was involved in a protracted and unpleasant dispute with university pedants in Holland.

The Appeal to Good Sense

Certainly Descartes and Galileo seemed to have thought that it was the sort of good sense that was possessed by intelligent men of affairs to which they could appeal with the new scientific reasonings, from which they could hope for understanding. However, were such abilities sufficient to *produce* scientific reasonings; was the scientist just the man of everyday good sense who applied it in the right way to science? Sometimes Descartes, at least, writes as though it were so; indeed, he goes further. The *Discourse on Method* famously begins:

> Good sense is of all things in the world the most equally distributed, for everybody thinks himself so abundantly provided with it, that even those most difficult to please in all other matters do not commonly desire more of it than they already possess. It is unlikely that this is an error on their part; it seems rather to support the view that the power of distinguishing the true from the false, which is properly speaking what is called Good Sense or Reason, is by nature equal in all men.

He then goes on to say that this being so the reason why some men understand and learn more things than others is that the others do not properly use their natural gifts, but if they are given a method for using these gifts, they may each be as good judges of the truth as others. Such a method, of course, he will propound. This, at any rate, is Descartes' professed view: the mark of science is the method: this method can be learnt and employed by any man, in the light of the natural reason which all men possess.

It is not clear, however, how far Descartes really believed this. The dry joke about everyone's satisfaction with his good sense—a well-known saying, incidentally, to be found already in Montaigne—immediately suggests irony; and certainly there is little to be found in Descartes' own attitude to other researchers which suggests that he thought them of equal ability to himself, only needing acquaintance with the method to set them on the path. Nor, if he did think so, did he exactly go out of his way to help them on to the path; thus he deliberately wrote his *Geometry* in an obscure style for fear that its originality would not be recognized if he made it too easy, and it gave him special pleasure to think of the difficulty it would give to distinguished French geometers. It is not unfair to say that Descartes' general attitude to science was that it was a business for geniuses, and that there were, at least, very few of them besides himself.

No Feeling of Scientific Community

The self-absorption which is very noticeable in Descartes, the lack of interest in the scientific efforts of others, is not peculiar to him; on the contrary, the absence of a sense of a scientific community is characteristic of the earlier seventeenth century. In part, it was due to lack of communications: the institutions designed to further communication, such as the Royal Society in this country, are the product of the sixteen-sixties and later. But this is not the only reason; even when the channels existed, the messages were often ignored. Thus Galileo, having been sent Kepler's book, left it unread—disastrously, if not (in this case) altogether surprisingly. Descartes, again, was sent some important work of Galileo by the Abbé Mersenne, whose indefatigable scientific correspondence made him almost a single-handed Royal Society; 'I have no time to read Galileo', Descartes loftily replied. There is a deeper reason than lack of communications here. It is that in the first part of the century the men in the front of the new advance tended fantastically to under-estimate the size of the scientific task before them, and were able to believe that in outline at least the shape of all scientific explanations might be discovered by one man of genius, or a few, in their own lifetimes. Granted this, it is not surprising that they should have not carried very far any belief which they had, that science was really only the methodical application of the good sense which was latent in the common understanding. Genius, or a genius, was enough.

Nevertheless, in their rejection of the academic professionals which I have already mentioned, there did arise the notion that it was some sort of unprofessional good sense or natural light of reason that, given the right method, could discover the truth. Nowhere do we find this element more pronounced than in the writings of Galileo's English contemporary, Francis Bacon. He was much inferior in scientific and philosophical powers to Galileo and the other leaders of thought—'he writes philosophy like a Lord Chancellor', William Harvey tartly said of him; but he busied himself in projects for the spread and utilization of science, which, precisely perhaps because of his lack of scientific genius, bring the subject nearer to the worlds of politics, committees, and economic organization. Bacon did indeed believe that there was a scientific method which anyone of moderate good sense could employ; and though he, too, tended to share the illusion that the main scientific discoveries would be made very quickly, he did have a view of the scientific process which would allow of an indefinitely prolonged effort by the combined activities of sensible men who had been properly trained. His views have correspondingly had a wide appeal at different times to societies in which these qualities were at a premium; as the American scholar C. C. Gillispie has admirably put it in his recent book, *The Edge of Objectivity*:

> Baconianism has always held a special appeal as the way of science in societies which develop a vocation for the betterment of man's estate, and which confide not in aristocracies whether of birth or brains, but in a wisdom to be elicited from common pursuits — in seventeenth-century England, in eighteenth-century France, in nineteenth-century America, amongst Marxists of all countries.

Two Attitudes to the Scientist

Thus in the rise of modern scientific method at the beginning of the seventeenth century, and its displacement of appeals to authority in such matters, we find lurking two different attitudes to the scientist himself. On the one hand, there is the natural emphasis on the genius who invented the method, or at least applied it with conspicuous brilliance and success, and who may hope to apply it to all principal problems in his lifetime. On the other hand, there is the notion of a common understanding between men of good sense uncorrupted by traditional learning, to which the genius may appeal as an audience of his discoveries, and who may, once the method has been discovered, be able to apply it and carry on the business of scientific inquiry by a suitable division of labour. Neither of these attitudes contained the truth about science: it is not to the point here to examine the relations of the scientific genius to the vast body of scientists who are not geniuses; it is enough to say, contrary to both the Baconian and the genius-centred views, that both of these types are needed.

There is one feature of this situation, however, that demands a final word. In the adjustment over the last three centuries of what might be called the genius element and the journeyman element in the scientific process, one set of people who have tended to be excluded are those that are neither geniuses nor journeymen scientists: those non-scientific men of good sense, whom Galileo and Descartes had in mind, seem to have become scientists themselves, and have had their good sense suitably trained, or to remain non-scientific and find their good sense not adequate to understanding what is going on. The plain man seems once more, by a characteristic historical circle, to be set against authority, only this time the authority is that of the scientist: whether he is regarded as the genius whose processes of thought are beyond ordinary reach, or as the journeyman who, even if his talents are not much stronger than the plain man's, has had a formal professional training in techniques of thought and inquiry which are incomprehensible to the untrained mind, however good its sense.

For a plain man who suffers from this well-known feeling of exclusion from the world of natural science, a look at the history of scientific ideas in the seventeenth century can be most rewarding. For one thing, it can actually remove some of the grounds of the feeling: to see men of genius painfully constructing ideas which are now commonplace, in order to solve problems which are now, thanks to their efforts, simple, is to learn in fact a good deal about the processes of scientific thought. But even if it did not cure his present sense of exclusion, a visit to those years would fortify, retrospectively, as it were, his plain man's self-respect. For at some points in the seventeenth century, if he were lucky enough to be at the right place at the right time, he could for a short while see the world of scientific discovery clearly with his own eyes, under a brilliant sky in which the clouds of traditional authority had dispersed and the clouds of expert authority had not yet gathered.

8

What Is Existentialism?

It is not easy to explain Existentialism, for two reasons. First, it is by any standards an obscure philosophy, whose exponents tend to express themselves in a very dark style. Second, there is a great variety of thinkers who might be called in the broadest sense 'existentialists', but whose views are very different one from another—some are Marxists, some liberals; some are atheists, and others Christians. Not all of those often called 'Existentialists' will accept the title.

Nevertheless, some threads run through this range of thought. To pick up the threads, it is probably best to look at the historical influences that have produced Existentialism. Of these, the most important is perhaps the nineteenth-century Danish thinker, Søren Kierkegaard. Kierkegaard was a deeply religious man, dominated by the idea—an extreme Protestant idea—of man's inadequacy in the face of God. In particular, he

THE BRITISH BROADCASTING CORPORATION

HEAD OFFICE: BROADCASTING HOUSE, LONDON, W.I

BUSH HOUSE, STRAND, LONDON, W.C.2

TELEGRAMS AND CABLES: BROADCASTS, LONDON, TELEX ∗ INTERNATIONAL TELEX: 22182

TELEPHONE: COVENT GARDEN 3456

Ref.: Asian/07/LPB   24th January 1962

Dear Mr. Williams,

      I am writing to ask if you would be willing to write a
script for one of our programmes in Vietnamese.

      We broadcast a weekly programme of answers to listeners'
questions, and among the questions we have recently received for
inclusion in this programme is one from a listener in South Vietnam
on the subject of existentialism. He asks us to explain what
existentialism is, who are its leading exponents and whether it
has any important following in this country. I am hoping to include
an answer to these questions in a programme to be broadcast on
either 17th or 24th February, and I am wondering if you would be
willing to write a script on the subject which we could use in
our programme. The script would ideally be between 800 and 1,000
words in length and should reach me at the above address a little
before the actual date of transmission in order to allow adequate
time for translation, etc.

      I do hope you will be able to write a script for me on
these lines, and I look forward to hearing from you whenever you
may have an opportunity of writing.

                Yours sincerely,

                (L.P. Breen)
        Vietnamese Programme Organiser

B.A.O. Williams, Esq., M.A.,
Department of Philosophy,
University College,
Gower Street,
W.C.1.

This letter has been included as a reminder of the extraordinary work of the
BBC World Service in more generous times.

rejected with great vehemence and impressive intensity the philosophy then dominant in Europe, the philosophy of Hegel. Hegel's system he regarded as abstract, intellectual, inhuman, and as offering false comforts: it tried to absorb man and his individual experience into a generalised picture of the world, and this concealed what Kierkegaard saw as a gulf between men and the world, and between men and God, which could only be bridged by an act of faith, a leap in the dark, which had to be taken in 'fear and trembling'. To lose oneself in the generalised notions of an academic system like Hegel's was to evade reality and responsibility.

A certain influence from Kierkegaard can be found in all existential-ists, even those who, unlike him, are atheists. Among such existentialists, the best-known is the contemporary French philosopher, playwright, and novelist, Jean-Paul Sartre; his views are largely shared by his friend, the woman writer Simone de Beauvoir. Sartre's central view is that 'man has no essence'—that there is nothing that he *has* to be, no fixed pattern laid down for him to follow. The basic fact about man is just that he *exists*: hence the name 'existentialist'. He exists, moreover, as a conscious being, someone who can be aware of what he is doing—aware, moreover, of this fact that there is no fixed pattern laid down for him, no values given to him from outside. This awareness gives man freedom to choose: and he has to choose, to commit himself, to certain values, and a certain way of life. This choice is, however, arbitrary: there is nothing to show a man how he must choose, but choose he must. Hence the despair or anxiety which writers like Sartre find at the bottom of things—it comes from the fact that man must choose, when his choice must in the end be arbitrary. Man must make his own values—out of nothing. There are indeed ac-cording to Sartre some people who attempt to conceal this state of affairs from themselves, by persuading themselves that some way of life or sys-tem of values is absolute, dictated by the world: but this is an illusion, and such people are merely trying to deny their freedom. They are, in Sartre's phrase, 'in bad faith'.

Existentialism is essentially concerned with problems of choice and personal commitment; and it is indeed one of its beliefs that it is only through direct personal living, the agencies of real choice, that anything can really be understood. Not surprisingly therefore writers like Sartre express their outlook as much through plays and novels as through for-mal works of philosophy, though Sartre and others also write such works.

Existentialism is a movement largely centred in France and Germany, and has very little influence in Great Britain. This is in part because the more philosophical or theoretical parts of Existentialism belong to a tra-dition of obscure metaphysical writing, having its origins in Germany, which has never appealed to the more pragmatic and literal-minded Brit-ish thinkers. The most obscure of Existentialist thinkers, the German

Martin Heidegger, would be thought by most British critics to be often writing what is quite literally nonsense. The more dramatic parts of Existentialism, on the other hand, its emphasis on the terrors of moral choice and the absence of any absolute principles of life, while they have relevance everywhere, naturally strike home hardest in countries where the political structure has in the recent past disintegrated or been overthrown. The French interest in Existentialism arose in the first place chiefly from the moral problems of the Resistance to the Germans in Occupied France.

These dramatic and personal aspects of Existentialism are probably of greater significance than its metaphysical theories. Even though Sartre and others have produced some important theoretical ideas, the main body of Existentialist theory is likely to appear to the future as a special and extreme type of German Romantic metaphysics rather than as a central contribution to the history of philosophy. The notion of 'existential living', however, with its emphasis on commitment, has certainly had a considerable impact on many people's thoughts about values, and on their actions, and may continue to do so.

9

Sketch for a Theory of the Emotions, by Jean-Paul Sartre

This is a translation of a brief work that was published in 1939, and it is an excellent thing that it has appeared.[1] It is of considerable interest in its own right, and also serves as a comparatively luminous introduction to some of the themes which Sartre pursues more portentously in *Being and Nothingness*. Not all readers may entirely agree with the blurb when it says that the essay 'is nowhere an obscure or difficult work,' but it is true that it has a special briskness and lightness of touch.

Sartre starts by criticising three existing theories of emotion—a 'theory of emotion' being a theory about what emotions essentially are, of what distinguishes them from other psychological happenings. The theories criticised are those of William James, that an emotion consists of consciousness of an internal physiological disturbance; of Pierre Janet, that emotion is 'the behaviour of defeat'; and of certain Gestalt psychologists, that emotion (the example particularly considered is anger) is an escape from tension experienced in trying to 'structure' a recalcitrant environment. Of these theories, Sartre regards the third as better than the second, and the second as better than the first; we are approaching, without reaching the truth.

He then turns to criticism of psychoanalytic theories, the point of attack being the concept of the unconscious; this is a theme he has developed in later writings. From this, he moves to his own theory, which occupies the last forty or so pages of the book. The central idea of this is that emotion is a more primitive state of consciousness or way of seeing the world, the essence of which is that it embodies a belief in magic. The object of a fear, for instance, may be seen as horrible quite independently of any powers for harm it may be believed to have; the fact that the horrible face at the window is on *the other side* of the window just disappears in the state of terror.

More basically, the magical element occurs in the reactions of the man in the emotion; in fear we may faint, and this is a magical way of seeking to annihilate the object of fear—like a man faced with a difficult problem who just goes to sleep. The account is not supposed to apply only to negative emotions; with great ingenuity, Sartre applies the same ideas to joy, for instance, which he identifies as a magical way of trying to make simultaneous and complete satisfactions incomplete and successive.

As so often with Sartre, I find myself left at the end dazzled but doubtful. The cleverness and imagination are enormous, and sometimes one is convinced. But even where one is, there is a doubt about what one has been convinced of. This doubt goes back to Sartre's method, the so-called 'phenomenological' method, which he took (with adaptations) from Husserl. The philosophy of this method is complex and not easy to make clear. Mrs. Mary Warnock, in a brief but helpful preface to this book, goes some way to making it clear, though I wonder whether—despite her disclaimers—she has not overestimated the genuine influence of Descartes on Sartre. For Descartes, mind or consciousness is something to be investigated independently of the world, by way of reflexion. With Sartre, for whom it is essential that consciousness does not have to be reflexive, that we can experience without thinking that we experience, we discover the activities of consciousness by giving a description of the world as it appears to consciousness: the activities of mind are, as it were, 'read back' from the world as it seems in different states of mind.

There are two great difficulties with this method. One is that the 'activities' of mind which are posited seem so often to be fictional; in Sartre all the time we are doing things—and, in one sense, consciously doing things—of which we are not aware. The other difficulty lies in evaluating the descriptions of the world as it seems. The world of, say, a frightened man may be described in many ways; is there any method of deciding which description is, for the purposes of this philosophy, the best, the one that gets nearest to the essence of fear? We may be able to get no further than seeing that some descriptions 'come off' and others do not. At any rate, some of Sartre's do most resoundingly come off.[2]

Notes

1. *Sketch for a Theory of the Emotions*, by Jean-Paul Sartre, translated by Philip Mairet (Methuen, 1962).

2. This review originally appeared as "World As It Seems," *Spectator*, August 3, 1962.

10

Sense and Sensibilia and *Philosophical Papers*, by J. L. Austin

Sense and Sensibilia consists of a course of lectures that Austin gave for several years, mostly skilfully stitched together from the notes by Mr Warnock.[1] It is a remarkable book: original, clear, forceful, entertaining and salutary. It is bound to have, as Austin's personal influence had, a considerable effect on the terms of philosophical discussion. After it, the philosophy of perception cannot be discussed in ways it usually was discussed before.

It is one of the peculiarities of philosophy, however, that the influence and genuine importance of a philosophical work can be remarkably independent of its actual success in doing what, in the narrower terms of its thesis and argument, it sets out to do. In the case of *Sense and Sensibilia*, it is not easy to determine just what it does set out to do; but of various aims that might plausibly be ascribed to it, only one really comes off.

This is the aim, which serves as a thread running through the book, of showing that certain of the arguments used by Ayer in *The Foundations of Empirical Knowledge* do not work. Austin's more important criticisms of these arguments are very effective; in particular he brings out, very briefly and clearly, an important circularity in Ayer's approach (p. 60).

But Austin's purpose, of course, was not just to criticise Ayer: he did not merely want to give, in lectures year after year, a hostile review of certain passages in a twenty-year-old book. A wider purpose, it seems, was to destroy a thesis of which Ayer's book was one expression: the thesis that there are certain objects called 'sense-data', which we perceive in a way more direct or immediate than that in which we perceive tables, chairs, and so forth. This more general aim of refutation, if he really had it, Austin cannot be said to have accomplished. For one thing, he explicitly leaves out of consideration one important type of argument for sense-data, used by Ayer, and also by Price, whose book *Perception* is occasionally referred to: an argument from the causal conditions of perception (cf. p. 46, note 2). For another thing, he blandly ignores certain difficulties on which some philosophers (notably Moore) put a lot of weight in arguing for sense-data. We speak of seeing a star, and also of seeing a silvery speck; this silvery speck is one sort of thing that people have wanted to call 'a sense-datum'. But, Austin asks, 'wouldn't we be prepared to say, and quite correct in saying, that the silvery speck *is* a star?' (p. 92). Isn't it just like kicking a piece of painted wood, and kicking Jones' door (p. 98); or like seeing Hitler, and seeing a man in black trousers (p. 99)? Answer: no; for the reason that Austin himself gives us, undisturbedly, in discussing another example (p. 98, note)—that though I may say 'that white dot on the horizon is my house', this does not license the conclusion that I live in a white dot. But if I live behind Jones' door, I live behind that piece of wood, and if (alarmingly) I lived with Hitler, I lived with that man in black trousers. That is to say, the analogies supposed to show *simple identity* here do not work; and it is precisely this fact that has inspired an important sort of talk about sense-data. Sense-data are, in fact, a pretty dead duck by now; but if the duck has any life in it, Austin's arguments are not enough to finish it off.

However, this may not matter so much. Perhaps, after all, his concern with the sense-datum theorists is only incidental. He has a still more general aim: to illustrate how philosophers tend to obliterate important distinctions, to ignore the diversity of the facts, and to take little notice of how our language actually works. For this aim, the examples of *some* arguments about sense-data will do. Austin repeatedly claims that these arguments fail because they ignore the vast variety of relevant situations, and also the distinctions between many different linguistic expressions, and uses of the same expression, that apply to those situations. Now it seems to be Austin's thesis that the first of these neglects is in some way due to the second: that the crude *Gleichschaltung* of importantly different situations has been caused by philosophers' neglecting subtle distinctions in the ordinary use of language. Part of the general aim of the book might be taken to be that of showing this connection.

If so, it is once more very doubtful whether Austin succeeds. His own practice does not do much to bear out the connection. For instance, Austin points out that Ayer and others have tended to use 'material object' merely as a foil to 'sense-datum', and have implied that anything that (roughly) is publicly perceptible is a material object. This he rightly criticizes—not, however, by talking about the uses of 'material', or of 'perceive', but by just reminding us of how many sorts of things we can see, hear, etc. Conversely Austin does some subtle work of distinguishing uses of 'looks', 'seems' and 'appears' in their various constructions, displaying in this the fine linguistic ear which was one of his outstanding gifts. But this set of distinctions is not at all closely tied into the argument; in particular, he does not show at all how neglect of them has misled the sense-datum theorists. It would be odd, *prima facie*, if, for some of these usages, he could do so, since they have nothing specially to do with perception at all.

In general, it is remarkable how little Austin uses his methods of close linguistic observation to support the specifically philosophical points that he makes, such as his claims that there are no incorrigible statements, and that there is no intrinsic relation between two statements which is that of one's being evidence for the other. Correspondingly, the linguistic observations seem often to be pursued for their own sake. This impression is borne out by various pieces in the *Philosophical Papers*, in which Messrs Urmson and Warnock have assembled all Austin's published, and three unpublished, papers.[2] Moreover, there are in this book some pointers to why this detachment of philosophy and linguistic study should occur: there is a good deal to suggest that Austin actively wanted in his linguistic studies, to get *away* from philosophical problems. This, then, is why the sense-datum theorists get such incomplete treatment; Austin's aim was to remove, not so much belief in their answers, as interest in their questions.

There was, however, to be a way back to philosophy. The linguistic study would lead back eventually to the subjects which the philosophical theorists had over-rapidly attacked—it was to be, in a famous phrase, the 'begin-all'. How was the 'begin-all' to be pursued? Austin's answer to this seems to have been a Baconian one: that one patiently assembled distinctions in ordinary use, and then elicited from them a pattern or theory—perhaps at that stage, but only at that stage, introducing some technical terms of one's own. The trouble about this is, that if it is taken literally, it is just impossible. There is no classification without a purpose—in theoretical matters, without a theory or a problem. Without some pre-existing notion of what one wants the distinctions for, their number is entirely indeterminate: one can go on making as many as one likes. Some-times, indeed, Austin seems just to be making some distinctions which take his fancy. Often, however, Austin in fact had a firm idea at the be-ginning what he wanted the distinctions to do, and assembled them ac-cordingly; and because he was a man of great philosophical insight, the assembly is often illuminating. Without the insight, the same activity is boring and pointless; he had not discovered, any more than Bacon had, a method that could be handed over to mechanics to churn out results.

Apart from the way in which the activity was to be conducted, what was the point of it? Why all this close scrutiny of ordinary uses? Here we meet a curious view of Austin's, which might be called his 'Wisdom of the Ages' thesis: that our ordinary speech contains a battery of distinctions that men have found useful through the centuries, and which have stood the test of time, and that these are likely to be sounder than any which a theorist can—at least when in a hurry—think up. There is a strong *prima facie* case for thinking that our ordinary working distinctions are very good anyway; and if we are to improve on them—as it is possible that we might, in some cases—we have at the very least to discover what they are first (cf. *Sense and Sensibilia*, p. 63; *Papers*, p. 133 *et al.*).

This view, of course, already presupposes some substantial posi-tions about the nature of philosophy, to the effect that a certain kind of speculative philosophy, the kind that tried to show that men were *quite mistaken* about some fundamental features of the world, is im-possible. If all these distinctions had been elaborated under a gigantic misapprehension, there could scarcely be much point in studying them. Thus the view takes for granted a whole lot of arguments right from the beginning. But since it shares this presupposition with most views at the present time, and with many at others, and since (to put it mildly) it is a presupposition for which there is something to be said, this is not the most interesting point about Austin's view. A more interesting question is that of its conservatism, even within the range of philosophy that is not enormously speculative. Now the charge that Austin was a linguistic conservative has been made, and has been rebutted by reminding us that the study of existing uses was indeed a 'begin-all'—after the investiga-tion, then possibly reform. But this is still, in fact, conservatism. It is particularly so if conjoined with the Baconian thesis about the meth-ods of investigation, for on that thesis, the investigation will be literally interminable. Even without that, it is conservative. It amounts to the proposal that no revolution or even reform can be mounted without a thorough sociological investigation of the *ancien régime*; and this is a proposal which in other contexts is rightly regarded as amounting to the proposal that there be no reform.

If Austin's advice had prevailed in the past, there would have been very little philosophy. This, perhaps, he would not have deplored. But there is a further question: if these Burkean counsels had been followed, would we now have a good number of the distinctions and usages that we do have in *ordinary language*? For *who* was it who laid down this intricate web of linguistic institutions? Austin writes vaguely of 'the inherited experience and acumen of many generations of men . . . [in] the practical business of life' (*Papers*, p. 133). But don't we need some real historical material about the changes in language? Above all, about the repeated impact on it, particularly in the fields Austin was most concerned with, of the despised hasty theorists? In language, as in politics, the conservative runs into the fact that the old is only what used to be new.

There are other ways in which Austin's attitude to language seems historically unrealistic. Sometimes his respect for the old seems to cloud his natural appreciation of the realities and vaguenesses of lexicography, and his tone reminds one almost of another Burke, that of the *Peerage*; as when he writes of 'our vast and, for the most part, *relatively ancient* stock of ordinary words' (*Sense and Sensibilia*, p. 63: my italics). What is the antiquity of a word? How ancient, for example, is the word 'idea'?

I suspect that the Wisdom of the Ages thesis is in fact a *myth*, a fanciful picture of the past designed to justify certain activities in the present. Austin was fascinated by, and extraordinarily gifted in detecting, nuances of ordinary speech. He also had great philosophical imagination and acumen. He sought to bring the two together, by urging the study of ordinary use as the method of philosophy, or at least a method necessarily preliminary to philosophy. At the theoretical level, I do think he succeeded. In his practice, it is notable that he often scarcely tried. When he did try, and succeeded, it was above all at the level of *persuasion*, in his extremely skilful deployment of fine linguistic distinctions as a weapon to encourage—or, more characteristically, to discourage—the holding of certain philosophical beliefs.

In this use of philosophical dissuasion, there is an obvious parallel with the later Wittgenstein. Neither had any faith in the older aspirations to philosophical proof; both urged patience and the recognition of untidy complexities; both substituted for older styles a persuasive method that was more effective in their own hands than it is (at least in a pure form) in the hands of others. They were, however, at completely opposite ends of the psychological spectrum in philosophy. The aim of Wittgenstein's method was illumination; its highest term of commendation, 'depth'; its fault, allusive obscurity. Austin—who carried to really remarkable lengths the English dislike of pretentiousness—sought plain truth; by way of accuracy; and the danger was pedantry. To which of these ways one is more attracted must be a question of temperament. But it must be said—as Popper rightly insists—that no branch of human thought has ever advanced by making its watchword just the accumulation of as many truths as possible, accurately expressed. These two remarkable books would not be as interesting and valuable if Austin had taken himself, as he insisted on taking other philosophers, literally.

Notes

1. *Sense and Sensibilia*, by J. L. Austin, reconstructed by G. J. Warnock (Clarendon Press, 1962).

2. *Philosophical Papers*, by J. L. Austin, edited by J. O. Urmson and G. J. Warnock (Clarendon Press, 1961).

11

The Concept of a Person, by A. J. Ayer

This book of essays (four new and five reprinted) gives a very good view of Professor Ayer's present philosophical situation, which is an interesting one.[1] It is now a long time since he gave up any large-scale adherence to the logical positivism that he originally expounded in that dazzling book, *Language, Truth, and Logic*, but he retains a loyalty to certain features of positivism. This can take the form of a nostalgic attachment to specific doctrines, and then it tends to have a Quixotic ring. In the first of these papers, which was his inaugural lecture at Oxford given in 1960, he says 'for my part I have no wish to disown the verification principle, though it suffers from a vagueness which it has not yet been found possible to eradicate'; and this indeed is pure loyalty, since it is a long time since anyone, including Ayer, has worked to improve the verification principle, and it is obvious, from this paper itself and also from others in the book, that he is no longer interested in it.

These infrequent gestures towards the Clause Four of his philosophy are unimportant. What is important, and very stimulating, is his adherence to something else: a general temper of philosophical argument which he showed in his positivist period, and which is not that most frequently met with today. Although positivism did, in an untypical way, have this tone, it belongs most typically to a philosopher who has never been a positivist, Bertrand Russell. The literary style of this book—which contains some of the best of Ayer's excellent writing—often reminds one of Russell, though with less surface brilliance, fewer jokes, and a greater devotion to painstaking argument. There are also beliefs that he shares with Russell: for instance, that philosophical conclusions can be straightforwardly (well, fairly straightforwardly) true or false, and can be shown to be so by argument; and that it is appropriate to speak of those conclusions that have not yet been shown to be true or false as though they were *hypotheses*, probable or improbable, well or ill-supported.

These are not the most prevalent beliefs in philosophy today; the ways of speaking that go with them cause many philosophers discomfort. The two thinkers who have most influenced British philosophy in the last 15 years, Wittgenstein and J. L. Austin, both did a lot, in different ways, to bring this about. Wittgenstein, though entirely involved in philosophy, doubted whether it could offer truths; Austin, in pursuit of truths, doubted whether they were to be found in philosophy. Wittgenstein developed an informal but very powerful style of reflection which sought insight into the origins of philosophical problems; Austin, up to his untimely death in 1960, devoted himself in good part to the accurate study of certain linguistic expressions in common use, hoping, it seems, by these means to by-pass traditional centres of philosophical argument and confusion.

Ayer is evidently sceptical about both these influences; and the interest of his situation is that, Wittgenstein and Austin having gone, he finds himself, at the height of his powers, sustaining philosophical methods that both of them had known very well, and had rejected. With Austin, there is perhaps no very great difficulty: his considerable, though unfinished, contribution is something that one can to some extent take or leave, and Ayer leaves most of it. With Wittgenstein, the problem is harder. His impact, both on the spirit of philosophy and on some particular issues, was enormous, and cannot be ignored. The problem, of the departed genius who has apparently dissolved one's own idiom, is just there—Ayer is the Brahms to Wittgenstein's Wagner.

The most superficial difficulty about this situation is that one may appear to the modish a bit old-fashioned. Ayer does not mind this at all, but on the contrary enjoys it; his enthusiasm for shocking the establishment (another resemblance to Russell) has merely found a newer object. (This enthusiasm has indeed led him, in this book, to make a curious slip: in the paper called 'Names and Descriptions' he criticises, from a Russellian point of view, what he calls 'a fashionable theory of reference', which, although it has been recently favoured, in fact belongs essentially to Frege, and is older than Russell's.) However, an enthusiastic refusal to succumb cannot be enough by itself; it needs substantial backing.

Ayer provides backing; his methods justify themselves, if not always to the same extent. Some of the pieces treat topics over which Wittgenstein's shadow falls less densely, and most of these are a great success; the ones on probability, laws of nature, and fatalism, for instance, are splendid examples of clear, straightforward and powerful argument. Elsewhere, as in the title piece and one called 'Can there be a Private Language?', he is nearer to Wittgenstein's main topics and his influence, and here I find that although the same virtues are often displayed, the outcome is less satisfactory. There is one particularly important reason for this. Ayer is still very attached to what was a thesis of positivism, and before that, of Hume, that any connection between two propositions or states of affairs must be either purely logical, a matter of meaning and definition, or else merely contingent, a matter of fact. Wittgenstein in effect rejected this axiom: the connection, for instance, between a feeling and its overt expression he regarded as neither of these (and not 'synthetic *a priori*', either). Now it is certainly true that his views on this have never been clearly formulated. But too much of what he says, it seems to me, is illuminating for one to suppose that there is nothing there at all, that it is all a big mistake. Whatever it is that is in the shadow, Ayer has not finally come to grips with it.

His failure to do so, however, is not an evasion. For what is particularly impressive about this book is its honesty. Even when Ayer hurries, as he sometimes does, he is not hurrying by on the other side. In the self-conscious commitment to his methods, there is nothing fake or fudged or done merely for effect. In this also, as in historical position — if in nothing else whatsoever — Ayer is like Brahms.

Note

1. *The Concept of a Person*, by A. J. Ayer (Macmillan, 1963).

12

Two Faces of Science

What are the two faces of science? At one level, it is just that we have a notion of science as technological power, which is by its very nature ambiguous, and which can be used, as preachers and others remind us every day, for good or for ill—bacteriological research for saving life or for germ warfare, nuclear energy for power-stations or for bombs. This is the most familiar form of the conflict between two aspects of science—the contrast between good and evil uses of technology. But although it is the most familiar form, I am sure it is not the only one, and fairly sure that it is not the most fundamental. Because, first of all, one certainly has not given an adequate account of the fear that many people have of technological progress if one just points out that technological discoveries can have evil uses. What may frighten them more deeply, in a way, is not so much the evil uses of technology as the evil consequences of its good uses; for we all know that we ought to be avoiding the evil uses, but of course are only too happy to pursue the good uses, with the alarming consequences they may entail: consequences which in the popular imagination may run all the way from the relatively immediate problems of unemployment due to automation, through to pictures of a future society in which we may be able to live indefinitely, construct in advance a genetic programme for our children, and educate them by direct causal action on their brains: all with results that we are afraid to dream about.

But even when one has added in these elements, I still do not think one has fully expressed the conflict between the light and the dark sides of our latent idea of science. For all this is still concerned with science as a means; it is concerned with science as technology. But I do not think that on either side, the positive or the negative, can the conflict be put as simply as this implies. For, on the one hand, there is certainly a prestige, an excitement, a cultural and intellectual value, which is thought, and rightly thought, to attach to science independently of its technological output. And on the negative side there is the point that this very excitement and human satisfaction involved in the scientific process can undermine the simple relations of means and ends; it can bring it about that we never find ourselves just in the situation of being able to decide how or whether to use certain scientific means. There is the fear, at least, that inherent in the impetus of scientific advance itself is a certain necessity that those means which are possible will be discovered, and those means that have been discovered will be used.

But let us go back to the positive side. There is in present society a genuine cultural enthusiasm for the idea of science itself, and in particular for the pure sciences. Why this *is* so is a complex question, involving, among other things, the economic basis of modern society, and its effects on people's attitudes. But why it *ought* to be so seems to me, on the other hand, a very easy question to answer, at least if you are prepared, as I am, to answer it in an unabashed high-minded way: it is because the achievements of the natural sciences represent in our age the highest intellectual and imaginative achievements of man, that is to say our highest cultural achievements.

As soon as I use the word 'cultural' like that, there are people who, like Hermann Goering, reach for their gun; and we immediately find ourselves in the now desolated intellectual no-man's land of the so-called 'two cultures'. I am not going to attempt the discouraging task of putting together the ruins that litter the ground there. But since this is a personal view, let me dogmatically state a position. Sir Charles Snow was quite right, in my view, to draw attention, as Lord Russell and others had done before him, to a certain anomaly in our intellectual life. One is not generally regarded in intellectual circles as an educated or cultivated person unless one has, for instance, some conception of what the Middle Ages or the Renaissance stand for, or of what was done by Dante, or Titian, or Goethe, or Beethoven; and so too, for contemporary artists. But it is not in the same way always regarded as an occasion for cultivated embarrassment if ignorance is shown, or even declared, of the achievements of Galileo, or Newton, or Mendel, or (in the present time) of relativity theory or molecular biology. This state of affairs is certainly absurd: absurd for more than one reason.

The Enemy of Parochialism

I take it that a chief aim of culture and education of any kind is to be the enemy of parochialism: that by knowledge both of fact in general and of man's achievements at other times and in other places one can form a juster assessment of one's own place and the place of one's society in the scheme of things. These general considerations about any sort of culture evidently apply to science, both in respect of the history of science and of certain present conclusions, theories, and also methods, of the sciences. The history is important, as part of what man has achieved; the present state is important, because parochialism will hardly have been resisted, if while one has some general conception of how one's society has evolved from other societies, as may be taught by the humane discipline of history, one nevertheless has no conception, or at least no living and effective conception, of how man himself evolved, for instance, or of the place of his planet in the universe.

But this is not the only point: for there is another sense of 'culture' in which to speak of a common culture is to speak of men sympathizing in and sharing some common aim, and living in an environment which is commonly understood. And whatever the difficulties of such conceptions in modern society, it is certain that men cannot fare well if they are cut off from an understanding of the methods and results of those activities that provide the central achievements of their time; or even, to go to a lower level, if they cannot comprehend, at least in outline, the nature and workings of the mere mechanical devices with which they are surrounded. They will be living in an alien world.

To these sorts of arguments—and they are familiar enough—it is often replied that there just is a barrier against understanding; that those not formally educated in the natural sciences can never attain to anything but superficial misunderstanding of them, and that this is on intellectual grounds disreputable, and worse than useless. The merit of this reply seems to me to depend on who advances it. If a specialist in one branch of science condemns as superficial the understanding of that branch by a non-expert, I will sympathize with him; for one knows that any expert in anything will inevitably so regard non-expert understanding, and, within his frame of reference, rightly so. But this point, of course, applies as much to relations between different scientists as it does to those between scientists and others. We have got into the habit of talking about 'science' as though it were one big thing that you are either inside or out of, but this is a mistake: there are sciences, and branches of the same science, and experts in one may have at most nodding acquaintance with the work in others. Yet scientists in different disciplines, unless themselves very narrow men, do think it worth while to have a little understanding of other scientists' work. So why not others? When the objection—nowadays usually put in the tempting form 'it is an insult to science to treat it superficially'—is advanced by non-scientists, it has all the characteristics of a psychological defence-mechanism. For they are demanding in this case what they do not demand in any other: expert knowledge, or no knowledge at all. But in no other cultural field whatsoever is such a ridiculous demand made. The knowledge that most of us have of the Middle Ages would be regarded as shallow and inadequate by an undergraduate specializing in that period; our knowledge of the history of art, by an art-historian; of music, by a musicologist: yet those bits of knowledge, giving us some general sense of how things go in those areas, are worth having.

But I do not accept the 'two cultures' formulation, and in particular I do not accept that the issue is at all just about those who have had some sort of scientific training versus those who have not. For in the sense that I care about the cultural significance of scientific achievement, a feeling for this may be as effectively lacking in those who have had scientific training as in those who have not. I have myself talked to groups of students in the sciences, both in technology and in the pure sciences, and been alarmed by the lack, in some of them, of any such feeling. Competent technically, they had no feeling for the history, role, or basic nature of their activities; science as one great human activity and achievement among others—for this is what it is—meant little to them.

Nor is this entirely confined to students; nor—and this is actually more dangerous—does this lack of understanding only take the form of *having no views* on the human significance of scientific and technological processes. There are some people—and I must emphasize, in case it is not already totally obvious, that I mean only a very few among the scientists and technologists I have met—who do have a set of very passionate views on such issues; views, however, which are not illuminated by any general understanding of historical or social matters, and which these people falsely think can be supported from science itself. These views come roughly to saying that technological progress is all; that a tough-minded utilitarianism is the only acceptable social philosophy; that there cannot be any free will and hence, it is supposed, present conceptions of justice and so forth are archaic, and to be replaced by techniques of social control. And occasionally, in their headier moments, they add that since only technologists understand these matters and are free from archaic illusions, they ought to have a much larger say in what happens. This set of views, just put baldly like that, is a caricature; but in a few cases at least the caricature comes uncomfortably close to the truth. And what is certain is that such a caricature plays a role in what I called earlier the negative aspect of our latent idea of science; this is one thing that frightens, when we think about a certain impetus in technological advance itself to produce an inhuman world.

Though it is a familiar point, it cannot be said too often that the sorts of views I have just caricatured, whatever merits they may or may not have, are in no sense whatsoever part or consequences of any natural science or technological application of it, and to suppose that they are is not only a philosophical mistake but grossly unscientific as well. To make it clear that science by itself cannot give us the clue to the social future is one task of those who educate scientists; just as it is a task for those who educate the others to make it clear that without some knowledge and sympathy with the sciences no one will understand the social future, or the past or present either. I do not think that these educational tasks need be quite as difficult as many people have been making out. Looking more closely at the ambiguous face of science, it is not so hard to see how it is in the highest sense one among human activities.

13

The English Moralists, by Basil Willey

This book has emerged from a course of lectures which the author gave, as he rather dauntingly informs us in the Preface, for more than thirty years in the University of Cambridge.[1] The course of lectures and the examination paper that it serves were conceived at a time—as Willey mentions—when the remnants of a pure aestheticism made it less than fashionable to attempt to relate literature and morality. They continued—though this he does not mention—through a period when his colleague in Cambridge, F. R. Leavis, was indeed relating literature to morality, but in a way that still gave little scope to the reflective history of moral ideas: the morality to which Leavis relates literature is *a* morality, a particular kind of outlook which, being identified with the essence of creative literary sensibility itself, becomes the basis of a peculiarly timeless kind of criticism.

Thus Willey, in more than one climate of opinion, has kept alive the connections between the study of English literature and the history of ideas. From his efforts there has come a string of sturdy and not unworthy books: the *Seventeenth* and *Eighteenth Century Backgrounds*, the *Nineteenth Century Studies*. They, too, got some of their matter from this persistent course of lectures, and the lecture-room tone, it must be said, is often present in their helpful summaries of reported writers. Now, in the year of his retirement from the King Edward VII Chair of English Literature, Willey has cleaned up the rest of his accumulated notes and published them as *The English Moralists*, both as a memorial of the years' activities, and with the hope (typical of a certain Cambridge introversion) that the book may help his successors, "if only as a historical atlas or as an awful warning," in guiding the future course of these same lectures.

It would be ungracious of Willey's successors, whoever they may be, to take him up too peremptorily on the second, at least, of these preferred interpretations. Yet perhaps it will be better if they do. There is, very obviously, no recipe for valuable writing in the history of ideas, no substantial maxims to make sure that what is written will be helpful or illuminating. But there are at least a few crude necessary conditions that one may look for, such as accuracy (to a reasonable degree) and absence of prejudice (of an unreasonable sort), and these conditions Willey satisfies only intermittently. This is because there are two substantial matters which, in quite different ways, he has not got under control: philosophy and Christianity.

Philosophy he puts down right at the beginning with some bravado:

> The "English Moralists" paper has been criticized as "amateur moral science," but I find it difficult to take that criticism seriously. It has been demonstrated over and over again that the "history of ideas" is not something which people with a literary training cannot grasp. They do not need to be professional philosophers in order to attain such knowledge, or enough of it to enrich and illuminate their literary studies.

("Moral science," I should perhaps explain, is Cambridge's term for philosophy.)

What Willey says here is not exactly untrue; but the extent to which it is true depends very much on what sort of history of ideas is in question, both the sort of ideas, and the sort of history. The kind of approach that comes from a concentration on philosophy will not perhaps be at a premium in studying ideas whose chief and most influential expression is not to be found in philosophers: the idea of progress, possibly, or the contemporary idea of honesty with oneself as a supreme moral ideal (the history of which is not yet written). Again, there may be a point for the history of ideas in not approaching even philosophers too philosophically; too nice a concentration on what they actually meant may disguise the influence that derived from their being misunderstood, and with some philosophers, Rousseau for instance, this is all-important. Yet while this is so, there will be some paradox in ignoring philosophy too much; for how is one to chart the misunderstandings, without philosophical understanding of what the philosopher really meant? At this point, there emerges the shallowness of Willey's approach, with its academic classifications of "literary training" and "professional philosophers." The truth, though simple, is more complex than the syllabus: that philosophical insight is not something separate from the *literary* understanding of philosophical writing, because it is not separate from understanding philosophical writing at all. Nor can there be a history of ideas without identification of ideas; and to identify *what* ideas are embodied in a text, particularly a philosopher's text, is no less a matter of philosophical comprehension than of anything else (which does not mean that those with "a literary training" are debarred from reaching it).

Willey in fact adopts, of all possible courses, the one for which his professed lack of philosophical knowledge, and his evident lack of philosophical sense, least suits him: he gives up a good part of his book to trying just to state, as briefly as possible, the views of various philosophers. This is not a fruitful activity at best; under the present auspices, the outcome is a sustained exercise in missing the point. Two of the more important sufferers are Locke and Hume. Locke's views on primary and secondary qualities, on substance, on revelation, and on the will, are variously mis-stated, misunderstood, or over-simplified; while some dark hints about "moral relativity" in his ethics are left untroubled by any statement of the fact that Locke actually aspired to make ethics into an *a priori* science. Locke is a confused thinker, indeed, but not boringly so, because his confusions are those of a highly intelligent and honest man trying to stand upright on intellectual ground that is shifting under his feet; Willey's disservice is to make him dreary.

Hume inspires a rather more lively treatment, but it is no more accurate: important arguments (on the sense of duty and on miracles) are so stated as to omit precisely the basic idea, and Willey seems ignorant of important work on the interpretation of Hume, notably Kemp Smith's on the *Dialogues on Natural Religion*. Hume is not in any case likely to get discriminating treatment, since, apart from the subtlety of his philosophy, he is an ironist, and irony seems in general to jam Willey's apparatus: both *Gulliver's Travels* and *Candide* are very crudely handled.

Willey's insensibility to irony is equally apparent in his dealings with Aristotle, whose Magnanimous Man he takes for the ideal of the system. This interpretation has been accepted by some people; but it is surely mistaken and it scarcely gains much authority from Willey, who is prepared to say that the *Ethics* is one of "the world's most boring classics."

Aristotle is in fact the victim of something more interesting than misinterpretation: he is the prime casualty to Willey's ideology, a sternly Protestant Christianity, which is expounded, relied on, and—consistently with its own spirit—very little analyzed. It sets the tone for the whole historical enterprise, the basic tradition of our civilization being found in a Platonic-Augustinian dualism, very disadvantageous to the flesh: man is a composite being, torn between impulses towards the higher and the carnal. No wonder that Aristotle, of less Manichaean disposition, gets such short shrift. Bad luck on the history of ideas that identifies either of these traditions as the guiding thread of Western thought. Even in the Middle Ages, the doctrine is in trouble, trouble which Willey gratuitously compounds for himself by claiming that "throughout the Middle Ages [Aristotle] was not merely an authority, but *the* authority." This falsehood is mildly qualified on a later page; but Aristotle stays in the center, and it remains obscure whether Willey *allows* the Middle Ages to have been Aristotelian, because they were Christian, or is ready to *admit* that they were Aristotelian, because he himself is Protestant.

The ideologue can write history, even the history of what he rejects; the Enlightenment, for example, can be effectively studied by one who, as Willey does, regards the doctrine of Original Sin as a sure demonstration that all its ideals are hopeless. But such a study requires a complex feat of self-denial, a willing suspension of belief, a determination not to preach. In this Willey totally fails, with the result that parts of his book read like the grotesque sermon of a school chaplain warning the senior boys against the spiritual shortcomings of purely secular writings.

It is an ironical point that another of Willey's Cambridge colleagues, Herbert Butterfield, shares Willey's religious outlook, but bases on it an attitude to history which is totally, indeed extremely, the contrary: because of the pervasive sinfulness of man (as well as for other reasons) the historian must make no moral comment. A word from Butterfield would be valuable to any zealot who succeeds Willey in that famous course of lectures.

Note

1. *The English Moralists*, by Basil Willey (Norton, 1964).

14

Universities: Protest, Reform and Revolution

It seemed right to try to say something about the discontents and student protests which have been, in Britain as elsewhere, troubling the universities; and certainly to undertake some discourse on the nature, purpose, role or whatever of universities, which did not take seriously the basic questions raised by what is going on, would be an idiotic evasion. However, I realise that in giving a lecture on these issues one runs a special risk of being tedious: on the one hand because events are running very fast, and problems which seem absolutely central at one point may even shortly afterwards seem less urgent or important; on the other hand, because many of the issues which obviously are central have already been so extensively discussed in public, and by many of us almost obsessionally in private, that one may well wonder whether anything remains to be said, and whether one may not be too groggy to recognise it if there is.

At least, in face of that difficulty, I shall be selective, and will leave out a lot of relevant things, resisting in particular (you may be relieved to hear) the temptations of *a priori* sociological explanation—why student protest has specially appeared so far at some institutions rather than at others, and at this time rather than earlier; to what extent, also, the causes to which it addresses itself are also the causes of its happening. On this last point, I shall assume only that many at least of the causes to which it addresses itself are worth taking seriously; this would seem to me to be so even if some of the motive power of protest comes from deeper or more general sources. I don't think that any theory—historical, sociological, or even perhaps zoological—of why the banners are being raised is going to absolve one from honestly considering what is written on them.

Recent student protest has, obviously enough, been directed to two different sorts of issues, some of them concerned with how the university itself should be run, some of them with international or national political issues and a critique of the society in which the university exists. This last phrase itself shows, of course, that the two sorts of issue are by no means distinct, a point which radical protest insists upon. For one thing, internal disciplinary issues and questions of student freedom are very often precipitated by protests directed at the political issues; for another thing, protests against the university's system are often seen as protests against features of society itself. I shall be saying some more about those more radical endeavours later on. For the moment, however, I should like to consider one or two of the issues that bear most directly on the university's own structure and operation.

The joint statement of the NUS [National Union of Students] and the Vice-Chancellors, though it showed at various points, not surprisingly, thumb-prints from the heavy hand of compromise, seemed to me to offer many sensible suggestions; and I am going to start from the assumption that *at least that much* should be acceptable to university teachers and administrators. Anyone who is root and branch opposed to student participation in any university body except student societies and, perhaps, a joint catering committee, I shall not seek to persuade. The question seems to me about methods and limitations, and what principles should govern them, and the lines to be found between student participation, student freedom and student control. One such line that looks inviting, and is often invoked, is a line between the academic aspects of student life and its social aspects. It is often said, and very reasonably, that university authorities should be less fussed than many of them have been in the past with the regulation of students' private lives, and that we should see an end to the battery of regulations still to be found in some places concerning where students go, when they come in, where they sleep and with whom. Moreover, where regulation is required, that a lot more of it should be totally delegated or left in the hands of students themselves, rather than handed down from on high. It looks as though many of us, though doubtless not all, may be able to agree on that general direction, without prejudice to what we may think about courses, examinations, syllabus and so forth.

I certainly think the general direction a sound one; and when the recommendations of the Latey Report on the age of majority are put into law, the legal decks will be cleared for treating students as adults. But in taking that view, one has got to be aware of certain consequences, and also of certain limitations which are going to be encountered, at least unless the system is changed in remoter respects. If one is not aware of these limitations, one courts the illusion endemic to mere liberalism, that change can be quite painless, and that the mere removal of old-fashioned restrictions will leave everything in just the same space that it was in before, only with a bit more room to move around in it. One courts also the nemesis of that illusion: the situation in which, discovering change after all to involve some pain, and that it all has a tendency to go further and in different directions than expected, panic sets in, the wheels of liberalisation are thrown into reverse, and one has the classic formula for a revolution. I offer here no argument for conservatism—only against sentimentality. Conservatism indeed has this one true premiss, that significant changes have unexpected consequences; but from that it invalidly derives its own illusion, that you can avoid unexpected happenings by seeking to avoid change. I am only saying that if introducing significant change, one had better expect the unexpected; and it helps to give some thought about what directions one should look in for its arrival.

In this matter of student freedom and self-determination in social matters, I shall mention just two directions in which I think we ought to be looking; there are certainly others besides. First, I think we have to give some thought to the question of how we reconcile this line with another aspiration that many have, towards a greater involvement of students and teachers together, and a less distant, less purely functional, relation of teachers to students than is found in some universities. For as things actually are, it looks as though the two things do not go together, but rather the contrary. The universities in which there is least fuss and control, by the very nature of things, over students' private activities, are large, non-residential, urban institutions, in which students cram into lodgings, flats, studios, attics, in an unsupervised way, and lead—if they are lucky and not just doomed to loneliness—some autonomous kind of student life. Equally, and by the same token, they roll up for classes with teachers with whom they do not share (except in special cases) much of their private life, the teachers having likewise rolled up from leading, in the suburbs or wherever, some autonomous kind of teachers' life. Opposed to this, we have a picture of the residential, organic university, with college life and free timeless converse between students and teachers; and those are just the places with the gating rules, one-sex colleges, and the Senior Tutor hiding behind the dustbins to catch them climbing over the wall.

Of course, both of these pictures are caricatures—and very much so the second. Nevertheless, they stand for a genuine conflict of aims which may not be irresoluble, but does need to be resolved. A very senior teacher from my university was reported in *The Times* recently as having criticised, in a speech to a society for the very intelligent, the younger generation of university teachers for being too concerned with their academic careers, and not enough with their pupils; married young, with small children, concentrated on research and publication, they left the undergraduates alone as much as possible. He was comparing the situation, I believe, with an older Oxbridge style, and of course in terms of that comparison there is much in what he says. But is that older style what a student would want now? Would the splendidly dedicated old don make much sense in the style of student freedom which is now sought, or in the institutions required to realise it? May not students, in a good number of respects, *like* being left alone to an extent which the older school would regard as involving a failure of tutorial responsibility?

I am afraid the answer to that last question is both *yes* and *no*, which is why there is a conflict of aims here. There is indeed one replacement for the old bachelor don, in terms of the more liberated and autonomous student life: namely, the young bachelor—or at least unfamilied—teacher, little older than the students, who spontaneously shares the style, social or political, that they favour. But his, in the nature of things, cannot be a general solution, for mere reasons of age; and we know from recent experience that the situation has its own difficulties, sometimes involving—to put a contentious issue in the antiseptic language of the social sciences—a certain confusion of roles.

I do not want to suggest that there is any large-scale or insoluble difficulty in these points. I do think, however, that one image of a university which goes very naturally with the aspirations to a less regulated student life clashes with an image which is on other grounds favoured; and such a conflict of images, if not made conscious and resolved as best it may be, is just the sort of thing that can leave people disorientated and in disarray.

The other matter that I think we ought to keep carefully in mind when moving towards student control of social arrangements refers particularly to discipline. Student participation in disciplinary committees and provisions of that type commands much assent; and it may be suggested further—indeed, it certainly has been suggested—that in some areas it is perfectly reasonable to put disciplinary control entirely into the hands of students. It may be that arrangements of this sort will prove, for certain purposes, entirely workable, and I myself certainly would not want to discount them in advance. But I felt that a colleague of mine had a point, who remarked that what chiefly worried him about such proposals was a fear that student bodies might prove too severe: a certain Jacobin dogmatism might make it go hard with students whose way of life or interests went in the currently disapproved direction. If there is anything to this, there may well be a case for retaining senior member participation in disciplinary procedures.

There is in any case the administrative point that the exaction of the penalties (unless they are of a very rough and ready sort) is likely to devolve on university authorities. But there is also the more general reason, that this may well be one of the areas in which the difference between senior members and junior members, that senior members go on for longer while junior members come and go, has some immediate relevance. This difference has been cited so often in connections where its relevance is not very obvious, that it has become a somewhat discredited observation, and its utterance virtually identified with a conservative reflex. But there are some connections in which it really is relevant, and this looks like one of them. For a student who finds himself in a certain climate of opinion, this just is the climate of the university: his experience of what it is like to be in a university is necessarily shaped by it. Senior members have an experience shaped by changes of climate, and while this can no doubt contribute to all those middle-aged deformations of cynicism, conservatism and so forth, it can also give rise to a fairly lively sense of the sorts of institutions and practices which can go on working fairly under shifting conditions, as the ideological wind blows with varying strengths in varying directions.

I turn now to one or two questions about student involvement in more academic matters, in particular matters of syllabus. Here again, there are some directions of reform which I for one, and I should suppose many here, would regard as highly reasonable. Thus it is entirely reasonable that students' opinions and doubts about what is taught, should have some serious notice taken of them; and if it is felt that no notice gets taken of them if they are voiced individually and informally, then one will have, even if reluctantly, to invent some rather more formal machinery to convey them.

Two qualifications: of which the first is, that students must realise (and almost all students I have talked to do realise it) that they themselves have to see to it that the channels of communication are not overloaded with vast quantities of repetitious material. It really is not an essential test of an academic's good faith, that he is prepared to be bored into the ground. If things get like that, anyone who is any good will go away, certainly from the meeting; and in the really long and terrible run, from that university.

The second qualification is that if students have the right to say to staff that they do not like the courses in these or those respects, and that they would like things to be done differently, the staff also has the right, if they happen to think that the students are talking ill-informed rubbish, to tell them so. It should hardly be necessary to say this; but there is a very odd view which one sometimes meets, some paternalist hang-over, according to which students should be allowed to say anything they like, but—since they are only students, after all—one should refrain from harsh criticism of what they say. This seems an utterly half-baked position. If academics are to be prepared to take student comment seriously, as they should be, they should extend to students the treatment they are happy to extend to their colleagues, of pointing out that something is idiotic, if idiotic is what it is.

I do not include among *qualifications* to projects of reform in this area, that students should discuss and not dictate, and that this is not a matter of student *power*. This seems to me, not a qualification to reform, but an absolutely necessary and limiting condition of it; and academics should regard this point as strictly non-negotiable, as they should regard the question of the appointment of university teachers. There are two reasons for this, both excessively and unsurprisingly well-known. One is the 'boot-straps' problem. It is straightforwardly a functional and relevant difference between junior and senior members that the latter know more about something, and are there to teach it to the former; and whatever advantages the junior members may or may not possess over the senior in moral enthusiasm or purity of heart, that difference is not cancelled out.

The second point is one that is usually put in terms of academic freedom: that academics should be free to teach their subjects as they see fit, free from pressures, particularly ideological pressures, from governments, churches, big business, populist movements—or mass meetings of students. This is indeed a fair way of putting it. But one may also put it in terms, not so much of freedom, as of integrity. Some very radical opinion seems sometimes to suggest that a teacher is morally at fault if he is unresponsive to demands that he should teach some particular kinds of material. Admittedly, he is at fault, and in very old-fashioned academic terms, if through narrow-mindedness he remains obstinately ignorant of important and serious developments. But, beyond that point, suppose he seriously thinks that the material is not so important as all that? Or what he is doing is more important? Or merely that, while the material may be interesting, he is not the man to do it justice, or that to do it justice would take him too much away from matters to which he thinks he has something to contribute? In short, what if he does not believe in it, or does not believe in it for him? Will it be a mark of virtue to give up what he does believe in, in order to put on some fashionable or well-regarded act of pursuing what he does not believe in? I should have thought that those who regard integrity as a cardinal virtue, and phoniness as a cardinal vice, would recognise to which category that performance would belong.

This last point is important, I think, even if we get away for a moment from the high ground of ultimate principle, and consider once more the area of desirable and possible reform. It is a very important limitation on proposals for syllabus reform in a given department, not only what the staff of that department can competently do, but what they can do *genuinely*. To take for a moment my own subject, which notably, though by no means uniquely, raises these problems: it would be an excellent idea for a philosophy department to provide, if it could, classes on certain thinkers not widely studied in this country, such as Nietzsche. But if, as things are, there is no one in the department who really cares about Nietzsche, to whom he means very much, it will be pointless to try to make them do it: a course on Nietzsche which is worth having cannot just be 'laid on'. Nietzsche is to some extent a special case, but the same point applies more generally, and particularly to the sorts of subjects for which there is at present a lot of demand. Of course, this means that there is some reason, if further appointments are being made, to look out for someone who is good and can genuinely and at a serious level meet these wider demands; but, there again, one has (obviously enough) to watch that one is not preferring the fashionable to the creative, nor succumbing to the danger of producing, as in some American universities for instance, an anthology of points of view rather than a set of people who can actually do something together. 'Non omnia possumus omnes' is a maxim which applies to departments as well as to persons.

Perhaps a professor of philosophy is likely to be particularly conscious, among demands presently made on the syllabus, of what are, in the broadest sense, ideological demands. But it is important that there also exist demands, not least among students, that courses should be 'relevant' in a rather different sense: that they should be more relevant to what people are going to do after university—at the limit, that they should be more vocational. Some recent student demands give the impression that they embrace both these aspects of 'relevance' to the point of contradiction:

on the one hand rejecting a university which allegedly churns out trained personnel on an assembly line in response to the needs of a mechanical society, on the other hand demanding that university courses do more to fit people into slots in society than they do at the moment.

There is indeed a kind of revolutionary outlook which would claim to overcome this contradiction, by seeking to change society in such a radical way that its slots (if it still had slots) would be filled precisely by people who had had a politicised, non-technical and unstructured experience in a radically changed university. I think in fact that this dream, besides its evident unrealism and the absurd picture it presents of the future of creative thought, contains a contradiction on the matter it cares most about—the avoidance of the mechanical. The contradiction, excessively briefly put, is this. Unless the theory belongs to the long series of agrarian fantasies—as Marxists used to say, utopian and reactionary fantasies—which have been a feature of much British socialist thought, it looks to a time when technology has not been abandoned, but rather has triumphed, and the labour of men has systematically been replaced by the operations of sophisticated machines. But either these machines are looked after and programmed by people, or they look after themselves. If they are run by a small number of people, not only will those people be technologically educated, but they will be the ultimate élite, the rulers of the world: contrary, surely, to the dream. But if the machines run themselves, then it will be machines which, in innumerable important respects, determine the living space of humans, and the machines, in effect, will rule the world: also, surely, contrary to the dream. One thing we can be fairly clear about, even with regard to these remoter prospects, is that if sophisticated machines are to replace a lot of labour we shall need a lot of people to be their masters, and a lot more people who will be at least their match; and that will require people who will be able to think technically about machines, and in a disciplined way about society. To abandon the more disciplined and rigorous intellectual activities on a large scale for more purely expressive and unstructured enterprises in education would be to prepare, not the liberated beneficiaries of that future society, but its certain victims.

If all this is to peer dimly into hypothetical futures, it is not wholly irrelevant to present discontents. In any case, no dream, even a better dream than that one, is going to get round the *present* conflict between demands for less vocationally functional, and for more vocationally functional, education. It is of course easier to point out the conflict, and to pinpoint some contradictions in student demands, than it is to respond adequately to the real frustrations that underlie them. But whatever thoughts we may arrive at about the relation of university courses to what students will later do (and a lot needs to be said here about the role of postgraduate courses, for instance), we certainly need to get the immediate diagnosis right about who, if anybody, is imposing what sort of pattern on whom. It is important to see that, in terms of what is actually happening now in this country, the universities are demonstrably not having imposed upon them demands of government or industry with regard to the needs for technically trained man-power. On the contrary, the agencies which bear most directly on universities, the DES [Department of Science] and the UGC [University Grants Committee], are busily engaged in that old liberal activity, of providing the means for people to realise their individual choices. Many committees, some headed by prominent academics, have shown that the country has an unsatisfied need for technologists and scientists, and tried to persuade universities to reflect this need; and in the late 50's the UGC intended some two-thirds of new places in universities to be devoted to these subjects. As is also well-known, the proportion of potential students demanding those subjects first ceased to rise, and then fell; and, instead of trying to devise means by which screws could be put on universities or students to force people in the required direction, 'society'—that is to say, in this case principally the UGC—heavily revised its allocations in the direction of providing more places in the humanities and social sciences. Much the same goes for the policies of the DES and local authorities towards Colleges of Further Education; when I visited a very prominent and expanding College of Technology a few weeks ago, I learned (with some surprise) that less than half of its students were doing technology or science. These developments seem to me important for an honest evaluation, both of revolutionary rhetoric about universities being the tools of a technological society, and also—as the Vice-Chancellor of Cambridge forcefully pointed out in his lecture in this series last year—of petulant and ill-informed complaints by some academics about inroads from these agencies into academic freedom.

There is a strong tendency in the most radical quarters, at least, to regard facts of this order as beside the point, and as at best expressions of a kind of a liberalism which happily puts up with, indeed (on the most radical view) actively fosters, the evils which political protest is directed against. This sort of critique borrows a lot from recent American experience, and radical American students are, not surprisingly, among the most prominent in certain universities here in pressing this sort of line. It would be absurd for me to embark here on a discussion of the failure of liberalism, if that is what it is, in American society, or of the extent to which basic problems of theirs are or are not paralleled here. Nor shall I try any serious evaluation of American academic troubles, such as the complex events at Columbia; that would itself be a very long job, even if I were capable of it. I think it is worth pointing out, however, certain differences in the university situation which for the most part obtains here, and that which has been the focus of criticism and protest in certain places in the United States; whatever one thinks of certain actions that have been taken there, what is certainly just false is the assumption that there is something called the 'late capitalist university' whose relations to society and to its students are the same in both countries.

There are several important points of difference. First, in the case of those prominent centres of university trouble in the United States, Berkeley and Columbia, there have been four sets of people involved: the trustees (or regents), the administration, the faculty, and the students, and the relations between all these four parties have caused difficulties—the regents (in the case of Berkeley) having political interests even against the administration, the administration taking decisions without concurrence of the faculty, and the faculty being—it is alleged—too remote from the students. This kind of set-up is not in general paralleled in this country, though one or two institutions may get rather nearer to it than the others. Correspondingly, if one takes the faculty and the students together, there is less ground for the feeling that their joint academic interests are being operated on from outside; and if one considers the relations between the faculty and the students, the claim that students are neglected or merely processed has less to feed on. Both points come out, if one remembers what—besides the money, the secretarial help, and the research apparatus—are the two great bribes extended to potential brain-drainers: that they will not have to teach, and that they will not have to administer. Of course American academics themselves do a great deal of teaching—more, for the most part, than the prestige British import who has been offered this inducement; but certainly they have handed over more in the way of administration than we have, and with it (some seem suddenly to have realised) control over what happens in their own institutions.

Another very important area of difference lies in the relations to money—both private money and defence money. There is nothing evil about private and industrial money in universities, and there is a lot of reason to be grateful for it, so long as the conventions that govern it keep it under control. But it is my impression that in certain American universities the trustees and administrators find themselves so deeply entangled in commercial and financial connections that freedom is lost. If one studies some of these situations, one may well feel that our arrangements for public money, so long at least as they are administered in the derided spirit of liberalism, can confer a greater degree of genuine independence than do these other arrangements, which are sometimes supposed to give greater freedom. The public money must, however, be in large part money devoted by society precisely to the purposes of education, and what it cannot be, in particular, is money devoted to defence. The lines between research devoted to military purposes, relevant to military purposes, and having nothing to do with military purposes, are famously difficult to draw; but the minimum principle, crude as it is, that universities should contain no classified research, seems to me of absolutely basic importance. This principle may seem to some to smell of the attitudes of Pontius Pilate, since (it may be said) the classified research goes on somewhere else, and one is merely squeamishly spared the embarrassment of having it on the premises. But, in any case, the principle that such research should not go on in universities is independent of whether one disapproves of classified research or not: even someone who approves of it will see the point that the distortions in the academic body set up by having it in universities are dangerous, and also that it is desirable that people should make it clear, by where they work, what their relations to it are. And if one does disapprove of it, or some of it, it is not hypocrisy to wish it to happen, if at all, somewhere else. One cannot eliminate everything one disapproves of from society, but one can do the best one can to see that those things are not done by bodies of which one is oneself a part, and for whose doings one is in some part directly responsible. The involvement of some American universities in defence contracts seems to me to have been a legitimate ground of protest.

I am not trying to say that American universities have been in all sorts of ways wicked, and we are marvellous. My point can be put merely by saying that even if there were equal grounds of protest in both places, they certainly could not be just the *same*, since factors which have figured very prominently in American protest are evidently different here. If those grounds are just transported across the Atlantic in a can, like a Hollywood film, and run here, it looks, to that extent, like another example of cultural imperialism.

So far I have spoken in large part about the *grounds* that protest may have in relation to a university, and about how those grounds may be, in certain areas I have singled out from many, met by reform. I should now like to look more closely at the *activity* of protesting in a university, and the relations of that activity to ideas of revolution—relations which are rather more complex and interesting than may appear on the surface. I think we can understand more or less what we mean by 'a student protest': they range from something slightly stronger and more irregular than merely sending a round robin to the Dean, and have many degrees of escalation up to sit-ins, strikes (a very ineffective weapon for students, incidentally), occupation of buildings and at the limit violence and destruction. They can be concerned, as I said at the beginning, with two different sorts of things: issues about the university itself, and wider political issues.

Now whatever one thinks of protests in general, one thing I think is clear is that one has to attach a special significance, from the point of view of a university, to *continuous* protests; and this applies to both types. So far as what we may call academic protests are concerned, it would be dishonest to deny that they do on occasion work, and produce some results that would not have been achieved, or so quickly, by the old channels of communication. The point about speed is of course particularly significant for students, who are not going to be there all that long, and may well have gone altogether by the time the unhurried processes of academic deliberation have dealt with the issue; even teachers can take this point, particularly when confronted with the kind of senior figure who always says, at the prospect of some reform, "it will come", as though that relieved everyone of bringing it about that it come. But, if, by the very fact of being students with a short career, students have an interest in the speed that protest can occasionally secure, it is also true, and by the very same fact, that they have an interest in protest not being continuous. Protest being by definition to some extent disruptive, the price they pay for continuous disruption during their university career must be, by the same argument, proportionately high. If some protest shifts a blocked system, and in particular encourages reforms which themselves may make protest less necessary to get later reforms, continuous protests designed to get reforms must be progressively self-defeating. So, granted at least that some results have been achieved, continuous protests will, if they have any rationale at all, probably have to have a rationale which is not primarily concerned with securing reforms, but with something else.

A similar point can be made with regard to political protest, but in slightly different terms. It might be said that in this case continuous protest had a much better justification, since, first, it is much less likely to have produced any results, and, second, the subject will be of greater national or world importance, indeed of greater moral importance, than arrangements in a university. These two points are true, but they do not make the case. The war in Vietnam, world hunger, the bomb, are issues vastly more important than anything I or any student will do; but it doesn't follow from that that protesting about these issues is more important than anything else I or he can do. If one is overwhelmed by the appalling feeling that what one is fiddling around with is completely dwarfed by such issues, one might think, as a few do, in terms of a more adequate individual response, such as working in famine relief or serving in some capacity in Vietnam. Few make such a response, and there are very few of whom one would think it was positively *demanded*; for most of us, making a protest may have to serve as a symbolic substitute, and it would seem to me quite frivolous and facile to say 'no protest — either complete dedication, or shut up'. But what is equally frivolous and facile is to suppose, granted that one is sticking to symbolic protest, that the more one protests the nearer one approximates to the unrealised dedication. Either one feels that there are values and aims which can honourably be pursued despite the world's sufferings, or one does not. If one does not, there is only dedication. If one does, then one has to realise that that is what one is doing, and not muck up those aims and values for oneself and others by confusing persistence in the symbolic with dedication to the actual.

If I am right so far, it just does not follow that if protest is occasionally a good thing, more protest must be a better thing; with both academic and political protest, continuous protest is by the very nature of the cases, a relevantly different thing, and not just more of the same. So for continuous protest, a rationale is demanded which goes beyond the justifications for occasional protest. What may it be? One, on the academic side, is if things are outrageously bad and no-one will move at all; another, on the political side, is if there is a real chance of actually securing a large change about the matters to which the protest is directed. I shall leave these, since I do not think that either of them is the case with virtually any situation which presently concerns us. There is another: that, on the academic side, of aiming at a change which is itself radical to a degree which no amount of mere reform could meet, and which the present authorities could not possibly grant. When I say that this would be a possible rationale of continuous protest, I do not mean that I agree with it: all I mean is that it is an objective in terms of which continuous protest might make sense, as it does not without some special objective. It looks, from reports, as though some student groups have such an objective with regard to the LSE [London School of Economics].

I myself think that the sort of institution which some members of the RSSF [Revolutionary Socialist Students' Federation] seem to want would, if imaginable at all, be a nightmare, which would make impossible the things that have to be sustained in a university (such as finding out the truth), and would also rule out the sort of critical understanding of society which can support genuine programmes of social action. Although the principles involved in these points are of course of the first importance, I shall not go on about them; I want just to make the point that in any case the objective of trying by continuous protest to turn an institution such as the LSE into that sort of place is an absurd as well as a destructive objective.

It is absurd, because there is no conceivable mechanism by which such groups could inherit an institution such as the LSE. One cannot quite see the UGC, for instance, complacently supporting an LSE which, if that final day came, would have been deserted by its administration, most of its teachers, and large numbers of its students. This is obviously true anyway; and it must be at least as obviously true on the extremists' own views of our society. If the aim is to have a certain sort of school—let us, just for the sake of a label and no more, call it a 'revolutionary school'— the aim of making the LSE, a place with certain buildings, a library, resources, government support, and a body of teachers, into that school is a very unrealistic way of going about it. But I doubt in fact whether the aim is just to have a revolutionary school. This is based purely on a suspicion, but I think a well-founded suspicion, which is this. Suppose someone came up and actually offered to provide premises and resources for a revolutionary school (a proposal seriously advanced by a weekly paper some time ago): how many students or staff in the LSE or elsewhere who are in favour of such a school would go off to it? I suspect that many would not. If that suspicion is right, it seems to follow that the aim is not in fact just to get a revolutionary school. To work on an existing institution is not just regarded as the only available way of bringing about a revolutionary school: to work on an existing institution is probably essential to the project—presumably as being either symbolic or anticipatory of a wider revolutionary project.

'Symbolic' or 'anticipatory' is here a vital distinction, and just as vital to potential revolutionaries as to anyone else. With revolutions, as serious revolutionaries know, it makes a great deal of difference whether a revolution is actually likely to happen, and if so who is likely to win. There seems to me only one thing more certain than that a revolution is not going to happen in this country: and that is, that if it did, the Right would win. There are indeed suppressed political feelings in this country which are not adequately expressed in our politics; but they are very largely feelings which support more and not less authoritarian, chauvinistic and xenophobic measures. Nor can the fantasists of the revolutionary Left, with the slightest vestige of plausibility, embark on those age-old strategies of aiming first at Rightist power, and eventually, by politicization of the oppressed masses, to the revolution they want: that is not how it would be, either.

Disruption of universities as *anticipatory* of real revolution is a project patently insane. The activity has to be seen rather as symbolic; but how, and to what effect? I think I must leave the answer to 'how' to those who support these views; the questions of what this symbol is supposed to symbolise, and what its value is, seem to me questions well pressed on those who advocate these courses, by those who immediately have to suffer from them. But one can certainly give some answers to the question 'with what effect?': the effect, noted by very many students, that every less liberal attitude in the country gets aroused against students' interests in general.

To choose a university, in any case, as the object of either symbolic or real revolution is basically pretty mad, as some speakers pointed out to students at Columbia; a lot of what it stands for is nearer to the ideals of the revolutionaries themselves than are other institutions. And to reply that the university is where one is, and is notably easier to deal with than those other institutions, is straightforwardly childish; it is on all fours with admitting that the reason one is nasty to one's father is that, while he is actually a bit nicer than the people one really hates, he is the one who is at home and gets upset.

While real revolution is not on, and symbolic revolution has little obvious point and many counter-productive results, the confusion of the real and the symbolic from which some evidently suffer is disastrous from every point of view. It can breed, in particular, a special kind of moral confusion. It is a platitude that, confronted with a real revolutionary situation, certain constraints go to the wall: intimidating the unenthusiastic, breaking up the meetings of those on the other side, and so forth, begin to look not only permissible but imperative. But whatever one may do if the revolutionary situation is really there, to get to this point in the interests of a fantasy is totally destructive, and self-destructive. I believe that very few have got to this point, but the emotional power of the fantasy situation makes it possible. I said that to reach this point was self-destructive, and I mean that in two senses. First, by generating an atmosphere in which belonging to the cause alone counts, and disagreeable voices are made inaudible, the individual loses his own sense of self-criticism, ceases to listen to what he himself says, and loses his grasp on reality. Second, he destroys his own cause, and any like it; for (as I have already said) in anything like our situation, it is in the end the other side that can shout louder and kick harder. Letting people be heard is a good policy anyway, but it is a particularly good policy for minorities.

One last point. Rousseau said that he regarded as the best state, that in which the citizens spent as much time as possible in thinking about public matters, and as little as possible in thinking about private matters. It has always seemed to me a good test of certain basic political attitudes, whether one spontaneously finds that a sympathetic remark, or, as I do, a repulsive one. Either reaction, but particularly that second one, is going in fact to need qualification; one qualification (by no means the only or most important) is that one may have to turn aside from legitimate private activities for a bit if those very activities, and those of other persons, look like being jeopardised. Now I don't in fact think that the activities of the most militant in universities have a very significant effect, as they would claim, in making people more concerned about genuine public issues of war and peace, hunger and oppression; what they do is to make the people around terribly concerned about *universities*, which is something else. Though that is a fairly private concern relative to those other problems, it is a public concern relative to one's own work and teaching; and faced with real militancy, those who do not believe in it do have, for a time, to get actively moving in the public terrain. Those who just want to be able to do what they want to do, will certainly, in order to secure that, have to do a good deal of what they don't want to do.

15

Has 'God' a Meaning?

People are often tempted to think of questions about meaning as though they were all on the level of the most trivial disagreements about the use of a particular word, the sort of disagreements that are rightly called 'merely verbal': exemplified, for instance, in the fact that Americans use the word 'suspenders' to refer to what we call 'braces'. Obviously, no sane person would waste time arguing about which was the right word to use, or what the word 'suspenders' *really* meant. But most questions about meaning are not nearly as superficial as this, and in issues of metaphysics or religion we cannot proceed in this way.

Philosophers have become extremely conscious of the fact that it is possible to use language in an impressive and profound-seeming way, without what one says having any meaning at all, or at least—and this is an important point—without its having the sort of meaning that the speaker would like it to have.

Some speaker may think that he is making an important statement about the nature of the universe, or of history, or something, and it may turn out, when he is pressed, that no meaning has been given to his sayings which is determinate enough for him to be making any recognizable claim at all. In particular, this will be so if there is nothing definite to distinguish what is involved in this man's claim from what would be involved in denying that claim. There has to be a difference between what things are like if it is true and what things are like if it isn't. If there is really no difference between what things are like if a certain claim is true, and what they are like if it is not true, we can say that that claim has no content at all.

One very simple example, from the field of religious belief: and I should say at once that I don't think that to criticize the sort of view I am going to mention is, in itself, to criticize any serious form of religious belief, since few serious religious believers would believe anything as simple as this. But there have been people who have thought that God's purposes were positively manifested in natural disasters such as eruptions and earthquakes; for instance, by the punishment of wicked persons overwhelmed by these catastrophes. It is pointed out that the same catastrophes tend rather indiscriminately to involve also innocent persons, such as small children; or presumably virtuous persons, such as members of religious orders. The simple believer then replies that this manifests God's purpose in another way, since it is good that the innocent and virtuous should go to Heaven.

He is then asked, presumably, why other innocent and virtuous persons are not given this benefit to go to Heaven quickly, but left to suffer on earth to a hearty old age; and many of the wicked, indeed, seem to do quite well and are not despatched. Something is then said to the effect that it is also good that the virtuous should have life on earth, and that the punishment of the wicked be delayed for a while, and so on. And after all this we see that absolutely anything that happened to the virtuous, the wicked, or the in-between will count equally well; natural calamities directed by God turn out to be utterly indistinguishable in principle from natural calamities not directed by anyone; and the content of the claim that the happening of such incidents reveals any sort of Divine purpose dissolves in thin air.

As I said before, I don't think the very naïve view I've just mentioned would be held by serious religious believers; in fact, I believe it would be condemned by them, as superstitious. The fact that this superstitious view turned out to be vacuous and have no content would be held by many sceptical philosophers to be the case, in a more sophisticated way, as regards the central tenets of a religion such as Christianity. One form of this more general sort of philosophical criticism was advanced by the 'logical positivists'.

Logical positivism started in the early years of this century, and was developed principally in Vienna in the 'twenties. It became known in this country through a very remarkable book by Professor A. J. Ayer, called *Language, Truth, and Logic*, which was published in 1936. The positivists held that there were only two sorts of statements that genuinely have meaning. One sort were statements which were true merely because of the definitions of the terms used in them: a boring example is 'all bachelors are unmarried'. These need not bother us. The other sort of meaningful statement consisted of those that could be shown to be true or shown to be false by some possible sense-experience: for instance, by some possible scientific experiment or observation. All other remarks not of these two types were considered by the positivists to be meaningless. This doctrine obviously dealt pretty hard with statements of religion, which certainly don't seem to be typically verifiable by science.

Many philosophers now would agree that a principal criticism of logical positivism was the very narrow view it took of something's being meaningful. It is obviously wrong just to lump together as meaningless everything that fails the positivist test; pieces of poetry, commands, expressions of wishes, and lots of other pieces of ordinary meaningful language fail the test and yet have meaning. The positivist challenge has helped to make philosophers more conscious of different sorts of meaning. While this is so, I do not think that the positivist position, in an essential respect, is just to be dismissed. For even if it overlooked a lot of kinds of meaning, it seems to me at least roughly right about one central sort of meaning: the sort of meaning which belongs to statements which one can claim to be true or false. This point can be made in terms of belief: that to believe is to believe *something*, and if there is anything that one believes, one ought to be able to say in some way—if not in the very narrow terms of sense-experience—what the difference is between what one believes being true and what one believes not being true. In the case of religious statements, in particular statements about God, the important question, to my mind, is not whether they have a meaning, or no meaning: the important question is, what sort of meaning they have.

And this is a question which affects whether one wants to go on making such statements or not.

There is no doubt that some people at some times have given a meaning to the statement that God exists, and to other statements about God, which came very near to making those statements into a sort of supplement to science: God came in where science left off. This is the God which the Bishop of Woolwich called in his book *Honest to God* 'the God of the gaps'—the gaps, that is to say, in science. Taken in this way, statements about God were certainly not empty or vacuous in the sort of way I have been talking about before. They made a fairly definite claim: that certain phenomena, such as the adaptation of animals to their environment, or, again, the existence of living things, did not admit of a scientific explanation. These negative claims that certain sorts of scientific explanation were impossible were certainly not empty; the trouble was that they have turned out to be false, since such scientific explanations are forthcoming and there is every sign that they will go on being forthcoming. So if that was the sort of thing meant by religious statements, if that was the sort of meaning they had, they would have to be written off as a hopeful bet against science, which science won.

At this point, some modern theologian may come along, and say something like this: 'I agree that the attempts to make God fill in holes in science is hopeless: the existence of God is not a hypothesis, supplementary to science, and never should have been regarded as such.' I also think the theologian may justly add that these sorts of arguments do a disservice to religion by making God into an abstract or scientific object, instead of something of living concern to people. 'Christianity is about people caring; it essentially involves taking a serious attitude to the world, to personal relationships, to society. When someone says he is a Christian, and that he believes in God, it is such an attitude that he declares. His statements of his religion are not meaningless: they have just this meaning, that the speaker declares such an attitude to life.'

This modern theologian I have made up is at best a composite figure; he is probably a caricature. But the tone is familiar. And my reply to him is this. 'If that is what Christian remarks mean, and only that, then people should stop making them. The Christian vocabulary is unnecessary; if you want to say "I care about personal relationships", we have a very good English sentence for saying that, which does not mention God—namely the sentence, "I care about personal relationships". What is worse, the Christian vocabulary is, for the purpose you give it, actively misleading. For it is quite obvious that historically the claims of Christianity have not just been ways of expressing certain attitudes to the world and to other people: they have been taken to be, if true, very important truths which *give reasons* for having those attitudes towards personal relationships and so on. To represent the words of Christianity as merely expressing these essentially secular attitudes is in fact to have given the thing up, while retaining the vocabulary.'

It may be objected that I am engaged in the old sceptics' game of insisting that Christianity be represented in the most conservative and implausible forms so that I go on disbelieving it. I hope that that is not what I am doing. What I am rather trying to do is to insist that if Christianity is to be Christianity at all there has to be something to be believed or disbelieved, and that this has to be something over and above a mere belief about the secular order.

Christianity is a religion which is very historically articulate; one knows a good deal about what has been believed at different stages of its development. It is also a religion which is tied to certain texts, in particular, of course, the Bible and of course to a particular figure, Christ, about whom one is told something in those texts. Given this, it seems to me possible to identify certain beliefs which must be held if it is Christianity that is being believed at all. I will suggest just one—very unambitiously and, one would hope, platitudinously. This is that God is transcendent to human affairs and to human attitudes in a sense which has the following consequence (though it is supposed to mean more as well): that God would exist whether human beings and their attitudes existed or not— even if there were no human beings or human aspirations, there would still be a God.

To believe this is certainly not enough to constitute one's being a Christian, as I understand it. A Christian has, for instance, to go on to say something very special about Christ (and not just that Christ was a better moral teacher than Socrates). But I shall leave the rest, and concentrate on this one point: that to believe what I just very roughly spelled out is at least *necessary* to having Christian beliefs. And I think it is worth asking oneself very carefully when confronted with some reinterpretation of Christian doctrine whether it passes this test: that it represents God as a being who would be there even if no human beings, or indeed other finite conscious beings, were there. If it does not, then I suspect you no longer have any form of Christianity, but probably some form of religious Humanism.

All this is still about meaning. I said the problem was about *what* Christian and other religious statements are said to mean. There is a limit to what they can be made to mean; when their meaning has changed too much, in particular when it is identified too closely with a meaning which refers *only* to human life, there is no point in going on making them in the religious form. Sometimes of course—perhaps one must say, very often—it is not at all easy to discover whether this has happened or not: clouds of ambiguity stand in the way. In this connection I think we should look extremely closely at a famous passage from Paul Tillich's *The Shaking of the Foundations* (pp 63 f) quoted in *Honest to God*, which seems to suggest that to deny that God exists is to deny that life has depth. Tillich wrote: 'The Name of this infinite and inexhaustible depth and ground of all being is *God*. That depth is what the word *God* means. And if that word has not much meaning for you, translate it, and speak of the depths of your life, of the source of your being, of your ultimate concern, of what you take seriously without any reservation. Perhaps, in order to do so, you must forget everything traditional that you have learned about God, perhaps even the word itself. For if you know that God means depth, you know much about him. You cannot then call yourself an atheist or unbeliever, for you cannot think or say: Life has not depth. Life is shallow. Being itself is surface only. If you could say this in complete seriousness, you would be an atheist; but otherwise you are not. He who knows about depth knows about God.' This raises many questions. In the sense in which 'life has depth' is a statement which only superficial people are going to reject—can it really be enough to represent what 'God exists' is supposed to mean? When people said that God exists were they really saying just that life has depth?

Is Tillich really saying that believing in God is just the *same* as not being superficial? If not, what more? What sort of thing does his pervasive phrase, 'the ground of our being', mean? Is the 'ground of our being' something that would be there even if we were not? Or is the 'ground of our being' something more like our deepest aspirations, which presumably would not be there if we were not?

I do not think that 'God', or statements containing that word, have no meaning. I think they can have all sorts of meanings. On some, they are very difficult to interpret indeed. On others, they seem to me to make claims which can be at least well enough identified to be seen to be substantial; in those meanings, which are various, the claims seem to me personally, I must say, to be false. But at least there is something to be false, and something to be disbelieved. In yet other meanings that are given to them, they say nothing, or too little, or something of the wrong sort—representing, for instance, merely some human aspiration. Then there is nothing to be false, nothing to disbelieve. But when that is so, there is nothing to be true, nothing to believe, either.

16

Russell and Moore: The Analytical Heritage, by A. J. Ayer

In the annals of twentieth-century philosophy, the early alliance of Bertrand Russell and G. E. Moore is famous, as the principal contribution to the undermining of the temporary and untypical influence of Idealism on British thought. Moore, at that time, influenced Russell; at various times Russell's work provided Moore, who was always disposed to start from other philosophers' sayings, with material to criticise. They each greatly influenced analytical philosophy. But they were very different philosophers, with extremely different temperaments and types of achievement. Ayer indeed treats them separately in this book (which is derived from his William James lectures at Harvard), dealing first with Russell and then with Moore.[1]

Bloomsbury, famously, favoured Moore, mainly (it seems) because of the intensity and purity of his personality, and on the strength of 'Principia Ethica,' which found intrinsic good notably in aesthetic experience and personal relations; Russell it seems to have regarded with the same suspicion as Keynes—he gave signs of being busy, worldly and liable to contribute to some positive science. Ayer's book, however, does not deal with any of that: it sticks sternly to the philosophers' arguments on logical questions and topics in the theory of knowledge, intellectual and cultural history left firmly on one side.

It does, however, deal with the more recent and professional reasons for favouring Moore, which have had some currency among British phi-

losophers. This attitude has insisted that Russell, for all his great achievements in logic and the foundations of mathematics, is both a more traditional and a more slapdash philosopher than Moore: more traditional,
because he took the brisk advancing of theories, sometimes surprising,
to be philosophy's business, while Moore saw that there was a problem
about both the nature and the extent of the philosopher's power to refute
common-sense; more slapdash because he lacked Moore's intense kind
of unflashy seriousness in trying to say *exactly* what he meant. Russell, it
has been said, looks back to Hume; Moore looks forward or sideways to
Wittgenstein and J. L. Austin.

Ayer, who is sympathetic to both his subjects, but more (it is fairly
evident) to Russell, has some interesting things to say in criticism of this
by now familiar view. In particular, he shows how little is defended by
Moore's celebrated 'defence of common-sense'—a good deal less than
is often ascribed to it by some subsequent enthusiasts for 'ordinary language.' Moore thought that while there were various beliefs of common-
sense, disputed by philosophers, which were certainly true, the question
of the analysis of those beliefs—what they really involved and meant—
was almost entirely open; and as Ayer reminds us, he was prepared to entertain some peculiar and indeed theory-laden suppositions about what
their analysis might involve.

I think that there are also some questions to be raised about Moore's
famous care and precision, to which virtues he raised an ugly monument
in his grinding style, which reads often like some legal document. This
style assists sometimes the appearance rather than the reality of precision, and is capable of conveying a kind of emphatic vagueness which
curiously co-exists with the marks of solicitor-like caution. Moore's definition of 'x *in this usage* is an incomplete symbol,' which Ayer quotes,
provides a rich example:

> In the case of *every* sentence, p, in which x occurs *with this mean-
> ing*, there can be formed another sentence, q, for which p is short,
> such that neither x itself nor any expression for which x is short
> occurs in q, and p always *looks as if* the rest of it expressed a propo-
> sitional function, such that the proposition expressed by p is a value
> of that function, whereas in fact it never does.

Such a sentence in fact just does not have the virtues which could alone
compensate for its vices.

Ayer does not range very widely beyond the exposition and criticism
of particular arguments and positions of the two philosophers, and there
are points at which the book tends to sink a bit discouragingly between
two stools, where the treatment is too analytical to give much historical
insight, but the philosophical rewards are too slight to make the discus-

sion of the Russellian or Moorean topic worthwhile in its own right. But this is only at points; he has organised and set out with great lucidity and skill a great deal of material, and puts us in control of the philosophers' arguments. If not all the arguments are equally fascinating, it is not Ayer's fault for reminding us that both these men worked their way in their time over some peculiarly unfruitful territory.

Note

1. *Russell and Moore: The Analytical Heritage*, by A. J. Ayer (Macmillan, 1971).

17

Immanuel Kant, by Lucien Goldmann

Lucien Goldmann is best known in Britain for his study of Pascal and Racine (*Le Dieu Caché*, 1955; translated as *The Hidden God*, 1964). He died in 1970; he has been commemorated in Cambridge by the Memorial Lecture which Raymond Williams gave last year. This book[1] is a translation of Goldmann's first book, his doctoral thesis at Zürich, which was published there under the title *Mensch, Gemeinschaft und Welt in der Philosophie Immanuel Kants*. A French translation was first published in 1948, followed by a second French edition in 1967, with the rather less informative title *Introduction à la philosophie de Kant*.

When Goldmann wrote this book he was very much under the influence of Lukács, an influence which indeed continued, but which he came to put into a longer perspective; thus even in the introduction to the 1948 translation he modifies the extravagance which in the first version placed Lukács alone of twentieth-century philosophers alongside Hegel and Marx. The book constitutes a 'humanistic'-Marxist interpretation of Kant, and in both respects it is unusual. It is unusual among interpretations available to English readers in being Marxist and it is unusual among Marxist interpretations in being genuinely devoted to Kant, both in the sense of being actually, if eccentrically, about him, and also in the sense of saluting him and his thought as a recognition at the deepest level of humane values which (in Goldmann's view) were later to be more fully and adequately expressed by Marx. Goldmann denies the aim of writing a work of Kantian scholarship, seeking rather to produce a work of philosophy, yet in fact there is a good deal of reference to and exposition of the Kantian texts, and the book even has the overall structure of an expository outline, starting with an historical background chapter (of a sort), and proceeding via the theory of knowledge and ethics to political and religious doctrines.

The key concept for Goldmann in Kant's thought is *totality*, a concept associated intimately with that of *community*. Goldmann's thesis is that Kant, both in his theory of knowledge and in his ethics, shows himself sensitive to the limitations and ultimate emptiness of 'bourgeois' and individualist conceptions, and strives towards a conception of a human community which will indeed be based on reason, but which will transcend the limitations of these atomistic conceptions. However, owing to the limitations of his time and place—the particular limitations of late 18th century Prussian intellectual life play an important role, both negatively and positively, in Goldmann's account—he could not conceive of such a community, as later it was to be conceived by Marx and (very imperfectly indeed) by Hegel, as lying in the *future*; he conceives it rather as lying in the region of the *ideal*, and the role which should be played by the philosophy of history is still, in Kant's thought, played by the philosophy of religion. As Goldmann puts it: 'In the critical philosophy, where man's limitation and the problem of his destiny predominate, only secondary importance is ultimately accorded to the philosophy of history; there is only a *present*, *duty*, and an *eternity*, *religion*, but no *future*, no *history*; this is the clearest expression of that ultimate limit beyond which, despite all his efforts, Kant was never able to pass.'

To some extent, Goldmann brings his account into relation to humane values as they can be perceived outside Marxism, and this not only makes him more sympathetic, in all senses, than many Marxist writers, but sustains some awareness of seemingly paradoxical elements in Marxism itself. Thus a constant theme, particularly among some American historians of ideas, has been the amount that many progressive or revolutionary philosophies have had in common with chiliastic and religious outlooks of the past: an observation deployed usually in a reductive spirit, and often justly so. But someone wishing to use that implement against Goldmann will need a firmer hold on it, since he clearly recognizes that to regard Kant's religious and moral aspirations as prefiguring Marxist revolutionary hopes is equally to see those hopes as expressing something in common with religious aspirations: the critic's observation is accepted, and the critic is seen as, too often, merely having begged the question about which way round it is to be used.

Goldmann is, in this work, exceedingly unabashed about the extent of historical aspirations. He quotes Heine: 'Wir wollen hier auf Erden schon das Himmelreich errichten' and adds that he 'thus expressed the essential content of modern humanism'. The statement is surprising enough. It remains surprising, even when two points have been allowed for: first, that the statement is in some part definitional of what Goldmann means by 'humanism', and second, that the 'essential content' relates to a hope, not to a prediction, so that part of humanism may be, as Goldmann claims it is in Kant, and was later to find it in Pascal and Racine, a *tragic* vision, which combines a belief in the pointfulness of human effort—and hence (Goldmann claims) at least not a certainty that it will be unsuccessful— with a deep lack of certainty that it will or could be successful. Goldmann is exciting and suggestive on a tragic element in Kant's philosophy, and I shall come back to that.

His own explanation of it, however, is intricately involved in his Marxist structure; for he has to explain why the aspirations after a human community take this tragic form in Kant, and this turns out to be connected with the social situation of the German bourgeoisie in that period. He has to go further, since even if that type of explanation could make a dent on the questions concerning the moral philosophy, it would seem conspicuously to underdetermine Kant's theory of knowledge. He does go further; and while one gets the impression that the application of specifically Marxist categories to the *Critique of Pure Reason* is a bit episodic, it is not exactly half-hearted, and although Goldmann's outlook (so far as I can see) is flexible enough to leave room for a good deal of internalist or non-ideological explanation of a philosophical work, he has not here systematically made use of it. The result is an irritating mixture of extreme vagueness on general points, and a reckless disregard of historical truth on a lot of particular ones; and it is a pity, since a reader may be put off by all that before he gets to some excellent insights.

Some of the more knock-about treatment of the history of philosophy is not so much connected with any specifically Marxist approach, but is rather a general feature of certain European philosophical styles, of the kind amusingly if cantankerously castigated by J.-F. Revel in his *Pourquoi des Philosophes?* and elsewhere. Like the 18th century Paris orchestra, so the 20th century Paris philosopher must start with a *coup d'archet*, and a fortissimo burst of surprising assertion takes one's breath away in the first chapter. 'All the great German philosophical systems start out from the problem of *morals*, from the "practical", a problem virtually unknown to French philosophers before Bergson' (p. 41). What about Rousseau, on the one side, or Leibniz on the other? Well, Rousseau is never mentioned at all, which is quite remarkable in a work covering this ground; as for Leibniz, it is claimed that 'the problem of morals already occupies a preponderant place' (p. 42), which is a bit weaker than the claim made on the page before, but is still quite untrue. Yet more remarkable is the explanation of why Germany, as opposed to France, has so few comic and satirical writers: '. . . one can only laugh at that which is already virtually overcome and brought down; one laughs when the future is open, when one has the whole people behind one. That is why laughing has become almost a national virtue in France' (p. 45).

One might, I suppose, charitably take it that this kind of remark in this genre of work does not actually aim at truth at all, and that it is an error of literary judgement to suppose that it does. What is said in cafés in Paris is not, in point of seriousness, so unlike what is said in saloon bars in London—it is merely that in Paris there is a greater disposition to print it. But this principle of interpretation cannot be extended too widely, and a point soon comes where the distinctive Marxist thesis of the book has to be called in question.

In general, the Marxist treatment of Kant's theory of knowledge which Goldmann offers depends on a kind of analogical thinking which is exceedingly mysterious in its backing, and hence, often, in its content. He claims that Kant in his analysis of the limitations on human knowledge 'lays the philosophical foundations for a most penetrating critique of bourgeois individualist society' and that 'this critique of the thought and action of individualist man is to be found in the Aesthetic of the *Critique of Pure Reason* and the two Analytics of the *Critique of Pure Reason* and the *Critique of Practical Reason*' (p. 110).

These claims seem to be based on, and to offer, no more than a loose structural or symbolic analogy between certain features which supposedly obtained in Prussian society, and certain features of the Kantian philosophy, as for instance its insistence on the notion of the 'synthesis of a totality' being 'set as a task'. That Kant himself saw his enterprise in quite a different light, and precisely and emphatically claimed that his results obtained for humanity as such, is of course admitted, but dismissed as a familiar kind of limitation. A few remarks about the sociology of knowledge do nothing to make these procedures less arbitrary.

This is of course excessively familiar ground. But in reading Goldmann, I am struck forcibly by something which can strike one also in the pages of phenomenologists, or, again, of Lévi-Strauss: the degree to which this is essentially *magical* thought, the primitive conception that similarities must point to powers, and analogies in thought stand for a kind of causation. As magical, it is also at a deep level comforting: and in more than the way in which Goldmann, very frankly and explicitly, makes it a demand on a philosophy that it should hold out hope for the future. (The element of comfort makes this kind of philosophical thought a weak candidate, in the long run, for radical critics of analytical philosophy to run as an alternative, since in *that* contrast the bleak elements of analytical philosophy must appear as witness to its being more honest and more grown-up: while in other connexions, that is not all that is to be said about its bleakness.)

Goldmann in fact, at a more particular level, has some difficulty in stopping the supposed Marxist explanations from collapsing into something too indistinct to be of any use to him. Thus one application he makes of Lukács' concept of *reification* (a very close relative of alienation) is to thought which radically separates *a priori* judgements from the empirically given; and this reification is closely associated with 'the modern bourgeois individualist order' (p. 127), an association filled out by references to the stock-market, the prices of commodities, etc. This seems to face the difficulty that perhaps the most notable example of this type of thought in the history of philosophy was Plato, who was not modern, nor bourgeois, nor confronted with a stock-market. Later on (p. 150–1) the possibility of reification seems indeed to be admitted to the rise of theoretical philosophy in ancient Greece—a rise itself associated, by a familiar Marxist tack, with Ionian trade patterns. So now 'modern' and 'bourgeois' seem to have given way to a more generous category, of persons engaged in trade; and in terms merely of Marxist theory itself, the question arises whether the association of these patterns of thought with the bourgeois stage of development was not a mistake, and the association should be, much more basically, with the division of labour. But if that, then much of the distinctive thesis of this book evaporates. Moreover, since these associations are anyway made in the most abstract terms, one might ask whether the 'conditions of production' with which these patterns of thought are to be associated may not turn out to be the conditions of any production whatsoever, in which case one will be rapidly returning to the original Kantian claim, that his theories were valid for humanity as such. Many different views, in principle, might be possible along this route: Goldmann does not in fact provide us with the materials to make anything determinate out of any of them.

Much of the theoretical material of this book is at best empty. But in among the theoretical materials there are certainly living and interesting things. One question in particular about Kant gains illumination from what Goldmann says, even though he does not directly approach it: why is it that Kant, who emphasizes over and over again that his theory of knowledge applies only to creatures who, like men, learn about the world through sense-perception, offers on the other hand a *moral* philosophy which purports to apply to any rational creature as such? Why not the same restriction for both theory and practice? The answer to this question leads into the heart of Kant's views about freedom and rational agents as ends; Goldmann offers interesting thoughts in this area. Again, he brings out in particularly striking ways the difference between Kantian and utilitarian thought, and equally the divergence between Kantian enlightenment and general 18th century views about progress. Above all, he convincingly brings out, as I mentioned before, a tragic aspect to Kant's thought, embodied particularly in the *aspiration* to a rational ethical world. Kant said: act as if the maxim of your action were to become through your will a universal law of nature. Goldmann writes: '"As if through your will"—in those five words Kant expresses in the clearest and most precise manner the grandeur and the tragedy of human existence. "Through your will" expresses the grandeur of man . . ."As if"— that is the tragic limitation, for nothing essential in the external world really depends on this individual action. It will not change the world, still less other men . . .'.

One of the sourest discords between what Goldmann finds here in Kant's idealism, and the Marxist onward march in terms of which he interprets it, lies in the consideration that in practice few movements in history can have been less disposed to 'futile' or 'Utopian' Kantian gestures than Marxist movements have been.

Note

1. *Immanuel Kant*, by Lucien Goldmann (New Left Books, 1971).

18

A *Theory of Justice,* by John Rawls

"Justice is the first virtue of social institutions, as truth is of systems of thought," Rawls writes at the beginning of this most remarkable book.[1] The sentence contains the seeds of a lot that is to follow. A social system may have many other properties that we can recognise as advantages—as that many people are content or getting what they want, or that a class of outstanding artists is supported—but without justice it is not acceptable. There are many social values, but they can be ordered: and justice comes first. Justice itself, moreover, is various: both in the sense that there can be various conceptions of justice, several of which Rawls very carefully explores, and also in the sense that the conception of justice which he favours, which he calls 'justice as fairness,' itself embraces more than one principle, and these principles are themselves ordered, with a scale or precedence rationally determined between them.

I pick on this matter of the ordering of social principles first, because it is an outstanding feature of the kind of system that Rawls has produced, and also one which makes this very long and densely argued book, not merely a great achievement of intelligence and moral reflection, which it certainly is, but also notably heartening. It is heartening because it not only promises, but concretely presents, a systematic body of thought about the principles which should govern society, in a manner which manages to be at once complete and humane enough to satisfy moral demands, and rigorously unified enough to meet the rational requirements of one who wants more than disconnected insights. Up to now the main streams of reflective thought about social ends have tended, with the exception of Marxism, to flow into one of two channels. They have been in some cases *pluralistic* (the kind of outlook which Rawls, making an individual but very pointful use of a traditional term of moral philosophy, calls 'intuitionist'): these believe that there is more than one independent social value, and that there can be no general and systematic way of ordering priorities between them—each case or type of case has to be viewed in itself, and some compromise contrived, between fairness and growth, for instance, or liberty and efficiency. To this the more rational and ordered alternative has seemed to be uniquely utilitarianism, which promises to reduce all social values to one: to some variant or another of the 'greatest happiness of the greatest number.' Since this aim is exceedingly obscure, both for empirical reasons and because the central concepts are very fishy, utilitarian calculation is muffled by pluralism, common-sense and half-heartedness, which is doubtless a mercy, since its unrestricted consequences, especially for justice, can be seen to be alarming. Nevertheless utilitarian patterns of thought carry great rational prestige, not only for social or economic reasons, but because it has often seemed to *embody* rational and systematic social thought as against the disconnected reflexes of prejudice or habit.

What Rawls has produced is an elaborate system of thoughts on social principles and the demands of justice in society, which can be put alongside utilitarianism in terms of providing a rational ordering of priorities, and yet, being founded on the central role of justice rather than utility, preserves values which have been emphasised by pluralists queasy of utilitarianism's willingness to sacrifice rights to efficiency. Any such enterprise, obviously, must make its basic moves at a level of high generality; to suppose otherwise would be to misunderstand the nature of the enterprise, and certainly utilitarianism could make no reproach to Rawls on this score. But Rawls does not remain merely at such a level, and the second part of his book contains sensitive and careful reflection on such subjects as civil disobedience and the rights of conscientious objection. In fact—and it is a point remarked by Rawls himself—his method allows more specific conclusions to be reached by philosophical or theoretical means than does utilitarianism. For the utilitarian, almost everything really depends on empirical facts, since he only has the one principle and everything else depends on how satisfactions will empirically work out; while for Rawls more specific considerations are worked into the basic principles themselves and there is correspondingly more ground that can be covered by reflection at the level of principle.

Rawls has two basic principles of justice. The first—and it is the first, having priority of application—is that "each person is to have an equal right to the most extensive total system of equal basic liberties compatible with a similar system of liberty for all." The second principle, in its final form, is that social and economic inequalities are to be arranged so that they are both to the greatest benefit of the least advantaged, and attached to offices and positions which are open to all under equality of opportunity: allowance being made by what is called the "just savings principle" or responsibilities towards the future (here, as elsewhere, Rawls deals very sharply and sensitively with matters which have been the concern of economic theory, and he returns to a great tradition of Mill and Sidgwick in joining these concerns with those of moral philosophy). The general conception of the two principles of justice taken together is this: "All social primary goods—liberty and opportunity, income and wealth, and the bases of self-respect—are to be distributed equally unless an unequal distribution of any or all of these goods is to the advantage of the least favoured."

Rawls offers an elaborate set of arguments in explanation and defence of these as the fundamental principles of justice. His arguments are designed to unfold their content, which turns out to be less obvious than one might have first expected; to compare them with alternative embodiments of justice, and also to compare different interpretations which can be given of these principles themselves; and to justify them, in the sense at least of showing that they satisfy certain basic moral opinions or intuitions which his readers may be expected to share with him. Whether the arguments are meant to justify the principles in a sense yet stronger than that, as for instance by showing that they should, or very plausibly should, be assented to by any rational agent—where 'rational' is not taken as *already* importing a suitable range of moral opinions—that is something that I am less than clear about. Why I am unclear about it will perhaps come out better if I look first at the role of the very striking model which Rawls uses to ground and explicate his system, the model of the 'original position.'

Rawls belongs to the tradition of contract theorists of society, and particularly associates himself with the later and more explicitly moralised version of the contractual model, as it is to be found above all in Rousseau, and also in Kant, the moralist whose influence is most evident in this book.

Rawls of course makes no appeal to any historical or actual contract as underlying society, nor (if I follow him) does he appeal to the idea of a contract in *justification* of allegiance to the state; as in Rousseau, it is not some tacit consent to a supposed contract which commands allegiance, but rather the moral properties of society, which properties can best be laid bare in the model or analogy of a contract. Rawls's model is of a set of persons settling jointly on a set of social principles and institutions to which they and their descendants will then be committed. They are to be pictured as making this choice under a certain set of conditions: apart from standing features of their initial situation, as that their powers are limited and roughly equal, scarcity a real but not overwhelming factor, and so on, they are to be understood as making their choice in accordance with certain principles: that their choice is to be in universal terms (that is to say, will apply to everyone), and does not mention any particular persons as, for instance, beneficiaries of the outcome; that the rules and institutions agreed on will be public, and known to all participants (this prevents, among other things, a cynical take-over bid from utilitarians, who often claim that any system which is ultimately best for everybody must really be utilitarian, even if its content is not); and that the choice will be binding and unchangeable. Above all, this imagined choice is pictured as occurring behind a 'veil of ignorance' as Rawls calls it: the parties in the original position—as this set-up is called—are pictured as ignorant of their own identities, history, and character, even, indeed, of their own tastes or preferences; though they are to be allowed knowledge of *general* empirical principles (a departure from total Kantian purity which Rawls is at some pains to justify). Most significantly of all—and this is the central point of the veil of ignorance idea—they do not know what position they will occupy in the social set-up which they are collectively to decide upon. It is Rawls's claim that in the circumstances imagined, what a rational man would decide upon is a set of institutions arranged on the basis of the two principles of justice he has formulated.

In this light, in particular, we understand the emphasis that those principles put upon the idea that inequalities are to be justified only if they are to the benefit of the least advantaged: the *maximin* principle, as it is called, of considering each possible set-up from the point of view of the worst-off in each one, and choosing that one in which the worst-off are better off than the worst-off in any other set-up. This emphasis is extremely important in Rawls's system, and it is one of the things that markedly distinguishes his outlook from that of utilitarian procedures (a point which is rendered absolutely precise in Rawls's treatment). If you run a risk, behind the veil of ignorance, of ending up in the worst position in the eventual outcome, and you do not even know how big that risk is, it indeed seems rational to make sure, very high among your priorities, that the worst offered in the outcome should be as good as possible.

So Rawls argues. But the first, if not the most basic, question that his treatment suggests is whether that is necessarily rational; or rather, perhaps, granted how underinformed the persons in the original position are, whether we, or they, have enough to decide what is rational. A man who chooses a system in which there is a risk of degraded slavery, but also a chance of tremendous power and prestige, is not evidently more *irrational* than one who opts for some more Attlee-like alternative—he just has a different temperament. In order to try to block this objection, Rawls cuts his persons off from a lot of basic information about the chances of ending up in one situation rather than another, and also (as I have said) about their own talents and temperament. But then the question arises, of whether in cutting them off from everything that could give a rational edge to the gambler's approach, he has not cut them off from so much as to make the whole model unintelligible. Rawls tackles the problems of trying to give his hypothetical parties enough information to make the exercise comprehensible, but not too much: there remains a real doubt about whether he has succeeded.

There is one set of theorists to whom Rawls will perhaps have little to say. Rawls's model of the original position is a striking monument to something which contract-theorists and (in *this* respect) utilitarians have in common, the belief that particular historical situations enter into political and social calculation only secondarily, along with particular empirical information about the wants and interests of the persons involved. Thus Rawls's parties are pictured in total abstraction from history, equipped like their Lockean and Rousseauite predecessors only with the draughty coverings of rationality and (perhaps) morality. This presents certain internal difficulties for Rawls's system: thus I think he is committed to talking about social *classes* at a stage in the proceedings where he has not provided any conditions for picking out a *class* as opposed to any arbitrary set of persons within society: what constitutes a class, and a class-interest, is a question that cannot be answered at the level of abstraction from history that Rawls seems to require. Nevertheless, those of us who have felt rather hopelessly that only an untidy pluralism could get anywhere near the complexities of social value must be led to wonder whether what they took for an insightful pessimism may not have been in some part just laziness. Utilitarians, again, will have to salute someone skilled in economic and systematic thought, with a genuinely alternative view. Others of us who may still feel that there is something dauntingly and unrealistically pure about the Kantian principles which Rawls employs, must recognise the extent to which Rawls's work has raised the level of what is to be expected of any alternative picture. Like all notable philosophical achievements, it will change the basis of discussion over a large area for a long time to come.[2]

Notes

1. *A Theory of Justice*, by John Rawls (Clarendon Press, 1972).
2. This review originally appeared as "Bernard Williams on Rawls's Principles and the Demands of Justice," *Spectator*, June 24, 1972.

19

Beyond Freedom and Dignity, by B. F. Skinner

B. F. Skinner is an American psychologist who is famous for a number of things. He pioneered a particular kind of behaviourist theory, based on the idea of selectively reinforcing by reward certain spontaneously produced patterns of behaviour: the model for learning is thus fundamentally that of evolutionary natural selection. He conducted a famous series of experiments with pigeons. He invented, among other things, an experimental device called the Skinner Box, which provides a totally artificial environment for the study of animal behaviour. He has written a Utopian novel. He has been extensively attacked by Chomsky, originally on the subject of language acquisition, who argued, extremely convincingly, that Skinner's theories were totally incapable of explaining the learning of language; this controversy extended, no doubt with some help from Chomsky's own political concerns, into larger areas of discontent with the theories, methods, outlook and ethics of the kind of behaviourism of which Skinner is the outstanding representative.

This book is described on the jacket as 'the summary of his life work in the scientific analysis of behaviour.'[1] This it scarcely can be, since it summarises no actual scientific results at all, but it is presumably meant as a summary of what Skinner thinks the results of his life's work offer for mankind. It is rambling, repetitive, optimistic, rather well written, and dauntingly stupid.

It is a mixture, in about equal proportions, of ninth-rate philosophy, ill-defined values, and non-existent science. The science is non-existent, it is important to emphasise, not just in the sense that it does not here appear on the page; it is not that Skinner has somewhere else demonstrated what he here repeatedly presupposes, namely that there exists a body of scientific work which enables us to explain and control complex human cultural behaviour in terms of his behaviourist reinforcement theory. No such work exists, and there is very little reason to think that it could exist. Because the accounts given here all rely on promissory notes drawn on a behaviourist bank which we have reasons for thinking is bankrupt, Skinner's supposed technical terminology in which he naively describes human affairs is exactly what he—in a rather hurt tone—denies it is, a jargon. It is just as scientifically worthless, and a good deal less amusing, than Mr Desmond Morris's attempts to describe human activities in terms drawn directly from the activities of other primates.

Skinner's main idea is to move our attention from attempts to explain and control individual behaviour by acting directly on the individual, to a concentration on the environment. A myth which he finds a great obstacle to this is that of what he calls 'autonomous man'—'the inner man, the homunculus, the possessing demon, the man defended by the literatures of freedom and dignity.' As will be gathered from these phrases, it is not easy to discover what exactly Skinner means by 'autonomous man.' He makes it harder by starting the book with a set of formulations which are perhaps unnecessarily absurd.

The Greeks, we are told, had a physics which 'personified' physical things, and which did not work; physics got going when it stopped treating things as persons. We have not made the same step in psychology and the behavioural sciences: we still talk about human behaviour in a 'prescientific' and 'personified' way. That is to say, Skinner's opinion seems to be that since it was a mistake to treat things as persons, it must be an equal mistake to treat persons as persons, and the sooner we stop the better. The Greeks (it used to be said) tried to explain the behaviour of things in terms of purposes, because they projected on to the world their own purposes. Now it appears, they made a more basic error, of thinking that they had any purposes themselves.

It may be that Skinner does not have to say anything as silly as this: but it is impossible to tell, because he constantly muddles up the questions of whether we are to speak in terms of individual intentions and purposes at all, with the question of whether social arrangements are best designed in terms of individual intentions and purposes.

The latter, at least, he denies: the 'literatures of freedom and dignity' have done great harm in insisting on such ideas as individual responsibility, in particular in its emphasis on punishment, which is, among other things, inefficient—'much time and energy would be saved' if other methods of controlling behaviour were adopted. Indeed, there is much to be said against punishment, and the myths that go with it; but Skinner has got nowhere at all in saying it, since he does not even consider most of the issues that bear on the matter: for instance, whether there is any kind of value in having methods of social control which persons subject to them can so far as possible rationally understand.

What values will replace the archaic and pre-scientific myths of freedom and dignity? What will the 'time and energy' be saved for? 'For more reinforcing activities,' we are told: 'reinforcing,' it should be said, is Skinnerese for 'enjoyable' or just 'good.' What these are, is left in the dark: it is perhaps up to us, though that might seem to Skinner to smell too much of autonomous man.

Central chapters on values and culture offer nothing on the central question except the vaguest kind of co-operatively directed evolutionary ethic. More insight into what Skinner would really like emerges in fact from a book much more revealing than this one, his Utopian novel 'Walden Two,' in which the community formed by scientific behaviour control is represented. The general tone is that of a particularly mild and genteel Adult Education Centre, with the performing arts and Sunday painting to the fore. In the present book, Skinner for one moment glimpses the possibility that his social technology might make a difference to art, when suffering danger and 'the struggle to be good' have been removed. He is unworried: 'the art and literature of a new culture will be about other things.'

This is not really a malign book, though it is a profoundly obtuse one. Its jaunty jargon is so pathetically removed from any social reality that it could scarcely produce, directly at least, much evil in practice, though the know-all reductive tone may encourage some enemies of freedom and dignity. More theoretically, the pity is that it can only encourage the idea that the values of humanity, and the scientific understanding of human beings, stand necessarily opposed to one another. If Skinner's reinforcement theory were really the science in question, that would indeed be so; but in fact scientific understanding is no more present in this book than any other kind.

Note

1. *Beyond Freedom and Dignity*, by B. F. Skinner (Cape, 1972).

20

What Computers Can't Do: A Critique of Artificial Reason, by Hubert L. Dreyfus

Electronic machines of the kind generically called "computers" can now do a number of things at least as well as human beings, and in some cases better. Many of these tasks are boring, such as finding addresses or counting things. Immunity to boredom is one thing that helps to give computers the edge over human beings in some tasks. Another is speed of operation: only a computer could do the calculations necessary for landing a module on the moon, since only a computer could do the sums in less time than it takes the module to get there.

In some cases, the computer's program guarantees an answer to the problem in hand. Whether this is so depends on several things: first, whether the problem is one for whose solution a determinate procedure (called an algorithm) can be specified. An algorithm is a set of instructions which when carried out is bound eventually to yield what is required. Looking things up in lists and doing addition are two among many tasks for which there exist algorithms, and computers spend most of their time on just such things.

But even if a task can be specified in an algorithm, there remain vitally important questions of whether a machine could complete the task in an acceptable time or within the limits of the amount of information it can process. These restrictions are so important that the question of whether there is an algorithm for a given task may be of little practical interest. Thus, in principle, there could be programs for playing checkers that involved counting out all possible future combinations of moves and countermoves (though even this would not by itself provide the way to choose the best moves). But assuming that at any given point five moves on the average are possible, the number of possibilities twenty moves ahead is greater than the number of microseconds in a year—which forecloses that way of going about it.

For most interesting tasks either there is no algorithm or it is not a practicable one. So machines must be programmed not to grind through the task but to proceed "heuristically"—to search intelligently (as we would put it), to show some insight into what is relevant and promising, and to learn what is useful and what is not. Such programs, of course, are in themselves as determinate as the others, and the machine's states are still determined by the program and its earlier states: the difference is that the program does not contain instructions which lead inevitably and by exhaustion to a solution, but rather is designed to throw up routines and strategies which should prove fruitful in finding a solution.

In talking of "computers" here I have in mind, as Dreyfus has throughout his book, *digital* machines, that is to say, machines that represent all the information they handle by combinations of elements each of which can be either of two states (on or off, for instance), and are thus machines which conduct their procedures in a series of discrete steps.[1] In saying that a digital machine goes in discrete steps one is saying something about how it represents information; one is not saying that it goes from one physical state to another by instantaneous magic, without going through places in between, but only that the places in between do not have any significance in representing information. When a digital device such as an adding machine is contrasted with an *analogue* device such as a slide rule, the point is not that one clicks and the other creeps, but that any points that the latter creeps through, however close together, do represent something.

Some still hope, and more fear, that foreseeable developments of these techniques will yield digital machines which over an impressive and growing range of human competence will equal or surpass human ability. In this book Dreyfus aims to refute these expectations and to allay these fears by showing on general philosophical grounds that the aim is impossible and that the research which seeks to develop machine intelligence so that it can solve interesting and really complex problems is doomed to failure, except perhaps in solving some very narrow problems. He starts with the record and claims that there has been over the last fifteen years a repeated pattern of initial minor success, grandiose promises and predictions, then disappointments, diminishing returns, and finally silence as the research bogs down and the promises remain unfulfilled.

Similar patterns can be seen in various fields of computer research. Following Minsky, a leading worker whom he extensively criticizes, Dreyfus distinguishes two main branches of inquiry that have seemed at one time or another very promising. One is Cognitive Simulation (CS), which takes tips from the ways humans actually solve problems and from the short cuts they use, and seeks to provide methods for machines which will significantly reproduce some psychological features of intelligent human behavior in solving mathematical problems, for example, or translating from one language to another. The other, Artificial Intelligence (AI), is, in Minsky's words,

> ... an attempt to build intelligent machines without any prejudice toward making the system simple, biological, or humanoid ... one might first need experience with working intelligent systems (based if necessary on *ad hoc* mechanisms) if one were eventually to be able to design more economical schemes. [Quoted by Dreyfus, p. 43]

With both these approaches, initial small successes led to overconfidence: Dreyfus rehearses numerous instances of this. But there is a real question about how significant much of this now aging material is. Even if early predictions of computers' chess competence were wildly overoptimistic, it really is not very interesting to be told again that a certain chess program was beaten in 1960 by a ten-year-old: it is even less interesting than the fact (a trifle gracelessly admitted by Dreyfus) that more recently a program called MacHack beat Dreyfus.

Artificial Intelligence has gone through a sober process of realizing that human beings are cleverer than it supposed. It has turned to a more cautious and diversified strategy of accumulating "know-how" rather than mounting frontal assaults. These developments—of which one will gather little from Dreyfus—are more appropriate to the sort of phenomenon intelligence is, and the boasts and disappointments which Dreyfus tirelessly rehearses are of decreasing relevance to assessing prospects now.

The more important part of Dreyfus's case lies not in the references to past history and slow progress, but in the general considerations which, he claims, show that the failures are inevitable and that it is to be expected that relatively trivial initial success will run out when one tries something more complex. The predictions of large success on the basis of small are not just examples of technologists' euphoria or grant collectors' publicity, but rely on a principle which is itself fundamental to the kind of analysis that goes into CS and AI, namely that moving from simple to complex is just moving from less to more—that the development of *more of the same* can be expected, in one way or another, to crack the problem. This principle Dreyfus rejects.

Dreyfus cites a number of features of human experience in problem solving that he claims are essential to problem solving and could not conceivably be reproduced or imitated by a computer. They are all of what might, very loosely, be called a "*Gestalt*-ish" kind, and include the phenomena of "fringe consciousness" (as when one is dimly aware of the relevance of some ill-defined factor), "zeroing in" (as when a problem-situation "organizes itself around" a promising approach), and tolerance of ambiguity, under which, for example, the mind can succeed in disregarding in a certain context a possible significance of a word which in another context would be the one to present itself. In general, the human mind can seize on what is essential in a given situation and mentally organize the whole problem in the light of this understanding.

It is I, and not Dreyfus, who have assembled this set of requirements for problem solving in such short order, though it must be said that he himself runs through them briskly and successively in his own exposition. But when they are brought together, one gets the first glimpse of a problem which grows throughout Dreyfus's book, that is, the exact status he assigns to such phenomena. Dreyfus tends to present them as though they were special ways human beings have of going about solving problems, ways not employable by computers but which have to be used if problems are going to be solved. But it is not clear that the requirements are all this, or indeed that they all have any one kind of relevance to problem solving. Thus an ability to distinguish the essential from the inessential does not provide a *special way* of solving problems, available to humans and lacking to machines: solving a complex problem is itself an exercise in telling the essential from the inessential, and to say that machines cannot do this is not to uncover a deep reason why machines cannot solve that kind of problem, but is just to say that they cannot. Dealing with ambiguity seems to be similar; and it certainly is, if we assume that one aim of the exercise must be to produce machines that can handle natural language.

"Zeroing in," on the other hand, seems to be of a different, though perhaps rather ambiguous, status. It could just refer to the human ability to arrange the data of a problem in a way conducive to a solution, seeing the relevant ways to use the data, and so on, in which case this ability seems once more logically indistinguishable from an ability to solve the problem, or at least (what is wanted) to solve it economically. But it could, as characterized by Dreyfus, refer to a certain kind of *experience*, of a *Gestalt* character, in which the data "turn round" and "structure themselves" and "present themselves" in a relevant way. It is the sort of experience, perhaps, that may be helpful to humans in problem solving. There are many reasons for wondering whether any machine could have an experience of that sort; but also, there are few reasons for supposing that it would have to in order to solve problems.

The confusion here is encouraged, I think, by Dreyfus's own philosophy, which does the best it can to obliterate distinctions between the problem situation itself and how it seems to the problem solver—a distinction without which the whole issue and some of Dreyfus's own assertions become unintelligible. He presents certain capacities as at once indispensable to problem solving and inconceivable for the machine. But, on inspection, these items tend to dissolve into some things that are certainly essential to problem solving (as being indeed in various degrees restatements of what problem solving is) but which are not shown to be inconceivable for the machine, and, on the other hand, things of the *Gestalt*-experience kind that may well be inconceivable for the machine but are not shown to be in themselves essential to problem solving—at least, for machines.

If one lays aside the covert appeal to *Gestalt* experience, most of Dreyfus's arguments look thin. He may well be right in claiming that many tasks that are simple for human beings would need systems quite undreamed of in practice for their machine simulation. But his claim to have *proved* the limitations of computers is exaggerated. If one shakes together the considerations that Dreyfus brings forward, one can extract, I think, three kinds of arguments for his conclusion; and all, it seems to me, leave the issue still open.

First, there is the general "anti-Platonic" argument. This is not so much one argument as a class of considerations, the general upshot of which is that both machine simulations of human skills (such as CS) and machine reproductions by other means of human skills (such as AI) depend on an assumption which is pervasive throughout Western, modern, or at least technological thought, namely, that rationality consists in reducing experience to discrete atomistic elements and handling them by determinate rules of procedure which can be clearly and discursively spelled out.

This assumption Dreyfus repeatedly calls the "Platonic" assumption, thus making a historical claim which it would be tedious to go on about, but which in some of its applications at least is downright amazing; as in the apparent suggestion (pp. 123–124) that Plato had the quasi-technological ambition of reducing the empirical world to determinate rule-governed order—something which the historical Plato repeatedly claimed to be impossible. (Though Dreyfus frequently quotes Heidegger, he does not in this historical connection; but the picture of Western intellectual history of course comes from Heidegger, who holds that Socrates and Plato with their clanging inhuman essences scared off the pre-Socratics, those shepherds of Being.)

Dreyfus contests what he calls the "Platonic" assumption on several planes. At the psychological level, his point seems to be that human beings do not in fact think about things, and could not solve problems, just by a "Platonic" style of step-by-step discursive thought. This seems true, but of doubtful relevance; it may tell against some machine men who claim to be guided by actual psychological data, but beyond that it seems to loop back into the *Gestalt*-experience consideration. Even when it is the aim of a machine intelligence researcher to construct a program which will solve problems "the way we do," it cannot be a requirement that the program should have the same sort of shape as our experience of solving problems—indeed, it is not in the least clear what such a requirement would mean. Admittedly—and here Dreyfus makes a good bit of capital—the idea of a machine solving problems "the way we do" is itself very unclear; but, as we shall see, Dreyfus has neglected to look in the obvious direction from which content might be given to that idea.

In any case, for AI researchers the aim is not to get a machine to solve problems "the way we do," but just to get a machine to solve problems. Against them also Dreyfus applies his "anti-Platonic" argument, on the ground that their assumptions about the possibility of modeling intelligent activity on a digital machine involve the "Platonic" assumption, not this time about the processes of human thought, but about what the world is like and what an explanation or theory about the world, and about intelligent behavior, must be like. A theory about intelligent activity might be "Platonic" without that activity itself being "Platonic," as the movement of the planets can be described in differential equations without the planets themselves solving differential equations; but, Dreyfus argues, there is no reason to believe that such a theory, which might enable one to model the behavior in a digital machine, is possible, and it is only the "Platonic" assumption that makes people think that it is possible.

The trouble in evaluating Dreyfus's argument here is that he leaves it unclear exactly how a theory can be said to be "Platonic," and how strong a restriction on the theory this is. His argument requires at least that any theory which can be modeled in a digital machine is "Platonic"; but he himself mentions the important result that any analogue theory can, if it is sufficiently precise, be modeled in a digital machine as well. He has an argument apparently designed to get round this fact, but I have not been able to understand it. It is not even clear how far round it he wants to get.

Dreyfus's rejection of the "Platonic" assumption seems to boil down to the usual antimechanist, antiphysicalist, or antideterminist claim that intelligent behavior cannot be scientifically understood, which it will be no surprise to find is rejected by AI researchers. I do not think that Dreyfus wants it just to come down to that, but I have not found enough in his characterization of the "Platonic"—once the *Gestalt*-experience element is laid aside—to stop it from just coming down to that.

Dreyfus's second general argument might be called the "all or nothing" or "form of life" argument. The clearest application of this is in the centrally important matter of understanding natural language, and the ability of speakers to cope with a high level of ambiguity, to catch on to what is relevant, and so forth. The sad failure of the project, much vaunted at one time, of constructing programs to translate from one natural language to another has revealed among other things how much information about the world a machine has to have available to it in order to make sense of even very simple human communications; and also how flexible and open-ended the deployment of that information has to be if the computer program, even when it seems to be getting along quite well, is not to collapse into breathtaking idiocy.

Dreyfus rightly emphasizes the importance of this sort of consideration but his treatment of the point is exaggerated. On matters of fact, he fails to acknowledge the extent to which current work on natural language programs shows greatly increased sensitivity to context; and on questions of principle, his treatment tends to distract attention from some of the most interesting questions that might be asked. He claims that the ever-present need of interpretation, and the indefinite range of knowledge and understanding that the human has to call upon, mean that we have to take a human being's "world" as a whole; Wittgenstein's celebrated remark about a language being a "form of life" is used here to suggest how much a whole way of being would have to be given to a machine if it were really to deal intelligently with its environment and properly understand what was said to it.

But might not this just be overdoing it? For one thing—to mention an issue which is hardly ever touched on by Dreyfus—even if the human world of understanding has this vast and indivisible complexity, perhaps the intelligent activity of some simpler organism might be adequately simulated? Some of Dreyfus's other arguments would no doubt aim to exclude that as well; but so far as this argument goes, it is as well to remember that machine intelligence would already have had a vast triumph if it could simulate on any substantial scale the intelligent activity of creatures less culturally elaborated than man.

Another, and more important, point is that Dreyfus's exclusive insistence on the ways in which human abilities, when all are present and working, are tightly interrelated, and on the extent to which information of different types is brought to bear on interpretative questions in various and plastic ways, distracts attention from the question of the extent to which abilities might be separable from one another, and of the kinds of simplifications which might yield a recognizable *fragment* of human intelligent behavior. Dreyfus seems, indeed, to think that the idea of such a fragment is nonsense; but we need more than phenomenological descriptions of the experience (or "world") of the functioning human being to convince us of that. We need detailed theoretical and experimental study of simpler animals and partial abilities, and Dreyfus's argument, which is all about a world both whole and human, neither proves its impossibility nor anticipates its results.

Dreyfus seems to make the demand that machines, in order to be intelligent at all, should be unfailingly at least as intelligent as human beings sometimes are. That demand is absurd; and, further, there is little reason to believe that the ways in which machines will succeed and fail in displaying intelligence will be just the same as with human beings or other animals. We should expect neither that machines will make no mistakes, nor that their mistakes will necessarily be related in a familiar human way to their successes.

The third general argument, or type of argument, is the "infinite regress" argument, which rests on the idea that the rules or principles of understanding that human beings use need interpretation and that their application is in various ways relative to context. Now rules or principles of a higher order can be used, which determine the application of the ones of a lower rank, and sort contexts into different kinds; but then these rules will themselves need interpretation. If every rule needs another rule, this leads to a vicious regress; it has to be stopped. It cannot be stopped, Dreyfus argues, by an appeal to rules that are intrinsically independent of the context they are to be applied to, or are self-interpreting—there are no such things, and the idea that there are is a fiction of "Platonic" thinkers. Rather, the regress stops, as Wittgenstein (once more) claimed, in certain concrete facts of human life and practice: we do just "go on" in certain ways, "catch on" to some things rather than others; justifications come to an end in a shared form of life.

I find this argument difficult because it is not clear to me what exactly these concrete facts are, and in particular whether they apply to the species as a whole, or culturally differ between societies, to mention only the crudest alternatives—a difficulty which I also have with Wittgenstein's own account of them. The impression often given by such arguments is that these facts—which no doubt exist—are in some basic way *inexplicable*: an impression much helped by the very fact that one is given no adequate directions about the level (cultural, psychological, zoological) on which one should look for them, and hence for their explanation. But while facts of this kind no doubt exist, there is no reason at all to expect them to be inexplicable. Until it is made clear why they have to remain inexplicable, it is likely to remain unclear why knowledge of them, or of some weak but adequate version of them, cannot be modeled into a machine.

I have already mentioned Dreyfus's own philosophy, which provides the basis for some of his criticism, and which he even claims is capable of producing *explanations* of intelligent and purposive behavior more adequate than any available to "Platonic" theories. The philosophy in question is a type of phenomenology owing much to Heidegger and to Merleau-Ponty. It is not, at least in this offering, very easy to take it seriously, or even patiently. One of its characteristics is its reliance on terms which sound explanatory, but which in fact conceal in their ambiguity many of the real questions that need to be asked:

> But what if the work of the central nervous system depends on the locomotive system, or to put it phenomenologically, what if the "higher," determinate, logical, and detached forms of intelligence are necessarily derived from and guided by global and involved "lower" forms? [Pp. 148–149]

What indeed? "Derived from" and "guided by" here are sheer bluff, and will remain so unless some more "Platonic" work is done.

Another trait—almost definitional of the method—is to offer a graphic, and often pointedly inaccurate, description of a perceived situation which allegedly reveals its nature:

> Thus, in ordinary situations, we say we perceive the whole object, even its hidden aspects, because the concealed aspects directly affect our perception. [P. 153]

That contains at least two straightforward falsehoods, and unhelpful ones: to suggest that such characterizations could helpfully replace scientific investigation of why and how things look solid under certain conditions is absurd.

Such untruths have a built-in defense mechanism: they are so obviously untrue that anyone who protests of their literal falsehood can be accused of having missed their nonliteral point. But that mechanism is not enough to keep them alive in a world of hard questions; nor, incidentally, to justify their use by Dreyfus, who earlier in the book has gone in for a great deal of donnish nit-picking against formulations, loose but often adequately intelligible, offered by people on the other side.

Another characteristic feature of phenomenology that deeply affects Dreyfus's argument is its traditional tendency, despite heroic efforts on the part of its leading exponents, to slide inexorably in the direction of idealism, the view that the world can only be coherently regarded as the-world-as-it-seems-to-us, or, worse still, the-world-as-it-seems-to-me. Dreyfus constantly uses formulae that present the world which men perceive and act in as already constituted by their experiences and perceptions: thus at page 136 he seems to accept that "only in terms of situationally determined relevance are there any facts at all"; and at page 184 writes, "We are at home in the world and can find our way about in it because it is *our* world produced by us as the context of our pragmatic activity . . . [our] activity has produced the world." Even my personal memories are "inscribed in the things around me" (p. 178).

Of course, there are ways of taking these sayings. But it seems that Dreyfus wants to take them in such a way that the whole idea of a scientific theory which regarded the objects of the human world—such as trees, for instance—in abstraction from human interests would be absurd. From that, I am inclined to think, he derives his most general "anti-Platonic" opinions: if the objects of the human world cannot be regarded in abstraction from human perception, activities, and interests, then there can be no scientific account which takes such objects and human beings, and inquires how they interact.

But if that argument is going to work, it looks as though the idealistic premise from which it has to be derived must be taken in an enormously strong and indeed lunatic way. It has to be taken, in fact, in such a form as to imply that, since trees are "produced" and so forth by human interests, a world in which there were no humans would be a world without trees—indeed, it would not be a world at all. If one objects to this, naïvely, by saying that it must be possible for there to be a world without humans, because there *used* to be a world without humans (including, however, trees), the reply will be that one has misunderstood.

But the use that Dreyfus makes of these idealist formulae for his purposes seems to me precisely to require the crude, indeed laughable, interpretation which he would immediately reject. For if we can conceive of trees without humans, why cannot we scientifically investigate their interactions with humans? If the sense in which the world is "produced" by humans is just the less hectic sense in which the world must be described from a human point of view, why is it impossible that among the things described from that point of view are the causal relations involved in the human perception of trees?

Dreyfus does not, however, surrender everything to the realm of production by human experience; apart from our experience, and really "there" in some sense, is a flux of energy, atomic particles, things as described by physics. Indeed, he admits that man is a physical system interacting like others with his physical environment, and that "inputs of energy of various frequencies are correlated with the same perceptual experience" (p. 95). Moreover, according to Dreyfus, the impossibility of digital simulation is not supposed to exclude the possibility of artificial organisms, if these are conceived of in terms of analogue systems, no doubt embodied in biological materials. But Dreyfus makes these concessions very lightly and clearly regards the levels of physical or neurophysiological explanation, which he is happy to concede, as something quite detached from the possibility, which he rules out, of the simulation of intelligent activity by digital means.

But Dreyfus does not see how much his offhand concessions to science may have cost him. For if we can gain enough physical knowledge to construct an artificial organism, and if *construct* it is what we do, as opposed to growing it *in vitro* from ready-made biological materials, then we understand it. And if we understand it so that we can construct it to behave in certain ways, then we understand the relation of its physical structure to its possibilities of behavior, in the sense at least that we understand what kinds of physical differences underlie what kinds of differences in behavior.

Moreover, there is no a priori reason why the possibility of yielding certain behavior should be restricted to structures in one given sort of material; it would rather prove, perhaps, to be indeed the *structure* of a system which provided the required potentiality. And if we got to that stage, then even if it were an analogue system that we had uncovered, it is unclear why in principle it should be impossible to model it in a digital machine. I see nothing in Dreyfus's frequent complaints against those who have confused physical and psychological levels that blocks *this* road to the positions he supposes himself to have cut off. This is the direction in which content can be found for the notion that a machine physically very different from us might solve problems or do other things "as we do." It also provides the sense—the only interesting sense for these investigations—to the question "*How* does man, or another animal, produce a given kind of behavior?"

Dreyfus says at one point (p. 144) of the question "How does man produce intelligent behavior?" that

> . . . the notion of "producing" behavior . . . is already colored by the [Platonic] tradition. For a product must be produced in some way; and if it isn't produced in some definite way, the only alternative seems to be that it is produced magically.

Well, one ambiguity, rather tediously, has to be removed: of course it isn't necessary that a given sort of behavior must on every occasion be produced in the same definite way, nor would a machine have to produce it always in the same way. But if the thought is that a given piece of behavior can appear on a given occasion, and not be produced on that occasion in some definite way—then yes, indeed, it would be produced magically. That is the magic Dreyfus is calling us to from his counter-Platonic cavern. But however depressed we may sometimes be by the threats and promises of the machine men, we are not forced in there yet.

Note

1. *What Computers Can't Do: A Critique of Artificial Reason*, by Hubert L. Dreyfus (Harper & Row, 1972).

21

Wisdom: Twelve Essays, edited by Renford Bambrough

John Wisdom, who this year retired as professor of philosophy at the University of Oregon, for many years taught at Cambridge. The most important fact of his philosophical life has been the influence of the later Wittgenstein, to which his publications bear strong witness from 1937 onwards; though he had published a number of things before that, including a book, *Problems of Mind and Matter,* it is as an exponent of Wittgensteinian ideas that he has, perhaps, most generally been regarded, and indeed has given the impression, in some of his most influential works, of regarding himself.

It is not an adequate assessment of him, as Renford Bambrough insists in the preface to this book of papers by various authors; and it can be added that if it were, Wisdom's writings could not now be of much interest.[1] When Wisdom wrote his best-known pieces on Wittgensteinian themes, the later work of Wittgenstein was largely unknown, confined to disciples, and transmitted by eager rumour and clandestine notes; but since Wittgenstein's death in 1951 publication of an extensive *nachlass* has, if not exactly enabled Wittgenstein to speak for himself (since much of it, seemingly, Wittgenstein did not wish to be heard), at least enabled each of us to cope more directly with the question of what Wittgenstein had to say.

Regarded just as a source, or as a display of Wittgensteinian ideas, Wisdom's work was in any case always stylistically too idiosyncratic; and the publication of Wittgenstein's work, again, does not help, since if one is forced to a comparison of these two ways of writing philosophy in a style without exposition or the apparatus of proof, Wisdom's jokiness runs the risk of coming out of it as English things do from some other comparisons with Viennese things (music, for instance). Quite apart from Wittengensteinian comparisons, Wisdom's style is rather perilous; at its most extreme, in the remarkable series of articles *Other Minds* (reprinted in a book of that name), though often it can be funny and revealing, it runs risks of being coy or facetious or resonantly vague—signs of strain, I suspect, generated by the difficulties in Wisdom's basic philosophical enterprise of accommodating to one another imagination, common sense, and what was in its origins a strongly positivist theory of knowledge.

Wisdom developed his philosophy in a climate in which positivism and logical empiricism were particularly lively influences, and while his work can be seen as a reaction against or move away from positivism, with its view of science as a summary of observations, its sharp distinction between verbal and factual truth, its verificationist view of meaning, nevertheless positivism recognizably shaped its interests. Positivism condemned metaphysical remarks as meaningless: Wisdom expounds kinds of meaning for them, which consist in their being paradoxically illuminating or reminding us of overlooked truths by saying what is literally absurd, or using words in a way which makes us see things which some theoretical obsession has obscured. Such an approach leaves a place for the imagination, and also a role for philosophy, which will at the very least always find some balance that needs redressing, some exaggeration that demands a counter-reminder. He has also stressed those forms of human rationality which were of least interest to positivism's scientific outlook, such as those deployed in legal argument, the comparison of one case with another.

Yet for all that, this philosophy seems to share with positivism a view that, whatever the value of philosophy, it is certainly something quite special, different in particular from the sciences: the idea that philosophy could be *continuous* with other activities, and that there can be no special problem about the meaning of philosophical propositions *as such*, remain equally remote from both outlooks, and in the same direction. That impression is strengthened by the nature of the role that Wisdom found for philosophical remarks, which was peculiarly protreptic: their meaning had to be explained in terms of their ability to make us see things differently, and in this they stood in important and explanatory contrast to some class of factual propositions whose meaning lay more directly in how they related to the world.

There is also the issue of scepticism. Positivism, like all forms of empiricism, centred itself on the theory of knowledge, and had a series of encounters with skepticism; its task was to find the warrant in sense perception for various kinds of supposed knowledge, and where that warrant seemed to be defective, the evidence not to reach up to the conclusions; there was a sceptical vacuum. Wisdom has himself constantly returned to issues about scepticism, in particular scepticism about other minds, the worrying doubt that we do not really know that anyone else has experiences. He has patiently circled round and round this issue, and has given ingenious and memorable help with it. He has resisted positivist, as all other, theories.

But the problem is set for him in a quite positivist way. One moderately primitive answer that might be given to the question of how we know that other people have experiences is that it is an empirical hypothesis which explains very well how they behave. When we are disposed to give this answer, Wisdom discourages us by saying that our belief cannot be an inductive analogical argument, an extrapolation from observed instances: for if it were, it could not (if adequate) be based on just one case, and moreover there would have to be independent verification of the conclusion, which is here in principle impossible. But the assumption that an empirical hypothesis would have to be based on such an argument and satisfy these conditions, is the straight positivist assumption that empirical explanation depends on inductive generalization, which work in the philosophy of science gives us no reason to accept. It is interesting that the exposition of Wisdom's philosophy by Gasking which forms the first chapter of the present book (the only piece to have appeared before, and now twenty years old) itself takes the inductivist and verificationist assumptions so totally for granted that in its formal setting out of Wisdom's argument they do not even appear as a separate premiss, but are presupposed in the conclusion.

In tone, Wisdom's philosophy is not at all like that of positivist philosophers. It gained its complex allusiveness and rejection of explicit doctrine from the later Wittgenstein. It acquired from another Cambridge source, G. E. Moore, a belief in the plainness of certain plain facts and in the oddness of philosophers' professing to doubt those facts—the weirdness, in general, of philosophical scepticism. Wisdom does not just reject that scepticism, he seeks to interpret it, explain it, see its illuminations. But while we should be sympathetic, grateful indeed, to sceptical aberrations, he will not let us forget, or at least for too long, that they are aberrations.

This approach does well to remind us that, and how, metaphysical remarks are not merely some additional remarks about how the world is, to be treated flatly like other putative additions to our knowledge. But it has the disadvantage, in particular, of making all forms of philosophical scepticism seem basically the same, and implying that the patient, sympathetic, diagnostic and possibly grateful attitude which is obviously the best that can be expected by some forms (such as scepticism about the material world, or the past, or other people's pains) is equally appropriate to others (such as scepticism about free will, or morality) which not only have a quite different claim on our attention but might actually be right. "Philosophy is the conflict of the obvious with the obvious", Mr Bambrough writes here; but the idea that the world may be in certain very important respects altogether different from what it seems is both sound and an important motivation to serious philosophy.

It has been said that all of Wisdom's philosophy is about what philosophy is. Though his best single piece ("Metaphysics and Verification", 1938) is about philosophy, the claim is in general not true: as witness the series about other minds which, despite many dicta about philosophy, is certainly about knowledge of other minds. Yet, for all that, there is reason behind the false claim. Wisdom's underlying outlook provides no direct way of addressing oneself to a philosophical view, or just arguing with it: one diagnoses it, or sees it as helpful, or illuminating, or misleading, and those attitudes are higher-order in a way in which to say of a view that it is true or false is not, except formally: to say that a view is true is to say that *things* are so, to say than a view is illuminating or helpful is not—it is nearer to saying something about those who hear it.

The tendency of the Wisdomian method to lead discussions back to the nature of philosophy is manifested in a few of the pieces in this book. The book is in effect a Festschrift, with some pieces about Wisdom, others about topics in or near his interests. It has the faults of the genre: there is a good deal of overlap, some central subjects get left out (surprisingly, there is nothing on Wisdom's concern with psychoanalysis), there is no criticism of Wisdom at all, and the pieces are of very uneven merit. Among the good ones, M. R. Ayers refreshingly introduces broader theoretical perspective, in relating some Wisdomian considerations to Chomsky's views; and Keith Gunderson says some very interesting things about physicalism, and even, since he can write well, earns a place for his jokes. Judith Jarvis Thompson contributes not only a paper but the frontispiece; her paper is good, but her fond photograph of Wisdom is a masterpiece.

Note

1. *Wisdom: Twelve Essays*, edited by Renford Bambrough (Blackwell, 1974).

22

The Socialist Idea, edited by Stuart Hampshire and L. Kolakowski

What is socialist thought? It is the attempt to work out systematically the consequences of the three revolutionary values of 1789, in the context of a world transformed by industrialism and capitalism. It is in effect the only systematic political thought we have. Most of the alternatives really come, in one way or another, to saying that there can be no systematic thought at all about the realisation of political values. There has been in the past intellectually elaborated conservative thought, but there is not much of it around today; while nationalism, when it comes to express its further hopes for society, has few of its own terms in which to do so: more often than not, it turns to something it calls 'socialism.'

Socialist thought displays divergent varieties and manifest tensions. This is hardly surprising: its problems are due, not so much to a special weakness of socialism, as to the difficulty of any political thought which aims to be at once ambitious, coherent, and realistic.

The tensions are certainly daunting enough. The demands for equality, justice, rationality in the deployment of resources, and the harnessing of industrial power to give material elbow-room for the free development of personality, point in the direction of centralised power; the need for a sense of control over one's environment, liberty in work, a decrease of alienation, and a greater sense of community, point to decentralised power, industrial democracy, and possibly syndicalist solutions. (It is a good thing that Tony Benn reminds us of these various aims; it is less good that he supposes that by looking zealous enough he can make the evident conflicts among them go away.)

Again, there is no reason to think that industrial democracy could increase anyone's freedom outside institutions of a wider political democracy, nor has anything proved better than parliamentary democracy in guarding the most elementary freedoms. Yet it would be idiotic to deny the doubts inspired by the gap between its pretensions and reality. Parliamentary democracy claims not just to manage society, but to embody and provide freedom, but it is in the area of that value, let alone in that of equality, that its response is found by many to be thin.

The present book is a collection of papers which explores, unevenly but with some real success, these and other such tensions, and the prospects for socialist thought.[1] It grew out of a conference held at Reading University in 1973: the title, 'What Is Wrong with the Socialist Idea?' was later changed, by a revision worthy of a Fabian drafting committee, to 'Is there Anything Wrong with the Socialist Idea?' That original note of discouragement is not altogether absent from the volume; and the collection is set off rather powerfully, in fact, in that direction since a piece which is both the first and one of the most powerfully presented, by Leszek Kolakowski, offers reflections which are discouraged at a deep level. The point and power of socialism in the form of a (humanistic) Marxism, he argues, lay in an idea of the restoration, or perhaps the first creation, of a human self-identity, a wholeness of human personality, not attainable under existing social and economic formations and this idea he is disposed now to see as a myth, simplistic, Rousseauite and dangerous.

Kolakowski's background (a leading exponent of critical Marxism, he was expelled from Poland in 1968) does not permit triumphant remarks from non-Marxists; and certainly there is no room for condescension from those of us who work for social democratic improvements and just postpone, or take for granted, the question of what picture of human life might be served by the society within which those improvements are defined. Yet, the modest degree of encouragement which Kolakowski permits himself in his introduction might receive a certain impetus from a tradition originally more sceptical: he offers as almost an anti-socialist admission the truism that not all human values can be rendered compatible, but that truism, true as it undoubtedly is, means a *defeat* only to the most optimistic kinds of socialism—to others, it helps to define the task.

The shadow of socialism as it has developed in Eastern Europe hangs heavily over quite a lot of this book. Practically no one has much to say for it and several Eastern European writers have impressive things to say against it. Mario Nuti finds himself more or less alone in his perception of Eastern European societies as at least farther on the way to genuine socialism and freedom than mixed Western societies, a position in which he finds mysteriously comforting the idea that, the party managers not being in Marxist terms a class, the exploitation of the workers 'will . . . not be a *class* exploitation, and their condition will be capable of being redressed by a "cultural" revolution. . . .' I should have liked to hear him discuss that proposition with Kolakowski.

Despite the critique of the Eastern party bureaucracies, however, this book is refreshingly free from the old, and typically British, idea that Marxist and non-Marxist strains of socialism have nothing to say to each other. There is only a small amount of biblical exegesis of Marx; at the same time, even those writers who make least use of strictly Marxist doctrine show themselves sensitive to the effects of Marxist ideas in the present situation: so Richard Lowenthal, in a beautifully set out and clear-headed piece on the future of socialism in the advanced democracies.

One form that the old idea of the separation of Marxist from non-Marxist traditions has taken, again typically in Britain, is the very general form of saying that non-Marxist socialism can be metaphysically pure, free from broad world-pictures, as Marxism cannot. This view must surely contain more falsehood than truth. To the important, and difficult, job of establishing their proportions this volume gives some help, if only intermittently; Charles Taylor, in particular, brilliantly argues that an ideology of an 'expressive' rather than an 'instrumentalist' kind, is what is needed to make sense of any form of socialism faced with late capitalism.

Stuart Hampshire, on the other hand, is disposed to see the dependence of much socialism on general pictures of man as a weakness; and argues, discouragingly, for both the necessity and the non-existence of detailed social scientific knowledge to govern political planning. But—apart from the question of whether there could be such pure knowledge—there is the vital issue of who, how, and with what authority, would apply such knowledge in planning whom: that is also an issue of which the socialist tradition is, happily, aware.

Note

1. *The Socialist Idea*, edited by Stuart Hampshire and L. Kolakowski (Weidenfeld and Nicolson, 1974).

23

Anarchy, State, and Utopia, by Robert Nozick

Why is there a state at all? Or, rather, why *should* there be a state at all? What is the justification of the state? The sense that these are real questions has come and gone and come again at various times; when that sense is present, the questions step in as the basic or first questions of political philosophy. It is not *obvious* that they are real questions, that the demand for a justification is a sound one. For one thing, one might be prepared to spend time on the justification only if one had an idea of some alternative to the state, and it is reasonable to feel that there are, at least now, no real candidates for that.

Differently, one may reflect that thoughts about justification could get a grip only if there were some set of principles or values which were sufficiently independent of the state (in general) to give one some leverage on the question. If the ideas by means of which the state is to be levered into or out of the arena of acceptability themselves presuppose the state, we shall effect nothing. But some, with Hegel somewhere behind them, will feel that there is fair doubt on that score—the moral ideas which supposedly provide the leverage will seem to them not only to be the historical product of the state (which is certainly true, but may not be damaging), but also, in some damaging sense, to get their life from the context of the state. This last group of doubters have also their Marxist relatives, who can, dimly, discern a better world without the state—it is, after all, what the revolutionary process should eventually lead to—but who regard present moralizing about the existence of the state as footling, and ideologically polluted.

Doubters of these last kinds are not going to be reassured by Robert Nozick's original, remarkable, and strikingly intelligent book.[1] He has nothing directly to say to their worries, though they should have things to learn from various of his arguments, and they should at least be forced by this energetic and inventive undertaking to put their claims in a clearer and better-argued form. As should anyone who wants to think effectively both about the existence of the state, and about what goes on in the state: for Mr Nozick not only revives the exercise of justifying the state, but comes out with some startlingly unfashionable conclusions about what it should be up to—or at least, what it should *ideally* be up to. This qualification, I shall suggest at the end, is of huge importance: the "ideally" is the clue to why Mr Nozick's book is not what it seems, nor (still less) what some unsavoury people will, with some encouragement from the author, undoubtedly take it to be.

Mr Nozick goes back to the traditional business of justifying the state from the ground up, the ground being provided by an imaginary set of circumstances in which there is no state; this is called by Mr Nozick, as by the tradition, the State of Nature. This, in his presentation, helps us to understand what the state is being justified *against*: drawing on some particularly American elements in the anarchist tradition, he spends much more time and ingenuity than anyone else has ever done in spelling out how things might go in a partly moralized State of Nature, where various private "protective associations" do the job, for a fee, of protecting people's rights of life, property, and so on, against force and fraud. It is partly moralized in the sense that the people in it do, for a good bit of the time, but not unfailingly, abide by moral considerations, where these are identified by Mr Nozick with a hard-core set of notions about rights, linked rather loosely with Kantian ideas about treating people as ends and not purely as means. (Utilitarians, of course, will not accept the moral starting-point: Mr Nozick assumes, I think reasonably, that no one with whom it is worth having the argument of this book will be a Utilitarian (really), and he makes on the way some excellent remarks to encourage people to realize that they are not.)

In taking the partly moralized starting-point, Mr Nozick is in line with Locke (an author to whom he closely, and surprisingly often, refers back). More explicitly free, of course, than Locke from any historical implications of the model, he differs more deeply by excluding any idea of a contract: this is State-of-Nature theory without the social contract.

In its place, he aims to derive the state from the starting-point of the model by a chain of events which involve no intentional intervention: by what he calls an *invisible hand* mechanism, adopting in this the language of classical economics, which alone of the social sciences is used in the book and whose methods provide some important parts of its intellectual structure. The mechanism which eventually, and after some pretty densely presented speculations, delivers the state without anyone intending it embodies an important idea of Schelling's in decision theory (and has some similarity to David Lewis's recent work on convention). It is an elegant idea to apply to classical State-of-Nature theory a mechanism by which one can arrive at a convention without (so to speak) holding one.

The state which is delivered is, as once more with Locke, the minimum "night-watchman" state of classical liberal theory, doing no more than protect its citizens from force and fraud and such like, leaving them free to pursue their individual projects. Mr Nozick shares Locke's distaste for taxation, and there is a tough-minded economic argument to represent it as a form of forced labour (though I must warn the CBI [Confederation of British Industry], before they prematurely rejoice over this liberating intellectual event, that we shall see that the consequences of all this *for things as they are* are very far from clear). Traditional State-of-Nature theorists, in justifying the state, inevitably justified a state of one kind rather than another, with one set rather than another of powers and restrictions: that was a main point of the exercise. Mr Nozick is no exception, and the argument in the first part of the book, which justifies against the anarchists the existence of the minimal state, is followed by a second part (as ingeniously argued, but more relaxedly written) which claims against socialists, nationalists, and indeed most people that the minimum state is the *most* that can be justified, and that more ambitious moral claims for the role of the state, in particular to produce justice by redistributive measures, are mistaken. Such powers, which are of course claimed in varying degrees by all modern states, have, according to Mr Nozick, no moral basis and offend against people's individual rights.

The major effort in the second half of the book is the attempt to argue against conceptions of justice (in particular, but not exclusively, that of John Rawls) that yield redistributive conclusions, and to give another conception, which does not: we shall come back to it later. The book ends with an engaging sketch of a pluralistic, libertarian Utopia, which has the unusual property of really carrying through the libertarian ideal by not laying it down even that people should live in a libertarian manner. The libertarian arrangements exist at the higher-order level of permitting a large number of very various communities between which people may move—they are all ordered within the merely Lockean framework, but in themselves they may be as restrictive or unpermissive as you (or rather they) like. Some of the difficulties which might spring to mind about these arrangements are rather disarmingly foreseen.

There is also, it should be mentioned, a bravura short chapter in which it is argued that the modern state *might*, after all, be justified (that is, in Mr Nozick's terms, could come into existence without violating anyone's rights). However, the squeamish reader should be warned against pressing this argument against the general tenor of Mr Nozick's conclusions. For the construction proceeds via everyone's selling himself into slavery; and while Mr Nozick himself, more permissive here than Locke, thinks that everyone has the moral right to do this, and hence that the results of it are not for that reason impermissible, it is typical of this structurally sophisticated and self-aware book that the reader should find himself in an ironical stand-off with Mr Nozick on this way of getting to the modern state.

The two major parts of the book, the minimally positive and the ambitiously negative, are connected with each other in more than one way. The aim of the second part is to show that no larger state is justified, by removing what Mr Nozick takes to be the major moral arguments in favour of such a state, namely arguments from distributive justice (only the larger state can be in a position to redistribute, in the interest of what mistaken theories take to be justice). Other arguments, and indeed other moral arguments, might be thought of to support the state. But Mr Nozick is interested only in a relatively narrow range even of moral considerations: those, roughly, to do with rights, justice and the crossing of one person's "moral boundaries" by another. It is this which dictates the narrow compass of what he thinks has to be said about the more ambitious state; equally, it controls the construction of the minimal state.

Now there is an argument for using the absolute minimum of hard-core moral notions in the first part of the book in the justification of the minimal state. For here one is arguing with someone like the libertarian anarchist, whose ideas these are, and the shape of the argument is to say: "Look, even with those (few) moral ideas one can get to the state" (though of course the rest of us, neither libertarian anarchists nor very tempted by them, might say right at the beginning that the anarchists' bag of moral ideas was too small anyway, and that we saw no interest in trying to cram that morally elaborated item, the state, into it). But, even if one is prepared to defend the state against them on the strength of this moral hard-tack, one is not bound to say that this is *all* the argument, even of a moral character, that can be brought to bear on the state; nor, correspondingly, are we bound to think that the only defence of the more elaborate state is to be found in applications of those, or closely related, notions. We might think that there were other values besides justice which the more elaborated state alone could advance: and that there was nothing in the intuitions employed in the first part of the book which will exclude these other values being weighed in the evaluation of the state. Mr Nozick's defence of his negative claim, that the more elaborate state is not justified, is inevitably weakened by the restrictions imposed on the range of arguments which he considers in favour of such a state.

Not just the second part of the book, but the first part as well, would be weakened if it could be shown that even the hardcore values, the minimal moral package of notions about rights, derived some essential support from sources outside the limited repertoire of the State of Nature (one form of that view, of course, would be held by those theorists I mentioned at the beginning, who think that in one way or another the minimal moral notions themselves derive their life from the state—indeed, from the elaborated state). Locke's treatment has often been criticized on that score; Mr Nozick's sophisticated reversion to Locke collects sophisticated versions of the criticisms, and it is surprising he has not done more to head them off.

In particular, he has tried—using, obviously, much ingenuity in the attempt—to get to his destination while avoiding any general discussion of a notion central to his views: *property*. He does have something to say about Locke's requirement that, when those in the State of Nature acquire things, there should be "enough and as good left over" for others. But, apart from that (which presents certain special problems for his theory of entitlement), he does not really address himself to the issue of what is an originally just holding at all, or of property as (what he requires) a purely *moral* notion. Hence, while there is a great deal in the discussion of the State of Nature about people's "boundaries" and how they get crossed, there is no discussion of where their boundaries are, or of how they get drawn. There is thus a persistent doubt about whether the State of Nature can really be got off the ground without taking for granted conventions and institutions of a kind which the State of Nature does not itself provide. Certainly we cannot hope to get clear about this just by using such intuitions as we have *as things are* about non-legal and informal ideas of property—they can too readily be seen as extensions of more institutionalized notions.

Another difficulty with the State-of-Nature argument is what its rules are. Mr Nozick reckons to have succeeded in his task against the libertarian anarchist if an invisible-hand mechanism would produce the state without violating anyone's rights, granted that the individuals are (partly) moralized. But there is an obscurity about why this thought-experiment operates as it does (why, one might equally say, *this* is the thought-experiment). Mr Nozick presents us with a set of persons who behave like economic men, but within the side-constraints, for the most part, of minimal morality; only "for the most part", since a lot of the machinery is designed to deal with persons who do violate others' boundaries, and not all such violations are unintentional. Now the steps in the development of the thought-experiment, though many and complex, are notably unrealistic, if judged from the position of social or psychological credibility. Thus, to take just one of many examples, the protection agencies, which are in economic competition with one another, show a commendable zeal in establishing the rights and wrongs of claims against their clients; but even a modest lack of optimism about human nature would suggest that in fact they would be partial towards their clients, hypocritical towards potential clients, and horrible towards confirmed non-clients.

Now Mr Nozick is not an optimistic idiot who disbelieves this; the point is, these considerations *do not count*. But why not? What weight is there in the fact that we *could*, relative to certain wildly idealized psychological assumptions, reach the state without violating anyone's rights? The motivation seems to be, that the (minimal) state will have been justified if it can be generated by steps each of which satisfies moral demands; and this is taken to mean that we can get there without anyone doing anything wrong. But how is this to be taken? The condition cannot be that we should be able to get there without anyone doing anything wrong *at all*, since it is a fact that some people sometimes do wrong which essentially contributes to our getting there and helps to power the invisible hand. By the same token, the condition cannot be that there is no wrong whose happening is essential to our getting there. So what exactly is it? How much wrong goes into the model, and where? Why cannot a sceptic resist the invisible-hand derivation, on the ground that its pictured working is too free of wrong to be plausible? As it stands, Mr Nozick seems—though I am not sure of this—to have settled for individuals in the model sometimes doing wrong, but associations not doing wrong; if that is correct, the model seems arbitrary. In any case, the derivation as it stands lacks any evident ground for being precisely as un-Hobbesian as it is.

Still less, of course, does it justify any existing state: for no state arose in this way, and it is Mr Nozick's thought, certainly in his theory of justice, and I take it here, that how a state of affairs *actually* arose is crucial for its acceptability. This is the basic idea of his theory of justice as entitlement, and of his criticism of Rawls (and many other conceptions). A holding is just, on this view, if it has been acquired by a just process from a holding which is itself just: at the beginning is a notion of just acquisition (on which, as I have already said, Mr Nozick has notably little to say). Supplementary to the processes of just acquisition and just transfer are processes of rectification for situations which are unjust in one of these respects (holding, or transfer, or previous rectification): and that is all there is of the basic theory of justice.

Mr Nozick makes elegantly clear the difference between such a *historical* theory of just holdings, and an *end-state* theory, which concerns itself essentially with the pattern in which holdings end up, and seeks to adjust the pattern to some desired paradigm: Utilitarianism, and egalitarianism, and Rawls's view are all end-state views. (There is a very nice demonstration that the State-of-Nature model which Rawls uses, that of the Original Position, is so designed that it could only yield an end-state conception of justice.) It will be clear how, at an ideal level of politics at least, Mr Nozick's conception, as against end-state views, favours a strongly conservative outlook.

What are the intuitive merits of these ideas? There are questions, right at the beginning, about how to argue these issues. Mr Nozick's basic method, throughout, is to take some everyday, non-political situation about which we are likely to agree, and apply our judgment in it to the larger issue of social principle—a method which, it might be argued, begs the question in his favour, since it presupposes his view that no new moral principles arise (should arise?) with the state. But even running the argument by his rules, his conception of justice does look like an enormous exaggeration of at best one aspect of our moral ideas. It is hard to know how far this is so, in fact, because, once more, we lack any theory of original entitlement. But suppose that, when the *Mayflower* arrived, some foresighted fellow, crouching by the gang-plank, jumped off and bagged a good area of what is now Massachusetts, before his companions, more cooperative, pious, idle, or enfeebled, got going; it looks as though Mr Nozick, if we assume there were no prior holders, would grant him just title. Do we agree? Would it be *unjust* to redistribute in favour of those others (even the idle)? Wasn't it *unfair* of this man to take advantage of the fact that the others did not spend those crucial moments thinking about property rights? Would a certain fact about the end-result, namely that the nice guys came (nearly) last, have no effect at all on our estimate of the justice of this man's holdings?

These are questions for Mr Nozick's theory of *justice* (and its application to this case); but we can notice more broadly that, even if we eventually agreed that this pushy settler was not to be faulted in justice, that would only underline the point that we could hope that the Pilgrims, and ourselves, would have arrived with more virtues than justice. We are reminded again of that richer range of moral resources (of the kinds of character, for instance, that we want to have in society) which Mr Nozick's treatment systematically leaves out.

There are other ideas and sentiments relevant to justice, which his treatment also passes over. What advantages, and their rewards, are candidates for redistribution is a real question, which egalitarians should face more honestly than they mostly do; but the fact that we should agree (most of us) with Mr Nozick that compulsory plastic surgery was no just reaction to inequalities in good looks, need not commit us all that quickly to agreeing with him on the evidently different matters of money and power. Again, and near the heart of Mr Nozick's view, the very matter of *distance* (in time, over successive transfers, or whatever) does *in fact* affect the sentiments of many about injustice: the luck of the talented commands more respect, some find, than the luck of those who merely had a talented father. These are also "our" notions, in as good standing, at least, as those to which Mr Nozick appeals, and his conception of justice merely as a pipe for the rightful delivery of rights over any distance is not tested against enough notions to be really persuasive.

This is a book of a very highly theoretical character; indeed its theories themselves have a tendency to pursue the virtues of formal elegance rather than of concrete realism, as witnessed by the presence of much economic theory and virtually no psychology or sociology. This leaves the conclusions rather high in the air, particularly above present political realities. These views leave undetermined to a high degree what should now, in current political practice, be done—to a greater degree than most political theory, including Locke's; they are in a deep sense Utopian, and the third element in the title is rightly juxtaposed with the others. This is not necessarily a failing: but it should be written in larger letters what the book does *not* offer. Above all, its theories do not, except in a very general and associative manner, offer any particular comfort to contemporary capitalism. For one thing, contemporary capitalism is a statist enterprise. For another, Mr Nozick's derivation theory of justice does not imply that contemporary property holdings are just; on the contrary (though it is a matter of unrecoverable fact), it is 99 per cent probable that almost all of them are not. (Mr Nozick may well think that much of America rightfully belongs to Indians.) And in a vitally important but unemphatic passage (page 231) he makes it clear that redistribution by the state may well be, as things are, necessary for the rectification of past injustice. There is little comfort in these pages for contemporary friends of business; but Mr Nozick hardly makes it as clear as he might that this is so.

Within this abstract, complex, clever, and always stimulating, structure there is to be found, one suspects, a robust and romantically creative individualist outlook which, though undoubtedly tough, is in quite a different street from that of the friends of business's nastier friends. But it will be partly Mr Nozick's own fault if they, and their enemies, think otherwise.

Note

1. *Anarchy, State, and Utopia*, by Robert Nozick (Blackwell, 1974).

24

The Ethics of Fetal Research, by Paul Ramsey

There is a contrast between American and British life which applies not
only to politics: while American practice is often harder, tougher and less
inhibited than British, so are the protests and analyses that it elicits. Some
frontier thought is at work, that before (or after) force all we have is argument, and that one cannot just rely on the rightness of what already
exists. Questions of practical ethics take on an urgency, and a sense that
something might actually turn on the results of an argument, which are
lacking in our own fully saturated culture, with its depressing combination of complacency and dissatisfaction. It is one of several reasons why
American philosophy is now a more stimulating, creative and high-class
business than British philosophy.

The contrast shows itself in the domain of medical ethics—meaning
by that, not the issues of professional propriety about sending in one's
bill and not sleeping with one's patients, but such questions as abortion,
euthanasia, experiments on patients, trust and deceit, and—not least—
the institutional morality of medicine and the rights of doctors to make
money. In some—not all—of these areas American practice has been less
muffled by convention than in Britain (while in the matter of the cash
nexus the American medical profession has famously displayed a degree
of naked greed which would, at least till recently, have been found un-
gentlemanly in Britain).

Equally, analytical thought elicited by these questions has begun in
America to take off in an energetic manner. It can bring with it, of course,
a considerable investment in academic light industry—workshops, insti-
tutes, projects. Some of them have deeply suspect pretensions, particularly those which aspire, as some do, to cast the philosopher as ethical
consultant, the intellectual chaplain of the terminal ward. Even if there
is some coherent intellectual basis for drawing lines between the acceptable and the unacceptable experiment, between the permissible and the
impermissible death—and whether there is such a basis at all is a real
question—it is certain that the answers cannot be carried into the hospital
in the form of the philosophical adviser. If philosophical reflection is to
aid practice in such matters, the route will be less direct; but perhaps it
would not need to be too long and hard, for all that, since one thing that

is clear about these questions is that people need something coherent to believe about them, and any set of reflections that makes some sort of sense of them is likely to get a hearing.

Paul Ramsey is an American theologian who has written a lot on these matters; he is identified with a rather conservative, but not dogmatically extreme, set of positions on them. *The Ethics of Fetal Research* contains some reflection, some history, and some attempts at clarification, rather than any very strong conclusions, though conclusions can be heard not far off. Its subject is the limits of permissible research on the human foetus, whether *in utero*, or when separated from the mother, as for instance (but not necessarily) as a result of a decision to abort.[1] It is the increase in legal abortion which has brought these problems to the fore. Among other possibilities, abortion can give rise to a foetus which is still living and which can temporarily be kept living, though it is not viable, i e, is not capable of independent life. Some valuable medical results, some of them concerned with the survival of foetuses, can be obtained by experiment on such foetuses, as also on the foetus *in utero* when it is intended to abort. (As usual, it is not easy to determine to what extent, and with what difficulty, the results might be obtained by other means.) The question arises of what limits should be imposed on research of this sort; and indeed there are questions about what medical uses can properly be made of dead foetuses which are the products of abortion—for instance, whether the mother's consent has any standing in the case.

In Britain these matters are presently regulated by rules laid down by the Report of the Peel Committee which appeared in May 1972. This report defines a class of pre-viable foetuses; anything too old or too large to be included is, if living, to be regarded as viable, and can only be treated in ways compatible with promoting its survival. There are further restrictions about what can be done even in cases of pre-viability; thus the report rules as unethical any procedure administered to a pregnant woman designed to find out what harm it does to the foetus, even if there is an intention to abort and the woman has given her consent. This fairly conservative document seems, as Professor Ramsey says, to have closed the debate in Britain; in America, however, discussion is still growing, and there has been a series of directives and draft regulations of varying degrees of permissiveness.

There are some interesting questions here on which Professor Ramsey briefly touches, about how such rules should be laid down. In this country a respectable committee led by a well-known non-researching doctor evolved some extensions of established professional practice. In America, equally typically, there is more debate and open intervention by interested groups. But there is a systematic difficulty in all matters of this kind, which has not been discussed enough, about what exactly is a proper interest, in particular a proper moral concern, on the part of the public. Does public opinion have a right to be heard if it is upset about what is going on? Yes, it may be said, if it is informed (if it is not informed, it has a right to speak, of course, but not a right to be heard). But what counts as being informed? Certainly if people were shown on television some of the experiments carried out on foetuses, they would be very upset—but then they would be similarly upset, no doubt, if shown abortions. Here we have the site of the tension that has arisen about the publication of certain aspects of abortion: those opponents of abortion who publish these things are accused of sensationalism, to which they reply that they are showing people what abortion is.

And in saying that, they are not saying anything untrue. The trouble is that a spectator who lacks any context or preparation will not acquire any all-round view of what abortion is. But then where do you hold the line about an informed opinion on foetal research, short of saying that the only persons who have an all-round view of what foetal research is are foetal researchers and their medical colleagues? And with this public opinion disappears again from the scene.

Professor Ramsey comes back repeatedly to the relation between the abortion argument and the question of foetal research, and the central theme of his book is that these are two different issues. Not here discussing abortion itself, he wants to be able to resist those who say to the public: "Since you have already agreed to abortion—a gross, destructive assault on the foetus—it is just irrational to resist much less drastic procedures on it which moreover bring experimental benefits." He does not aim to make any definitive case against the more drastic forms of foetal research; he does want to say that it is a separate issue from abortion.

He has raised an important and complex issue, and reveals a number of its complexities. It is a pity that, in what often looks like a hastily written book, he has not had greater success in unravelling the muddles. Those who use the tough and very plausible argument which Professor Ramsey confronts will not, I suspect, be moved away from it by this book, though they should be moved to look at the argument again. Professor Ramsey's treatment is bedevilled by two separate confusions of his own making. The most important question here is: "If you believe that abortion (on social grounds, or at will) is permissible, are you committed thereby to thinking that unrestricted experiment on foetuses (or at least voluntarily aborted foetuses) is permissible?" This question Professor Ramsey fails to concentrate on adequately because he allows himself to be distracted by a different question, which is whether the mere fact that abortion is *widely accepted* commits us to thinking foetal experimentation is permissible; here the answer is "no", and Professor Ramsey spends time berating adversaries who (he claims) think two wrongs make a right, rather than directly discussing the question whether either could be wrong if the other were not.

Secondly, in so far as he does take on that question, he tends to take on only a small part of it, making the point that there are moral issues about foetal research which arise even outside voluntary abortion, as for instance with miscarried foetuses. This of course is true, but it still does not answer the main question.

Although Professor Ramsey says that there are two issues, in fact the way he discusses foetal research strongly suggests that, in his view, the desirable restrictions on it properly imply restrictions on abortion. His favoured analogies for the foetus under research are the dying, and—for those not yet, but about to be, aborted—the condemned. Such analogies press very hard on the question of by what right these human beings have been killed or condemned, and it is surely impossible to accept straightforwardly these analogies without more discussion than Professor Ramsey permits himself here of their relation to the abortion issue.

Although Professor Ramsey has not really succeeded in separating these two issues, he may well be right in believing that they can and should be, to some degree, separated. None of the received ways of thinking about these things makes it easy to separate them: neither the Utilitarian way, which makes it all a matter of benefits to mankind, nor the classificatory way, which makes it all a matter of what kind of thing a foetus is. But we have no reason at all to believe that our received ways of thinking about these things are at all adequate to them; we have to invent ways of dealing with them which will fit as honestly as possible with what we know about human nature, what we hope for it, and what we care about in it. Though that is not quite Professor Ramsey's way of looking at these problems, and though here he seems not to have got things into the order that even he himself wants, his book displays a certain tart humanism and dislike of cant which help to remind us that everything we invent has got to give us not only ways of thinking coherently about these matters, but ways of feeling coherently about them.

Note

1. *The Ethics of Fetal Research*, by Paul Ramsey (Yale University Press, 1975).

25

The Moral View of Politics

Twenty years ago, the prevailing view in English-speaking philosophical circles was that political philosophy would never flourish again. Now by contrast, the subject is very active, the predicted funeral seems to have been indefinitely postponed, and the sources of this new life are largely to be found in the United States of America.

The moribund condition of political philosophy at that time was due to more than one cause. Some of the causes were internal to the state of philosophy itself; in particular, there was a prevailing theory that statements of value were sharply to be separated from statements of fact or theory, and, in addition, philosophy chastely refused to come out with statements of value. Living political philosophy, moreover, needs a context of political urgency, and the decline of political philosophy in the Fifties and early Sixties was, to that extent, a phenomenon of a period of political stagnation, one which prematurely saluted the end of ideology.

The situation has now changed in all these respects. The harsh theoretical disjunction between fact and value has been modified; the reluctance of philosophers to come out with normative statements is much less apparent; and the political context itself has also changed.

There has been a real revival in political philosophy, and this has been particularly conspicuous in the USA, where the revival of serious political conflict in the later Sixties has, in a traditional manner, helped to revive philosophical political thought. Three sorts of issue in particular contributed to this. The Vietnam war raised questions about the rights and wrongs of warfare; and not only the idea of a just or unjust war, but those very phrases (moving out of the Catholic tradition) came to play an important part in controversy. Because many students faced or feared they would face the draft, the war presented, in a very urgent form, questions about the right of the state to demand service, the duty to obey, and the right to individual conscientious objection: and the rights, equally, to protest by civil disobedience. All of this constituted what might be called the area of rights and allegiance. Second, there is an area of social justice: the application of reflective philosophical theory to moral and social issues presented by the injustices of Western society, assertion of which, in the late 1960s, unsettled conservative belief that those injustices had gone away, and liberal faith that they gradually would do so. This is an area which has produced the outstanding single work of political philosophy since the war, John Rawls's *A Theory of Justice*—a work on which Rawls had been working for a long time before recent political developments, though it is by no means unmarked by them. Third, among several other kinds of active social influence, one should mention, in particular, conservationist anxieties, and also the women's movement, which has given rise to a particularly active philosophical debate about abortion. Both of these influences bear on population policy, and this, in turn, relates back to the issues of social justice; conservation affects future generations, and questions arise about how to think about justice between generations: particularly when, as under policies of population control, the question of what the future generations will be is, in some part, itself a matter of social decision.

In speaking of the impact of these events on philosophy, I have in mind what, in a broad sense, may be called analytical philosophy—philosophy which, while not committed to the restrictive conceptions current in the 1950s, nevertheless shares with them a belief in analytical methods and a discursively argumentative tone. Rawls's book is in this style, and so is another striking book which I shall come back to, Robert Nozick's *Anarchy, State, and Utopia*. It is also the prevailing style of a journal which has succeeded, for several years now, in discussing at a high level a wide range of these problems, a journal called *Philosophy and Public Affairs*.

This broadly analytical type of philosophical work is intellectually important, interesting in its relation to the development of philosophy, and is certainly influential on public and student opinion, through publications and the work of individual teachers. But a more dramatic influence, it must be said, was shown in the late 1960s by a different style of thought in social philosophy—the kind of post-Marxist critique pursued, to particular, by members of the Frankfurt school who were transplanted to the USA in the 1930s; work which came to much wider and more excitable public notice in the form of Marcuse's writings, particularly *One-Dimensional Man*. Some effects of this type of work, and of the events of which it became part, have certainly remained; but the interest in this style of philosophical writing has somewhat receded with the radical movements which it helped to inspire.

One of several ways in which the work of Rawls and Nozick differs from this kind of work is that their values are overwhelmingly of an individual and moral character; the attitudes appropriate to society are seen as extensions of individual moral conviction, and this approach takes, moreover, a rather startlingly pure, non-historical, and unsociological view of the nature of moral conviction, and the role of moral conviction in the determination of what happens in society. In this regard, the works of Rawls and of Nozick are strikingly alike, though they radically disagree in their conclusions.

Rawls's book, *A Theory of Justice*, is an elaborate work, which shows very clearly the effects of many years' discussion and revision. It offers a theory of social justice which is grounded in the moral notion of fairness; its argument proceeds, for a great deal of the book, by working out the consequences of a certain thought-experiment. We are to imagine a set of persons from whom the actual world, their historical and social position in it and their own personal characteristics, are hidden by what Rawls calls a 'veil of ignorance'. This state of affairs is called the Original Position; in the Original Position, these persons know no particular facts, but do know the general laws of economics and of the social sciences. (It is an interesting reflection on Rawls's basically Enlightenment outlook, that he assumes that there are such laws which, in principle, can be understood independently of particular facts of history.) In the Original Position, people are to choose a social system for themselves and for their families, and the argument turns on what principles they would rationally employ in doing that. Rawls argues that they would reject Utilitarian principles—for instance, a principle of the highest average welfare: for, after all, when the veil of ignorance was lifted, they might turn out to be among the least advantaged persons in the system, and a high average welfare in that system could still leave them very badly off indeed. Eventually, Rawls argues, they will rationally go for what he calls the Difference Principle, which says (very roughly) that if there are to be departures from equality in welfare, then those departures must be in the interests of the worst-off group.

There has been, and will continue to be, much argument about how Rawls runs his thought-experiment: whether any choice can be made under this degree of ignorance. But the most basic question concerns the force of the thought-experiment itself. Even if a determinate conclusion could be reached about what would be rationally chosen in the Original Position, what would that signify? Well, the answer to this is that it imports a moral conclusion—the self-interested preferences of these abstract agents (insofar as they still have a self) are supposed to be a model for the moral and impartial preferences of actual agents, what actual agents would choose if they were choosing disinterestedly. The basic idea is the very simple one that a fair division of a cake is one you would make if you were selfish but knew nothing about which piece you would get yourself. It is, thus, an approach to social justice which appeals to, and has to be checked against, our moral sentiments. These sentiments, which Rawls standardly calls moral 'intuitions', are supposed to be elicited from us rather as the knowledge of our language is: as a linguistic theorist relies on the intuitions of a native speaker about what is an acceptable sentence of his language, so we try out the consequences of moral and social theory on our moral intuitions, and seek to achieve what Rawls calls a 'reflective equilibrium' between intuition and theory.

But there is a weakness in this analogy, and in the method it supposedly supports. It is not so much that Rawls is totally resistant to any kind of relativism, though it is notable how utterly untouched his work is by the kind of relativist anxieties which haunt all social philosophy which grows out of sociology and social anthropology, anxieties which surely express, however confusedly, some proper reflexive doubt about whether our current moral priorities can be universally applied. The trouble is, rather more basically, that there is no adequate analogy in the linguistic case for the situation of conflict and disharmony in our moral sentiments, where, necessarily, it matters to us in practice how the conflict is resolved. The relation of such conflicts to moral theory, in Rawls's sense, is unclear, and the analogy to linguistics which Rawls uses does not really help us to understand it. The moral theory contains consistent and maximally general moral principles, and they, by fitting our intuitions about a large number of cases where there is no conflict, are supposed to acquire the authority to solve the cases where there *is* a conflict. But how do they acquire this authority?

Here again, the lack of an empirical dimension to Rawls's thought shows itself. The fact is that we understand too much, in historical and social terms, about the origins of our moral sentiments and about the origins of our conflicts, for us to be able to accept the purely Kantian idea that an abstract structure of principles should, by its harmony and generality, and its ability to fit many of our sentiments, command our allegiance with regard to the sentiments which we are less sure about, and the conflicts in our moral thought which we actually experience.

Now, Rawls's theory of justice is one which regards justice as a property of outcomes or distributions — you look at the whole pattern of distribution to see whether each person's holding is a just holding. In this respect, Rawls's own view is like many other views whose principles are to be rejected in the Original Position, views such as Utilitarianism; they have in common that they all regard justice as a property of the outcome. Robert Nozick, in his book, distinguishes all such theories from what he calls an entitlement theory of justice, where the central question in considering whether someone justly holds something is not what everyone else holds, but how this man came by what he holds; if he justly acquired it from someone who justly held it, then he justly holds it. It is not the resultant pattern, but the legitimacy of each transaction in itself, which should be looked at. Ferociously conservative conclusions can, of course, be drawn from this conception of justice, conclusions opposed to all redistributive mechanisms; and Nozick draws such conclusions, with a good deal of intellectual ingenuity and a certain enthusiasm for upsetting *bien-pensant* liberals.

Nozick's theory of justice is only the second part of a book which first discusses—in utterly abstract terms, which make plentiful reference to Locke—the question whether the state is justified at all, and concludes that it is justified, but only in a minimal, nightwatchman form. Taxation, for instance, is regarded as a species of forced labour. What emerges in theory is a utopia which roots itself in an American tradition of libertarian anarchism. What would emerge, in fact, if these ideas gained popularity in the late 20th century, is certainly another matter, and, indeed, Nozick's relation to contemporary right-wing defenders of capitalism is ambivalent. He is committed to opposing them, both because modern capitalism is essentially statist, and also because holdings in contemporary America are quite certainly, by Nozick's own standards, unjust (a lot of it was originally stolen from Indians); but his denunciations of redistribution through taxation sound louder than any such considerations. He runs the risk of doing the same as many Goldwaterites, of heading nostalgically for an Old West state of nature, but doing it in a Cadillac.

But, in principle, both his and Rawls's views are radical: Rawls's because the Difference Principle is radically redistributive, Nozick's because it would be a radical change that got us away from redistribution. Rawls and Nozick are quite different in their views of justice, their understanding of the state, and the virtues they salute. But they have much in common. They both approach political philosophy from moral perceptions recovered in intuition (of which Nozick makes much the same use as Rawls does, but he takes and works into theory a different and a narrower range of intuitions). They both regard the enterprise of thinking philosophically about society in abstraction from history or concrete social conditions; and, connectedly, the social sciences they use, Nozick even more than Rawls, are economics and decision theory, both of which can be pursued at a high level of abstraction.

Falling back on such moral perceptions as you have, and starting from there; supposing that social principles can be elaborated independently of a determinate historical starting-point: these were conceptions of the Founding Fathers and, again, of the frontier situation, and it is not fanciful to see the willingness to start from historical scratch as an American disposition which, explicitly in Nozick but effectively in both these writers, conditions their works, and, indeed, lies behind the vigour with which a range of writers have been willing to tackle the questions of social principle which I mentioned earlier. In all of them, there is an approach from individual morality, combined with a readiness to school it to theory and to accept new consequences. An important contribution to this activity is undoubtedly made also by that respect for general theory which is now a very widespread and invigorating feature of American philosophy, as opposed to the piecemeal methods which were the ideal of British philosophy in the Fifties, and which did have, at that time, great influence in America.

While this work in political philosophy is often valuable and exciting, it does sit oddly to present discontents. It does seem rather late in the day to come so directly to politics from purely moral conceptions — though reasons for the vigour of this moral reaffirmation can themselves be found in recent American history. It is hard, again, to accept a political philosophy which does not start rather more determinately from the highly elaborated, and very densely occupied, social and political scene we actually have. Where the frontier was is now Cleveland or St Louis, and a situation in which we could really make a new start would be one in which alarmingly little would have to be left. People who were in that situation might not find themselves with just those moral responses on which these philosophers, in their different ways, markedly rely.

I have concentrated on American developments, and, in particular, on the work of Rawls and Nozick, because these seem at present to be the most strikingly original and influential developments in a field which shows signs of continuing to develop more broadly. Two kinds of development beyond the limits of their work are, I think, to be hoped for. One is that there should be work which is more closely based on the current historical situation and, correspondingly, grounded in a closer relation to the social sciences. Another possible development, a desirable one, is that the methods and standards of analytical philosophy should come closer to those concerns which have animated neo-Marxist and neo-Hegelian critics of our society, concerns which have, so far, been expressed in more archaic philosophical forms. Both possible developments have a requirement in common: that historical understanding should be brought into the picture in a way in which it conspicuously fails to be in the work that I have been discussing.

26

The Life of Bertrand Russell, by Ronald W. Clark; *The Tamarisk Tree: My Quest for Liberty and Love,* by Dora Russell; *My Father Bertrand Russell,* by Katharine Tait; *Bertrand Russell,* by A. J. Ayer

Bertrand Russell's *Autobiography* (which was published in three volumes in the 1960s) is a work that leaves one in more than one way winded. It is not altogether a book, bringing together a rather random collection of letters with a sketchy account of the author's life which, though sometimes alarmingly frank, omits much and hurries the reader on from one cursorily described event to another. It is not just the speed of travel that leaves one gasping, but the glancing view of some episodes that Russell puts in. One is several times confronted with a summary or dismissive account of central, professedly transforming, occurrences in his life, which cannot, surely, represent things as they were then lived, yet at the same time is not just the misleading product of a distant or oblique style of recollection.

There is no recognizable economy of narration which explains the effect produced by the *Autobiography.* The spiritual transitions which flash by, which are enacted between the striking of a match and the puffing of that ubiquitous pipe, do not seem as blank and unreal as they do because the structural outlines are left on the horizon, the emotional materials having burned or wasted away. On the contrary, it is the language of intense and overwhelming feeling, for a person or for the sufferings of mankind, that itself lights up these Polaroid snaps of Russell's past and leaves the reader with a problem about how Russell could possibly have understood himself, either when he wrote these pages or when what he wrote about occurred. The most famous, now notorious, case is his account of his deciding on a bicycle ride that he no longer loved his first wife, Alys, and pedaling back to live for years in accordance with that discovery. But there are many other passages in which references to extreme or drastic resolution leave the reader bewilderingly distant from any conception of Russell's self-understanding.

Mr. Clark's long biography does much to help us on questions of fact, to fill in holes in the story, and to correct some impressions left by Russell's account.[1] For one thing, his affair with Connie Malleson ("Colette") went on longer, and had more echoes in Russell's later life, than you would judge from the *Autobiography*. Clark has taken great pains with an enormous amount of material, Russell's widow having given him full access to documents. He makes a number of new discoveries and suggestions, very plausibly proposing in particular that the object of a passion in Russell's earlier life, whose identity he concealed, was in fact Mrs. Alfred North Whitehead. He is good, also, at sorting out more recent events, and gives a very reasonable account of Russell's involvement in the Committee of 100 against nuclear weapons, and his eventual quarrel with Ralph Schoenman.

The amount of work that has gone into producing this well-documented and clearly signposted account of Russell's life is not to be underestimated. But one cannot pretend that it is an illuminating or even a deeply enjoyable read. It has the property of large books sold at airports: the author judges that he has his reader for a long while if he neither lets him sleep nor makes him work, so that the style is by turns undemandingly bland and stridently chummy. "Bertie . . . was therefore denied the tempering ordeal of a public school and consigned to a mixed bag of governesses and tutors," he cheerily says near the beginning, and the tone is not untypical. Several reviewers have remarked that the style seems to get less embarrassing as the book goes on, and this is true, but it is hard to know whether the reason is that Clark is more used to his subject, we are more used to Clark, or Clark finds the events of Russell's later life easier to deal with.

One reason might be that Russell's contributions to philosophy in his later life were less fundamental, both to the subject and to Russell's view of himself. Clark's occasional dealings with Russell's philosophy are unsuccessful, and indeed it is not easy to guess what he takes himself to be doing. Many of his brief accounts of Russell's philosophical work can be read in more than one way, and one of those ways is usually not totally wrong; but it seems rash to suppose that that will be the one to occur to a reader who benefits from being told, as Clark tells him, that Leibniz was "Voltaire's Dr. Pangloss, the German polymath who had waltzed through the second half of the seventeenth century as philosopher, scientist, mathematician and diplomat." A basic weakness of such accounts is that they do not rest on knowledge of other philosophy; one reason why Clark makes a mess of the admittedly hard task of explaining what Russell's most famous logical article, "On Denoting," is about is that he is not familiar with Frege's treatment of the issues, from which Russell started. Clark falls back on identifying the main point of the article with its most prominent joke.

It is a pity that Clark has not got a better sense of Russell's major work; for one thing, it means that Russell's relations to others who affected him in that work, above all Wittgenstein, are very vaguely characterized— these geniuses engaged in deep and difficult subjects are presented as grand and quaint, like great physicists in a TV documentary. But Russell's major contributions were to very technical and abstract branches of philosophy and logic, and it is unreasonable to hope that his biographer will be an expert in those subjects.

Even A. J. Ayer's book, which gives a marvelously clear and of course utterly professional account of some of Russell's central ideas in philosophy, does not take on the hard task that lies beyond the recognition that Russell made a great contribution to the philosophy of logic: the task, that is to say, of assessing exactly how much difference Russell's work made to the development of modern work in the foundations of mathematics. Clark does best with Russell's more popular writings on ethical and social subjects—a department in which Ayer, for his part, mostly contents himself with a brief account of Russell's not very interesting theoretical opinions in moral philosophy, accompanied by some bleak tutorial comment on them.[2]

What is more unsettling than Clark's dealings with Russell's central philosophical work is his uncertainty of taste in assessing Russell's rhetoric. *A Free Man's Worship* is described as "a short but profoundly moving cry of defiance against the human predicament, couched in terms of romantic disillusion"; but it is not only a dated but also a hollow piece of oratory, and Clark's acceptance of it at its face value shows a lack of curiosity. Russell himself was later, in his more Voltairean period, to have doubts about its style, but the weakness of its costless heroics against cosmic indifference went deeper and further than he recognized. There is an absurdity in Russell's resentment at the universe's failure to live up to man's expectations, a resentment which seems an extension of his annoyance at mankind's not living up to him. "I am ashamed to belong to such a species," he wrote in 1916.

There is a fascinating page in volume two of the *Autobiography* dealing with that period, where, writing of making love to Connie Malleson during a Zeppelin raid, he describes sentiments about the war which he felt intensely at that moment, sentiments which show up as not totally free either of easy heroics or of contempt for the idiot mob. This love for humanity, coupled with a dismissive hatred of many of its deepest char-

.acteristics, is typical of Russell and is obscure enough to blur the picture of his love for a particular person, which he insists on bringing together with those general feelings. Of his relation to Connie Malleson, he said that it was "never trivial and never unworthy to be placed alongside of the great public emotions connected with the War." But where exactly does that place it?

Often, Russell writes of feelings as though they were unmeasurably overwhelming, and yet as though, in the next minute, he had quite straightforwardly got their measure. This phenomenon, so bewildering in the *Autobiography*, turns up in several curious passages quoted by Clark. Writing to Ottoline Morrell, Russell speaks of what he called his "first conversion," in the presence of a woman who Clark has given us reason to believe was Mrs. Whitehead:

> I came to know suddenly (what it was not intended I should know) that a woman whom I liked greatly had a life of utter loneliness, filled with intense tragedy & pain of which she could never speak. I was not free to tell my sympathy, which was so intense as to change my life. I turned to all the ways there might be of alleviating her trouble without seeming to know it & so I went on in thought to loneliness in general, & how only love bridges the chasm—how force is the evil thing, & strife is the root of all evil & gentleness the only balm. I became infinitely gentle for a time. I turned against the S. African war & imperialism (I was an imperialist till then) & I found that I loved children & they loved me. I resolved to bring some good & some hope into her life. All this happened in about five minutes.

Certainly thoughts relating to each of those things could intensely pass in five minutes. Perhaps one could even end up after five minutes in those states (though the discovery about children seems a bit ambitious). But certainly no grown-up person should write in retrospect as though a five-minute sequence of intense emotion was itself the entire enactment of all those life-transforming changes; any more than one expects him to be able to write, in all solemnity, of a different time:

> That was the only time when I completely lost faith in myself & thought of myself as a mere cumberer of the earth. I resolved to commit suicide as soon as I could get rid of certain definite obligations which for the moment made it impossible.

It was not just Russell's feelings, but the fact that he had feelings, that excited him, and this certainly contributed to the now well-known emergencies of his sexual life. Clark gives some idea of the different significance to Russell of different relationships, though he tends to adopt a rather breezy and knowing tone about some of it, and he leaves us outside the complexities and strangenesses of Russell's relations to Ottoline Morrell. Some of Russell's reactions, particularly in self-justification, are certainly surprising—sometimes it is hard to gather even what he thought he was saying. When he had just had a brief affair in America with the unfortunate Helen Dudley (who later followed him at his suggestion to England, but proved boringly unequal to Russell's feelings about the war), he wrote to Ottoline, with whom he was still intensely involved:

> I do not want you to think that this will make the very *smallest* difference in my feeling towards you, beyond removing the irritation of unsatisfied instinct. I suppose it must give you some pain, but I hope not very much if I can make you believe it is all right & that she is not the usual type of American. The whole family are extraordinarily nice people. . . .

But it must be said that he was able to extract strikingly long-lasting devotion from others: Alys, a pathetic figure in Clark's representation, still in love with him, apparently, until her death; Colette (who seems to have been marvelous) sending him red roses on his ninety-seventh birthday. And the autobiography of Dora, his second wife, though it sturdily sets out to live up to the self-reliant promise of its subtitle, in fact is a tribute to the power that Russell's presence had in forming her life.[3] In her book there is an implied, as well as a stated, acknowledgment of the sense of life that he obviously could, while he was still interested, convey. After he and Dora split up and he left the school they had started together, there were unceasing squabbles and pieces of litigation. While Dora Russell tells something of this tale, it lacks any great force of recrimination or self-justification or anything else—she seems to have lost interest. The pages of this book which stand out as vivid are those about their time in China together just before their marriage, when Russell was exceptionally happy.

Russell has been called a skeptic, and there is indeed a biography of him by Alan Wood (Simon & Schuster, 1958) subtitled "The Passionate Sceptic." Skepticism is concerned with the withholding of assent, the sustaining of a state of intellectual suspense; it is very hard to find any strain of real skepticism in Russell, as opposed to an occasional judicious tone of voice and an advocacy of the virtues of benevolent reasonableness. His opinions were often dogmatic, simple, emphatically expressed, and poorly supported by evidence. They were said to be skeptical merely because they were antireligious and unpopular; perhaps also he seemed a skeptic because he appeared to want to believe some of the things he denied, and made it seem such a heroic feat not to deny that the world is as it is.

In his technical philosophy he was not a skeptic but, after his first years, an empiricist, and the main guiding thread to his development is his attachment to empiricist principles and habits of thought. As in the empiricist tradition, his philosophy of language is always closely allied to the theory of knowledge. It is impossible to give an account of his logico-linguistic treatment of particular terms and definite descriptions that does not also involve his conception of knowledge by acquaintance, of what can be grasped with certainty. A. J. Ayer gives a very clear account of how this works, but (no doubt because his own sympathies lie close to Russell's) he does not bring it into such strong relief, or contrast it with contemporary alternatives, as D. F. Pears does in his book *Bertrand Russell and the British Tradition in Philosophy* (Random House, 1967). Related to that empiricist strain, but sometimes conflicting with its more radical demands, was Russell's attempt to make his philosophy cohere with what he conceived to be the general findings of the natural sciences—something which brought him back to a causal theory of perception from the more Humean type of position which he occupied in the *Analysis of Mind*.

This element of respect for the sciences in Russell's work might well prove more sympathetic to philosophers now than it has in the past twenty-five years, when Wittgensteinian attitudes represented any tendency of philosophy to be shaped by the natural sciences—and still more any attempt by philosophy to emulate them in method—as a basic indecency. A revaluation of Russell's theories of knowledge and their associated metaphysics will need a less squeamish temper. It will also need a certain relaxation of the insistence, particularly inherited from G. E. Moore, on the virtues of literal accuracy, which Russell, always a swift and careless writer, treated with some disdain.

The time has come for that revaluation, and there is room for doubt about what will emerge: whether Russell has been seriously undervalued in these areas (as opposed to the philosophy of logic, where his reputation is assured), or whether it is true, as many philosophers would say, that the larger bulk of Russell's philosophy is unfruitfully archaic. Unlike Moore and, above all, Wittgenstein, Russell was largely free of real worries, so characteristic of twentieth-century thought, about what philosophy is or could be. I think he regarded freedom from these reflexive worries as a mark of vitality, but it may prove to have been a kind of obstinacy which, together with his facility, led him to run up philosophical theories of just the kind that no longer have anything to offer. If Russell's epistemological work does prove, on the other hand, to retain real interest, then it will have been a triumph, in a certain sense, of his naiveté as against the self-consciousness of his contemporaries.

In practical life, politics, and social opinion Russell was yet further removed from skepticism than in his formal philosophy. That moderation of assertion which is supposed to characterize the skeptic he used more as a rhetorical device than in a discipline of self-criticism, and the temptations of indignant emphasis often seduced him. Sometimes his published opinions were the victims of a haste imposed on him by the heavy journalistic routine which he sustained to keep himself and his family — Clark has a good quotation from a letter to Stanley Unwin:

> It has been drawn to my attention that on page 209 of "Marriage and Morals" I say "It seems on the whole fair to regard negroes as on the average inferior to white men." I wish in any future reprint to substitute for the words: "It seems on the whole fair," the words "There is no sound reason."

For a man who often insisted that practice should be guided by thought, and thought controlled by evidence, his enthusiasm for acting, and advocating action, on the basis of some flimsy bright idea was remarkable. It lay behind his advocacy of a preventive war against the USSR in the late 1940s, an episode particularly carefully investigated by Clark.

In a way that was, in its effects on other people, more painful, an amazing confidence of this kind seems to have attended the experiment of a progressive school at Beacon Hill which he and Dora undertook. Their daughter Katharine was one of the pupils, and her touching and unpretentious book gives a very real if avowedly subjective view of what it was like.[4] Though he could also be great fun, theory in the form of some dire amalgam of Rousseau, Pavlov, and the Puritan conscience seems to have filled the judicious philosopher with an alarming degree of conviction, both in the general conduct of the school (which not altogether surprisingly came to bore him), and in his dealings with his own children. Mrs. Tait tells of a small, but to me chilling, episode when her brother John as a small boy had to stagger on a long climb from the beach with a rock which he wanted to keep and which was too heavy for him, having been told on clear and reasonable grounds of principle that he could keep it if and only if he carried it home by himself.

Whether it was enthusiasm for a new libertarian yet disciplined world, or political indignation, or sexual passion, or pantheistic surges, there emerges the impression that Russell was so relieved that he had powerful feelings that he was only too happy to take them at their face value. His theoretical philosophy, moreover, offered not much value to such feelings beyond their face. He made a harsh disjunction of reason and feeling, and held a simply deductive or instrumental view of reason. Such views offered him little space in which to understand feeling critically, or to deepen or enrich it. "He was especially prone to accept Hume's theory that the emotions are detached, because he himself exemplified it," as David Pears has said in his admirable review of Clark (*The New Review*, London, December 1975). If feelings did not mean what, at the reviving moment of their onrush, they seemed to mean, then perhaps they meant nothing at all; and if they meant nothing, then nothing meant anything. In this inability to detach the significance of feeling from its immediate aspect, there is something adolescent. D. H. Lawrence, who said a lot of silly things about Russell, and in some ways got the worst, from Russell's well-known memoir, of their inevitable quarrel, nevertheless was centrally and deadly right when he wrote to Ottoline Morrell of Russell, then aged forty-three:

> he is vitally, emotionally, much too inexperienced in personal contact and conflict, for a man of his age and calibre. It isn't that life has been too much for him, but too little. Tell him he is not to write lachrymose letters to me of disillusion and disappointment and age; that sounds like nineteen.

This lack of a real relation to his feelings, his attachment to their surface meaning, shakes confidence in Russell. We cannot take him as a touchstone of things, and when he is presented, as he occasionally was by himself and more frequently by others, as the *channel* of reason or humanity or human dignity, there is reason for distrust. It is not as a selfless embodiment of rational principle that he is to be seen, nor is he one of those figures who divine, transmit, and shape feelings which are shared by others but elude those others' formulation. Even in his stand against nuclear warfare, though it was important and impressive and admirable that he stood where he did and extended an emblem of reason against what is offered as rationality by technocrats and politicians, he did not gain his dignity in this by having any deeper understanding of things than they, or a more insightful conception of reason. He just obstinately, and valuably, placed himself where he did because that is how he then felt.

Even in this case, and still more obviously elsewhere in his life, it is not moral penetration that gives Russell's life its extraordinary quality, nor is it understanding, whether of himself or of anyone else. It is his will, in the purest sense of willfulness. His embodiment of the aristocratic characteristics he was aware of in his conception of human excellence—"fearlessness, independence of judgment, emancipation from the herd, leisurely culture"; the sheer arbitrariness of his choice, on a considerable scale, to do what he wanted—these, together with his philosophical achievements, actually carry greater authority than his reasons for the social ideals he was always preaching, or the powerful cosmic and personal passions which so impressed him.

Notes

1. *The Life of Bertrand Russell*, by Ronald W. Clark (Knopf, 1975).

2. *Bertrand Russell*, by A. J. Ayer (Viking, 1972).

3. *The Tamarisk Tree: My Quest for Liberty and Love*, by Dora Russell (Putnam's, 1975).

4. *My Father Bertrand Russell*, by Katharine Tait (Harcourt Brace Jovanovich, 1975).

27

Reflections on Language, by Noam Chomsky; *On Noam Chomsky: Critical Essays*, edited by Gilbert Harman

Since the publication of *Syntactic Structures* nineteen years ago the general shape of Chomsky's position in linguistic theory has become familiar. The subject, as he conceives it, is a branch of cognitive psychology; its basic problem is posed by the human capacity to acquire a natural language, something which Chomsky has insisted we should see as remarkable, with regard both to what the child experiences and to what he acquires. What he acquires is an indefinitely extensive creative capacity to produce and to understand an open-ended set of sentences that he has never heard before. What he is offered by his elders (or rather from them, since Chomsky thinks little importance can be attached to directed language teaching) is evidence, as he has put it, "not only meager in scope, but degenerate in quality." The actual performances the child is exposed to are fragmented and distorted relative to his recognition, apparent in the competence he acquires, of what would be an acceptable sentence of his language.

To explain the gross disproportion between what is acquired (in the form of competence) and what is experienced (in the form of speech) we need to posit a strongly constrained, internal, innate mechanism which, when triggered by the experience of speech, builds a cognitive structure, a grammar of the language, within limits set by very specialized schemata. Any human child, moreover, can learn naturally any human language, so the schemata must be universal, and when Chomsky refers to the properties of the innate mechanism, he often indicates that each of us possesses, indeed knows, the principles of a universal grammar. His model, though cognitive, is also biological, and in the present book, which consists of three lectures given in 1975, together with a long paper which is a revision of one submitted for a *Festschrift*, he particularly favors an embryological analogy, in which development of language is compared to the genetically controlled development of an animal.[1]

As Chomsky has tirelessly pointed out to his critics, the mere idea of an innate component in learning a language is undisputed and uninteresting: the blankest theory of behaviorism requires some innate mechanism, however minimal. The important question concerns how complex and how specific to language acquisition the mechanism is supposed to be. In particular, Chomsky has differed from the empiricist tradition in regarding the mechanism as not simply one that applies a general learning strategy to language. Discussion over the past years, however, has made it clear that this particular difference between Chomsky and the empiricists is ambiguous, and some recognition of the ambiguity can be traced in the present book.

A "general learning capacity" might be defined in terms of some very simple learning theory, such as the traditional empiricist theories of "association" or of "inductive" generalization. In this sense, Chomsky convincingly insists that no one has offered a plausible or even coherent way of representing the learning of language by such empiricist learning theories. But it might also be true that very little that is learned can be represented in these simple empiricist terms: maybe most learning requires innate mechanisms more complex, and with more defined limits, than empiricism traditionally has allowed. If this is so, then the important question for language concerns how specific the capacity for language acquisition is, not the extent to which it is, peculiarly, innate.

The general issue is to some degree, but only to some, independent of what exactly the principles of the grammar of a human language have to be. Chomsky has retained, of course, his original picture of grammatical rules as being "generative." They include transformational rules which turn abstract "deep structures" into "surface structures." These surface structures take on a particular phonological form and emerge as the sentences one actually hears.

But many other more particular aspects of the theory have changed over the years. Above all on the matter of the relations between syntax (how and why a sentence is well formed or, in most everyday senses, "grammatical") and semantics (what a sentence means, what it refers to, what has to obtain for it to be true), Chomsky has abandoned the "standard" theory of *Aspects of the Theory of Syntax* (1965), by which semantic interpretation was applied to deep structure. He now applies semantic interpretation to surface structure, a notable modification of his earlier views. On a verbal matter, Chomsky in these pages proposes giving up the well-known phrase "deep structure" for those initial abstract base sentences to which the transformations are applied. His grounds for doing so are revealing of what he cares most about. He argues that not only these base sentences, but processes applied at the level of surface structure as well, are "deep" in the only interesting sense—namely, expressive of important and hidden human powers.

On the questions of the relations of syntax and semantics, many other positions are possible and have been vigorously discussed. Some expressions of these disagreements about the place of semantics in transformational grammar are to be found in some of the papers collected in the book edited by Gilbert Harman;[2] other papers take the discussion further, into questions about how semantics in general is to be understood and pursued—by using a theory of truth, for instance, as proposed by Donald Davidson, or by certain abstract structures of "possible worlds," advocated here by David Lewis. It is exceptionally difficult for someone like myself, who is not engaged full-time in the technical literature of these subjects (difficult, also, I suspect, for those who are), to have any full sense of how these various approaches relate to one another and to generative grammar, or to understand how far these and other semantic theories exclude one another, or are rather dealing in complementary questions.

Harman's collection, though it contains much good material, is not going to help anyone with this problem. His introduction is useful as far as it goes, but it does not go nearly far enough; and while the book is called *On Noam Chomsky*, in the case of one or two papers it would take someone with a sophisticated understanding of the subject to grasp why the matters discussed bear on issues raised by Chomsky at all.

Even when proposals about the nature of semantics are explicitly related to Chomsky, the size, weight, and exact location of disagreement can remain obscure. Harman valuably reprints John Searle's admirable piece "Chomsky's Revolution in Linguistics," which appeared in this journal in 1972. In it Searle criticizes Chomsky for not associating semantic study with the notion of communicative intention; he urges his own and Grice's theories of speech-acts, which link the meaning of the sentence to the intentions of the speaker, to fill what he sees as a void in the Chomskyan system—the *point* of language. Chomsky, in the present book, replies to Searle, but chiefly to deny, once more, the necessity of communicative intent, and to insist that uses of language can be thoroughly and seriously meant though not intended to influence any hearer.

> As a graduate student, I spent two years writing a lengthy manuscript, assuming throughout that it would never be published or read by anyone. I meant everything I wrote, intending nothing as to what anyone would believe about my beliefs, in fact taking it for granted that there would be no audience.

But how could the existence of such cases possibly be the main issue? One would like to know whether, if what Searle says about the connections of meaning and intention were true, much or any of Chomsky's views would be upset. It might be true that, despite exceptions, language is primarily or centrally connected with intentions to influence hearers' attitudes; and yet some Chomskyan account of the capacities to produce and understand those utterances could also be true.

All through this field, as in other places where exciting work is going on, views which may well be compatible nevertheless struggle with one another. This is because they struggle for attention; the research programs may be compatible in content, but the thought that goes with each of them, "this is the way to go on," excludes the others. This thought may be essential to the researcher—the synoptic peacemaker who pleads for compatibility is up in the observer's balloon, not engaged at the scientific front. In Chomsky's own case, however, a further dimension is involved, and a more important one. He associates his own approach with an affirmation of the depth of the human mind and the value of the individual, and he is suspicious on more than theoretical grounds of many styles of opposing theory.

    Chomsky's arguments with his opponents are painstakingly reasoned and academic in tone (though he is unduly given to that polemicists' put-down, "unfortunately," as in, "Unfortunately, X is rather careless in his references," page 218). It is only after technical argument—but still too soon, granted some complexities we shall come to—that he falls back on ideological explanation, associating empiricist opposition to his views with social reaction. But through the laborious and sometimes peripheral self-defense, one can see that he is deeply distrustful and disapproving of some other ways of doing linguistics and the other human sciences, and that his linguistic theories, in their central contentions, have an ideological significance which relates them in some unclear but powerful way to his political and social outlook. This comes to the surface in a few pages of Chomsky's present book, and it gets very brief consideration in the last item in Harman's collection, Dell Hymes's informative review of John Lyons's book on Chomsky in the Modern Masters series (Viking, 1970). It is worth exploring further.

What exactly is involved in the innate component, what principles the language-acquisition device is armed with, are of course technical matters. But whatever they may exactly turn out to be, the more general question comes up of how to describe their presence. Chomsky has favored the terminology of unconscious, innate, *knowledge*, and this has helped to connect his theories with those Rationalist thinkers of the seventeenth century and later whom he has claimed, always with some caution, as his intellectual ancestors. Whether "knowledge" is the right concept, however, is a hard question. Certainly many objections which have been put to Chomsky, such as that, on his principles, a falling stone must know how to fall, entirely miss the point, and ignore the cognitive character of the states governed by Chomsky's innate schemata, as Thomas Nagel well argues in Harman's book. Yet, as Nagel also points out, there remains a long step to accepting the concept of knowledge as applying to the presence of the schemata themselves, and there are theoretical embarrassments in the use of that concept.

There is, for example, the question (raised elsewhere by Harman) of the vehicle by which this knowledge is represented in the mind, a vehicle looking suspiciously like another already mastered language. There is also the related problem that knowledge which is more than merely skill should imply the possession of concepts, and we have no reason to ascribe to the language-learner, at any level, the theoretical concepts of universal grammar. Chomsky's own embryological analogy hardly points unwaveringly in the direction of a model that uses the notion of knowledge. In the present book he suggests that whether we call these potentialities "knowledge" is a verbal question, and he is prepared to let the word go; but how slight a concession this is becomes clear when he agrees to put, in place of "know," the word "cognize."

Chomsky's insistence on a cognitive vocabulary to describe the presence of the innate schemata seems to be sustained by one of his strongest convictions, the power of linguistic theory to reveal the depth of the human mind. It implies an uncovering of lower, but continuously related, levels of human thought, and historically it helps to tie his theory to earlier Rationalist speculations. These, however, usually took a less naturalistic view of the mind than Chomsky does—the idea of a cognitive study as a branch of human biology is for Descartes's own system unintelligible. But their views can, like his, be handily opposed to an empiricist outlook, which takes a shallower and more mechanical view of the psychological. That empiricist outlook can, moreover, Chomsky believes, be easily associated with a denial that there is a human nature, and with a manipulative and authoritarian conception of what can be done to human beings.

This opposition between rationalist and empiricist approaches (though, as Hymes says, Chomsky's own theoretical work has transcended it) has great ideological significance for Chomsky. The empiricist conception of human beings as unpredisposed objects for conditioning he associates with potentialities for technological oppression. Chomsky admits that empiricist systems of ideas do, as a matter of historical fact, strongly resist being categorized in the way he requires, since the idea that there is no fixed human nature, but that man is a social product, has very often been associated (for instance, by many Marxists) with "progressive and even revolutionary social thinking," while the opposite view has supported conservative and pessimistic outlooks.

"But a deeper look," he goes on (page 132), "will show that the concept of the 'empty organism,' plastic and unstructured, apart from being false, also serves naturally as the support for the most reactionary social doctrines." "Serves naturally" here is pure ideologists' sticky tape, no better than "goes with." Similarly unreliable connections are made when Chomsky goes into historical interpretation:

> Empiricism rose to ascendancy in association with a doctrine of "possesive [sic] individualism" that was integral to early capitalism, in an age of empire, with the concomitant growth (one might almost say "creation") of racist ideology. [Page 130]

In so far as this offers anything except evasive insinuation, it invites a quick answer: in any sense in which classical empiricism was "in association with" early capitalism, slavery, etc., so was its near contemporary, classical rationalism. No historical speculations of this sort can effect anything, and Chomsky's other admissions show that he is, or at least has good reason to be, uneasy with them. He is likely to find better ground in certain features of the present. Now, when psychological technology is a conscious weapon of political power, and the notion of human needs as opposed to contingent preferences has been moved by many forces into the center of serious social thought, there really is a case for saying that the spirit of empiricist and, above all, behaviorist outlooks must, apart from their intellectual inadequacies, turn us in the wrong direction. Here Chomsky's negative view, at least, seems to have real power.

But even so, it is more doubtful whether Chomsky's own innatist doctrines can turn us in the right direction: they might even help to do the opposite. For here the question of the specificity of the language capacity, mentioned earlier, takes on a considerable and unexpected ideological significance. Chomsky's claims have always been for the special character of man's capacity for linguistic learning, and part of his evidence for this has precisely been that, the grossly defective apart, men are equal in this capacity, while differing in general intelligence and in their capacities to learn other things, such as physics. But now why should these distributions of innate capacities have any tendency at all to encourage belief in the foundations of libertarian socialism? Chomsky speaks of his hopes for progress toward human self-determination and genuine freedom; but the basic linguistic competence, as he describes it, has no connection with notions of progress at all—it is perfect as it is. What does leave room for progress, and indeed progress toward self-determination and freedom, is man's lexical sophistication and conceptual grasp—but that, precisely, is a linguistic dimension in which men do differ, and in which the results of learning are not the same for all, and the innatist element correspondingly weaker.

Again, why should Chomsky's theory have any power against racism, association with which was one of his more sinister charges against empiricism? In so far as racism has any coherent relation at all to opinions about different intellectual capacities, why should the fact of an equal innate capacity for language acquisition be thought to help against it? No theorist of apartheid is likely to be daunted by being reminded that the African child can effortlessly acquire Xhosa—or, come to that, Afrikaans.

If, on the other hand, the innatist claims are substantially extended from the field of language acquisition into other forms of learning (for instance, as Chomsky seems to speculate at one point, into moral capacities), the charge of their irrelevance to racist issues may decline, but the possibility of an unfortunate and destructive type of belief in their "relevance" might increase. It seems odd that anyone should need reminding at the moment that it is the environmentalist view on matters of "intelligence" which has been identified as the liberal one. The entire question of the ideological significance of such studies is now a notorious moral and intellectual mess, but to accept their ideological significance while cleaving to innatist styles of explanation may not necessarily be the most progressive way out of it.

An important point here is that in the field of language acquisition, Chomsky has good reason to equate what is genetically determined with what is common to the species. That equation may very well hold for all innate human cognitive capacities, but there is no a priori guarantee from the nature of genetics or anything else that it must be so.

The ideological implications of Chomsky's theories are by no means straightforward or unambiguous, and Chomsky himself moves with dangerous speed and simplicity between his theoretical preoccupations and the political ideals for which he has so conspicuously stood up. In fact, the ideological effect of Chomsky's work in language seems to me not so much to support or express distinctively socialist aspirations for society, or opposition to oppression, but rather, a stage further back, to assist a humane revaluation of tough-minded inquiry in the psychological sciences. His work, apart from its spectacular and ongoing effect in linguistics, constitutes the most powerful and encouraging reassurance that a psychological science which is recognizably continuous with the natural sciences does not have to treat human beings as very boring machines.

The recognition that human beings might be scientifically understood but are yet not just machines could well coexist with more than one kind of social or political view, not all equally liberal. But as well as being a vital truth in itself, it is a necessary step to any adequate views on these issues at all, including any adequate liberal views. It is here, in the humane understanding of science itself, rather than in more direct ideological interpretation, that the most general significance of Chomsky's deeply impressive work is likely to be found.

Notes

1. *Reflections on Language*, by Noam Chomsky (Pantheon, 1975).
2. *On Noam Chomsky: Critical Essays*, edited by Gilbert Harman (Doubleday/Anchor, 1974).

28

The Selfish Gene, by Richard Dawkins

A philosopher, H.W.B. Joseph, who 50 years ago was (as Richard Dawkins now is) a fellow of New College Oxford, used to set as a first essay for philosophy students the problem: "what evolves?" Joseph's question was a notably unfruitful one, but with the large and exciting development recently of both ideas and information in evolutionary biology, questions of that general sort retain their place in that they put a large premium on reflective power and intellectual imagination.

The sense that there are intellectual problems here which are both exciting and accessible, even if only imprecisely, to non-specialists, is well conveyed in Dawkins's introduction to recent work in social biology.[1] He discusses, with great clarity and an obvious flair for exposition, such subjects as the evolution of altruistic behaviour, and indeed of selfish behaviour; natural selection for sexual differentiation, the maintenance of sex ratios, and the evolution of the menopause; the importance of kinship, and its vital difference for genetic theory from mere group-membership. He throws light also on such things as deceit, mimicry and reciprocal altruism. He extensively and perspicuously uses decision-theoretical ideas, in particular Maynard Smith's elegant concept of an evolutionarily stable strategy.

Dawkins is refreshingly free of two connected errors which rampage through popularisations of these subjects: that there is a straight extrapolation from the behaviour of systems under natural selection to anything at all about human society; and that nothing basic about human life is determined by culture. He explicitly and repeatedly denies both these falsehoods, and is very cautious in tracing any analogies between human social habits and genetically determined behaviour patterns in other species. He does, in a last and admittedly speculative chapter, try something different: not extending genetic theory itself into cultural phenomena, but applying to the explanation of cultural patterns a structure similar to that of genetic theory, using the notion of a cultural atom or "meme", which is transmitted from one generation to another by education and socialisation. The bad experiences that the history of ideas has had with "atom-idea" concepts does not encourage one to believe in much future for this type of analysis.

The part of Dawkins's account which will cause most trouble to the layman (I gather, to some experts as well) is the insistence, expressed in his title, that the unit whose "selfish" behaviour provides the motive power of evolution is the gene. Gene selection is the operative concept in evolutionary genetic explanation. Individual selection is, for quite a lot of the book, permitted, as an acceptable "approximation". Group selection is throughout criticised and replaced by more basic modes of explanation.

This emphasis Dawkins presents in a good deal of rhetoric, some (like his dustjacket) of SF provenance. Animals and plants are "survival machines" which genes have built for themselves; a monkey is "a machine which preserves genes up trees"; "they swarm in huge colonies, safe inside gigantic lumbering robots . . . they created us, body and mind; and their preservation is the ultimate rationale for our existence". He takes care to say that purposive language about genes is not to be taken seriously: it can all be translated out into statements about differential probabilities of survival and so forth. On this he does not mislead. But there are other objections. One is that the *War of the Worlds* image, apart from being (unlike the ideas themselves) rather boring, could leave an impression that even if genes do not really have purposes, evolution (after all) does, namely to make the world safe for genes—a purpose which is likely to seem obscurely threatening.

More seriously, the metaphors have not helped Dawkins to make entirely clear his answers to certain basic questions. In particular, I do not understand how exactly he sees the relation between three propositions which he asserts:

- that the genes which "struggle for survival" are pieces of chromosomal material;
- that a given piece does not always confer the same character—what it confers depends on context;
- that what are selected for, under evolutionary pressure, are characters.

In this connection, he does not give the reader the sense of seeing right into the question as much as he does with other issues in this successful and stimulating book.

Note

1. *The Selfish Gene*, by Richard Dawkins (Oxford University Press, 1976).

29

The Fire and the Sun: Why Plato Banished the Artists, by Iris Murdoch

In this short book, based on her 1976 Romanes Lecture, Iris Murdoch takes up Plato's celebrated attack, from the point of view of philosophy and truth, on art and the artists.[1] She considers where its weight lies, and compares its inner workings with other distrustful placings of art against morality, notably Kant's and Tolstoy's. She offers some thoughts, lastly, on the theme of how we might take something like Plato's point and yet defend art, resisting his demand that such art as may be allowed by the state to exist should be socially useful, morally celebratory, or at least decently minimal—and *minimal* would mean really modest: 'the paintings of (for instance) Mondrian and Ben Nicholson,' she excellently says, 'which might be thought of as meeting his requirements, would I think be regarded by Plato as histrionic and dangerously sophisticated.'

The book is not just an aesthetic argument on Platonic themes. It aims to go a good deal into Plato's philosophy, to such an extent that the publishers claim that it 'comprises in an accessible form a general view of the development of Plato's thought'. This emphasis is in more than one way a pity. It curtails to a fragmentary and tantalising brevity Miss Murdoch's suggestive remarks on what she rightly claims is a real question: in what way serious art can be understood as anything but threatening by a view which puts a conception of human goodness—as distinguished from human achievement—at the centre of life. In the place of pursuing that question in its own, and our, terms, Miss Murdoch's chosen plan gives much room to a very curious account of Plato's philosophy.

It is, first of all, in no obvious sense 'accessible'. It is allusive and off-hand: for one thing, no one will find it at all easy to follow unless he already knows something of the order in which Plato's dialogues are supposed to have been written. Barely intelligible references to one or two works of scholarship, not further documented, are scattered in parentheses. Remarks about different themes in Plato are put together in ways which are quite often imaginative but, equally, bewildering. She has not been helped, further, by the printer, one of whose many misprints issues on p. 3 in the misleading information that Plato's Forms are 'part of an argument for the immorality of the soul'.

If the account of Plato is hard to follow for those who do not know about Plato, it must be said that for those who do it is hard to credit. She relies on a resolutely simple account of the development of Plato's thought about the Forms, of a kind which has been indisputably modified, and many would say quite discredited, by modern scholarship. It is central to her story, to take just one example, that the strange cosmogonical dialogue the *Timaeus*, to which she gives a lot of attention, be placed unequivocally at the end of Plato's life; but for the past 25 years at least this date has been strongly disputed, and anyone who puts so much on the old dating owes the scholars an argument or two.

It is a pity that all this has to be said, since the interesting questions could emerge without any commitment on these issues. Plato in one period, Plato in one mood, or merely Plato as he has often seemed, would serve better to set out her central themes than the elaborate involvement in speculative history and creaky scholarship. Among the several ideas that curl about in the rather cramped space left for them, a main stem is this: for Plato, beauty is a conception which, properly grasped, is allied with truth, knowledge, and moral demands, *against* art, pleasure, and the indulgence of the ego. The image of the Forms, unchanging intellectual objects, stands as a picture of the moral world, of the world of goodness, which makes an unyielding demand on human beings who, considered merely in themselves, are, in a phrase of the old Plato which is quoted more than once, 'nothing much'. Platonic Eros, the passion for pure beauty, aroused for him in the first instance by boys and perhaps also by nature, but not (unlike us) by art, reaches out to that order of things that lies beyond us. The hardness and necessity of that moral order is linked also with the necessity of the natural order. For us, this necessity is, no doubt, just the necessity of how things are; for Plato, it is the necessity of the Cosmos, of the world conceived as created by and expressing 'passionate selfless unenvious mind'. (No disjunction of fact and value here, no mere equivocation on the 'must' of what we must do and of what must be.) Reality and goodness must after all be one—Plato's central doctrine: not because what is tangibly real, here and now, must be good—quite the contrary; rather, because both truth and goodness stand opposed to fantasy, distortion, the imaginative indulgence of the ego.

Miss Murdoch moves Plato, in his moral aspects, as close as she can get him to Kant, so that the Forms seem like a Greek façade surrounding that Gothic image, the Categorical Imperative. I think that this is a mistake about Plato's moral psychology, which is in fact more egoistic, and more illuminatingly so, than she makes out. As an issue of general principle, not of history, this is an important point: much can turn on whether we picture morality in terms of abandoning ego in favour of reason, reality, or duty, or see it rather in terms of the formation of an ego on which the claims of morality can constitute reasonable demands. The Greeks generally, and rightly, preferred the latter, though there is a line in Plato, the line which Miss Murdoch exaggerates, which leads indeed in the direction of the former.

Suppose we are seized, as well we may be, by that line, and rest the weight on a conception of the good as something external to the 'greedy' ego (as Miss Murdoch often calls it), something inherent in a hard order of reality. What will we or she say to the claim—a pressing one, after all—that there is no such order of things, that what she would have us yearn for is not there? This is an embarrassment which has been latent in other of Miss Murdoch's writings, and not solely in her philosophy. Faced with the historical retreat from a conception of the moral order as transcendental, one who nevertheless insists that goodness lies in correct perception and freedom from error will inevitably tend to locate the subject-matter of that knowledge or error merely in the world around us: the misperception which is sin will have to consist in a misunderstanding not of the cosmic order of things, but (for instance) of other people. In that direction, in total and ironical contrast to the original spirit of the thing, lies cosiness. Only connect, understand others, you cannot will evil. It is a pity—though, granted much else of what he said, hardly a surprise—that Nietzsche has not yet succeeded in persuading us what a hopeless thought that is.

Miss Murdoch, retaining a schematically Platonic language at least, but with something of a modern blank where the Cosmic Thing used to be, defends art against Plato. But her defence, in the last pages of the book, is notably thin and, to tell the truth, distinctly easy-going by the standards earlier praised. One thing art does is to stand in for the life of the Platonic sage. 'It is just as well that there is a high substitute for the spiritual and speculative life: that few get to the top morally or intellectually is no less than the truth.' (I wonder where she puts the moral top.) 'Art is a great international human language, it is for all.' (Why? Are the qualifications for understanding art lower than for understanding people?) 'Of course art has no formal "social role" and artists ought not to feel that they must "serve their society". They will automatically serve it if they attend to truth and try to produce the best art (make the most beautiful things) of which they are capable.' (Two gigantic questions are begged there. One— that to serve art is to serve society—is centrally raised by Plato himself; the other—the equation of good and beautiful art—is raised by most modern art, at least.) 'The connection of truth with beauty means that art which succeeds in being for itself also succeeds in being for everybody.' (What—*now*?)

These are sentences which, carefully considered, would not have been written. It is a bit unnerving that, consecutively, they should be among her concluding reflections. It also belies many good things in the book— she has excellent things to say, for instance, on the morally destructive powers of irony, and on religious imagery in art. But on what we can and should now think on the largest issues she has raised, she sinks from the high and icy Platonic challenge to a very undemanding level of comfort. It is a striking fact that her most eloquent writing in this book is in the cause of a world view which we and she must know is an illusion.

Note

1. *The Fire and the Sun: Why Plato Banished the Artists*, by Iris Murdoch (Oxford University Press, 1976).

30

The Logic of Abortion

I want to take up some of the moral and philosophical issues involved in present controversies about legalised abortion. The puzzlement that people feel about this issue, and the deep disagreement that obtains between different people, are of the kind that invite philosophical reflection, and, in fact, a great deal has been written by philosophers about the issue in recent years, both here and in the USA. Though I shall not try to conceal my own views, what I shall try mainly to do is separate and point out some of the main threads in this discussion, rather than present a case.

A lot of the most important questions about the abortion issue I shall not try to discuss at all. Apart from some important practical issues, there are also some leading moral issues I shall have to leave aside. For instance, is it fair that women should find it easier to get an abortion in some districts rather than others? Again, how can we reconcile a woman's right, under the law, to have an abortion with a doctor's right not to perform an operation he morally disagrees with? These questions I shall have to leave aside. I shall consider only some of the most general questions raised by the principle of abortion.

One thing to be said about this debate right away is that it is, at no point, distinctively a debate about religion. It is, indeed, a fact that, among those who oppose the deliberate termination of pregnancy, many are Christians, and, in particular, Roman Catholics, but the views that they bring to bear on the issue are not uniquely Roman Catholic views. You do not have to have religious beliefs to be against murder, and it is not peculiar to Catholics to classify abortion as murder. Since the issues are not essentially connected with religious beliefs, I shall not make any special reference to religion from now on.

The shortest moral argument against abortion is the one I just mentioned—that abortion is, simply, murder. This very traditional line of argument will say: murder is the deliberate killing of an innocent human being; that is exactly what abortion is; it is therefore wrong. Let us call this the 'murder argument'. It is a very simple argument. To those who offer it, that seems part of its virtue—it is a mark of its truth, which sophisticated qualifications are only designed to evade. To other eyes, its extreme simplicity seems to be bought just by assuming the answers to all the important questions before one begins to look at them.

Among those who want to crack the smooth surface of the murder argument, there are, of course, many different approaches. They can be usefully divided, I think, into two camps. The first camp shares a certain belief with the murder argument itself: that the central question here is a *definitional* question, in the sense that the important point lies in defining what class of beings the rule against deliberate killing applies to, and whether the foetus belongs to that class. This approach agrees with the murder argument in method, by treating the issue rather like a legal question about the application of a law, though it disagrees, of course, about what the verdict should be. The second camp of those who reject the murder argument want to get away from that type of debate altogether.

The main definitional issue has been whether the foetus is, within the terms of the moral law against murder, a human being or not. In one way, the answer to this question seems to be 'yes', and, indeed, obviously 'yes'. The foetus is, after all, a living thing, and it does not belong to any other species. But then we are faced with the familiar fact that the foetus is, up to a certain point, not a formed human being, and, even after that point, it is not a fully formed human being. If one pursues that kind of consideration, one can naturally arrive at the conclusion that it is when the foetus is viable that it is properly or fully a human being; and drawing the line at this point will, of course, yield a more permissive abortion policy than the murder argument originally anticipated.

If the murder argument is going to insist absolutely on the humanity of the foetus before viability—its humanity, that is to say, in the sense relevant to how it is to be treated—then certainly it will yield a quite strikingly conservative abortion policy. If you consider a separate, already born, human being—consider, for instance, one who is already grown—it would be generally agreed that one cannot just kill him because he is likely to contract some disabling disease, or, again, because his mother runs a risk of death or injury if he is not killed; and since the point of the murder argument is to insist on the equal humanity of all human beings, it could not permit even very early termination, even in cases where deformity or disablement of the infant is indicated, or, again, serious harm to the mother.

The murder argument, then, in its use of the concept, 'human being', seems to yield either a very permissive abortion policy or an absolutely rigidly negative one: a permissive policy if 'human being' implies viability and a negative one if it does not. In this second, rigidly negative version, the argument is using one undoubted biological fact—that the foetus is a developing member of the species—to do all the work, while many will feel that their problem starts from that fact and cannot simply be solved by referring to it.

A different definitional question arises if one applies the prohibition on murder not to human beings as such, but to *persons*. Even if the foetus is a human being, it seems easy to deny that it is a person, where this implies faculties of communication, relations to others, consciousness of a fairly complex kind, and so on. Some philosophers argue that it is not human beings as such, merely biologically determined, that we should be particularly concerned with, but rather with persons; and the foetus is not yet a person.

The trouble about this—or, rather, what I find the trouble about this, since the philosophers in question seem to be pretty unconcerned about these consequences—is that, if the foetus is not yet a person, then neither is the newborn baby; nor again, if the requirements of personhood are made sophisticated enough, will small children be persons. What is more, the senile, and other adults in a defective condition, will be, on this sort of showing, ex-persons or sub-persons. Of course, those who think in this way will urge other rules with respect to non-persons, and will doubtless urge us not to cause unnecessary suffering to any sentient thing. But if failure to qualify in the person stakes is enough, as this argument would have it, to eliminate restrictions on killing the foetus, it is presumably enough to remove restrictions on killing those other non-persons as well, and the results of taking this line will be wide-ranging indeed.

There is a deep fault with the notion of a person, as used in these connections. It sounds like an all-or-nothing matter, whether a given creature is a person or not, but, in fact, the term turns out just to mean that the creature displays, to some extent—it seems, an arbitrary extent—some psychological and social characteristics which lie on a sliding scale. Unlike the matter of degree presented by the physical development of the foetus, questions raised by the variable scale of psychological characteristics arise all over the place: with the old, for instance, as I have mentioned.

The 'person' approach to abortion presents, perhaps more than any other, the danger of the slippery slope, by which one's decisions about abortion leave one with no way of resisting other policies about killing and death about which one would have the gravest qualms. Some tough philosophers would say that this merely shows that we should not have qualms about those policies, such as infanticide, suppression of the senile, and so on. I find it quite unclear, however, what is supposed to give their arguments more authority with us than is possessed by our sense of humanity, as it is significantly called.

I have already touched, implicitly, on the notion of a right, and the language of 'rights' is indeed involved quite deeply in this debate. It is invoked, of course, by both sides. Thus, on the one hand, there is talk of the rights of the unborn child; on the other, one hears, sometimes, of the right of the woman to do what she likes with her own body. These particular ways of talking about rights very obviously presuppose, each in its own way, answers to the definitional questions I have just been discussing. If you can dispose of the issue by saying that it is just an issue of the woman's right to do what she likes with her own body, then you are implying that the foetus is to be regarded just as part of the woman's body, which is to answer the definitional question one way. If you treat the matter in terms of the rights of the unborn child, then you are answering the definitional question the other way, seeing the foetus as a human being, like any other, with rights. So these particular ways of bringing in rights are very closely tied to the definitional issues.

Another line of argument, however, makes an effort to get away from the definitional issue, and belongs rather to what I called, earlier, the second camp of those who resist the murder argument: the camp of those who try to get away from the question of defining the foetus, whether as a human being or a person. They may say: 'Let us agree, if you like, that the foetus is a human being, and killing the foetus is a case of killing a human being. The question is, in what circumstances one is justified in doing that.'

One way of trying to answer that question has, again, invoked the idea of a right. It asks whether we can think of circumstances analogous enough to the situation in which abortion is at issue, to help us decide whether we could have the right to kill a human being in such a situation. A bold argument on these lines has been advanced by the American philosopher Judith Jarvis Thomson. She suggests that, if one woke up one day and found oneself strapped to another adult human being, with his life-systems dependent on one's own, so that the only way to get rid of him was to kill him, then one could have the right to kill him—even if one was partly responsible for his being there. I have presented the example very baldly, without Ms Thomson's striking and chilling elaboration, which makes it more plausible than perhaps I have done, that one would have the right to kill this incubus.

But even if one were persuaded that one had the right to kill the incubus, it is hard to see how that conclusion could merely carry over to the abortion case. One difference between the cases is that pregnancy is normal and not freakish. Another is that, in itself, it only lasts nine months. Another is that, because it is normal, and normally issues in a baby, it has sentiments and reactions attached to it which could not be attached to the freakish case of the incubus. These differences do not all cut the same way with regard to the abortion issue, but, in my view, they do discourage the idea that we are going to get much insight into the rights and wrongs of abortion by considering what we might say about rights in such imaginary situations—situations which may have some structural resemblance to the pregnancy situation, but are, at the same time, freakishly unlike it.

This brings out a question which has been gradually pressing itself on us all the time: whether pregnancy, the situation in which abortion is in question, is enough like anything else at all for us to reach answers about it by analogy from other situations. While the definitional approach was faced with the problem that the foetus is neither just like nor just unlike an independently existing human being, argument by moral analogy faces the problem that pregnancy is, at once, highly familiar and also very unlike any other situation.

There is one school of thought which, at any rate, is better placed to acknowledge that fact than the others I have mentioned. This is the utilitarian approach, which considers the issue entirely in terms of consequences, the consequences being measured in terms of happiness and unhappiness. This approach does not need to get involved in the definitional issues; nor does it find it helpful to think in terms of rights.

That it does not have to worry about the issues of definition comes out clearly when one reflects that, if we can think about social questions in terms of consequences at all adequately, we must, in general, be able to think in terms of the consequences of various policies for merely possible people, people who may not exist at all. In thinking about birth control and population policies, for instance, we have to think about how things would be for people who, if those policies are adopted, will never be conceived. All the more, then, we should be able to think about the possible welfare of someone who, if a pregnancy is terminated, will never be born, and it does not matter for this consequentialist argument how the foetus itself is classified.

Those who feel strongly that the foetus is an actual human being, with actual rights, will, of course, reject the utilitarian approach, which attaches little weight to whether this is an actual human being, and, in general, is not very concerned with rights. Utilitarians tend to regard the language of rights as an obscure and unhelpful way of discussing matters better considered in the light of the all-round consequences.

If we reject the view that the foetus is unqualifiedly a human being who has rights like any other—and I suggested, earlier, that the consequences of accepting that could be very conservative indeed—we will, to that extent, agree with the utilitarians about the abortion issue (though we may well not agree with them more generally in their unconcern for rights). But even those who agree thus far with the utilitarians may well have other worries about the utilitarian approach. Does utilitarianism pursue its study of consequences far enough?

Obviously, in a matter such as abortion, we must be concerned not just with the consequences of each particular case, for the particular mother and the particular child, if it is born. The more general consequences of having certain sorts of laws and practices also come into it. Here, it is a valid question to ask what sort of society the practice of abortion on a wide and liberal basis would fit into; what general outlooks would naturally go with it; what attitudes to birth and to killing you would have to teach young people if they were to live easily in such a society. Moreover, in asking that sort of question, we need to look to a wider range of values than utilitarianism admits—values which go beyond happiness, or, at any rate, involve a deeper conception of happiness than utilitarianism usually admits.

The situation we actually have now, it seems to me, is that this wide range of questions is most characteristically raised by opponents of freer abortion, who answer it by predicting a society indifferent to human life and to human values if abortion is widely sanctioned. Those on the other side often seem indifferent to the issues of how a certain practice demands an appropriate outlook and set of values to go with it, and what that outlook might, in the case of abortion, be. They urge the particular miseries of the particular cases, which is forceful enough, but this, often conjoined with an emphasis on individual freedom, does not meet the anxieties of the other side. Thus, each of these opponents feels that the other side is indifferent to what should most be cared about. This leads to something characteristic of this controversy: that each side honestly regards the other as heartless.

Clearly, the larger question must be raised. What sort of society would it be that had got thoroughly used to the institution of relatively liberal abortion? What kind of life goes with that? Would it threaten other values, such as the rights of the senile not to be tidied away? The question must be raised, but I do not see why the answer to it has to be hostile to a liberal abortion policy. I pointed earlier, to the fact that the pregnancy situation, the situation which raises the question of abortion, just is markedly different from others, in particular from others that involve life and death. This is not a problem which has to invite the slippery slope—even though it easily can do so if it is wrongly treated. A social context in which liberal abortion laws are both in effect and easily accepted may not have to be one in which there is general indifference to human life.

Whether it is actually possible, in the long run, to have a society which combines full acceptance of liberal abortion institutions with humane attitudes to such things as birth, death and killing depends, in part, on whether it is genuinely possible for most people, without either self-deception or brutality, to feel that the killing of a foetus is something basically different from the killing of a separate human being: to *feel* that, not just to think it. Whether that is possible for most people I do not claim to know. But there is one significant piece of evidence on the subject which does not seem to be often mentioned: that there is a difference between the *death* of a foetus in early pregnancy, and the death of a separate human being.

This is a difference, above all, in the experience of women. A genuine psychological distinction, for most women, exists with regard to spontaneous abortion: for most women, to miscarry at two or three months is not at all the same experience as a stillbirth, or an infant dying in its first weeks. I speak of the emotional or psychological difference, not just of the obvious physical difference, though that itself no doubt contributes. If there is that difference with regard to spontaneous abortion, it is no good, on the question of induced abortion, advancing theories or fears which involve the consequence that the difference should not exist, that miscarriage and stillbirth should seem the same. Yet many moral theories about abortion do seem to have that consequence.

This is a point about the experience of women. In the end, this issue can only come back to the experience of women. This is not because their experiences are the only thing that count. It is because their experiences are the only realistic and honest guide we have to what the unique phenomenon of abortion genuinely is, as opposed to what moralists, philosophers and legislators say it is. It follows that their experience is the only realistic guide to what the deepest consequences will be of our social attitudes to abortion.

31

On Thinking, by Gilbert Ryle

Gilbert Ryle, who died in 1976, was for many years a professor of philosophy in Oxford. He was a man of genially military appearance, with a knobbly, cubic head; rather soldierly in speech and manner, he punctuated his sentences with an abrupt half-cough, highly characteristic of him and much imitated. He was an exceptionally nice man, friendly, generous, uncondescending, unpretentious, and, for a well-known professional philosopher, startlingly free from vanity. He affected an amiable Philistinism, which to some degree was also genuine: 'no ear for tunes,' he was disposed to say, if music was mentioned. He was often amusing. He once said of a philosophically-disposed senior Tory politician that he stood like a light out to sea, firmly beckoning ships on to the rocks.

He gave very sensible advice, telling his pupils, for instance, not to do a PhD unless they had to, since it was 'better to write a short good book later than a bad long book earlier'. He also gave excellent advice in philosophy, and communicated some good philosophical habits. His example was borne along on a certain anti-theoretical breeziness, but he showed philosophy to be a serious subject, and he conveyed a sound contempt for 'isms', schools, and mechanical party loyalties. He told a story, which he claimed to be true—and he was a truthful man—to the effect that when he had lectured in Germany after the war, a young man came up and said: 'Doctor Ryle, I admired your lecture, and should like to join your school: unfortunately I am a Kantian.'

I first encountered Ryle myself as a student, around the time that he published his major book *The Concept of Mind* in 1950. The book had considerable influence, creating both a style and a focus of discussion. It was a professedly anti-Cartesian tract, aimed at 'the ghost in the machine', and against theories which represented the mental life as a hidden immaterial process duplicating or paralleling observable doings (as Ryle was disposed to put it). In pushing against such models, it inclined, to put it mildly, in a behaviourist direction. It seemed to suggest that there was no conscious inner life at all. This impression was not intended by Ryle, and was denied by him, but it was encouraged both by the general style of the argument and by the briskly commonsensical tone in which the mental life was treated. Along with the philosophical aim of reducing, so far as possible, the hidden inner to the obvious outer, Ryle seemed to have a more general project of replacing the less workaday with the more workaday.

Ryle had started out, in the late 1920s, with an interest in Phenomenology. He even wrote a quite favourable review of Heidegger's *Sein und Zeit* when it first appeared. There are historical connections between these interests and some features of *The Concept of Mind*, but by the time he wrote that book his methods had become 'linguistic', and his style one of those that constituted what has been called 'linguistic philosophy'. He dealt in uses of words, and his arguments rested heavily on considerations of what did and did not make sense. Since he wrote in English, it was a question of what did and did not make sense in English, but he always dissociated himself from the minute interest in fine points of usage which some of his colleagues displayed. He claimed that any sound argument of the kind that he used reached below the level of a particular natural language, and could be translated. *The Concept of Mind* has indeed experienced, and perhaps survived, translation into other languages, most recently—very recently—into French.

The idea that the results transcended any local language was expressed in *The Concept of Mind* in terms of a notion of *categories*, which allowed Ryle to say that certain terms stood for dispositions, or processes, or occurrences, and so forth; and he thought that the errors underlying the dualistic view of mind stemmed in good part from what he called 'category mistakes'—in particular, from a tendency to interpret as a hidden or inner occurrence something that was correctly understood as an overt or behavioural disposition. Many of Ryle's results took the form of allocations of concepts to categories, a style of conclusion memorably parodied by a student at the time in the dictum: 'shop-lifting is not a feat of strength.'

In later years, Ryle became suspicious of the category machinery, feeling, as he was disposed to feel with any technical machinery, that it created its own problems. By the time he wrote the pieces collected in this volume, he had largely given it up. This book gathers together seven papers and one review all concerned with the topic of thinking, and also a fragment about another philosopher's views of Wittgenstein. Three of the papers have not been published before; all the papers form part of the work Ryle had done for a book on thinking which he was planning when he died.[1]

The central question, variously and often obliquely approached, is one that he felt that he had left unsolved in *The Concept of Mind*: how to characterise that sort of thinking which consists in silent meditation or reflection, the activity, as Ryle constantly puts it, of Rodin's *Penseur*. *The Concept of Mind* had effectively attacked any idea that mental activity typically takes such a form, or that intelligent action is action monitored by such an internal process. The book gave no account, however, of what that activity itself might be, and indeed left little room for its existence. In pursuit of this question, Ryle takes up such subjects as talking to oneself, teaching oneself, and thinking as soliloquy.

The apparatus of categories did earlier provide some rationale, if an obscure and insecure one, for the linguistic arguments. If one thinks that there is a basic, universal framework of categories, then it is a sensible procedure, by examining language, to try to relate various concepts to that framework. In the absence of that apparatus, however, Ryle's linguistic arguments are scarcely tied to anything, and it is a persistent failing of these essays that it is quite unclear why given linguistic considerations are supposed to count for particular philosophical conclusions. Many of the arguments here fail, because they rest on no coherent conception of the relation between mental phenomena and the language that describes them.

Thus, supporting a conclusion of Zeno Vendler's (a conclusion contrary to a long philosophical tradition) that knowledge is not a kind of belief—for example, true and well-founded belief—Ryle cites the fact that one can know what ..., where ..., whether ... etc., but one cannot believe what . . . etc. But this does not prove anything at all. Leaving aside the important area of practical knowledge—and the tradition has not supposed that practical knowledge is a species of belief—the answer to Ryle's point will simply be that if someone knows, for instance, who stole the jewels, then he knows of some person that that person stole the jewels: that is to say, he *knows that* something, and this knowledge may indeed be a species of belief. The grammars of 'know' and 'believe' are indeed different, but more than that is needed to lead one to this sort of conclusion about knowledge and belief.

Other arguments in the book are just too blunt and brisk. One of the more startling conclusions that Ryle claims is that it makes no sense to assert or deny that someone thinks *in* English, say, or French—or *in* words, come to that. If that is a truth, it is a surprising one. But the only argument Ryle offers, so far as I can see, is that an orator considering words for a speech, or a translator for a translation, does not think 'in' the words he is considering for his purpose, but thinks about them. No general conclusion can follow from that: he may think about those words *in* other words. There is probably a truth lurking in what Ryle says, but his considerations do not bring it to light.

Ryle believed in arguments in philosophy. The tiny fragment about Wittgenstein interestingly, and convincingly, makes out that Wittgenstein also did so, though it has been said that in his later work he did not (Wittgenstein seems sometimes to say it himself). Ryle shared also with Wittgenstein, and no doubt in part derived from him, certain other things. One was the important belief that the philosophy of mind had to get beyond both dualism and behaviourism: in these essays Ryle can be seen explicitly trying to do that, as he had not successfully done in *The Concept of Mind*.

Another thing he shared was a hatred, not of argument, but of philosophical theory. This distrust of theory was typical of much linguistic philosophy of the 1950s; with it there went a rejection of the idea that philosophy could be continuous with theoretical interests of the sciences. Ryle was open to many new philosophical ideas, but these limiting conceptions he sustained into a later time. When he found a disposition to theorise joined to an admiration for Cartesian notions of innate knowledge, every hackle was raised, and the only intemperate piece here is that in which, disagreeing now with Vendler, he attacks Chomsky for his well-known view that a child's acquisition of language can be explained only by postulating a determinate innate mechanism for acquiring it, a mechanism which, Chomsky thinks, it is appropriate to call innate knowledge. It is a deep idea, and a powerful and illuminating debate has occurred about it. It is sad to find Ryle bluffly dismissing the whole business with a philistine diagnosis, clearly wrong, of why Chomsky thought that there was anything in it.

Ryle had a very distinctive style, marked by long lists of words, particularly adverbs, and by an epigrammatic turn. He seems to have developed the style without reflection, but he became very conscious of himself as a stylist, and the mannerisms eventually took over, and carried him at times beyond the bounds of self-parody. The most exaggerated example here is probably the first piece, in which he writes, for instance:

> If *Le Penseur* is trying to compose a melody, then he is very likely to be humming notes and sequences of notes, aloud, under his breath or in his head—not just humming them, of course, but humming them experimentally, suspiciously, cancellingly, rehearsingly, recapitulatingly, and so on. These very notes and note sequences that he hums composingly, he might, by chance, have hummed gramophonically and with his mind on something else. Or if *Le Penseur* is trying to render an English poem into French, while he is unlikely to be humming notes and note-sequences, he is likely instead to be murmuring them, of course, experimentally, suspiciously, cancellingly, rehearsingly, recapitulatingly . . .

The mannerisms seem to have provided a substitute for the theoretical backing which he was so reluctant to give his arguments. He taught his pupils, in the most honourable and impressive way, to sift argument from rhetoric, but his own philosophy came increasingly to depend on an idiosyncratic rhetoric. Having given up the only account he had of the relations between linguistic observation and philosophical subject-matter, he was left only with common-sense and the resources of a style: a style which, to some extent, in its consciously dry jokes, expressed him, but which, under pressure of what it had to provide, was driven at the extreme to a kind of compulsive incantation which was far from the nature of this clipped, controlled man.

I knew Gilbert Ryle quite well, and liked him very much. As many others do, I owe him a lot, both personally and intellectually. I am afraid that those who did not know him, although they will get an overpowering sense of a certain style, will not find the real quality of his intellectual presence in these mannered, empty and unconvincing essays. They are late work, and he left better and perhaps more lasting material in pages of *The Concept of Mind* and in earlier papers. But it may be that, more generally, it was the activity rather than the product that mattered. I do not think that that would have surprised or upset him.

Note

1. *On Thinking*, by Gilbert Ryle, edited by Konstantin Kolenda (Blackwell, 1979).

32

Rubbish Theory, by Michael Thompson

The author of this book was once a builder, working particularly for the 'knockers through', as he calls them, who turn two rooms into one in terrace houses and make other well-known changes to convert a collapsing slum into a thing of pride and a joy for ever. Thompson's sharp descriptions of these operations, and of the contrasts between the attitudes of those who own these gentrified residences and their working-class neighbours, who regard few of their possessions as things of pride or joy, and certainly not for ever, offer some of the few enjoyable passages in the book. They also contain one of the main ideas for it.[1]

The idea is that what was originally regarded as a transient object—something which would last for a limited time, and then wear out—can make a transition into a durable object, regarded as lasting, theoretically, for ever; and that it makes this transition by passing through the category of rubbish, in which an object has no value at all. This category is at certain points said to be covert or invisible, which seems sometimes to mean that the category, or at least its operation in the system, is hidden from us, and sometimes (even less plausibly) that the objects in it are unnoticed. Slums are rubbish housing. Another example worked out to illustrate the idea is that of Stevengraphs, a kind of popular Victorian woven picture which sold for small sums in the 19th century and then disappeared from the market, until, by a familiar modern process, they were 'discovered', and now fetch large prices, have a written history, and so on. They are nearing the state in which they can fly out of the top of the exchange system altogether, and enter the ultimate reserve of durability—a museum.

The transition from transient to rubbish to durable is said to happen only in that direction. Nothing changes, for instance, from durable to rubbish, or gets from transience to durability without passing through rubbish. These results are protected against counter-examples largely by definition.

This structure, and the changes that occur within it, are then related to systems of social control. 'Those people near the top have the power to make things durable and to make things transient, so they can ensure that their own objects are always durable and that those of others are always transient.' Just as there was a doubt whether rubbish is invisible, or unthinkable, or both, it is not clear what it is, according to Thompson, that people near the top can determine: whether it is the actual pattern of ownership, or, rather, the way in which society thinks about the things that people happen to own. Having said that 'slumminess is imposed by the social system,' Thompson seems to be arguing with himself whether this means (or principally means) that the social system keeps itself going by creating what are indeed slums, or, alternatively, that 'slum' is a classification which the system allows the powerful to apply to whatever buildings it suits their interests to apply it to.

The theory next incorporates the notions of production and consumption. 'Consumption' is treated in a puzzling way; and certainly not as it is used in economics. Transient objects are 'consumed' when they are used up; rubbish is said to be 'consumed' when it is disposed of or processed, as in a sewage farm. Durables cannot be 'consumed'. A certain amount of paradox flowing from the assumption that VAT is a tax on consumption—which, with 'consumption' used like this, it clearly is not—leads to reflections on art-objects, the resistance of artists to their works being treated as items of commerce, and so on. The structure of rubbish theory adds nothing to these ideas, and actually makes it harder for them to register their impact. The distinction between the transient and the durable is very poorly related to the distinction between what does and what does not have a market price, with the result that his vocabulary does not even help Thompson to make clearly a good point which, I think, he wants to make: that the attempted escape to auto-destructive or otherwise transient art-products will probably leave the artist still trapped within the commercial system.

At this stage of the book, rubbish theory, in its own name, steps back, and we turn to applications of catastrophe theory, a branch of mathematics developed by René Thom which provides descriptions of sudden and discontinuous changes. This is applied to a supposed cycle, suggested by Basil Bernstein, between a 'collection curriculum' in institutions of education, which consists of self-sufficient and separate subjects, and an 'integrated curriculum' which does not. The first of these is associated with authoritarian arrangements and Louis Dumont's *homo hierarchicus*; the latter with democratic arrangements and *homo aequalis*. They are expressed, indeed, in different styles of architecture: 'collection curriculum architecture emphasises the vertical; integrated curriculum architecture emphasises the horizontal.' Even the undemanding reader who is nodding these assertions into his mind and out again may be held up by the next one: 'the most complete and perfect example of the former is the Radcliffe Camera in Oxford: a Parthenon-in-the-round, presenting a perfect façade in all directions.' The circle of the Radcliffe Camera, like the colour circle, one might have expected to serve rather well as an emblem of the opposite thing, curricular integration. I suspect that there must be something about its age or place that inhibits Thompson from working his trick the other way round.

Catastrophe theory provides a geometrical model for the sudden collapse of 'boundary maintenance' between subjects, so a collective curriculum under stress turns suddenly into an integrated curriculum—leaving, it seems, a mess, out of which people have to crawl back into a new collective curriculum. No evidence is mentioned that this cycle in curricula actually occurs, let alone that the particular set of psychological motivations invoked to explain it are relevant. We come out from Thompson's wonder tunnel of three-dimensional graphs clutching no more than the recognition that if curricula developed, for any reason, in a cycle that involved sudden collapse, then catastrophe theory, the theory of sudden collapse, could be used to describe that cycle. Three minutes inside the Radcliffe Camera, or outside it, can give better rewards.

How the two main characters of this book, rubbish theory and catastrophe theory, are related to one another, is a question that is never discussed. The book ends with the modest claim that these theories will enable us to handle both persistence and change, both evolution and revolution, will substitute the 'Heracleitean hypothesis' for the 'cartesian', and, together, will 'allow us to embrace a less repressive style in which problems give way to capabilities'.

There is, indeed, one substantial piece of theoretical work in the book: one chapter which offers what might be a contentful and interesting explanation of what is said to be a genuine social phenomenon. This is an explanation of a complex cyclical interchange of pigs and pork between tribes in New Guinea. However, this is done largely with some ideas from Keynesian economics: it uses catastrophe theory only in a marginal way, and it has nothing to do with rubbish theory at all. That section apart, this book contains virtually no serious intellectual work at all. There is no such thing as rubbish theory. There is just a bright perception, taken up from the surface of our culture, which might have made a jokey article. As a phenomenon, however, the book is striking: it combines in a very obvious and concentrated form all the most poisonous features of bad social science.

There is, first of all, a pervasive methodological mess: general statements which may or may not be tautologies; supposed paradoxes or 'contradictions' which are only the product of some unquestioned and idiotic assumption; vague assimilations of one thing to another, presented as theoretical discoveries of great abstractness and rigour. Mere rubbish, however, as Thompson himself insists, should not be saleable. What may give all this some popular appeal is something else: a pervasive knowing-ness, self-deprecating in tone, but suggesting at the same time a large and dangerous daring. Masks are being removed, threatening truths revealed, and a conspiracy of misdirection thwarted.

There is a particular trick which is used at several points to create this effect of risky revelation. It is one possible and appropriate aim of social science to provide a sociology of belief. From the starting-point that be-liefs are to an important degree socially determined—something more widely recognised and more deeply discussed than Thompson seems to realize—he moves, usually in one sentence, to the suggestion that beliefs are *politically* determined, and serve some class or similar interest: with a flick of the wrist he manages to insinuate something hard-working Marx-ists are still struggling to define and establish.

The idea that beliefs are socially determined has well-known reflex-ive problems: what of the theory itself that reveals the determination? Much thought has been given to that question, from Hegel and Marx onwards. You would not gather that here. The witness to the problem, in Thompson's text, is rather a characteristic tone: self-deprecatingly aware, at some points, of its environment, while vastly ambitious, at others, in transcending that environment; sometimes reflexively and tolerantly rel-ativistic, elsewhere condescending, deflating and snide. It is the tone of much contemporary writing about society.

I have entertained the idea, and not utterly rejected it, that this book is a brilliant parody, a perceptive send-up of the most degraded kinds of social theorising. If so, it is too long, but marvellous. However, I fear that that is probably not so: if not, there must be some other explanation of how the book came to be so concentratedly what it is. It may have some-thing to do with Thompson's experiences as a renovating builder. Writing about those, he is noticeably uneasy, as well as condescending, towards his customers. He tends to fall back on the easy case where they can be despised for their taste, for putting in the wrong doors and fireplaces. But there must have been some, and he shows that there were, who made genuinely decent houses out of slums; at the same time, their relation to the neighbourhood, and to the social process in which they were all embedded, was much the same whatever their taste, and made him (and no doubt many of *them*) uneasy. He helped them to do these things, and was paid to do so; reflecting on the process, he was, very understandably, ambivalent about it.

Later, when he was lecturing in social science—probably, to infer from the book, to art students—he had new customers, keen to knock through the last distinctions in the decaying intellectual terrace. They must have multiplied his ambivalence in several dimensions at once. In this case, he was himself required to inhabit the terrace; moreover, he had no means of telling which was a load-bearing wall. His book is perhaps best heard as a cry, aggressive but still ambivalent, from under the rubble.

Note

1. *Rubbish Theory*, by Michael Thompson (Oxford University Press, 1979).

33

Lying: Moral Choice in Public and Private Life, by Sissela Bok

In 1960, when a U2 spy plane was shot down over Soviet territory, the Americans first denied that the plane had been spying; later, Eisenhower publicly owned up. The incident raised some questions about political lying. It was clear that what made the Russians particularly angry was not being spied on, nor being first lied to, both of which they took for granted, but being publicly told the truth, which put them in a difficult position. It was not clear, admittedly, exactly why it put them in a difficult position, since everyone—or at least everyone whose opinion in any way bore on them—knew that the first story was a lie; but clearly there is something to appearances (or was, since things may have changed a bit), even those that do not appear to be more than appearances.

Ms. Bok, though she refers to the incident more than once, does not take up such questions as what is saved in saving the appearances. Indeed, she mentions only the fact of the lie, and says that many Americans were shocked when they heard of it—and I take her to mean that they were shocked that it was committed, not that it was admitted. It is characteristic of her book that she leaves out the politically interesting half of the event. Her approach is that of moral philosophy: and what above all emerges from her treatment of lying is that she is against it.[1]

She has a good subject, and within the rather severe limits set by her commitment both to moral philosophy and to morality, handles it well.

She gives useful materials on the history of the morality of truth-telling. She sets out clearly, and reasonably rejects, both the absolutist position which forbids all lying, and the consequentialist position which sees it as just one option among others. She considers, among many other aspects, excuses, white lies, lying to elicit the truth, and paternalism. She refuses to get bogged down in the excessive subtleties which have often been spun around the casuistry of this subject, whether it be about the exact difference between telling a lie and withholding the truth, or that between lying to someone and merely misleading them. She needs these distinctions, as the rest of us do, but she does not try to hang much moral weight on them. I take this to be a matter of moral as much as of philosophical principle with her: her severity falls as firmly on those who try to define their way out of lying as on those who go in for it. There are points at which she might usefully have been a little more philosophically insistent about the nature and boundaries of deceit. One small example comes up within the subject which is her usual field and which she discusses best, medical ethics. She is hard on the use of placebos, but she never exactly says why she supposes them to be deceitful. As the physician gives the starch pill he says (or his giving it says): "this will make you better". If the patient believes him, and the doctor has chosen the treatment well, what he says is true. So how can he deceive? It cannot be that what his giving the pill says is "this will make you better whatever you believe about it" — many medicines would fail that test. It is, of course, easy to think of other things that the pill-giving might say, which would be false: as, "there is something in this which is specifically related chemically to what is wrong with you". But why should we believe that the speech-acts of medical practice bear such precise pharmacological implications?

Ms. Bok's doubts about the use of placebos probably relate rather to the fact that their use implies a lack of openness with the patient. There is something the doctor knows about the efficacy of this pill which it is essential that the patient should not know, and which cannot be declared between them. But Ms. Bok herself admits that there are some situations in medical practice of which that can properly be true; and if there are cures which work through belief, and which, when they work, validate that belief, then surely they would afford another such case?

The idea of openness plays a central role in Ms. Bok's ethical thought. It is for her a vital test of the morality of a social practice, that the practice could be openly declared among all who are affected by it. A test of this kind has attracted a number of philosophers (it figures, for instance, in Rawls' Theory of Justice), and it is certainly significant, but in the application to lying, at least, it is not at all clear how it is supposed to work. The test shares an important difficulty with one of its prominent intellectual ancestors, Kant's Categorical Imperative, in that everything turns on how specific the rule is which is to be publicly understood. If there has to be a clear understanding between you and me that one may lie in the precise circumstances that we both know that we are in, lies are going to be less useful, at least, than they are at present. Indeed, it might turn out that they were no use at all. I suspect that Ms. Bok would subscribe to the maxim that one may lie only when one must lie, when there is no morally acceptable alternative. Granted this, it will follow that under conditions of sufficiently specific publicity, including your knowing that I am a conscientious moral person, my lies could not deceive you at all. At the other extreme to this, the conditions of the publicly acknowledged rule might be very unspecific, as that one may lie when the public interest is at stake: but then we are where we anyway are, in the ethical quagmire which Ms. Bok deplores.

There are, then, some theoretical doubts even about Ms. Bok's moral test. But there are some deeper and larger subjects, which she never touches on at all. Some concern the relation of the values of personal honesty to other social values; there are also questions about the extent to which a moral test can, in public life, reasonably be expected to be observed anyway, and under what political conditions. The shadows of the Vietnam War and of Watergate fall heavily across this book, but virtually none of it, in fact, is about politics. There is a brief and rather weak final chapter in which some institutional aids to public veracity are discussed, but the book hardly ever confronts the issues of how truth-telling should be related more generally to politics and to social institutions.

To take just one issue, Ms. Bok unquestioningly assumes throughout that the demand for honest politicians, and the demand for limitless information—the "right to know"—support one another, and do not conflict. This assumption is open to question. One may have secrets whose content is not discreditable, and if one is allowed one's secrets, one need not lie. Cases such as Watergate lead away from this issue. There, the secrets are indeed discreditable, and the lying simple villainy. From any moral point of view, in fact, Watergate is boring. No one doubts that those in power should not act like that. The interesting question—besides the issue of how such people come to power—is rather how one stops them so acting, and here the freedom of information must certainly help: the right to know is undoubtedly a weapon to discourage those in power from doing what they have no right to do.

The U2 incident, however, provides quite a different kind of case. If the right to spy is granted at all, then the right to know must be suspended; or if it is insisted upon, then its queries must be met with lies. Espionage, one must tautologously insist, is supposed to be covert. There are indeed questions, as that incident illustrated, about what sort of activity espionage is; what role it plays in national security; and what sorts of games, in the name of national security, are played between nations. But one thing that is clear is that so long as there are such activities, the more the right to know is insisted upon, the thicker the web of even domestic deceit must become.

A more trivial case, but with some similar lessons, is that of politicians' private lives. Ms. Bok says that if politicians are subjected to improper inquiries about their private lives, they may withhold information, but should not lie. This is pious and unrealistic. It depends on the practices of the media, and on how the right to know is concretely interpreted, whether there even exists an option of merely withholding information. If the popular Press is at once insistent, slovenly, sensationalist, stupid and contemptuous, as in Great Britain, the well known may find that the only alternatives to lying about their private life may be those of having no reputation or having no private life.

This small area illustrates the general, and indeed obvious, point that the morality, and the necessity, of lying must always be a function of at least two other things: the nature, including the morality, of what is truly being done, and the kind of information that is being demanded, including the question of what it will mean by the time it reaches its destination. American politics has traditionally subscribed to the belief that the best way to secure right action and honest politicians is to make politicians and other public agents accountable under conditions of maximum popular investigation. At the same time, however, and as firmly, Americans have believed that their politicians are dishonest, and would be even more so if not pursued by the right to know. But the same ideas can be turned round to yield a different result: if there were less faith that politics could be an entirely open business, perhaps politicians would not need to be so dishonest.

It is not merely that Ms. Bok's book suffers from an excessive confidence that the institutions which express the right to know can never conflict with the demand for public honesty. She tends also to overlook the role of institutions altogether, and to make the unpolitical assumption that what is principally needed to make political life better is more morality in it. There can be no doubt that it makes some difference what the moral character of politicians is. But beyond that, almost every question is open. There are questions of what institutions select for what kind of character, and of the extent to which the structures of power encourage politicians to exert moral pressure on each other. There are also questions about the variety of moral character that in given circumstances is most desirable. Ms. Bok more or less assumes, I think, that what is more desirable in rulers is a righteous character, and a scrupulous concern for principle. But I doubt that a Kantian Cabinet is really what we want; a certain honourable cynicism (though it is not all that we need) may serve better, for much of the time, to keep us out of the mud.

Ms. Bok should have been more impressed by Machiavelli's question, whether, granted the world as it is, politicians can keep us out of the mud if they altogether refuse to get into it themselves. Rulers who do not have to do nasty things are not simply the cause of an acceptable social order— they are also something to be achieved by it.

Note

1. *Lying: Moral Choice in Public and Private Life*, by Sissela Bok (Harvester Press, 1978).

34

Logic and Society and *Ulysses and the Sirens*, by Jon Elster

There are some pieces of logical or theoretical jargon which are marks of ideological allegiance—intellectual wind-socks to display which way the wind is blowing the author. While linguistic philosophers, at least of the older sort, 'analyse' some intellectual object, structuralists and their neighbours 'deconstruct' it. For Marxists, a set of interrelated problems is usually 'problematic'; and what gives rise to their problematic, is involved in it, and needs to be overcome, is, standardly, 'a contradiction', where that is not something in their or someone else's discourse, but an objective state of the world.

Logicians characteristically hate this use of the word 'contradiction', something which, they will insist, applies only to words or to thought: not, certainly, to the world. Even when the term is applied to actions or social states, items which at least embody or express thought, they will prefer to say something else, and speak of 'conflict', for instance, or practical impossibility.

The idea of contradiction which is not just an affliction of thought but is something real in the world, and which has to be overcome by progress or in thought or action, is due to Hegel, a fact which itself does not recommend it to the logicians. Great lengths of Hegel's work indeed go under the title 'Logic', but little of it belongs to that science which was developed by Aristotle, the Scholastics, Frege, Russell and many hundreds of current practitioners who work in Schools of Philosophy, Linguistics, Mathematics or Economics. Among the many things that Hegel understood, logic in that sense—that is to say, the real sense—was not one. His unwieldy, slithering notions of contradiction and negation were included in his legacy to dialectical materialism, and some very dreadful and obfuscatory rot by Engels or Plekhanov, in which the corn negates the seed and so on, is owed directly or indirectly to him.

All that may be thrown away, and only the demands of religious observance could want it kept. But along with it, logicians and their natural philosophical allies characteristically throw out an entire dimension of social, political and psychological thought: a dimension which was among the many things Hegel understood, and which, indeed—so far as such a thing can ever be true of anyone—he invented: 'Contradiction' is a property of thought, and the attempts to apply it to the cornfield can be forgotten. But it does not follow from that that it is an affliction only of descriptive thought: it can apply also to social or individual projects or attitudes. It is not very helpful to extend it to any kind of conflict whatsoever. Conflicts of interest between peasants and workers do not in themselves constitute a contradiction: though some political project may involve genuinely a contradiction if it essentially involves having to satisfy both of two sets of interests which are essentially opposed to one another.

A policy, a social situation, a frame of mind, can involve contradiction in this way if it necessarily involves objective or other kinds of thought which are necessarily irreconcilable. Thus, in Hegel's most famous and influential example, the master wants from the slave something he necessarily cannot have—'unilateral recognition', as Elster puts it in *Logic and Society*, a recognition *freely* accorded to him by someone who is a chattel, who cannot freely recognise anyone. This state of consciousness is essential to the master, and implicit in the historical forms that his institution takes.

There is nothing in all this inconsistent with real logic. In fact, however, the philosophers who live most intimately with real logic have not had much interest in these ideas, as Sartre's existentialism did, or some forms of phenomenology, or, of course, Marxism. There are many reasons for this: most superficially, the dubious associations I have already mentioned of the profligate use of 'contradiction'; more seriously, genuine difficulties, which indeed need investigation, as to the ways in which a particular thought form (a 'consciousness', as Hegel put it), or again a self-defeating project, can be necessarily involved in or presupposed by a social relationship or other historically-given development. Hegel had one big dark answer to that question; Marxists have lots of active answers, but they tend to scurry off when disturbed. That fact—together, of course, with the mere fact that the whole business has anything to do with Marxism at all—tends to keep the logicians away. A similar neglect is shown by the economic or social scientific theorists of rational behaviour. They are concerned with some kinds of logical difficulty which strategic thought can encounter: but their formal theories are characteristically too tied to simple conceptions of Utilitarian rationality, and their range of psychological and social reference is too narrow, for them to make much contact with this range of problem, grounded as it usually is in complex historical and psychological materials.

Jon Elster, in his brilliant, inventive, mercurial books of essays (as they both are, though only the second professes it), encourages these various parties to come and look at each other, and generates enough quick-fire excitement to make some of them surely want to do so.[1] His versatility suits the needs of the case. He is a Norwegian, and, by affiliation, a Professor of History. He is a totally idiomatic writer, further, in both English and French and perhaps other languages as well. He obviously knows a lot of mathematical logic, economics, political science and formal decision theory. He quotes in an unforced and relevant way from Donne, Stendhal, Emily Dickinson and Groucho Marx, to name a few; about the last he remarks that his famous dictum, 'I would not dream of belonging to a club which would have me as a member,' is a reversal of the Master-Slave paradox, and that it was indeed he who stood Hegel on his head.

Elster can overdo it, and a section of *Ulysses* about the paradoxes of love betrays, in a memorable phrase of Professor John Findlay, the rattle of machinery. He is also systematically infuriating, because his method in both books is to start questions and not to answer them; to throw out one or two good ideas, not to develop a thesis or sustain an argument for very long. He is interested in the vocabulary of discussions and the ways in which concepts can be put to use in various directions, rather than in solving any given problem. The effect is rather bad for the nerves: in terms which might be appropriate to his own style of paradox, it is like a brisk meditation. Yet it is very clever and inventive, and wonderfully clear; and brings the powerful instruments of modern logic to a rich range of social and psychological issues.

The issue of social contradiction and self-defeating projects occurs in both the books. *Logic and Society* considers more generally the application of logical notion to social description: the logic of possibility, for instance, as applied to politics, or the logic of 'counterfactual history', the activity of considering, for instance, how the USA might have developed without the railway, or the South without slavery (both actual projects of

Robert Fogel), a style of thought which seems bafflingly indeterminate yet at the same time is closely associated with causal claims in history which most people want to be able to make. These topics both get pretty short treatment compared with the central topic of 'counter-finality', the phenomenon of projects which are doomed to defeat themselves, as Marx believed the processes of capitalist development were bound to do. Elster is good both about the logical structure of such processes and about the various ways in which they have been related to historical development.

Ulysses and the Sirens mainly concerns the rich subject of rational strategies to deal with partial irrationality. The paradigm, revealed in the title, is that of *binding oneself* so that one will not be able to do things which one foresees oneself doing for bad reasons. Although Elster proceeds, as always, at a cracking pace, there is a lot of insight as well as brilliance in his discussions of this and related subjects. He is particularly good about the phenomenon of 'time preference' — that is to say, the fact that we characteristically attach more value to the sooner than to the later: a fact which is nervously repudiated by many philosophers, decision theorists, and (in so far as they are not the same people) evangelists of capitalist accumulation.

Besides his formal skills and his vast reading, Elster can bring to these subjects flashes of a distinct historical and political shrewdness. *Logic and Society* contains, in the middle of a fairly formal discussion of political possibility, some very suggestive remarks about Lenin, Rosa Luxemburg, and the theory of the 'necessary failure', in the sense of a failure which is indispensable to the success of the cause.

At three or four points in these books, there are hints of an extremely important idea: that directed and rational practical thought, whether in politics or in individual life — the rehearsing of possibilities, calculation of probabilities, devising alternatives — must for theoretical as well as practical reasons have a limit. This is not just because time or information runs out, but because there are necessary ambivalences of reason which can only be resolved by action rather than by further thought. To the extent that it is indeed a theoretical necessity, this will be a further point at which logical structure and social reality meet one another at some depth. It is one of several which Elster's plumb-line has touched in his rapid voyage. Let us hope that he will slow down his ship and survey in greater detail these underwater structures of social thought and action.

Note

1. *Logic and Society*, by Jon Elster (Wiley, 1978), and *Ulysses and the Sirens*, by Jon Elster (Cambridge University Press, 1979).

35

The Culture of Narcissism, by Christopher Lasch; *Nihilism and Culture,* by Johan Goudsblom

All around him in American society Lasch sees intellectual and moral feebleness, cultural decay, despair and inner rage.[1] There is no personal love, only a snatching at gratification, or domestic skirmishes in the war of all against all. There is no politics, only manipulation; no radical protest, only street theatre; no education, only organised illiteracy. The 'élitism' of earlier educational functions has been purged—by robbing the educational process of content. Sport is corrupted into mass entertainment. Therapy has replaced genuine moral reflection, and superstition has replaced genuine therapy.

This jeremiad is illustrated with many well-chosen and sometimes amazing examples of what Lasch detests. He treats some subjects with insight and an effectively energetic indignation; sport is especially well handled, perhaps because it is a rather less familiar theme for articulate cultural critics. But this is an unrelenting and repetitious harangue, with very little effective claim to explain anything, and its considerable success in the United States must surely owe something to its resemblance to the traditional minatory sermon, where the orator's words furnished the Calvinistic thrill of seeming to reach into one's own social and moral condition. In this case, however, they do not reach very far. In its attempt to give instant enlightenment about the deepest ills of American society, the book is—to a degree of which Lasch seems surprisingly unaware—an example of its own subject. At the same time, it is a replay of what is, in fact, a very old theme.

Since America has been a modern state, its decay has exercised its moralists. This nostalgia has by no means always had the 18th-century condition of America as its object, but almost always, like so much else in American culture, it has been an expression of 18th-century ideas. This has been particularly true when the resources of primitivism have been deployed, when the idea has been expressed that in some less sophisticated or less complex state of affairs things were—as perhaps they might be again—less dreadful than they are now. Among views of this kind historians of ideas have distinguished in the 18th century a 'hard' and a 'soft' primitivism, two different celebrations of the Noble Savage. The first, and more familiar, stands for rugged independence, simplicity of taste, loyalty, family virtue, and hardness of body and temper. Soft primitivism, a more socially threatening ideology, was encouraged by early reports from Tahiti, and pictured the uncorrupted state of things in terms of relaxation, gentle plenty, and an entirely amiable promiscuity.

These images have confronted one another in America within the last fifteen years: largely unchanged, except that the hard image has been brought nearer home, to the supposed history of America itself, while the soft image, in the fantasies of flower children and various religionists of pleasure, has been to some degree detached from falsehoods about the South Seas and projected into an accessible alternative culture: one in which, as Lasch points out in his discussion of such faiths, religious discovery and liberation are seen in terms of a technology.

Lasch is assuredly no soft primitivist—and he is not, strictly speaking, a hard one either, since what he sees as lost in contemporary America is a sophisticated urban style of culture, and not the qualities displayed within the ring of ox-waggons. Yet I suspect there is a lot of what he says which speaks to the same sense of loss as that touched by those who pine for a tougher past. Images of hardness, strength, and resistance to elementary oral gratification, run through his book: they are, in fact, largely what holds it together. What is supposed to hold it together is Lasch's use of the concept of narcissism. There is a certain amount of psychoanalytical discussion which describes in theoretical terms a special kind of character: insecure, dependent on others for self-respect, subject to grandiose images of the self, and filled with anger. This character Lasch explores to some effect: bringing out, for instance, the fact that its baseless self-glorification is quite different from a proper fostering of self, and deftly eliciting its 'secondary characteristics': 'pseudo self-insight, calculating seductiveness, nervous self-deprecating humour'. The total embodiment of modern narcissistic America is, Lasch suggests, Woody Allen.

This account of a kind of character, with its psychoanalytical formulation, offers a good number of suggestions. But it really does little to sustain Lasch's cultural critique. For this critique to be sustained, a link would be needed between the psychological description and some significant feature of present American society; and since the basic contrast is between the way things are and the way things used to be, some historical understanding is needed of relevant changes in American society. So far as I can discover, there is just one attempt at such an explanation, on page 176: 'The psychological patterns associated with pathological narcissism, which in less exaggerated form manifest themselves in so many patterns of American culture . . . originate in the peculiar structure of the American family, which in turn originates in changing modes of production.' (The radically—or merely historically—disposed reader brightens up.) 'Industrial production takes the father out of the home and diminishes the role that he plays in the conscious life of the child.' That is all. The account then goes on to explain how the mother cannot compensate for this, because of various weaknesses which are themselves part of what has to be explained.

Besides that hopeful reference to changing modes of production, there are various other signals in the book to indicate that Lasch is not merely—what he seems a good deal of the time—a disgruntled, though bright conservative. His lament over the decline of the work ethic also includes sneers at the work ethic, and his celebration, as against narcissism, of what are plainly bourgeois virtues tends to steer clear of their association with the bourgeoisie. In the last section of the book, Lasch admits that 'the conservative critique of bureaucracy superficially resembles the radical critique outlined in the present study.' He says that this resemblance is only superficial, on the ground, clearly correct in itself, that conservatives have a mythological view of the role of individualism in capitalist business. The content of his own radicalism, however, fizzles out in a sentence or two of almost Bennite vacuity about citizens having to create their own 'communities of competence'.

Lasch's complaints suggest no genuine explanation; more generally, for all his admirable concern about preserving a sense of the past, they lack any sense of historical structure. It is no good his just saying that his critique is 'radical': unless his account gives some historical meaning to present discontents, it is neither radical nor reactionary, but merely a complaint about present discontents.

This absence of any historical theory, which makes Lasch difficult to distinguish from any nostalgic malcontent of any period, leaves an obscurity over a question which must be central for any critique of modern culture: whether modernity is to be seen as a special category, and modern discontent as unprecedented. Of course, any set of discontents is going to be unprecedented if taken concretely enough: the question is whether the modern world is seen as presenting a crisis—it may also be an opportunity—radically different from anything in past history. Hegel and Marx, of course, took this to be so, and both associated the promise, as well as the distinctive character, of modern culture with its unparalleled degree of self-consciousness. It is a line of thought which lies behind Lasch's discussion, but it is one which he does not confront. If he had confronted it, he would also have faced the very real question whether, if one accepts that idea, one agrees with the ultimately optimistic interpretations of the phenomenon that Marx and Hegel gave, or sees it as bringing the destruction of European (and American) culture—a return to darkness, or a move to some state of society for which reflective self-consciousness will not be the value that it has been for us.

> And here again I touch on my problem, on our problem, my *unknown* friends (for as yet I *know* of no friend): what meaning would *our* whole being possess if it were not this, that in us the will to truth becomes conscious of itself as a *problem*?

> As the will to truth acquires self-consciousness—there can be no doubt of that—morality will gradually *perish* now: this is the great spectacle in a hundred acts reserved for the next two centuries in Europe—the most terrible, the most questionable, and perhaps also the most helpful of all spectacles.

This, needless to say, is Nietzsche, quoted in Johan Goudsblom's clear, learned and useful book, which was published in Holland in 1960 and has only now, with revisions, been translated into English.[2] It charts the development of nihilism, defined in the sense which Nietzsche gave to the word, and in terms of which he invented, in effect, the contemporary problem of nihilism: 'A nihilist is a man who judges of the world as it is that it ought *not* to be, and of the world as it ought to be that it does not exist. According to this view, our existence (action, suffering, willing, feeling) has no meaning: the pathos of "in vain" is the nihilists' pathos—at the same time, as pathos, an inconsistency on the part of the nihilists.' The problem lies in the fact that our culture is importantly devoted to the Socratic demand of the 'truth imperative' with regard to both 'being and well being', as the translators handily put it, and refuses to base action or a way of life on anything less than some absolute truth: at the same time, we acknowledge both that there are no such truths to be had, and that the very consciousness which makes that clear can make it at the same time harder to do without them. Nietzsche again: 'However, the tragedy is that one cannot believe these dogmas of religion and metaphysics if one has the strict method of truth in one's heart and in one's head, whilst on the other hand one has become so tender, so sensitive and so agonised through the development of mankind that one needs remedies and consolations of the most supreme type; this gives rise to the danger of man's bleeding to death from acknowledged truth . . .'

Not all of Goudsblom's book is about Nietzsche. The parts that are stand up better than much writing about Nietzsche to the danger of having the rest of one's text discredited by the power of the quotations, and they provide a persuasive account of centrally important aspects of his thought. There is some rather pedestrian history of philosophy in the book—the truth imperative through the centuries—but, in general, under a modest and steady manner, Goudsblom skilfully shapes substantive and illuminating information about nihilism, and makes it clear that both the 'truth imperative' itself and scepticism about our ability to satisfy it are cultural and not merely theoretical forces.

At the extremes of his prophetic disgust, Nietzsche did not foresee the precise deformations of social and personal life that Lasch holds up for castigation. But it may be that he understood a great deal about their structure. Was he right in his basic reaction—that the fault must lie with the Socratic aspiration towards moral truth and reflexive understanding? And if so, is there any way of overcoming that drive to ever greater self-consciousness without invoking a catastrophe? These questions are more pressing than ever.

Notes

1. *The Culture of Narcissism*, by Christopher Lasch (Norton, 1979).
2. *Nihilism and Culture*, by Johan Goudsblom (Blackwell, 1980).

36

Religion and Public Doctrine in England, by Maurice Cowling

This peculiar book belongs to a series called 'Cambridge Studies in the History and Theory of Politics', but one should not be misled by the name either of the series or of the book: there is very little about the history of politics and nothing about its theory, and not much direct light is thrown on the subject of the title.[1] *Cambridge*, however, it very much is. The acerbic parochialism, dislike of the modern world and its cultural effects, a distinct sense of Englishness, indeed put one in mind, oddly enough, of another Cambridge writer, the late Dr Leavis, as do some turgid writing and a violent dislike of Lord Snow. Oddly, since Leavis's intense moralism is the sort of thing that Cowling most detests: but that only makes it clearer how some spirit of the place managed to affect them both.

Leavis is not mentioned in these pages, but many Cambridge figures, past and present, are. The author relishes the utter inconspicuousness of some of them, and their parochial preoccupations. Welbourne, Smyth and B. L. Manning (author of a chapter on 'What the Boat Club owes to the College') all receive considered treatment, alongside better-known historians, and figures such as Whitehead, Toynbee, Eliot, Churchill and Evelyn Waugh. 'It was not until it began to be said in Jesus that Peterhouse was willing to get rid of Knowles that Butterfield was in a position to persuade Vellacott that Peterhouse had a duty to keep him,' writes Cowling with relish, and we know where we are.

The parochialism is partly related to an autobiographical intent: the author wishes to introduce us to the formation of his own opinions. However, this is a recessive note, and it comes out rather oddly because the most explicit autobiography occurs in the Preface, in which, by some obscure authorial convention, Cowling always refers to himself in the third person. 'For as long as he can remember the author has hated these modes of thinking,' he rather grandly says in the course of it. It must be said that what precedes this remark is not so much an account of any modes of thinking as a list of names (including, I should no doubt declare, my own), and that this sets the tone for quite a lot of what happens later.

Cowling's idea is to mark out a certain set of dislikes, opinions and attitudes, both by the intermittent element of autobiography, and by an account and assessment of these various writers. The treatment of them is very uneven and often very blank, particularly because so much of it takes the form of fragmented quotations from their writings. The device of quotation and semi-quotation has a function, and allows Cowling to sustain an ambiguous relation to what he is reporting. We shall come back to that. Merely stylistically, it has a deadening effect, particularly when Cowling is trying to deal with philosophical rather than historical writings: the account of Whitehead, for instance, and in good part that of Collingwood, are about as appealing and lifelike as a police photomontage of a wanted man.

All these writers, and the teachings of the forgotten dons, whether favourably or unfavourably treated, bear on the question of how the modern world should be viewed in the light of the religious consciousness; and the answer is that, at any rate, it should not be viewed as it usually is—within the pious and fraudulent constraints of liberal and humanist preoccupations. 'How shall we sing the Lord's song in a strange land?' was the title, mentioned by Cowling, of a sermon by Owen Chadwick, Regius Professor of History at Cambridge, and the object of some of Cowling's more condescending comments. In view of the prominent confessional stance that Cowling has chosen to take in this book, the question presses heavily on Cowling himself.

His colleague Edward Norman, who recently voiced in his Reith Lectures prejudices similar to Cowling's, is criticised for the 'wavering and inadequate expression that he gives to his conception of the Church of England', and it is said that he 'is in danger of abandoning—perhaps wishes deliberately to abandon—the only claims that make it possible to believe that the Church of England is a Church.' If the proprieties of Peterhouse permit it, Norman might point out that this is a bit thick from one who spends 450 pages in giving barely any idea of what these claims might be, or of the ways in which the Anglican embers might be kept glowing if not with the secularist hot air which he and Cowling jointly despise: Cowling may well reply that the second and 'larger' work which he promises will set out all these matters. If so, it will have a hard time.

At the end of this volume, at any rate, it is clear that Cowling's thoughts, when they extract themselves from the activities of merely quoting, commenting and sneering, are in a state of such abject confusion, and his relation to what he believes is so evasive, that some special infusion of intellectual and spiritual grace will be needed for him to do better than Norman, or to feel his own situation more clearly.

Anglicanism seems indeed to be the preferred form of his 'Christian conservatism', and that certainly fits well with his praise of splenetic military men and cantankerous parsons. But the hints we are given of the sentiments at the heart of his religious attitude seem to suggest some different and darker associations—nearer the scepticism and distrust of all merely secular improvement which can be found in the unliberated heartland of the Church of Rome. If all that one's religion offers is a sense of original sin, imperfectibility, and a recognition that eternity is 'as significant as time'; if one joins to that a scathing dislike of all liberal improvement; and if one is prepared to say that 'in face of the transcendence of God, no moral or political system has any authority, and more or less anything will do,' then one needs some extra agency to keep one from immediate and close association with the more unreconstructed sort of cardinal.

Anglicanism has presumably offered in the past such an agency in the form of certain relations to and within society, ways of going on in a predominantly English style. No dogma or even image of religious truth adequately determines, in this tradition, the religious life: historical contingency, social 'arbitrariness' (one of Cowling's favourite words), must give it substance. But the more that that is true, and the less that there is anything to work with other than what we historically and arbitrarily have, the less room Cowling or any other critic has to object to what we historically and arbitrarily have at any given time—for instance, now.

In a very brief epilogue to his book, Cowling says that Christian conservatism, for the moment, 'most certainly in England, must primarily exist as dissent, a Jacobitism of the mind, which can do little more than protest its conviction that the modern mind is corrupt.' But all minds, in Cowling's lapsarian perspective, are corrupt. In order to show that the modern mind is in some peculiar way corrupt—and in a way of which he, and Christianity, and conservatism, are supposed to give us some improved understanding—he needs a more reflective, more open and less defensive conception of truth than any that he displays here, or indeed, I believe, possesses; and not only of truth, but of truthfulness.

One of Cowling's objections to the liberal consciousness lies in its pretensions to objectivity, and in particular to historical objectivity. One of the things that the admired Canon Smyth is said to have 'done' 'pedagogically' is that he 'implied' 'that academic detachment is nonsense and that all academic statements are shot through with prejudice, partiality, and persuasive intention.' Objections to what is called 'the constricting positivism of professional historical truth'—like enemies of liberalism to the left, Cowling uses 'positivist' as a fairly general term of abuse—yield a poorly defined relativism, about which we are told not much except that it is a necessary defence of religion. Concerning what he learnt from Sir Edwyn Hoskyns, he writes, in a passage which is fairly typical of this book's prose: 'But I do not think, in terms of emotional engagement (let alone in terms of religious practice), that I grasped the connection that Hoskyns was making between the religion he was protecting and the relativism that he was using to demolish the Liberalism he thought was eroding it.' And of Toynbee, a special and early enemy, he says that he failed to see that 'what is needed is the realisation that relativism subverts eclecticism, that irony protects religion, and that reactionary bloodiness is needed for survival.'

But if historical truth is relative, and religious truth either is totally remote from the world or is embodied in circumstances which are themselves relative and arbitrarily shaped, then it becomes utterly unclear, not merely what the exact objection to liberalism is, but why there is an objection at all. It has, after all, been rather successful, a point which Cowling in his rather unconvincing guise of defiant Jacobite is only too ready to make, and he has left himself with little alternative to being overwhelmingly impressed by that fact. Cowling's own historical work mainly consists in illuminating the very small-scale politics of British history in this century by detailed use of quotations from documents, in a manner broadly unflattering to the motives of the agents involved. These studies, and the view of men and politics which is suggested by this book, hardly permit him any room for surprise that public life, particularly English public life, contains a high measure of humbug, and if that humbug is indeed effective, there is not much left, on Cowling's own premises, for the knowing and disillusioned old warrior to do, except to straighten the medals on his shabby greatcoat and salute it.

Perhaps, at the end of the line, it is not any public inadequacy of liberalism which Cowling has the right to deplore, nor even a public deceitfulness, but rather that the high-minded propounders of liberal ideals, the self-satisfied advocates of 'procrustean virtue', as he occasionally puts it, are self-deceived. But, once more, if that implies, as it surely must, that they are blinded to the reality of the world, then we need a rather more adventurous and certainly less relativist account of the reality that they conceal from themselves.

Cowling's posture, assumed with a self-conscious reticence, is one of realism, irony, courage, patience and withdrawn anger; and it implies, as against the liberal pieties, a style of personal truthfulness. It is, then, interesting to see what happens when Cowling gets near, for once, to an opinion which is indeed unacceptable in enlightened circles, which is more specific than his usual target of humanitarian claptrap in general, and which he himself residually suspects to be odious. Here his unheroic use of quotations can give itself away: a clear example is provided by what, in his discussion of Enoch Powell, he euphemistically calls the question of 'immigration'.

> In discussing immigration, Powell was careful not to express hostility to immigrants. In demanding a reduction in their numbers, he claimed to be defending their interests. He did not propose forcible repatriation, nor was his position a 'racial' one. He claimed simply that the national identity was in danger . . .

In the first sentence of this, Cowling is for once outside his usual hedge of quotation, and the robust commentator on this rough world immediately finds himself explaining, with an unction worthy of the purest liberal, what Powell was careful not to express, as opposed, presumably, to what his words were taken to express. In the next sentence, however, Powell only 'claimed' to be defending the immigrants' interests, while, in the sentence after that, the word 'racial' collects a pair of quotes, the moral and intellectual force of which remains wonderfully unexplained. Finally, Powell turns out to have claimed 'simply that the national identity was in danger'. That 'simply' is unambiguously Cowling's, and it would be worth knowing in more forthright terms how simple a matter this sceptical historian of political behaviour takes 'national identity' to be.

There is nothing very remarkable in someone's entertaining these opinions, and Cowling's doing so is less important (as Cowling would certainly admit) than Powell's. What is tiresome is the tone of heroic truthfulness with which Cowling throughout this book invests an undertaking of sustained equivocation: often, in an evasive relation to what he quotes, and all the time with an implied reliance on views of society, salvation and history which he smugly holds, rarely states and could not coherently defend.

Cowling seems to have the odd belief that (leaving aside the workers, who are thought to have got a number of things right) only he and the various reactionaries, famed or dim, whom he praises have noticed that much liberalism is optimistic and high-minded claptrap which carries its own intolerances, that survival needs irony, that values conflict, that most things in the world are determined by force and fraud, that political moralism is often self-indulgent, that progressivist utilitarianism is a barren creed. He should be better-informed: these things have got out, and many have noticed them. There are, however, two differences at least between others who have noticed these things, and Cowling. One difference is that some others regard these facts as part of the present historically-given problems of political thought and action, and in trying nevertheless to think and act, exercise that irony which Cowling so much commends—with the aim, for instance, of defending the conceptions of truth and objectivity which he himself both needs and despises. Cowling indeed admits that modernity has, in effect, to be accepted. It is merely superficial of him to suppose that those who equally 'accept' modernity, but instead of sitting in colleges writing clotted and ill-natured books, seek to shape its requirements in slightly better rather than worse directions, are necessarily victims of its more flatulent ideologies, or any less command the 'toughness, subtlety and illusionlessness' which he claims to use merely in living out the modern world.

Another difference is that those others may extend their lack of illusion to eternity, and to the supposed meanings provided by Christianity. It is indeed one of the oddest, and no doubt in this case consciously acknowledged, ironies of Cowling's outlook that the ruthless critic of complacency should want, so it seems, to slump onto the dusty hassocks of an older Anglicanism. But I wonder, in fact, how far he does want that, or how far some larger irony may encompass that advocacy as well. The religion in question is so little defined, and its relation, even potential, to our society—that relation mentioned in the title of the book—is so underdetermined, that one may legitimately wonder how far it may not be the vehicle rather than the inspiration of Cowling's rancour. His repeated claim is that irony is now necessary to Christianity: but it may merely be that the deployment of Christianity proves useful to sarcasm.

Note

1. *Religion and Public Doctrine in England*, by Maurice Cowling (Cambridge University Press, 1980).

37

Nietzsche on Tragedy, by M. S. Silk and J. P. Stern; Nietzsche: A Critical Life, by Ronald Hayman; Nietzsche, vol. 1, The Will to Power as Art, by Martin Heidegger

Nietzsche's first book, *The Birth of Tragedy*, was published in 1872, when he was 27, and while he was a Professor of Classics at Basel. It had the unusual effect, for him, of attracting some attention at the time of its appearance: after that, Nietzsche's writings virtually ceased to be noticed until the 1890s, by which time he was, for the last 11 years of his life, insane, virtually without speech, and out of touch with the world.

Nietzsche said to his sister that this book was a 'centaur', a description which emphasises its oddness, underestimates its beauty, and misleads about the number of its components, since it is a blend not only of scholarship and literary prose, but of philosophy and assertive aesthetic judgment. It makes some historical claims in answer to an old question, the origin of tragedy among the Greeks; more importantly, it tries to characterise the nature of the Greek view of the world, how that is expressed in Greek tragedy, and what significance both that view and those plays can now have.

According to Nietzsche, two contrasting spirits stand over Greek, and over all genuine, art—Apollo and Dionysus. Apollo represents order, civilisation and the determinate image; Dionysus represents nature, fertility, rapture, and the dissolution of individuation into collective expression. Greek tragedy was a highly stylised and formal art which arose nevertheless from the cult of Dionysus, and at its highest, in Nietzsche's view, it represents a peculiar moment at which the forces of Apollo and Dionysus were balanced—a balance which expresses a heroic understanding and acceptance of the destructive horror of things, a 'pessimism of strength'.

These elements, the Dionysiac and the Apollonian (a term surely preferable to Silk and Stern's 'Apolline'), by no means merely represent, as they are often taken to do, a dichotomy of passion and reason, or of emotion and form. The basic element of the Dionysiac is indeed *Rausch*— 'rapture' in Krell's translation of Heidegger, 'ecstasy' in Silk and Stern—

but the corresponding idea of the Apollonian is *dream*, and the order which Classical art can set upon things itself has roots in a realm of illusion. The balance between these forces, and the consciousness which the tragic outlook involves of the unity of destructive and creative forces, was embodied only in the earlier period of the Greek Classical Age—above all, in the tragedians Aeschylus and Sophocles. Of these, Nietzsche tends to emphasise Aeschylus, who was indeed the earlier, but (as Silk and Stern point out) it is certainly Sophocles who most clearly and unpityingly embodies what Nietzsche had in mind.[1]

The third great tragedian, Euripides, destroyed tragedy, according to Nietzsche, or rather helped it to destroy itself, in association with the spirit of Socrates, that spirit of 'Alexandrian optimism' which trusted in reason to make the most basic questions of living into matters of discursive knowledge. That same rationalistic optimism led inevitably to a depreciation of art, including Plato's celebrated rejection of it. The Platonic consciousness, and the later forms of moralism which in various ways Nietzsche assimilated to it, could not stand the power of tragedy, nor the metaphysical conclusion which, in *The Birth of Tragedy*, Nietzsche saw as implicit in tragedy: that 'only as an aesthetic phenomenon can existence and the world be eternally justified.'

That conclusion, like other elements of his earlier thought, was a response to Schopenhauer. An admiring interest in this thinker was one of the things Nietzsche shared with Wagner, with whom, at the time of this book, his association was at its closest, though he was later to break it off, in a reaction of independence which was self-protective and entirely necessary. One of the many interesting facts in Hayman's detailed and scholarly biography is that Nietzsche was present at the Wagner house on the famous occasion on Christmas Day 1870 when Richter and 15 musicians played on the staircase Wagner's birthday offering to Cosima, the piece later to be known as the *Siegfried Idyll*.[2] References to Wagner and to his art are present in *The Birth of Tragedy*, both in the salutation of Act Three of *Tristan* (a work which Nietzsche knew only from the piano score) as a modern embodiment of the tragic spirit, and, a good deal more problematically, in the form of echoing Wagner's own hope that his art might be the focus of a national consciousness, in some way comparable to the spirit of the Dionysiac Festivals at which the tragedies were performed.

Silk and Stern, the one a Classical scholar, the other a Professor of German Literature who has already written a rewarding book on Nietzsche, have produced a joint commentary on this remarkable work, which gives a vast amount of background information and relevant comment. They tell of the traditionally German sense of exile, *Heimweh*, from the ancient world, and of a fascination with Greece which went back to the

18th century, in the form of an image which Nietzsche, more than any other single writer, was to destroy: that of an untroubled, serene world of Attic sunshine. They explain how the book came to be written, and the controversy which surrounded its appearance—in particular, the ferocious attack on it by a scholar younger than Nietzsche, later to become the most famous Classicist of his time, Ulrich von Wilamowitz-Möllendorff, whose savage pamphlet, often right about details and mostly wrong about the larger issues, may have helped to produce the fortunate effect of Nietzsche's becoming a philosophical writer rather than remaining a philologist—though he was already set on that course before he published *The Birth of Tragedy*. Their commentary also provides information about such matters as the German understanding of tragedy; Nietzsche's Classical scholarship as displayed in the book, and how that now appears; and what Nietzsche himself later came to think of it.

The composite authorship has probably contributed to the book's being longer than it needs to be, and there are some sections of it—that on Aristotle's *Poetics*, for instance, rarely an inspiring subject—which are distinctly dutiful. They have between them permitted a slightly schoolmasterly tone at times, both in summary of useful points, and also in some of their criticisms of Nietzsche: 'Even here, we must admit, [Nietzsche] is liable to indulge his own inventive powers at the expense of his nominal subject.' But many of the criticisms are well taken and the book judiciously offers (to those who can afford it) a great deal of useful information, organised round a wonderful subject. The only really mad assertion it contains, so far as I can see, is that in the operas of Mozart 'music and drama merely alternate.'

In his last active years, Nietzsche came to take a poor view of much of *The Birth of Tragedy*. In 1886, he brought out an edition which had a new preface and a new subtitle. It was no longer *The Birth of Tragedy from the Spirit of Music* but *The Birth of Tragedy: or Hellenism and Pessimism*. The Preface was called 'Attempt at a Self-Criticism'. To some degree, Nietzsche exaggerated the degree of his distance from the content of the book, which contained some of the most fundamental ideas of his later work, even though it is true that he had little use later for the contrast of the Apollonian and the Dionysiac, nor did he take any further great interest in drama. Much of the self-criticism of the Preface is, in a searching sense, stylistic: 'Today I find it an impossible book: I consider it badly written, ponderous, embarrassing, image-mad and image-confused, sentimental, in places saccharine to the point of effeminacy, uneven in temper, lacking the will to logical exactitude, quite convinced and therefore disdainful of proof, mistrustful even of the *propriety* of proof, a book for initiates . . .' And the Wagnerian aspiration had gone: 'Meanwhile I have learned to look without any hope or mercy on this "German spirit", and also on contemporary *German music,* which is romanticism through and through, and which, apart from being the most un-Greek of all possible art-forms, is also a first-rate poison for the nerves, doubly dangerous for a nation which loves drink, and honours unclarity as a virtue . . .'

Granted these remarks and many like them from Nietzsche's later years, granted his attitude to pretentious obscurity and professorial self-importance, he really did not deserve Heidegger's lectures on him. Heidegger offered four lecture courses on Nietzsche at the University of Freiburg-im-Breisgau between 1936 and 1940. The present volume is the first of four volumes in English translation to be published, and carries an analysis by the translator, who clearly knows a great deal about Heidegger, can nevertheless write clearly, and might well have extended himself beyond the very limited role that he has taken.[3]

These lectures are directed to the same area as *The Birth of Tragedy,* but they barely mention the work. In all these lectures, it seems, Heidegger took as his text a book called *The Will to Power,* which is, in fact, a collection of aphorisms and notes, of very different dates, which Nietzsche's dreadful sister, the energetic anti-semite Elisabeth, put together from his *Nachlass* according to an outline—only one of many different such plans—which Nietzsche had written on one sheet of paper for a book of that title. *The Will to Power* is a deeply interesting and powerful collection of writings, but it is not really a book by Nietzsche at all, let alone his definitive work. The idea that that was what it was was propagated in the Thirties by Alfred Bäumler, who wrote postscripts to editions of Nietzsche's work and was a Nazi. Heidegger, it must be said, honourably repudiates in this volume Bäumler's Hitlerian interpretations, but he accepts Bäumler's account of the nature of the book called *The Will to Power;* nor is there any correcting comment by Krell, although he refers to the English translation by Kaufmann and Hollingdale (Weidenfeld, 1968), where Kaufmann's Preface sets out these matters in detail.

Heidegger has one or two interesting things to say—for instance, about the relations of Will and Power to Romanticism. He gives some suggestive interpretations, as when he suggests that Nietzsche's claim of 'philosophising with a hammer' means, not smashing things, but to 'tap all things with a hammer to hear whether or not they yield that familiar hollow sound'. Some other interpretations are interesting without being convincing, as when he says that Nietzsche's claim that 'we have art in order not to perish of the truth' refers to supersensible or transcendental 'truth' of the kind falsely offered by optimistic Platonist philosophers—a version which seems precisely to take the edge off Nietzsche's thought. Nietzsche did not remain satisfied with the redeeming power of art as expressed in *The Birth of Tragedy,* but that left him with the problem which the formulation had tried to answer—of the relations between the power of art and the demands, if not of truth, at least of truthfulness. Heidegger discusses at length what Nietzsche called the 'holy dread of the discordance of art and truth'—but only, so it seems to me, to disappear, when the going gets tough, into abstract nouns and gnomic metaphysical evasion.

Heidegger is the only world-famous philosopher of the 20th century about whom it can seriously be argued that he was a charlatan, not because he is obscure, but because it can seem that his obscurity is functional, and that his characteristic combination of an abstract metaphysical terminology with homely domestic metaphor (so that things 'stand in the clearing of Being' or such) is not a necessity born of the unequalled depth of his inquiry—something to which he insistently refers—but a purposive substitute for thought which in more perspicuous modes is harder. I genuinely do not know whether such critics are right, but these lectures at least, less densely written and so in some ways more revealing than his more finished publications, do little to disarm them.

There are passages, some quite long, about the history of philosophy, in particular about Plato, which are sometimes utterly dull and banal, and sometimes simply inaccurate: often past writers are tacitly bent to a Heideggerian purpose, 'a philosophy for initiates'. His use of 'therefore' startlingly 'lacks the will to logical exactitude': indeed, most of his discursively presented arguments are the dialectical equivalent (to adapt a phrase of Wittgenstein's), not of a clock that tells the time wrongly, but of a heap of junk. Perhaps that was his intention—to provide an affronting propaedeutic to real, non-discursive, philosophy. Heidegger's work on Nietzsche has been influential, particularly in France, but to me these lectures seem to do no good to the understanding of Nietzsche, nor to gain anything from it, but mainly to be a hideous example of several things that Nietzsche explicitly and rightly hated.

It is certain, even if not everyone has yet come to see it, that Nietzsche was the greatest moral philosopher of the past century. This was, above all, because he saw how totally problematical morality, as understood over many centuries, has become, and how complex a reaction that fact, when fully understood, requires. To help himself to understand it, he resourcefully explored, in twenty years of increasingly hectic activity, our feelings about art, guilt, violence, honesty, and indeed every element of that moral consciousness which the Greeks helped to invent.

It is not easy to write a book about Nietzsche. Two of the present books succeed, one as a learned and critical commentary on one special work, the other by offering great biographical learning and only modest philosophical ambitions. Heidegger in this volume does not display much learning, and no one can ever have supposed that his philosophical ambitions were modest. But above all it is in its style, in its lack of light and its dire assertiveness, that it shows no sign of having grasped the demands that Nietzsche managed to impose on anyone wanting to write about him, or about the subjects that he transformed.

Notes

1. *Nietzsche on Tragedy*, by M. S. Silk and J. P. Stern (Cambridge University Press, 1981).

2. *Nietzsche: A Critical Life*, by Ronald Hayman (Weidenfeld and Nicolson, 1980).

3. *Nietzsche*, vol. 1, *The Will to Power as Art*, by Martin Heidegger, translated by David Farrell Krell (Routledge & Kegan Paul, 1981).

38

After Virtue: A Study in Moral Theory, by Alasdair MacIntyre

MacIntyre's brilliant and deeply interesting book starts from a truth which is, as he says, not as obvious as some of its effects—that modern morality is in a mess.[1] The mess does not consist simply in the fact that there are many moral conflicts which we find it difficult to resolve. The point is rather that there are no agreed ways of thinking about these conflicts, so that claims of justice, for instance, stand in blank opposition to claims based on utility and welfare, and we do not know how to weigh arguments in terms of what people deserve or need against considerations of general happiness. Indeed, we do not even know how to think straight about what they deserve or need.

MacIntyre's explanation of this is that we are surrounded by disconnected fragments of a previously working morality, which has been progressively deprived of sense by the demands of modern society and its impersonal organisation. Such a society offers an intolerable opposition between a bureaucratic and technical world on the one hand, and mere privacy, the world of the individual, on the other. This encourages us to think of ourselves, in relation to morality, in purely individualist terms, and as not essentially related to any social structure or institutional duties. This utterly abstract picture of the moral self is shared by analytical philosophy, by Sartre, and by many social scientists. It is in fact only a reflection of our alienated social condition.

The only choice now left to us, MacIntyre claims, is between Aristotle and Nietzsche. The latter discovered the historical collapse of traditional substantial conceptions of morality, and was prepared to face the consequences (or some of the consequences) of there being no coherent basis to moral thought. If we do not accept that, we must try to reconstruct morality on the kind of basis offered by Aristotle, according to which the virtues constitute the central notion.

MacIntyre opts for Aristotle. He gives some account of how virtues relate to rules of society, and sketches foundations for a morality grounded in the virtues, by using the three notions of "a practice," "a narrative order" (which can constitute a whole human life), and "a moral tradition" which allows room for conflict and criticism. This new Aristotelianism will be free, he hopes, from defects which he rightly points out in Aristotle's own theory—for instance, that it implausibly implies that you cannot have any one virtue unless you have all of them.

Aristotle himself, of course, essentially connected morality and politics: the proper life for man can be lived only in a proper society. MacIntyre deeply agrees, and this is indeed one of his major claims; but at the same time he regards the situation of modern society as so hopeless that the new morality can be lived, for the time being, only on a private scale (it seems), and the book ends with a few brief and bewildering remarks in favour of St Benedict and Trotsky, offered so desultorily as to suggest that, as he wrote them, MacIntyre was packing to depart.

Much of MacIntyre's construction goes by very fast indeed, and one repeatedly wants to stop it with questions. But the feeling is sustained that one's question would get an interesting answer. Sometimes the jumps in the argument leave one with too little grasp even on what the theory is supposed to effect: I find this so with the treatment of narrative structure, where the relations of fiction to reality, and of prospective decisions to retrospection, remain firmly hidden in dazzling light.

The book is in fact a collection of highly suggestive pieces which are sometimes skilfully juxtaposed rather than connected by argument. One piece is particularly thinly connected to the rest. This treats the well-worn theme of the scientific unpredictability of social developments. It is supposed to earn its place by undermining claims made by managers to legitimate power in modern society in virtue of their powers of bureaucratic control, but it cannot possibly do this, since MacIntyre's own argument allows—it may indeed require—that there *is* such a thing as successful bureaucratic control, and all the argument can show is that it is not grounded in scientific prediction.

Some aspects of MacIntyre's diagnosis, and of his reconstruction, are, of course, not entirely new. It is surprising that he does not refer, among recent writers, to Charles Taylor, for instance, who in his book on Hegel (a writer himself neglected by MacIntyre) and elsewhere has expressed similar concerns. But *After Virtue* is still an original, as well as a compelling and imaginative book, and the major doubts that it raises are doubts on major issues. Much of MacIntyre's accounts of the virtues, and his claim that modern moral thought is deeply in a mess in a way that current philosophy is not equipped to understand, are surely correct.

But I find it hard to believe his historical diagnosis. Above all, it is surely not merely an effect of alienated modern society that we have the conception of a pure moral self which, abstracted from all social institutions, is able to stand back from, accept or reject any proposed pattern of affections or allegiances. On the contrary, this is an idea which has recurred in different forms at various points in the history of morality, in Plato and in certain forms of Christianity as well as in Kant. It itself represents, in fact, a certain moral demand—a demand of justice, that one should lay aside, in the search for ultimate moral worth, the determinations of society. What value you possess, it suggests, cannot ultimately depend on where, or who, in what social conditions, you were born.

Aristotle indeed does not have that idea; but it is not that the world in his time had not yet faced that demand, but that he seems to have forgotten it. Similarly, he seems to have forgotten the problem about vindicating morality against egoism, a problem which MacIntyre very oddly displaces to the 18th century, although it was manifestly faced by Plato and by Socrates at the very beginning of the Western tradition.

In its historical aspects, MacIntyre's account is a brilliant nostalgic fantasy. What we have now is not so much the collapse of a fine Aristotelian tradition under the deformations of the modern world, but rather the outcome, under those modern pressures, of faults which have always existed in the Western moral consciousness. If, at our present juncture, we do have to choose between Aristotle and Nietzsche, it may rather be Nietzsche who is right: it has finally *got out* that there is something wrong with morality. But it is itself one of MacIntyre's most illuminating exaggerations to claim that this is the only choice that we have.

Note

1. *After Virtue: A Study in Moral Theory*, by Alasdair MacIntyre (Duckworth, 1981).

39

Philosophical Explanations, by Robert Nozick

Toward the end of his talented, diverse, and very long book, Robert Nozick embraces the idea of philosophy as an art form, and of the philosopher as a literary creator who works with ideas.[1] This reinforces an idea that may have already occurred to the reader; if this book is in some way like a literary work, it is clear what kind of literary work it is like.

Nozick, when young, wrote several articles of startling brilliance, originality, and, in some cases, formidable technical resource, in such fields as the formal discipline of decision theory. He then produced the notorious *Anarchy, State, and Utopia*, a lengthy book which advocated individual rights, libertarianism, and a minimal state; attacked public welfare; discouraged redistributive social justice; and represented taxation as forced labor. It was very clever and not very pious, and gave a distinct impression of hard-talking heartlessness (though the genuinely heartless publicists of the right who welcomed it as a philosophical liberation failed to notice that Nozick was committed, most probably, to believing that most of America belongs to the Indians).

After the hard, scandalous success we should not be too surprised to find now a book that has deeper and more spiritual ambitions, which covers many large traditional subjects, and which devotes the same outstanding talents not just to solving puzzles or showing off, and not at all to slamming the pious, but to reaching toward more speculative and awesome reflections on the meaning of life. This is *Philosophical Explanations*. It is an attempt at the Great American Novel of philosophy.

Like most other such attempts, it fails. It is an extraordinary mixture. In part, it is as brilliant and exciting as anything in contemporary philosophy. Quite often it is suggestive and interesting. Sometimes it is very bad, and at moments it is so deeply awful that it is only by considering the Great American Novel syndrome that one can see how it came about. A feature of that syndrome is the disposition to take the size of the attempt for success itself. That can affect readers as well as the writer. Many large things have already been said about this book by commentators. One is that it introduces new philosophical techniques, and is likely to influence the way in which philosophy is done.

Nozick does offer some claims to a distinctive method, but he sensibly makes much less of his originality in this respect than the commentators do. The idea, borne by his title, is that philosophy should try to explain things, rather than offer proofs. It is not altogether clear what he means by this distinction. He wants to avoid "coercing" people with attempted proofs to inescapable conclusions; he does not want to proceed by rigorous deduction from self-evident premises. But it is not obvious how that aim is related to offering explanations: some explanations (some mathematical ones, for instance) themselves proceed in that way. He recommends something else again when he tells us to proceed in a tentative rather than a dogmatic spirit—there can be tentative suggestions of proofs, and there can be dogmatic explanations. Nor is any of this the same as the aspiration, which he also expresses, to make a philosophical work that is more like the many-columned Parthenon than like a tall, thin tower, so that when bits fall down, as they will, something of beauty may be left. That analogy poses the question, not whether the work consists of proofs, but whether it all consists of one proof.

One kind of thing Nozick's various distinctions do exclude: a philosophical work that tries to deduce all its conclusions from a few axioms. That is excluded, but then virtually no philosophy has been like that. Spinoza claims to have done that in his *Ethics*, but no one believes him. At the very beginning of Western philosophy, Parmenides' poem (or half of it) may have tried to do that, but it is hard to tell from its ruins—except that they seem more like the ruins of a temple than of a tower.

In fact, almost all past philosophy has consisted of explanations, and has been known by its authors to do so. Plato's did, and the word *aitia*, the Greek for "explanation," is closely associated with its most notorious speculative construct, the Theory of Forms. Aristotle was obsessionally explicit in offering explanations. Even the rationalist Descartes can be seen as, much of the time, explaining—and he was aware, in the case of physics (at least), of something to which Nozick draws attention, the power of explanations that one knows to be untrue. Kant was centrally engaged in explanation: explaining, as Nozick reminds us, how something *can* be so (for instance, that every event must have a cause), but also, and very illuminatingly, how we can seem to be forced to believe things that are absurd or impossible. Kant and other philosophers, such as Wittgenstein, have believed something that Nozick mentions but does not in fact attend to very much in this book: that a good philosophical explanation, insofar as it corrects everyday belief, carries with it an explanation also of error, and of why incorrect everyday belief should seem true.

There are perhaps two distinctive things that Nozick particularly has in mind in emphasizing explanation as against "coercive" proof. He is telling us, for one thing, that philosophers should entertain ideas in a patient and imaginative manner, and not treat them, or those who offer them, as the local heavies in a Western movie treat the stranger in town. It is not the most creative approach in philosophy to shoot an idea out of someone's hand as soon as he picks it up. Here Nozick's conclusion is fine and good. Not everyone needs to be told it.

The second thing that Nozick encourages goes further and is less good. This—which emerges much more in the later part of the book, about value—is the idea that a philosophical conception recommends itself if, as well as fitting a number of our spontaneous practices of thought and feeling, it would be nice if it were true. At times, Nozick starts at quite a distance from the facts and constructs a model of how things might be, the main point of which seems to be that the world would be a better and less squalid place if that were how things turned out to be. Thus he offers a picture in which we have a dignity that lies in possessing genuine free will; in which there is an objective world of values that are not created, though they are in some way brought to life, by our thought; in which these cosmic values are what give meaning to life.

These are not contemptible ideas, and Nozick does not merely assert them. He puts them to some explanatory work—though that work is rather narrowly conceived—and he argues about them in some detail. But what gives the ideas their initial impetus does not lie in any explanatory power—at least any beyond their effortless ability to match the conviction we may have, some of us more than others, that we have the dignity of undetermined free will and that there are objective values. What launches them is the feeling that everything would be higher and more inspiring if things conformed to Nozick's model, and it is that feeling, together with a certain tone (of which more later), that grounds the fear that this book is trying to do a dreadful thing: to lead philosophy back to an aspiration from which the work of this century has done so much to release it, the aspiration to be edifying.

There are some important kinds of philosophical explanation that do not figure enough in these pages. One is that Kantian type of explanation I have already mentioned, the explanation of why what seems to us to be so should seem to be so if in fact it is false. There is a good example of this lack in Nozick's first section, on the identity of the self. Philosophers have much discussed issues of what differentiates one person from another and what it is for a particular person to continue to exist: is it continuity of body, of character, of memories, or what? An important slant to these questions is given when the perspective is the person's own. Suppose I am invited to reflect what person in the future would, under various imaginable transformations—e.g., if my memories or character or body should be radically altered — be *me*. Some philosophers (including myself) have claimed that the following principle applies to such cases: that the question whether a certain person in the future, let us call him Y, is the same as a person present now, X, cannot be a question of whether Y is merely the *best candidate* available at the time for being X.

Imagine two different states of affairs five years from now. In one of them, a certain living body, Y (not your present one), has been programmed to have your present memories and character (more or less), and your own present body has been destroyed. In the other state of affairs, Y exists, just the same, but your present body, X, also continues, with the same memories and character. Clearly in the second case, X is you, and Y is not. Y is just a copy. Does that mean that Y cannot be you in the first case either? I and others have argued that it does mean that. Nozick denies this, and claims that who one will be in the future depends on the available candidates. In the first case, you will be Y, since there is no better candidate; in the second case, you will not be Y, since there is a better candidate. He calls this the "closest continuer" theory of (personal) identity.

Nozick actually claims to *show* that the principle that he rejects is false, by producing a counterexample. This strays a bit, early in the book, from the protocol of eschewing proof, but in the event he does not stray far, since the counterexample is feeble and proves nothing. (It concerns a group of émigré philosophers who will be the Vienna Circle if there is no other and larger group of émigré philosophers elsewhere, but will not be if there is. But a group of persons is not the same sort of thing as a person. "Are you the Vienna Circle?" the welcoming committee asks. "At least some of it," the émigrés might reasonably reply.)

More interestingly, Nozick proceeds to find other kinds of philosophical issues which, he claims, have a similar structure, for example, the analysis of justice, or the meaning of sentences. This is worthwhile, and sheds light on a number of questions. But even if this is so, it will not answer the question that many will feel most needs answering: how *can* this be the right answer for personal identity? How can it be that the question whether I should fear for what happens to some future person (supposing that I care about myself) should depend on whether someone else has been killed off who would have had a better claim to being me if he had survived? Perhaps the question can be answered, but it is not answered here, and it certainly needs to be. If what Nozick claims is true, then some things that we very deeply believe about personal identity are false. We believe, for example, that our claims to personal identity do not depend on who else is around. And what needs philosophical explanation is why we believe them. That explanation would also help us to think straight about our future without believing those things.

One of Nozick's objectives is to respect and make sense of deep metaphysical and, in some cases, religious motivations that express themselves not only in some unschooled reflection but also in a variety of religious and philosophical traditions (he refers quite often to Indian thought). His way of confronting these traditional questionings, however, is often somewhat oblique. He takes up the question "Why is there something rather than nothing at all?" This has certainly in many traditions been felt to be a real and puzzling question: to such an extent that well-known attempts in philosophy to show that the question is misconceived tend to seem shallow and unconvincing. Nozick turns the issue into a subtle discussion of the theory of explanation. If it is claimed that a principle is explanatory of everything, can it also explain itself?

This is, once more, an interesting discussion, but the reader may feel that he or she has been left alone to work out the relevance of Nozick's immense ingenuity and logical inventiveness to the archetypal metaphysical concern which started the discussion off. (The reader, incidentally, will need not only close attention, but also some technical knowledge, to follow Nozick down some of his paths in this book—what a Gödel numbering is, for example.)

By far the most successful section of the book is that on knowledge. This is very vigorous and resourceful, wonderfully clever, and, at a rather technical level, highly instructive. It is also academically the most conventional part of the book and very directly rooted in the recent literature. The argument is at the same time very original in its application. The basic idea is that someone knows something if he "tracks" the truth, where this means, very roughly, (1) that he believes something true, (2) that he wouldn't believe it if it were not true, and (3) that if it were true, he would believe it—where the last clause adds the idea that not only is it true and he believes it, but his belief is "sensitive" to the truth. By "sensitive," Nozick refers not to a special capacity of the believer but to the existence of a factual link between a belief and that which the belief is about. This is all worked out in considerable detail and with a subtlety that does not, as often happens in discussions of this subject, lose touch with the point of our having such a concept of knowledge.

The most spectacular result is achieved when this definition is applied to dealings with the skeptic. Nozick writes, "We do not seek to convince the skeptic but rather to formulate hypotheses about knowledge and our connection to facts that show how knowledge can exist even given the skeptic's possibilities." The skeptic says, for instance, that we do not know that we're not in a tank having our brains stimulated by a mad scientist in such a way that it seems to us just as though we were in a room, seeing a table, and so on. So we don't know that we are in fact seeing a table, even though it seems to be there, in perfect view, and everything seems as it usually does. Nozick says, and derives it from his definition, that we don't know that we're not in the tank; we do know that *if* we're in the tank, then we are not seeing the table; yet we do know that we're seeing the table. (Knowledge, in the technical phrase, is "not transitive under known logical implication.")

This is the one argument that practically no one has used against the skeptic, and it testifies to Nozick's remarkable discussion that this conclusion, which might seem a desperate device, begins to look natural and plausible. If one wants to know how to deal with skeptics, or indeed what knowledge is, this discussion must be read.

I am less certain that Nozick's dealings with the skeptic get their strength, as he suggests, from his general objective of substituting explanation for proof. His point, as I've said, is that he is not trying to refute the skeptic, that notoriously discouraging task. But even if he is not trying to show the skeptic that the skeptic should not believe (or rather disbelieve) everything that he does, he is trying to show us that we need not accept what the skeptic says. If the skeptic is right, however, we should accept what he says; so the skeptic can't be right. It is not obvious that those who have attempted to refute the skeptic (notably Descartes) have wanted more than that. But this is not a simple question, and this section is not only one in which the argument comes vividly to life, but also one in which the distinction between explanation and proof may for once be doing some helpful work in its own right.

When this high point of the book ends, we are less than halfway through. All the rest belongs to a division called "Value," in which such things are discussed as free will, punishment, moral motivation, self-improvement, "the value of valuers," and the meaning of life.

The section on free will is at several places uncharacteristically hesitant, not just in conclusion, but in direction. This is particularly so in the passage on retributive punishment, a subject on which, it seems to me, if Nozick had applied the same trenchancy as he has done to banging more fashionable views, he might well have given up. Here he attempts another application of the idea of explanation. The aim is not to justify retributive punishment (or to give a retributive justification of punishment), but to give an account of what its underlying ideas are. Nozick starts with some distinctions between revenge and retribution, and gives an elegant account of what an act of retribution is, revealing it as a form of communicative behavior which does not merely hurt but shows someone something. He then considers the simplest view of punishment as "showing" someone—a teleological version of it, in which the aim is to produce a change in the offender by which he comes to recognize his guilt.

There are well-known problems with theories of this kind, which tend to go around in a circle. The painful element, essential to punishment, in such an instructional act seems gratuitous. If the point of hurting a man is to tell him, why not just tell him? Or, if the aim is not just to tell him, but to convince him, the rationale may well become the same as that of reformative punishment. Anyway the rationale will not apply to the unreformable—apart from the point that it will always be an open question whether he might not be more effectively convinced by other means.

So Nozick moves to a wholly nonteleological interpretation, as he hopes, of retributive punishment. The aim of retribution is not merely to produce certain consequences but to do something "right or good in itself." The aim, as he puts it, is to "connect the offender with correct values," where this is not an aim that is added on to the act of punishment, but inherent in it. Nozick's idea is to produce an effect on the offender, not necessarily *in* him: correct values are given "some significant effect in his life." But, once again, why painful punishment rather than something else? This, replies Nozick, is necessary for it to be a *significant* connection with values. Why then should only those who have actually done wrong be so connected with values? Because, Nozick would answer, the wrong they have committed shows them to be not just unlinked, but "anti-linked," to values. Is this, however, not also true of the dispositionally wicked? But, Nozick claims, if they have not committed acts they have not *flouted* values, and the aim of retributive punishment is to "replace flouting with linkage."

The effect of Nozick's criticism of the old arguments against retribution is simply to have reduced to the smallest possible circumference the circle in which the argument moves. He is not trying to produce a justification of retribution, but he does aim to produce its rationale, and the rationale provided moves round in so tight a circle that it is hard to see how the justification of retribution might eventually be applied. The "role of suffering in punishment," Nozick says, is "to negate or lessen flouting by making it impossible to remain as pleased with one's previous anti-linkage." That version, in fact, is not yet entirely purged of the teleological—for suppose he remains pleased with his previous anti-linkage? But even with that impurity, the account is so utterly wrapped in itself that it is not going to give much insight to anyone who was previously puzzled by the idea of retributive punishment.

Another feature of the discussion of punishment is shared by all the material on value: it is vastly removed from any actual social institution. There are one or two desultory references to the law, but virtually nothing that focuses on the fact that punishment is inflicted by some actual authority in some actual social circumstances. This characteristic, spread over the whole large discussion of value, issues in a level of abstraction that is often bewildering, and which utterly discounts many obligations which one might have thought to be precisely obligations of philosophical explanation.

Value, we are told (I suppose one should rather say: "it is suggested"), consists basically in the degree of "organic unity." We value, he implies, that which unifies diverse and apparently separate materials or experiences. Not much is done to give content to this old and uninformative proposal. For Nozick, as for earlier writers, it is based on the differing complexities of higher and lower organisms and on some selected considerations about aesthetic objects—despite well-known and indeed obvious difficulties about measuring "organic unity" anywhere, and, in the case of art, when we can supposedly detect it, doubts about necessarily preferring its increase. But such problems do not seem to concern Nozick very much. He is more interested in a set of logical devices dealing with the notion of value in the abstract. He discusses in detail such topics as what would be involved in "tracking bestness," as he puts it, and "why is being a value-seeker and responder to value qua value itself valuable?"

Very little of this offers a direction to a psychology of moral action. Nor does it stoop to recognize any of the well-known problems raised by social explanations of actual systems of moral value, for example the conflicts between different systems of value in different societies and the difficulty of achieving objectivity in describing or explaining them. Indeed Nozick barely pays much attention to any distinctively human category. The picture we are left with is of the objective cosmic dimension of value as organic unity, with our having the opportunity to link ourselves with this, and by that be transformed and elevated. These salutations to independent values, alternating as they do with very detailed formalistic arguments (on the conflict of obligations, for instance), give the impression of some beautiful nebula, at one time seen through the optical telescope, at another with its light broken down through the spectroscope. There is a difference, however, since a nebula sends light to us, but values are inactive, unless we make them active in and through us. As Nozick puts it, in a very typical passage:

> Value seekers and responders have a cosmic role: to aid in the realization of value, in the infusion of value into the material and human realm.

Can that possibly, one begins to wonder, be the way to put it—to put anything?

If we do take up our cosmic role, then we may, according to Nozick, be transformed. One of the most important features of his account, and one that he seems least prone to regard as peculiar, is his emphasis on the notion of spiritual superiority, and indeed on a kind of *ressentiment*, a destructive and belittling envy that can be aroused by the spiritual superiority of people who, as Nozick sees them, have excelled in this cosmic role. Many of his passages that are most genuinely passionate are about this subject. They have the same note, and the same animus, as was to be found in *Anarchy, State, and Utopia* on the subject of envy directed toward more mundane forms of superiority. The tone of the present account introduces more than a hint of a competition in spirituality.

There is something very wrong with the way in which these notions are deployed in Nozick's writing: that is to say, there is something wrong with the writing, and also something wrong with them. The theory itself does not give much content to these ideas of spiritual self-improvement, and the level of generality prevents his giving us any side illumination from the merely historical or psychologically particular. He tries to give us the idea directly, so to speak, and the fact is that we cannot trust him as a messenger from any spiritual height, because by the time that he is fully launched on his cosmic role he not only cannot hear anything that is happening on Earth, but cannot properly listen to himself.

It is not merely a matter of the occasional sententious banality: "It is better and lovelier to be moral"; "imagination has always been a faculty prized by students of literature and art"; "in our own biographies, at least, each of us is the leading character." Such phrases are alarming enough—as Anthony Burgess's narrator says in *Earthly Powers*, "If I could write so blatant a tautology, I could write also of the goodness of evil or the badness of good, and probably, somewhere or other, did." But it is more generally true that the nearer we get to Nozick's image of what he calls "spiritually advanced persons"—the arousers of *ressentiment* in those unwilling to be, as he puts it, "helped along" in this direction—the more his capacity to listen to himself seems to lapse:

> There are some individuals whose lives are infused by values, who pursue values with single-minded purity and intensity, who embody values to the greatest extent. These individuals glow with a special radiance. Epochal religious figures often have this quality. To be in their presence (or even to hear about them) is to be uplifted and drawn (at least temporarily) to pursue the best in oneself. There are less epochal figures as well, glowing with a special moral and value loveliness, whose presence uplifts us, whose example lures and inspires us.

There is a lot more of this. There is even more about people glowing. Such writing sounds like Close Encounters of Some Yet Higher Kind, or a commercial for breakfast food. Whether its defects derive from the state of the modern world or from the English language now or (as I believe) from confusion about values, it will not do. And Nozick, even if he has switched off the monitor to Earth, will know, since he is a very good philosopher, that the problem cannot just be a matter of finding some happier way of saying the same thing.

In fact I think that the part of this book that is about value is utterly misconceived, and that the whole enterprise of approaching the problems in this abstract way, virtually unrelated to human psychology or society, and assuming ill-defined and suspect notions of spiritual superiority, is a large error. I do not believe that there is any cosmic role, and I think that Nietzsche was right when he said that philosophy should stick close to the Earth. But even if I am wrong, and there is something to be recovered from such conceptions, it is a basic truth, which Nozick seems not to have encountered at all, that it could not be recovered in these terms, or by such ingenuous methods. It is not a new truth. The wise men to whom Nozick sometimes refers, rabbis, gurus, Zen masters, have known and shown that the cosmic role, if there is one, needs a high measure of irony, personal and indeed cosmic, in order to be presented or interpreted. A craftier route to the beyond will always be needed, if there is a beyond, and the mere combination of cleverness with earnestness is not going to find it.

Note

1. *Philosophical Explanations*, by Robert Nozick (Belknap Press of Harvard University Press, 1981).

40

The Miracle of Theism: Arguments for and against the Existence of God, by J. L. Mackie

The late J. L. Mackie was a notably clear and hard-headed philosopher who brought great powers of argument and a demanding intellectual integrity to a wide range of subjects. He wrote with force and insight about logic, theory of knowledge, philosophy of science, ethics and the history of philosophy, and now, after his early death, which was a great loss to the subject, we have a book in the philosophy of religion.[1] It is very largely, as its subtitle claims, a study of arguments for and against the existence of God, though it extends naturally enough, and disapprovingly, to the discussion of some believers who have written in favour of trying to get by without any arguments.

Mackie was an analytic philosopher, but his philosophy was not in any conspicuous or interesting sense linguistic. After all those books of the 1950s and early 60s which took up the "language" of religious belief, it is striking that Mackie dismisses in a line or two problems specifically about the meaning of religious statements. He finds it for the most part fairly obvious what they mean, or at least those that assert or deny the existence of God or express his more general properties; I think that Mackie might have had greater difficulty with the meaning of some more specific Christian claims, such as the Trinity or the Incarnation. Mackie's problem is not about what it means to say that God exists, but whether it is true, and what reason there is to think it true.

He had in general a great respect for the natural sciences and a lot of his work concerned the relation of the picture of the world that is given by them to our other beliefs and reasoning. In this, too, Mackie differed from linguistic philosophy, though not so much from the logical positivism that preceded it. What his work most resembled, in fact, was a kind of analytical philosophy that preceded both of them, the philosophy of Broad and of Bertrand Russell. It is very much the spirit of Russell—though I do not think that his name is mentioned—that is to be found in this book: a spirit which is rational, sceptical, benevolent and firmly failing to conceal, at crucial moments, contempt for the evasive and hatred for the fanatical.

Mackie differs from Russell inasmuch as his arguments are longer and more careful, the history is more accurate and the finish is a lot less brilliant. There are also far fewer jokes, though Mackie does turn one dry pleasantry about the American philosopher Alvin Plantinga, who is thought by some to have rehabilitated the Ontological Argument by his researches in modal logic: "So perhaps St Alvin will . . . take his place beside St Anselm; at least he will have no difficulty in meeting the miracle-working requirement for canonization, after the success he has achieved in subverting (as Hume would say) all the principles of the understanding of so many intelligent readers."

Some of the text seems a little dutiful, and the amount of explanation given to various subjects is sometimes surprising; Berkeley's arguments, and Descartes's proof of God from our idea of him, collect a lot of detail, though neither can now seem at all compelling, while, on the other hand, the inexpert reader who wants to consider Plantinga's claims to sainthood is not given much help with his apparatus of "possible worlds". But this is a minor oddness of a book which, so far as the arguments of natural theology go, treats them with very great clarity, accuracy and intellectual care. For a detailed and perspicuous account of how it now stands with the First Cause Arguments, the Argument to Design (as Mackie rightly calls it) and the rest, I know of no book that does it better than this, and anyone who thinks that these arguments do anything to strengthen their conclusion has very powerful negative considerations from Mackie to contend with.

What the book does is to deal with those traditional arguments—no less, and, just about, no more. Mackie is above all interested in the arguments, and, more than that, he loses interest in those defenders of religious belief who are not themselves interested in arguments. He says that he prefers the "clarity and honesty" of classical works on this subject, and among present philosophers of religion who are believers, he prefers and often discusses the work of Richard Swinburne, a writer of similar temper, who also considers God's existence as a hypothesis to be assessed, and who is prepared to give a judicious estimate of such things as the probability, if God exists, that he should have created a physical universe. Mackie, in the later part of his book, does engage with some writers who treat the subject in a less rationalistic spirit, but, with the exception of William James, they do not get much of a reception. Some Wittgensteinian fideists, if that is what they are, are justly told off for "evasion and double-talk". Kierkegaard is found simply baffling. Pascal appears largely as an advocate of intellectual dishonesty.

A book which is as admirable as this, in many and not merely intellectual ways, and which confines itself to working its way, with negative results, through these arguments, must raise the question of where these ways of going on now stand. Its approach, it seems to me, concedes at once too little and too much to religion. It concedes too much to these arguments in pretending that it is an open question whether they could deliver their conclusion. They may in their various ways have incidental logical and philosophical interest, as involving one or another fallacy or equivocation, but I wonder what unbeliever now could be swayed by them towards belief, or what believer, looking for intellectual reassurance, could find it in them? It is not so much that Hume and Kant, to whom Mackie with characteristic candour and clarity expresses his debts, broke up most of this furniture a long time ago, but rather that the world since then has drastically damaged the rooms in which it used to stand.

Someone who is drawn to religion now—here as least, and I do not speak of Teheran—will be drawn to it by needs which do not simply come before these arguments psychologically, as Mackie would concede, nor try to provide a new argument (which will, as Mackie insists, be a bad one), but which rather invoke a conception of what religion does which seems remote from the spirit of these arguments. It is here that Mackie's approach seems to concede too little to religion: too little, that is to say, to the needs that it has served. He does indeed consider possible causes of religious belief, but, once more, in relation to an argument about truth. Is it an argument for the truth of religious belief that it exists at all? Of course it is not, since many causes of religious belief have been suggested, some of which could be adequate and not at all involve its truth. Feuerbach, Marx, Freud and others are thus appropriately mentioned, and to deal with the argument, that is enough.

But as soon as one sees religion, as Mackie rightly does, as a purely human phenomenon, it becomes a matter of great importance what human phenomenon it is, and which of these explanations, if any, is true. In particular, it is a crucial question whether the account of religion that one eventually has is one that represents its content—above all, its more unnerving and anti-humanist content—as something alien to humanity and its needs, now simply abandoned by advanced thought, or rather sees it as expressing needs that will have to be expressed in some form when the belief in God has disappeared.

It is because of these questions that the issues remain with philosophy. It might be said, and Mackie himself might have said it, that after the issues of truth and argument have been laid aside, there is no philosophy of religion, or at least no decent philosophy of religion, but only anthropology or another social science to help us, or perhaps the imaginative powers of literature. That may be right, so far as something called the philosophy of religion is concerned, but it is not the end of philosophy's involvement with religion. For in moral philosophy at least, and in the reflections about society and about the mind that must be part of it, there must be some attitude involved towards the needs that religion has served, and some consequences to be drawn from the ways in which it has served them.

In one of his more Russellian moments, dealing with Kierkegaard, Mackie says, "We are, in effect, back with the god of the Book of Job, and whatever we may think of Job himself, there can be no doubt that Jehovah comes out of that story very badly." But the author of the Book of Job knew that; or at any rate he knew something that raised the question for him very clearly. That religion can be, as Mackie points out, a nasty business, is a fact built into any religion worth worrying about, and that is one reason why it has seemed to so many people the only adequate response to the nasty business that everything is.

That does not make it true, and Mackie's truthful, reasonable and humane book tells us that very clearly. At the end of its forceful and economical arguments, however, one faces a paradox which arises from its own destructive success. It is only if religion is true that the most interesting question about it is its truth. If it is false, the most interesting question about it is not the truth or even the reasonableness of what it claims to tell us about the cosmos, but the content of what it actually tells us about humanity.

Note

1. *The Miracle of Theism: Arguments for and against the Existence of God*, by J. L. Mackie (Clarendon Press, 1982).

41

Offensive Literature: Decensorship in Britain, 1960–1982, by John Sutherland

John Sutherland has produced 'a calendar following a series of events (mostly trials) from 1960 to the present day', which deals briefly and brightly with obscenity cases from *Lady Chatterley's Lover* and *Fanny*

Hill to *The Romans in Britain*.[1] The aim is to investigate changes in public attitudes to 'offensive literature'. It is a lively survey, but is not the useful history of that process which might be written.

First of all, as a calendar, it is inaccurate. I would not rely on it for the date of Christmas. It does not state correctly the grounds on which the conviction in the *Oz* trial was overturned (misdirection of the jury on the meaning of 'obscenity'). It says on page 3, wrongly, that in the same case John Mortimer defended Richard Neville, and on page 122 that he did not. In one of the brief excursions into cinema, there is a very muddled account of the French treatment of pornographic films. Pasolini's *Salo* was not assigned to the 'P' category and sent to the blue movie-houses like *Deep Throat*. It was dealt with by a special administrative decree, which confined its showing in Paris to two art houses—a restriction which was firmly enforced.

This slip actually shows a serious misunderstanding of French attitudes to pornography and its relations to culture. They came out well in a conversation that some of us on the Committee on Obscenity and Film Censorship[2] had with a French official about the criteria for a film's being pornographic. He found the question not serious: 'Everyone knows what a pornographic film is. There are no characters or plot, there is nothing but sexual activity, and it is not made by anyone that one has heard of.' But, we boringly insisted, what if these criteria diverged? What if a film of nothing but sex were made by, say, Fellini? Pause. *'Personellement, je le trouverais incroyable qu'un film de Fellini soit présenté dans les salles pornographiques.'*

Carelessness is not confined to the facts. The book is written in a weirdly slapdash style, and is full of phrases such as 'bowdlerised limbo' and 'buttressing Albion's floodgates'. Some sentences are very peculiar. A 'custodial fear of cheap literature' is said to have been 'very active in the 19th century and can be traced back aboriginally, to obstructions on vulgate Bibles' (a vulgate Bible is, in fact, a Bible in Latin). The reasoning, too, sometimes seems to have slipped past the turnstile of thought while Sutherland was out. 'Pornography, of course, grows old very fast, which is why skin mags customarily carry no date of issue' presumably should read 'Pornography hardly grows old at all, which is why . . .'

The 'of course' in that last sentence is revealing. The book displays an attitude which can, quite often, be seen as a sprightly independence, but which sometimes sinks into a manner which has become a standard and odious feature of the radio interview, a knowing condescension to whatever view is being interrogated, from the standpoint of some other, vaguely implied, view which would itself be patronised and ridiculed if it were being questioned. The journalistic sneer slides lightly over every opinion, leaving a desolating sense that they are all equally prejudiced, naive or self-serving. Judges, barristers, liberal critics, pornographers and poets are all put in what Sutherland presumably regards as their place, though it is not at all clear where those places are. It would be ungracious of me not to mention that one exception is the Report of the Committee on Obscenity, which is treated in a very friendly manner.

Here and there in the book Sutherland gives an idea of the story he might have told about the changes in spirit that have occurred between the *Chatterley* trial and the present day. That story would have to consider three notable transformations. Then, the issues seemed to be importantly about literature, and now they do not. Then, pornography was a good cause for liberals, and now it is at best a nuisance. Then, those who were much concerned about pornography were all conservatives, and now they include some radicals. Associated with all these changes is the decline in esteem of the Obscene Publications Act, which started the period as the saviour of Lady Chatterley, but now seems confused, unhelpful, and too dependent on a useless definition of 'obscenity'.

The main reason why literature is no longer the issue is that the liberals' cause is, for now, largely won. After the acquittal in 1976 of *Inside Linda Lovelace*, not itself a work of literature, the DPP [Director of Public Prosecutions] seems to have given up on works consisting only of the printed word, and our recommendation that such works should not be restricted at all on grounds of obscenity was, as Sutherland says, virtually a recognition of the existing state of affairs. But the Obscene Publications Act and the other confused provisions remain, and who knows whether the literary issues that Sutherland is able to chronicle as past may not come back again? If they do, it is very hard to believe that the 'public good defence' offered by Section 4 of the Act could any longer be seriously thought to provide a respectable way of resolving them.

On the question of nuisance, the obtrusive effect of publicly displayed pornography, the Indecent Displays (Control) Act has had some effect — much the same effect, so far as the outside of the premises is concerned, as we recommended. The effect in some places is certainly awful, and the blank fronts of closely ranged sex shops an urban blight. As Sutherland says, 'row upon row of shuttered shops all containing wares of matching uniform ugliness, is not the urban renewal one would wish on central London.' Without the shutters, however, they would also, as he puts it, fill him with a 'Kurtzian exterminatory rage'. Here the only cure, short of a regeneration of society and the disappearance of the problem, seems to be measures to reduce the density of the shops, and I think that there is a good case for introducing planning powers, as we did not positively recommend, of the general kind that the GLC [Greater London Council] is taking, to lighten this environmental oppression.

In some other hearts, however, the Kurtzian exterminatory rage has turned against the whole business. The most striking recent phenomenon, one that Sutherland takes up in his last chapter, is the vocal (and sometimes physical) opposition to pornography expressed by the radical feminist movement: already established in the USA, it was not to be heard very distinctly in this country five years ago. Some of its materials are the same as those of more traditional protesters, and some are reworkings of old misconceptions: for instance, that all pornography is basically the same, making the same appeal to the same fantasies, and that those fantasies are very simply related to reality and to action.[3]

Other ideas are more distinctive, such as the assumption that if 'softcore' pornography is very sexist (as it is), 'hard-core' pornography must be even more sexist. This is not true. While a lot of extreme pornography certainly expresses sadistic fantasies against women, the standard blue movie, too hard-core to collect a BBFC [British Board of Film Censors] '18' certificate, is usually less sexist, whatever else it may be, than the contents of *Playboy* or *Mayfair* or the unspeakable and endlessly popular *Emmanuelle*.

This is because the conventions that divide the soft from the hard precisely involve differences in the ways in which the sexes are represented, in who may be shown in a state of excitement, and so on. Blue movies may exploit everyone, but they do not markedly more exploit the women involved in them than the men. There is some truth, if only some, in the idea that mass-circulation soft-core pornography is sexist primarily because anything mass-circulated is sexist.

Have the ugly and assaulting fantasies presented by pornography any right to exist? Does anything need to be shown, beyond their content, in order to deny that right? The feminist Left standardly thinks not ('pornography *is* violence against women'), and in this it resembles the militant Right. Neither party, interestingly, is first concerned with the question that preoccupies those who sit on government committees — and those who subsequently sit on the committees' reports — namely, what should the law be? Conservative pressure-groups (but not Lord Longford) have often been reluctant to be tied down to any details for a replacement of the Obscene Publications Act, and radical feminism is at best uneasy, sometimes openly contemptuous, about the machinery of regulatory laws.

In this, the feminists are more consistent than the conservatives. The latter have the same interest as the rest of the bourgeois community in the processes of law, and in the application of administrative discriminations to an imperfect society. But radical feminism is professedly utopian, and not concerned with such temporising measures as the regulation of pornography. The aim is to eliminate these fantasies, and what they express,

altogether. But whatever the cause of pornography and its aggressive fantasies is taken to be—capitalism, or the male principle itself ('women do
not have violent fantasies, only men do,' a woman said to me in a public
meeting, trembling with rage)—its elimination will need at least time and
transformation, some regulation will be needed in the meantime, and we
are left with the doubtless boring question of what it should be. In face of
the radical feminists, I am left also with a less wearily gradualist thought.
Pornography may well be internationally a substantial criminal industry,
and that fact in itself demands attention. But from the point of view of
cultural criticism, when one is confronted with what is still the pervasive,
lying and destructive sexism of almost all our popular culture, to go on
about the particular nuisance of pornography is largely a diversion to a
more traditional and much less significant target.

Notes

1. *Offensive Literature: Decensorship in Britain, 1960–1982*, by John Sutherland (Junction Books, 1982).
2. The Report of the Committee on Obscenity and Film Censorship, chaired
and largely written by Bernard Williams, was published in 1979 by HMSO.
3. This, among other simplifications, is excellently discussed by Susan Barrow-
clough-Ignatieff in her review of the Canadian film *Not a Love Story*: *Screen*, Vol.
23, No 5 (Nov–Dec 1982).

42

Consequences of Pragmatism
(Essays 1972–1980), by Richard Rorty

Richard Rorty's recent book *Philosophy and the Mirror of Nature* is an
original and sustained attack on the idea that it can be the aim of philosophy, or even of science, to represent the world accurately. Neither
activity can reveal, as he sometimes puts it, a vocabulary in which the
world demands to be described. The book is remarkable for its learning
and for its powers of critical exposition. At the same time, some of it is

slapdash, and its program for what philosophy should do when robbed of its traditional conceptions of truth and objectivity is, to put it mildly, schematic.

The present volume consists of twelve already published essays written between 1972 and 1980, together with a new introduction.[1] The jacket says that it fills in the details of the story told in *Philosophy and the Mirror of Nature*, but it actually does something more interesting than that. It reveals Rorty's attitude toward questions bearing on the central theories of the earlier book, and offers his view of other philosophers and traditions, including Heidegger, about whom he says that he would now want to revise his view upward. The essays here also have a hero, who was less explicitly seen as one in *The Mirror of Nature*. This is John Dewey; and the pragmatism of the title is above all that of Dewey.

Rorty claims to free Dewey from dated associations, and to find him already waiting at the end of a road on which Michel Foucault and Jacques Derrida are now traveling. Dewey's "chief enemy," Rorty writes, "was the notion of Truth as accuracy of representation, the notion later to be attacked by Heidegger, Sartre, Foucault. Dewey thought that if he could break down this notion, . . . we would be receptive to notions like Derrida's—that language is not a device for representing reality but a reality in which we live and move."

The new book shares some failings with *The Mirror of Nature*, and at the end we still do not know much about how philosophy should go on without its old illusions. Rorty's style also provides some minor irritations, such as his tendency to parade lists of great names and of turning points in the history of philosophy (something that could be a legacy from his early days at the University of Chicago). But the essays are wide-ranging, informed, and above all interesting. Rorty has an unsettling vision of philosophy, science, and culture, and it matters to what extent he is right. Like others who have a large view, he sometimes seems to the analytical critic to have run different questions together. What is not always true in such cases, but is usually true of Rorty, is that when he has run different questions together each of them turns out to have its own interest.

"It is impossible to step outside our skins—the traditions, linguistic and other, within which we do our thinking and self-criticism—and compare ourselves with something absolute." That is one of Rorty's central theses. Or, rather, it is several theses. The least contentious is that we cannot think about the world without describing it in some way: the world cannot present itself uncategorized. Moreover, there is no way in which the world simply describes itself, or presents itself in terms that could not themselves be the subject of inquiry, reflection, and alternative proposals. Those claims, in themselves, are not too upsetting. They still allow us to think that there is an independent world that we are trying to describe, and that what it is actually like can control the success of our descriptions.

Rorty's pragmatist, however, reaches much more drastic conclusions than this, and claims (so it seems) that all we can ever do is compare one description with another. He denies that "deep down beneath all the texts, there is something which is not just one more text but that to which various texts are trying to be 'adequate.'" He does not think that we can say anything substantial about the purposes served by our descriptions, against which we might test them. Moreover, in addition to this, Rorty has a further, historicist thesis, according to which the categories that any human group uses are a function of its time, and are essentially formed through historically localized tradition. The historicist thesis plays a large part both in *The Mirror of Nature* and in the present essays.

If one says that any human thought is inescapably immersed in the traditions of its period, what counts as "a period" is an important question; and, in particular, what tradition performs this basic function for us. Rorty is not very definite about this. In *The Mirror of Nature* sometimes it is the period of "Western man" or "modern Western man." In the present book the relevant item, at least once, is "human thought since 1600." The question particularly presses, because Rorty is so insistent that we cannot, in philosophy, simply be talking about human beings, as opposed to human beings at a given time. In the course of a perceptive discussion of Thomas Nagel and Stanley Cavell, both philosophers who (in different terms) hope to recover from the tradition deep philosophical questions that relate to human experience as such, Rorty precisely contrasts the approach of taking some philosophical problem and asking, as they might, "What does it show us about *being human*?" and asking, on the other hand, "What does the persistence of such problems show us about *being twentieth-century Europeans*?" (his emphases).

The historicist ideas do provide one fairly natural way of interpreting Rorty's main thesis, but they do not merely follow from it, even in its most radical form. Basically, he accepts the historicist outlook because he believes that the history of philosophy has itself led us to it. He thinks that Dewey, Quine, Wittgenstein, Heidegger, and Derrida are the true descendants in their various styles of Hegel and the nineteenth-century philosophers who reacted against the Kantian claim that philosophy could discover "the a priori structure of any possible inquiry. . . ." As he interprets them, they have led us to see that there is not much more to be said about the ways in which we describe the world than that they are the ways that suit us, now. Of course philosophy, traditionally, has tried to say more than that. It has tried to overcome what it has seen as deep and persistent problems about the relation of our thought and action to the world. For Rorty these writers have, accordingly, led us to a point at which traditional philosophy should end.

Sometimes Rorty takes a slightly different turn in his insistence on historical self-consciousness and in his rejection of general groundings for his or any other method. That we should see philosophy and other intellectual activities in the way he commends is not a lesson of where we have come to in history—something that we should rationally conclude from it—but simply a product of that history. We are where we now are, and that is how we, now, go on.

Rorty is not a relativist. He has as crisp a view as any positivist in agreeing, for instance, that it was a good thing that the world that was based on religious conceptions and authority has passed, and he cheerfully describes a certain attitude as "merely a relic of pre-Galilean anthropomorphism." But is he really in a position to dismiss relativism and the problems associated with it, as he does in one essay? The sort of dialectic in which Rorty's self-conscious historicism places him is one in which everyone can try to undercut everyone else by asking others whether they have allowed for the ways by which their own consciousness has evolved the very thesis they are advancing. Self-consciousness and reflective awareness, when made into *the* distinctive attitude of a sophisticated philosophy, make it revolve ever faster; the owl of Minerva, robbed by later skepticism of Hegel's flight plan to the transcendental standpoint, notoriously finds itself flying in ever-decreasing circles.

Rorty's procedures, in these respects, are an odd mixture. Sometimes he seems quite knowing about the status of his own thoughts (though he is not as quick on the turn as the French writers, such as Derrida, whom he most admires, or as the poststructuralist critics are, who need these reflexes to keep alive). At other times, he seems to forget altogether about one requirement of self-consciousness, and like the old philosophies he is attempting to escape, naively treats his own discourse as standing quite outside the general philosophical situation he is describing. He thus neglects the question whether one could accept his account of various intellectual activities, and still continue to practice them.

Some of the nastier problems of this sort arise with his treatment of the natural and biological sciences. Rorty's characteristic tone about science is that there is nothing in the least special or particularly interesting about it.

> Pragmatism . . . does not erect Science as an idol to fill the place once held by God. It views science as one genre of literature—or, put the other way around, literature and the arts as inquiries on the same footing as scientific inquiries. . . . Physics is a way of trying

to cope with various bits of the universe; ethics is a matter of trying to cope with other bits.

In a similar vein he says, in an article called "Method, Social Science, and Social Hope," that it simply turned out that the Galilean picture of the universe worked better than, say, an Aristotelian picture, but that there is no "epistemological moral" to be drawn from this. In particular, he argues, it is a confusion to think that the success of physics since Galileo is somehow connected with the fact that it regards the universe as "infinite and cold and comfortless," and it is a mistake to look for any scientific method that explains scientific success. Indeed, the question "What makes science so successful?" is for him a bad question. He applauds T. S. Kuhn's notion of Galilean science "as exemplifying the power of new vocabularies rather than offering the secret of scientific success."

In the essay just referred to, and to a lesser degree in *The Mirror of Nature*, Rorty runs together two questions. One is whether the success of science invites or permits any interesting description of what the success of science *consists of*. The other question is whether, from its previous success, we can derive any general methods to secure its future success. The questions are distinct. Karl Popper, for instance, who, like Rorty, thinks that there is not much to be said about the second question beyond banal recipes of rational procedure, also believes, unlike Rorty, that there is something to be said about the objective progress of science in finding out what the world is really like.

It is harder than Rorty supposes to throw away conceptions of the *aim* of science such as Popper's, and it is harder in more than one way. It is harder, first of all, because it is not clear what Rorty wants us to put in their place. Science "copes," "is successful," its vocabularies have "power"; but they have power or success in doing what? In generating predictions, Rorty is sometimes rash enough to say, and that means better predictions. Here we find we are being taken on an old-fashioned philosophical ride. Doesn't "better" mean, for instance, "true"? On Rorty's view there is no point in getting off at that stop: "Truth is simply a compliment paid to sentences seen to be paying their way." But what is it that we see when we see that they are paying their way?

This is a very old subject of debate, and it is still going on in orthodox analytical philosophy. Rorty's pragmatist does not want to win that debate or to continue it, but rather to opt out of the whole thing, to change the subject. Some analytical philosophers will say that he *can't* do that. But Rorty is surely right in saying that much philosophical achievement has consisted simply in changing the subject, and if the pragmatist changes this subject, he changes it.

To me the weakness of Rorty's position lies in something else, that he sees all this as a matter simply for *philosophy*; he sees changing the subject as making a move within, or out of, philosophy. This seriously neglects the extent to which the descriptions that he dislikes come from within science itself. Science itself moves the boundaries of explanation and of what is explained, just as it moves the boundary of what counts as observation. It was always a mistake for philosophers to contrast in any absolute way the "observable" and the "theoretical" in science, since theory creates and constitutes new forms of observation. Scientific theory explains, moreover, how such an elaborately constructed image as an electron micrograph can be the record of an observation.

The sharp distinction between theory and observation was a mistake made by Rorty's enemies, the positivists, who celebrated science for its respect for brute fact. But such criticisms of the positivists turn against Rorty himself, because they are an example of something which, it seems, he should regard as impossible, namely of science explaining the reliability of its own observations. Similarly science can often explain the truth of its conjectures. Advances in scientific theory quite often, in fact, involve explaining why some predictions of previous theories were true, while others failed. Not all scientific advance does that—no recipe fits all scientific advance—but it is one important phenomenon that gives substance to the idea of objective scientific advance.

More generally, it is an important feature of modern science, not mentioned by Rorty, that it makes some contribution to explaining how science itself is possible, and how creatures that have the origins and characteristics it says we have can understand a world that has the properties it says the world has. To say that such achievements as evolutionary biology and the findings of the neurological sciences, for example, are trivial, and that any old theory could do what they do, is simply a mistake (though it is true that limitless numbers of theories could deal with the same questions trivially). These ideas contribute, *from within scientific reflection itself*, to an image of the objects of science which Rorty says we should not have; they contribute, that is, to a conception of the world as it is, independently of our inquiries. That conception may be an illusion, but if it is, it is not the product of a simple philosophical error to be explained in a line or two of reference to Kant and his successors; and, above all, it is not simply a product of philosophy.

Correspondingly, it is not just a question of philosophy whether it is hard to give up that conception of the world. The other sense in which it will prove hard to give up is one in which it will be hard to give it up even if it is an illusion. It will be hard to give up for those working in science.

There is an important contrast here, which Rorty seems not to see, between scientific inquiry on the one hand and Rorty's interesting ideas about the future of philosophy. In a revealing passage he says that "pragmatism denies the possibility of getting beyond the . . . notion of 'seeing how things hang together'—which, for the bookish intellectual of recent times, means seeing how all the various vocabularies of all the various epochs and cultures hang together." That may be a program for the successor of philosophy, or for the literary studies from which he does not want that successor to be distinct, but it is certainly no program for science. The sense that one is not locked in a world of books, that one is confronting "the world," that the work is made hard or easy by what is actually there—these are part of the driving force, the essential consciousness of science; and even if Rorty's descriptions of what science really is are true, they are not going to be accepted into that consciousness without altering it in important ways—almost certainly for the worse, so far as the progress of science is concerned.

But if that is so, then a dreadful problem confronts the pragmatist: whether his ideas can be, in their own terms, "true" at all. For the pragmatist to say that his formulations are true presumably means simply that they work out: and what reasons have we to think that the pragmatists' sentences about science will work out better in the practice of scientists than scientists' sentences do? The point here is not that scientists have self-revealing knowledge of what they are up to, but merely that the scientists' sentences help to keep them going—and that, for the pragmatist, is all that can matter.

Indeed, there is a question whether the pragmatist can even appropriately *say* many of the things that Rorty says. Here there is a problem that was seen more clearly by Wittgenstein than by any of the other philosophers whom Rorty admires, certainly more clearly than by Rorty himself. If it is impossible to provide grounds for, or get beyond, what, at a very general level, we naturally say; and if philosophy, as traditionally understood, tried to go beyond that, and so should now end; why should it not *simply* end, so that all we should say is what anyway we naturally say? In *The Mirror of Nature* there are passages to the effect that we have merely found it overwhelmingly "convenient" to say that physics describes a world which is already there, rather than, for instance, that the world changes in relation to our descriptions. But if that is overwhelmingly convenient, and the only consideration can be what is convenient, then what everyone should be saying is simply: physics describes a world that is already there. So why does Rorty go on telling us *not* to say that?

Here the Rortian pragmatist, like the follower of Wittgenstein, is likely to say something to the effect that without the startling reminders he provides one may be misled, and succumb to false images of our situation. Misled by what? The answer often is—by philosophy, or by similarly irresponsible kinds of discourse. Wittgenstein often gives this answer (though he also gives the materials for some better ones): it is what underlies his famous remark that philosophy occurs "when language goes on holiday," a remark which, one might say, is, like some others of his, deeply shallow. In fact, the "misleading" impressions are encouraged not just by philosophy but by such activities as pursuing physics. So unless science itself is revealed as an unnatural or holiday activity, it is part of our nature, and not simply a product of philosophy, that we should be "misled."

But then there is a real problem of what content is left, on the pragmatist's assumptions, to saying that we are *misled* at all, and of what basis he can have for saying it, unless he tries to reoccupy the kind of transcendental standpoint, outside human speech and activity, that is precisely what he wants us to renounce.

There is, then, more than one question about how to read Rorty's descriptions of scientific activity, if we accept his view of what such descriptions can be. There is a different set of problems about the self-understanding, and the future, of philosophy. The problems are different, in particular, because Rorty expects science to continue—its "discoveries form the basis of modern scientific civilization. We can hardly be too grateful for them." But philosophy should come to an end; or rather, as he often puts it, "Philosophy" should, where the upper case stands for philosophy as a distinct *Fach* or professional undertaking. There will be room for a kind of post-Philosophical philosophy, a kind of cultural criticism, for which there is no very special expertise. Occasionally Rorty's speculations about the future of this activity strike a Marxian-utopian note; the nonprofessional inheritor of Philosophy will be a new Renaissance polymath doing literary criticism in the morning and history in the afternoon, and doing them in a spirit of Nietzschean gaiety.

Yet here again there is a problem about how this activity is supposed to coexist with a consciousness of its own nature. It is hard to see how these new forms of intellectual life can thrive for long, when they are at the same time so professedly second-order, derivative, and parasitic on the activities of those in the past who have taken themselves to be doing Philosophy in its own right. "Philosophers could be seen as people who work with the history of philosophy and the contemporary effects of those ideas called 'philosophic' upon the rest of culture. . . ." The reference to the history of philosophy, and the quotes around "philosophic," immediately reveal the inherited identity that backs up this image. Even the Nietzschean gaiety relates to the use of these figures of the past; it is with approval, I think, that he says of Derrida (one of those who recognize where we really are) that he "does not want to comprehend Hegel's book; he wants to play with Hegel."

I doubt, in fact, whether Rorty has extracted from the ruins, as he sees it, of Philosophy any activity that will sustain a post-Philosophical culture of the kind that he sketches. It is not very realistic to suppose that we could for long sustain much of a culture, or indeed keep away boredom, by playfully abusing the texts of writers who believed in an activity which we now know to be hopeless.

Rorty's views, however, affect more than the future of philosophy considered as a distinct activity. They raise important questions about the significance for culture in general of certain intellectual ideals—above all, a certain image of truthfulness—which philosophy, in some of its styles, particularly cultivates.

One of Rorty's aims is to overcome the division between scientific and literary culture; he refers surprisingly often to the late Lord Snow, associating with him various distinctions that are considerably subtler than any that occurred to Snow himself. At the same time, he wants to overcome the divide between two kinds of contemporary philosophy, broadly called "analytical" and "Continental." I have already said that so far as the future of culture is concerned, the first of these aims is not going to be realized in Rorty's terms, since the business of engaging in scientific research, and the intellectual motivations that people have for doing so, are so totally unlike making comparisons within a web of texts that even if (in some sense that Rorty still needs to explain) that is what science *really* is, the activity will, so long as it flourishes, reject that description of itself.

But that was a point about describing the aims of science, not of adopting a specific methodology, and even if science successfully continues with the conception of itself as discovering what is really there—if, that is to say, science continues—this leaves open most questions about its connections with any wider cultural or social conceptions of rationality. Here the other divide, between the two kinds of philosophy, comes into the picture. There is something in what Rorty says when he claims that analytical philosophy and Continental philosophy have been the public-relations agencies of science and of literature respectively.

There is something in it, though much is left out. Positivism apart, analytical philosophy has not been committed to the supremacy of science, or to validating science's laudatory images of itself, and all of this Rorty himself explains very well, both here and in *The Mirror of Nature*. (He says, incidentally, in the preface to that book, that it could as well have been written in a Heideggerian as in an analytical style, and it is simply a matter of his own experience that he has chosen the latter. He may believe this claim, but I doubt that anyone else does.) But it is certainly true that the discourse of analytical philosophy, its argumentative procedures, are more continuous with those of scientists. It seems to its practitioners more responsible, more consequential, less open to arbitrariness, whimsicality, and rhetoric than other styles of philosophy, and I suspect that it seems so to scientists as well, insofar as it does not seem to them, along with most other philosophy, merely pointless.

If Rorty is right, there is nothing to these contrasts at all, and analytical philosophy's claim to greater intellectual virtue, of a kind that has some general cultural significance, is simply baseless. It merely mistakes articulateness for clarity of perception and argumentativeness for rationality. It derives no prestige from its relation to science, both because there is no methodology that it can share with science, and because science isn't in any case what this philosophy generally thinks science is. Its characteristic neglect of the imagination is not a contribution to objectivity but a self-inflicted limitation. If analytic philosophy is like anything else at all, it most resembles the activities of lawyers under an adversarial system, and its admired skills are mainly the forensic skills of courtroom debate.

"Forensic" might be thought at least minimally a compliment, but the complimentary element is missing. Granted a legal system, forensic practices can be thought to assist justice. But without any analogous system of rules, without any accepted standards of argument and evidence, the forensic practices of philosophy will be left, for Rorty, only with the worst aspects of the adversarial system. Thus analytical philosophy is not more rationally organized than any other sort of philosophy; it merely employs a different kind of rhetoric, and uses different methods to bully opponents.

Rorty has made a vigorous and entirely serious challenge, which raises a question more important than merely how to do philosophy. That question can never in the end be that important, and Rorty himself criticizes some philosophers he admires, such as Heidegger, for overrating the significance of philosophy itself for civilization. But the value of philosophical styles of argument goes beyond the value of philosophy, because of the virtues that they try to express. No one has to believe that the questions of philosophy are the most important questions there are, or that philosophy can discover what mankind should be doing. But analytical philosophy does hold that it offers a very abstract example of certain virtues of civilized thought: because it gives reasons and sets out arguments in a way that can be explicitly followed and considered; and because it makes questions clearer and sorts out what is muddled.

On this view, analytical philosophy asserts important freedoms, both to pursue the argument and, in its more imaginative reaches, to develop alternative pictures of the world and of human life. It is both a creative activity and an activity pursued under constraints—constraints experienced as, among others, those of rational consistency. Its experience of those constraints, and the terms in which it approves those who most imaginatively work within them, is one where its spirit overlaps with the sciences. Both in this philosophy and in the sciences, the ideal is the old Socratic ideal that mere rhetoric and the power of words will not prevail.

This is the image of philosophy and its virtues that Rorty radically criticizes. He seems to me, however, very unradical and excessively optimistic in his picture of an intellectual community that has got rid of this image. Certain "conversational constraints" (of roughly Habermas's kind: he does not say much about them) will keep things together as much as anything ever does, and we shall just have to do whatever we can to sustain traditions of open-mindedness and receptiveness to new considerations. He does not want us to get too excited or unnerved by, for instance, Foucault's vision of discourse as a network of power relations. " 'Power' and 'culture,' " he writes, "are equipollent indications of the social forces which make us more than animals—and which, when the bad guys take over, can turn us into something worse and more miserable than animals." *When the bad guys take over*: there are at least four different ways of intelligibly stressing the words in that phrase, and each of them expresses an equally shallow way of thinking about what happens to a society when rational civility collapses.

No more than in *The Mirror of Nature* does Rorty give many indications of how discourse should go on when freed of the illusions of truth and objectivity. In the general cultural context, he is just as optimistically neglectful as he was in the case of science about the effects of everyone's coming to believe what he has to say—effects which the pragmatist, least of all, can afford to neglect. But that still does not mean that he is wrong, except possibly by his own standards of what it is to be wrong, and his challenge to the standards of what analytical philosophy calls clarity and rationality remains one to be taken seriously.

His kind of questioning has great force in a field that he himself does not take up, that of moral philosophy. Analytical moral philosophy has now revived the activity of theorizing about what is right and wrong rather than merely analyzing ethical terms. What this activity urgently requires, and has never yet managed to provide, is some coherent understanding of the relations of such theory to practice, where this includes the relations of the theorists to the rest of society. In the work of such philosophers as Peter Singer, it seems merely to be assumed that the virtues of an intellectual theory, such as economy and simplicity, translate into a desirable rationality of social practice. That represents a Platonic rationalism of the most suspect kind. There is no advance guarantee of ways in which humane and just social practices may relate to philosophical theory of any sort. That is just one application of the question that Rorty rightly presses, of the relations between the discursive virtues of analytical philosophy on the one hand, and desirable forms of social rationality on the other.

These essays along with *The Mirror of Nature* should encourage philosophers, and not only philosophers, to ask and pursue that question. There are lessons to be learned from the new and unexpected forms in which Rorty puts the question. There is also something to be learned from the weak parts of his account. The two major weak points are the inadequacy (certainly the pragmatic inadequacy) of his account of science, and the very weak indications that he gives of the nature of a post-Philosophical culture. Perhaps this double weakness expresses a strength in the traditional idea that philosophy and science can share a conception of truthfulness that is not merely an application of the will to power.

An account of the relation of science to culture should still start, it seems to me, from that impression which so powerfully affects its practitioners, and which is so dismissively treated by Rorty: that science offers one of the most effective ways in which we can be led out of the web of texts, the archive of discourse in which Rorty finds himself imprisoned along with the "bookish intellectuals of recent times." In his optimistic dealings with Foucault, Rorty quotes the dreadful sentence "Man is in the process of perishing as the being of language continues to shine ever brighter upon our horizon." I suspect that unless we keep the sense (cherished but misinterpreted by empiricism) that science finds ways out of the cell of words, and if we do not recover the sense that pursuing science is one of our essential experiences of being constrained by the truth, we shall find that the brightness of language on the horizon turns out to be that of the fire in which the supremely bookish hero of Canetti's *Auto-Da-Fé* immolated himself in his library.

Note

1. *Consequences of Pragmatism (Essays 1972–1980)*, by Richard Rorty (University of Minnesota Press, 1982).

43

The Collected Papers of Bertrand Russell, vol. I, *Cambridge Essays 1888–99*, edited by Kenneth Blackwell and others

This is the first volume of a projected series of all Bertrand Russell's papers, published and unpublished, to be issued in 28 volumes between now and the year 2000.[1] The volumes will be divided into two major groups by subject, so that volumes II to XI will consist of strictly philosophical material, while volumes XII to XXVI, containing political and social papers, will be ordered chronologically. A paper, for these purposes, is a 'public writing,' including political messages and open letters as well as newspaper articles, book reviews and essays. 90 per cent of these papers, the editors claim, have never been collected, and 15 per cent are unpublished.

This vast enterprise is edited from the Russell Archive at McMaster University, Hamilton, Ontario, an institution whose quiet existence on a scarp by the Niagara River was transformed when it became, through the purchase in 1968 of Russell's papers, the world centre of Russell studies. The editors have provided a full-scale apparatus, with elaborate annotations and textual notes. This is clearly intended to be a great monument.

The first volume covers, among other things, Russell's adolescent years, undergraduate work at Cambridge, and material associated with his first and second books: 'German Social Democracy' (1896) and 'An Essay on the Foundations of Geometry' (1897). A good deal of the material is unpublished. Some papers that Russell read to the Apostles, that now excessively well-known secret society, are included, to some extent marked by what Paul Levy, in his biography of Moore, unkindly called the 'sophomoric' quality of the discussions. Russell, urging the cause of the admission of women (not entirely popular with his brethren), observes: '. . . when we divided last term on "Can we love those we copulate with?" the presence of women in the discussion would have been invaluable.'

From his years as an undergraduate, there is a 'locked diary' ('the dons are sad specimens of wasted power, and have persuaded me that emoluments for mere academical distinction are a very pernicious institution'), and there are also some essays read to his philosophy teachers which, perhaps unsurprisingly, are greatly impressive. His history of philosophy is more accurate than in 'The History of Western Philosophy,' but there are fewer jokes.

The overwhelming impression is not merely the fact of Russell's precocity, but how much of his later style and manner was already formed in these earliest years. In 1888–9, when he was 16, he kept a secret journal written in Greek letters. It is full of sentences such as 'I now come to the most difficult of subjects, immortality, a question I have already tried to answer in this book, but, as now seems to me, on false lines of reasoning. . . .' He seems to have had from the beginning an extraordinarily easy and elegant way of writing, and some of the earliest pieces here are a great pleasure to read, while one is less irritated at this stage of his life than one is in his later writing by those less happy characteristics of the bright youth which he was never to lose—the occasional condescension, for instance, and the unnerving briskness. He said that by the time he came to write anything down, almost all the work had already been done; but the impression he too often gives in his mature work is rather that the work is being done then, at the speed it takes to read it.

After he left Cambridge, his wit also found its natural shape, and there are some funny pieces in the book, particularly an unpublished item on the Uses of Luxury. The introduction to this, incidentally, shakes one's confidence in the editors, who seem to be better detectives than readers. They have tirelessly uncovered possible locations at which the paper may have been read, but they also say that it defends inherited income, which it expressly attacks.

This very interesting book contains, as all this series will, public and scholarly documents rather than personal ones. We do not have so much here as we do in the 'Autobiography' of Russell's chilly declarations of his emotions, but rather discover him looking brightly and busily outwards, at intellectual and political problems. It is rather wonderful to see him so fully formed so early, exercising just the weapons he would use for the next 80 years.

Note

1. *The Collected Papers of Bertrand Russell*, vol. 1, *Cambridge Essays 1888–99*, edited by Kenneth Blackwell and others (Allen & Unwin, 1983).

44

Reasons and Persons, by Derek Parfit

Ten or fifteen years ago, the complaint against moral philosophy was that it did not address practical problems, but concentrated on meta-ethics: that is to say, on questions about the status, meaning, objectivity and so forth of ethical thought. That complaint is now out of date. For a decade, analytical philosophy has been conspicuously concerned to display its credentials for being of use in helping us to think about concrete problems.

In doing that, it has escaped the charge of evasiveness, but has slipped back into the line of fire of other accusations. One is that it has disconnected itself from other speculative, critical or, indeed, philosophical thought. Philosophers have tended to turn to ethical theory, an enterprise that tries to resolve practical dilemmas by appealing to a structure of moral principles, a systematic framework which philosophical ingenuity can hope to apply to concrete issues. This raises the question why a set of ideas should be thought to have any special authority over our sentiments and our lives because it has the structure of a theory. Besides having this very basic problem of what might be called theoretical authority, ethical theory has sometimes been impoverished because it has cultivated too much the autonomy of ethics, and neglected other areas of philosophy, and (with the exception of some philosophers such as John Rawls) other disciplines.

Derek Parfit has written a brilliantly clever and imaginative book which treats in a very original way a wide range of ethical questions.[1] It spends virtually no time on meta-ethics (perhaps too little), but it avoids many of the deformations that sometimes afflict first-order ethical philosophy. It makes contact with other subjects, such as welfare economics. It is deeply involved with some other parts of philosophy, in particular with questions of personal identity and of what a person is. It also starts the subject, rightly, not within the sphere of morality but in the wider area of practical reason, setting out from the question 'what have we most reason to do?' rather than from any distinctively 'moral' question.

Within ethical thought, Parfit does not start off with any ethical system. Nor does he hope to conjure one out of nothing at all. He concentrates on questions of consistency, asking us, over and over again, in different connections, what is implied by our ethical judgments, and whether what is implied hangs together with other implications to which, equally, we seem to be committed. That is not his only method. He uses many methods of ethical argument, more than moral philosophers often acknowledge. It is only when in his concluding chapter he quietly displays a few of them, that one realises how naturally they have been deployed. In these ways he goes some way to meet the problem of theoretical authority—though not, I believe, far enough.

In starting with practical reason, and in some of his methods of argument, Parfit agrees with the Victorian moral philosopher Sidgwick, whom he greatly admires. Keynes thought that Sidgwick lacked intensity and was suffocated by respectability. Parfit would deny these charges against Sidgwick, but whether he is right in that or not, the charges certainly do not apply to this strange and excitingly intense book. It is in four parts. In the first, Parfit considers what it is for a theory of rational action to be, in any of various ways, self-defeating. He deals, very subtly, with such problems as this: if one believes that one's aim should be to produce the best outcomes all round, it is very unlikely that the best way to do this is to consider, on each occasion, how one can bring about the best outcome. The best outcomes are more likely to be produced if each person acts from motives which do not involve thinking directly about the outcome. This has been thought to be a problem for consequentialist theories of this kind. Parfit insists that it is not, and that this result does nothing to refute the theory that we should produce the best outcomes all round. It merely tells us how to produce them, by cultivating in ourselves other dispositions. In other cases, however, theories can be damagingly self-defeating, by enjoining on each of us courses of action which, when we all pursue them, collectively defeat the objectives at which the theory was aiming in the first place (which is not so, Parfit claims, with the innocuously self-defeating consequentialist theories).

In these connections, Parfit has a lot to say about problems that have concerned decision theorists, such as the famous Prisoner's Dilemma, which makes it distressingly clear how courses of action that are individually rational can be jointly damaging, and also that when the parties know that fact, they may still have good reason to follow them. These issues, and many others of the same kind which he discusses, have a good deal to do with politics. Parfit makes it clear that they do, but he does not for the most part discuss them as though they did. The discussion is detailed, quite hard, and very revealing, but in social or political terms it is rather airless. He does not consider what institutions would be needed, for instance, or what forms of social understanding, in order to do what he, like Sidgwick, recommends us to do, which is to induce in ourselves dispositions of action which serve the ends of an underlying ethical theory while not revealing its content.

It is perhaps a pity that this rather daunting section has to come before the winningly ingenious discussion of rationality and time that forms the second part. In this Parfit asks whether we should be more concerned with what will happen tomorrow than with what will happen years from now, and if so, why. That is only the most familiar of such questions. He also wants to ask, for instance, why we should be more concerned with what will (or rather, may still) happen than we are with what has happened. Why is it good news that the nasty operation has already happened? If one is disposed to think that this issue, at least, is perfectly obvious, Parfit, with a very light touch, can turn one round to see that it is not.

In this section, too, he makes some important moves in a campaign which runs throughout the book and helps to unify it—the war against the Self-Interest Theory, which holds that the rational thing to do is to be concerned with one's own aims and interests as viewed, so far as possible, over one's whole life. This war Parfit conducts on two fronts, as he puts it. On one side, the theory is harassed by Morality, which says that we should be concerned with more than ourselves—for instance, with everybody. On the near side, it is undercut by the Present Aim Theory, which says that what it is rational for one to do now is what one wants now. For this view of things, or rather for a slightly more respectable version of it, Parfit makes a very good case against the Self-Interest Theory. One of his main objectives is to show that prudence does not have the special priority in rational behaviour that is often given to it. This is a good objective, but feckless readers who hoped to be liberated by it will find their enthusiasm dampened when they learn later that there is something wrong with imprudence after all: it is not irrational but immoral.

The reason for this is that our later selves are properly to be seen as rather like other people. Parfit is trying to get us to see that in practical reasoning 'when?' is much the same sort of question as 'who?' We should get rid of the picture that dominates us, or most of us, that there is some special identity that one has, some underlying item which is really *me*. We should get rid of the very compelling idea that there must always be a fully determinate answer to such questions as: 'Will that person who will be in pain in ten years' time be me or not?' On the true view of things, according to Parfit, there may be simply no answer to that question. We should realise that, as Hume believed, a person is no more than a collection of experiences held together by certain relations, such as those of memory and continuity of character. When we see that, we shall understand that it is misguided to draw a sharp ethical or prudential line between ourselves and others.

These are the subjects of the third part of the book. In the final part, Parfit turns to problems raised by our concern for future generations, in particular by population policy and the question of how many people there should desirably be. As with personal identity, he has already published articles on this subject, and has made notable contributions to it — for instance, in discovering what he calls the Identity Problem. This lies in the fact that when we discuss whether future people will be better-off or not as a result of our policies, we cannot suppose that the same people will be there to be affected by one or another of our policies, since our actions will radically affect what individual people will come to exist. Parfit shows how arguments that may seem plausible in this area can lead to undesirable results, such as the Repugnant Conclusion, as he calls it, according to which an indefinitely large population of people whose lives were just worth living would be morally preferable to a smaller population of people who were a lot better-off. Parfit tries to find a theory that will avoid this result and at the same time certain other paradoxes. In the end, despite much ingenuity and refinement of argument, he confesses failure: but he can claim credit for identifying some remarkable problems along the way, which will undoubtedly generate discussion for a long time to come.

The intensity displayed by the book is in good part argumentative. Short, sharply-defined sentences are loosed at one in compact formations; the effect, at times, is of one who will not let you go. But there is an imaginative intensity as well, displayed above all in the examples, often simple, carefully designed, each presented with a title — a device that could have been arch if used with less skill. Many of these examples are fanciful, particularly in the personal identity section, where teletransportation, bodily fission and other fantasies are introduced to construct cases that challenge our everyday assurance that we know what would and what would not count as the same person. Such fanciful cases have often been used by the philosophers who over the past decades have helped to set the agenda of Parfit's discussion. Others reject them, saying that our concepts have developed to deal with the actual, not with worlds extensively different from ours, and there is no reason to expect those concepts to be able to breathe that alien atmosphere. To this line, Parfit has several sophisticated replies. One is that this idea could explain why in certain unlikely cases we might not know what to say, but it can hardly explain why, with other equally unlikely cases, we do seem to know what we would say. In some matters, again, and personal identity is one of them, the whole idea of not being able to give an answer is something that our common notions seem to exclude, and is a basic part of the problem.

They are good replies, it seems to me, when these are regarded simply as metaphysical issues. But it is less clear why they are adequate when we are concerned, as Parfit is, with supposed ethical consequences of metaphysical positions. To put it another way, it is not always clear why metaphysical positions, arrived at in this way, have ethical consequences at all. Parfit is encouraged by his metaphysics of the merely agglomerated self to accept an ethical outlook which abstracts from self-interest and sees other people, and stages of oneself, as more like one another than we normally suppose. He thinks that philosophy should move us to a more impersonal outlook. But the extent to which it should do that must surely depend on what the world is actually like. If the experiences which constitute one person are powerfully related to one another, and give their owner (as Parfit, rather riskily, allows us to call that person) a strong sense of his or her own identity and of difference from others, why should a metaphysical belief, that he or she is really a fuzzy set of experiences, provide a reason for feeling and acting in some altered way?

Connections between metaphysical and ethical issues are central to this work, but it is not always made clear how they run. In at least one case, one which Parfit touches only very briefly, they do not run at all. He says that if, as some metaphysicians have claimed, the passage of time is an illusion, it cannot be irrational in practical thought to have no preference for one time over another, such as a preference for the near over the far. But this does not follow. If time's passage is an illusion, so is the flow of time apparently involved in action and deliberation themselves; relative to the metaphysical truth of the matter, the whole enterprise of practical deliberation, and all the various principles that might be brought to it, would alike have to be bracketed. If time's passage is an illusion, we live that illusion, and finding out that it was an illusion would not provide us with a reason for deliberating in one way rather than another within it.

Parfit can convert the metaphysical into the practical so easily, I suspect, because the view that he takes of the practical, and of experience in general, is throughout the book so radically external. Philosophically speaking—it is not true of his literary allusions—he sees everything from the outside. In dealing with personal identity, this conceals from him one of the main reasons why people think that it must be a determinate question whether some future experience will be theirs or not: that if it will be theirs, they can, as well as expecting that it will happen, also expect it, in the sense of imaginatively anticipating having it; and there seems to be no room for the idea that it is simply indeterminate whether I can appropriately do that or not. If Parfit had discussed that particular point, it would not necessarily have harmed his case, and it might even have helped to reconcile us to it. But in other ways his neglect of the first-personal view, in the theory of personal identity as in his earlier discussion of one's need to induce certain dispositions in oneself, leaves a gap. When we think how the argument is to be understood and applied, a dimension is missing.

In one respect, Parfit leaves it unclear whether he has adequately applied his metaphysical conclusions to his own argument. In the last part of the book, where population policy is in question, the idea that people are only aggregates of experiences seems to have been left behind. The whole discussion rests on a notion which seems uneasily related to that idea, the notion of 'a life worth living'. All Parfit's paradoxes involve the question whether the people in various populations have lives which are, or are not, worth living. But the discussions of personal identity and of prudence have earlier led us to distrust the ethical importance of a *life* at all. Perhaps a life worth living need not be taken to mean a life which as a whole will have been worth living. Perhaps it just means some living which, at any given time, is worth living. But Parfit cannot, as things stand, simply contract it to that. Almost the only clue that he gives to what is meant by saying that a life is not worth living is that people who had a life very much not worth living would kill themselves if they could. But he cannot use that notion without reference to the identity of the life that such a person would be ending. On his own view, that involves the question of the lives which suicide would be preventing: meaning by that, not the children that the agent would not have, but the selves that he would not become. Parfit cannot use the willingness to commit suicide as a neutral test of how a person values his or her own life. If imprudence is, as Parfit says, immorality, then suicide is murder.

There is another question raised by the section on population policy, besides those that come from the metaphysics of persons. That section tests more severely than any other part of the book the reliability of our ethical reactions when we are confronted with extreme and very abstractly presented possibilities. Correspondingly, it is the part that most calls in question Parfit's refusal to raise questions of meta-ethics. Asked by him to say whether it would be better if there were two large populations, not connected with each other, each consisting of people whose life was just worth living, rather than one of those populations with a standard of life rather higher, or some yet more complex question of the same kind, I may wonder what I am being invited to do. What real substance can such judgments possess?

The problem presses all the more when I have, for once, a belief on these questions that seems very solid, but it turns out that theoretical argument may lay it aside. Very many of us believe in what Parfit calls 'The Asymmetry'. If any child that I had now would (very probably) have a miserable life, that in itself would be some reason against my having a child now. On the other hand, if any child I have is likely to have quite a happy life, that fact in itself is no reason for having a child rather than not. We do not think in terms of doing the child a good turn by bringing him or her into existence. Parfit argues that we should probably think in those terms. To me, I must confess, it seems that 'The Asymmetry' is as clearly valid as anything is in this area, and while we certainly need a philosophical account of that impression, I do not see how theory acquires the power to cancel it. If moral philosophy is to do as much as Parfit hopes, by his very abstract means, it badly needs an account of the authority of theory.

However, here as elsewhere, the conflicts that Parfit has discovered are entirely real, and his imaginative and powerful arguments have uncovered deep questions which have in most cases never been explored so thoroughly, while, in other cases, they have barely been thought about at all. They are important questions, for practice as well as for philosophy, and in a moving last chapter, Parfit makes it clear how important he takes them to be. This ingenious, unusual, compelling book fully meets the importance of its questions.

Note

1. *Reasons and Persons*, by Derek Parfit (Oxford University Press, 1984).

45

Wickedness: A Philosophical Essay, by Mary Midgley

Mary Midgley believes that too many people suppose there to be no such thing as wickedness, and in the first part of her cheerful and chatty essay she sets about various outlooks that encourage their error.[1] She criticises relativism, for instance, which makes people think that no-one is to be judged, and also a kind of fatalism supposedly based on science. We cannot do without morality, she claims, and hardly anyone thinks we can: those who claim to have got rid of it are really advancing some new morality, which in turn is likely to emphasise some selected parts of an old one.

If we have to believe in some morality or other, does it follow that we have to believe in wickedness? Mary Midgley assumes too readily that most of familiar morality, including a belief in 'wickedness,' stands or falls together. In particular, she seems disposed to think that any ethical outlook we might come to hold will not only preserve the institution of blame, but will continue to give it a special significance.

But this need not be so. We can be sceptical about some of our ethical thinking without giving it all up. We might agree that some people were nastier than others, more selfish, treacherous or brutal, and react to them appropriately, without thinking that these vices were their fault. Would we believe in wickedness?

We certainly would not have to believe that there was one state of the soul that all these odious people shared. Mary Midgley herself does not believe that. She is against a unitary account of wickedness, either in a metaphysical form, or in the scientific style that tries to find the roots of all undesirable behaviour in a force such as aggression. Wickedness, she believes, is a negation, consisting in the absence of the virtues. There are many different reasons why people do not act or feel as we would ethically like them to. This is surely correct: but then it is unclear why there is such a topic as the study of wickedness at all. There is no general account of people's inabilities. Why does Mary Midgley think that there is a question for her essay to answer?

She takes there to be a question, I think, because some of the time, at least, she means more than this when she says that wickedness is a negation. Even when it consists in what looks like mere failure, in indifference, inconsiderateness, or brutality, she thinks that it is not merely a question of the agent's being unable to do better. She believes, as many of us believe, that the agent could have noticed or cared, if only he had bothered to. In other cases again the agent's intentions are (one might say) positively negative; his aim is itself to frustrate and hurt.

Why, she wants to ask, do people have such intentions? One answer that impresses her lies in the idea that wickedness is born of negation in a still deeper sense, that it comes from an emptiness that issues in envy and destructiveness. Some of the most thoughtful parts of her book are directed to this idea.

She makes some use of literature, and besides the perhaps predictable figures of Iago and Milton's Satan, there is, interestingly, Dr Jekyll ('any crash course on evil,' she happily remarks, 'must acknowledge a great debt to the Scots'). Freud is acknowledged, if a bit patronisingly, and she speculates briefly and suggestively about evolution. But at the end it is not quite clear how much she thinks these enquiries can explain, because it is still not clear what it is, in her view, that needs explaining.

Sheer motiveless destructiveness and malice invite explanation—that is why they are said to be motiveless. If that is what wickedness is, it indeed needs some special understanding. But when Mary Midgley assures us— *reassures* us, in fact—that there is such a thing as wickedness, when she repudiates the relativistic or fatalistic critics of morality as a whole, she has something wider than this in mind. 'Wickedness' then covers many more enemies of virtue, a whole range of ethical deformations—greed, possessiveness, resentment, cowardice, inconsiderateness.

Moral philosophers should indeed be more interested than they are in these things, and her book very helpfully tells them so. But she has not made it clear why, and how, such characteristics demand to be *explained*. This amiable essay is in several ways optimistic, and particularly because it finds something surprising in the fact that these are often our motives.

Note

1. *Wickedness: A Philosophical Essay*, by Mary Midgley (Routledge & Kegan Paul, 1984).

46

Secrets: On the Ethics of Concealment and Revelation, by Sissela Bok; The Secrets File: The Case for Freedom of Information in Britain Today, edited by Des Wilson

It is often said that the British are obsessively interested in secrecy. It is less often said how deep and peculiar this obsession is, and how much more there is to it than the well-known fact that British authorities are exceptionally secretive. Our interest is in secrecy as much as in secrets: it is the process, the practices and irregularities of keeping and revealing secrets, that concerns us. This interest in process rather than in content, together with the unconstructive and unfruitful nature of the obsession as it is regularly displayed, for instance, in the Sunday papers' excitement about spies, makes it like an attachment to pornography. It is typical of it that we find it hard to distinguish fantasy and reality. The unceasing scratching at past espionage is obscene partly because fact and fiction have merged: Blunt, Bill Haydon, Smiley, Peter Wright seem by now all at the same distance.

This obsession with espionage is that of investigators, of unmaskers. Its motives even with regard to secrecy are complex. It is obvious that the need to unmask and then unmask again assorted Cambridge spies is concerned with more than the secrecy of the information they gave away. It is fascinated by their secrecy as spies; by sexual secrecy; and by the previously hidden life of a ruling class that excluded the rest of society from its secret garden. This rage of discovery is equalled by the obsession of people in charge to keep things secret, not simply with regard to espionage—something that is hardly surprising, particularly if one's spies were also other people's spies—but in all areas of government. As Sissela Bok's book illustrates, it is a deep and nearly universal desire of those in power; Des Wilson's collection of articles powerfully documents and eloquently attacks its special intensity in this country, the most officially secretive among democracies.[1]

Sissela Bok's thoughtful book is not concerned only with official secrets, though they get a lot of attention. She discusses such things as the relations between secrecy, intimacy and privacy; there are many interesting observations, such as that the German word for 'secret' is directly connected with the word for 'home' (it is one of the words concentrated into the acronym *Gestapo*). She discusses self-deception, confession, professional confidentiality, police and journalistic investigations. She has some notable horror stories. There was the Holy Vehm, a secret vigilante organisation which was founded in mid-13th-century Westphalia and lasted until Napoleon. There is the chemical company which, having shipped the wrong additives to feed-grain co-operatives in Michigan, as a result of which many people had their health ruined and very many cattle died, threatened to sack any employee who helped investigators. For those who think academics more virtuous than business, there is the story of the social science experiment conducted in Pittsburgh in the Sixties, in which the investigator left schoolchildren alone with the spilled contents of a handbag in order to investigate their disposition to steal.

The book shares with Sissela Bok's earlier work on lying a disposition to give an even-handed and very judicious appraisal of the ethical issues raised by these questions of public and private truth. It is not always quite clear, however, whom she is addressing. On gossip, for instance—an admirable subject in this connection—her sensible remarks take a slightly severe tone, but I doubt whether she expects to have much effect on the frivolous gossipers she condemns, while the others do not need to be told. Not that she is too severe. She is properly unreceptive to the extreme strictures of Kierkegaard, and to Heidegger, who wrote with all his characteristic deftness: 'by its very nature, idle talk is a closing-off, since to go back to the ground of what is talked about is something which it *leaves undone.*' With this kind of thing, she rightly says, 'they erase differences and deny meaning in their own way.'

Sometimes her moral discussion speaks fairly directly to people who have to decide what to do in relation to the institutions of secrecy. Her chapter on 'whistle-blowing', one of her best, seems addressed to potential whistle-blowers, and asks what considerations you should have in mind if you are deciding whether to go public with the iniquities of the organisation that employs you. On other questions, she is concerned with what rules or practices would best serve the wide range of interests and rights involved. She rightly says that while there are of course many reasons why information should not be divulged, there are no reasons at all why the general considerations that govern official or professional practice should not themselves be public. Living in a society with a constitution, a Supreme Court, and many articulate lawyers, she is always conscious of these ideals of social transparency; in Britain, she would find the very idea of discussing the subject fairly unfamiliar, except at the level of evasive platitudes.

The deformations, in the USA as here, are not all in the same direction. If too much is hidden, too much is searched for, and often the wrong kinds of thing. The public's 'right to know' is often called up in this connection: Sissela Bok is sharply critical of the way in which this idea is constantly misused. If someone has a right to know a particular thing, she argues, someone else must have a duty to disclose it. But often when the right to know is invoked, as the paparazzi swarm in the trees or reporters effectively prevent the negotiations they are supposed to report, it is perfectly obvious that no one has a duty to disclose—it is merely that they may be forced to.

The claim of a right to know is often bogus, but it is not always so. It does apply if the information you want to know is information about yourself held by some public body. It also applies to a lot of information relevant to public decisions. The book that Des Wilson has edited, on behalf of the Campaign for Freedom of Information in Britain, brings out, in a section on international comparisons, how remarkably far Britain is behind other countries in these respects: behind in legislation, and still further behind in the degree to which it is implemented. According to the claims made here, even France, that notorious monument of unaccountable state power qualified only by the unco-operativeness of its citizens, is more liberal in these matters than Britain.

Different problems are raised by freedom of information in the two kinds of case. In the individual case, there are some issues of protecting the administrative process from cranks and fanatical complainants, and from the sort of publicity which means that no one can ever write down a frank opinion of an employee or candidate. Beyond that, it is a matter of making sure that information can be known to those whom it concerns and not to others, and this is not easy, particularly when—as these books point out—information is increasingly held by many interrelated agencies.

In the case of information about such things as decisions of government and reasons of state, and issues of policy and administration, there are wider questions about what can properly be demanded and for what reasons it may be withheld, and both these books sensibly discuss them. This includes areas of research such as environmental pollution, where (an article by Maurice Frankel in Wilson's book makes clear) public bodies, as things are, can have not only the right, but even the duty, to conceal information which is directly relevant to public concerns, and indeed to nailing polluters. The Wilson book is appropriately the more combative of the two. It emphasises yet again the dire influence of Section Two of the Official Secrets Act, which can be applied to any official transaction of any kind. This unreasonable and oppressive provision has been repeatedly criticised by the most respectable authorities, and survives only because it is selectively and hypocritically applied—which does not stop its being applied with extreme ferocity, as it was to Sarah Tisdall.[2] I did not know until I read this book that it passed through all its Commons readings and the Committee stage in just thirty minutes, during a war scare in 1911.

There is another set of problems, though, beyond the general issue of reducing official secretiveness, and beyond the details of what can reasonably be concealed. This is the question of how things are to be made known. In the personal cases, once more, it is not basically too hard: someone who wants to know should be able to go and find out, without too much trouble, expense or bureaucratic obstruction. But it is a different matter with the issues of public concern. When the public indeed has a right to know, who exactly has a right to do what? If there is to be freedom of information, whose freedom will it be? Neither of these books faces up to these questions.

The point was illustrated when Crossman's diaries were published. In the dispute about their appearance, there was a good deal of talk about the right to know, but it mostly neglected the point that as a source of knowledge about political events, Dick Crossman's testimony—even his testimony to himself—needed, to put it mildly, a good deal of interpretation. His individual and sometimes malign preoccupations provided no surrogate for a Cabinet Hansard. It can rightly be said that more information, if not about the discussions in last week's Cabinet (supposing there still is a Cabinet), would lessen our dependence on the preemptive memoirs of rival ex-Cabinet Ministers: but then there is the question of who releases what, and, above all, of the style in which it is made generally available.

Much would be achieved if important information, which could be found by interested people with skills to make it known, were more available than it is. But the right to know will be fully operative only if the media—the *means*, as they are supposed to be—are able to convey knowledge. Very little of the British press is willing to do that. It is not so much that it is untruthful or inaccurate, although it certainly is. It is rather that most of it makes truths meaningless, by presenting them in an instantaneous, superficial and fragmented way that defeats understanding. The state of the press is as much a problem for freedom of information as official silence is: it is the problem of making genuine information possible. TV in Britain is a more responsible and helpful medium than most of the press, but because it is transitory it cannot do things that only writing can do. No one has found a substitute for the coherent press that now barely exists in Britain.

These books are right: here as elsewhere, modern government is either deeply dedicated, or lazily attached, to concealment, and it is damaging and dangerous and deplorable. But the reluctance to let things out which is natural to all authority is wonderfully encouraged by the spectacle of what happens in Britain when they are let out. Many serious interests are defeated by excessive official secrecy, but it is not made easier for officialdom to remember that fact when most of the press does not represent any serious interest, or show any concern to make anything understood. The public, in some matters, does have a right to know, but the press cannot claim that right for itself until it makes itself able to provide the public with knowledge.

Note

1. *Secrets: On the Ethics of Concealment and Revelation*, by Sissela Bok (Oxford University Press, 1984); *The Secrets File: The Case for Freedom of Information in Britain Today*, edited by Des Wilson, foreword by David Steel (Heinemann, 1984).

2. Sarah Tisdall, formerly a clerical officer in the British Foreign and Commonwealth Office, was jailed for leaking British government documents to a newspaper in 1983.

47

Choice and Consequence,
by Thomas C. Schelling

This is a collection of papers that Schelling has written in the past twenty years or so, on subjects ranging from the general nature of game theory to nuclear deterrence, and from the psychology of self-control to the economic and corporate structure of organized crime.[1] The pieces are grouped by subject, not ordered by date (you have to do some digging in the book to find out when they were written). They are of varying weights and depths. Some contain detailed pieces of analysis, while in other places Schelling goes on in a more ruminating style, praising Thucydides as a strategic analyst or reflecting on the problems of giving up smoking. They are well written, always interesting, sometimes brilliant, and demand little technical knowledge: some, notably the essay on game theory, in fact offer it, in a very handy form.

Some of these papers demonstrate remarkably how economic concepts can be used intelligently to raise new questions about society and to suggest answers to them, in a way that can provide understanding without necessarily deploying new facts or even very unfamiliar ones. Particularly striking are the two articles (which slightly overlap) about crime, "Economics and Criminal Enterprise" and "What Is the Business of Organized Crime?" In these very clever and illuminating pieces Schelling first defines organized crime, as not merely crime that is organized, in the way that a squad of cooperative burglars with complementary skills might be, but as crime which seeks a monopoly. He goes on to discuss a whole range of questions, considering for instance what the structural conditions of an activity are that make it an appropriate business for organized crime; who its economic victims are; the resemblances of extortion to taxation; the reasons why those engaged in extortion may prefer to overcharge for an unwanted service, rather than merely removing money. These articles are interesting for more than the insight they give into crime. They should be read by political philosophers, for sobering thoughts both about the limits that may restrict legitimate power, and also about the nature of that power.

Differences in outlook between academic professions can parallel variations in what each finds surprising or unsurprising. Philosophers and others are often surprised (until they become old, cynical and well-read in the work of strategic analysts and decision theorists) at what those writers, like others who belong to the economic professions, can find surprising: such as the oft-overlooked fact that human beings seem actually not to measure the value of people's lives in terms of their discounted production potential or some such criterion. In this respect, Schelling is one of the most honorable exceptions, and sturdily refuses to be astonished by humans behaving like humans. A famous essay of 1968, "The Life You Save May Be Your Own," discusses ways in which lives, and in particular various possibilities of lives being lost, can be assigned prices.

The worth of that discussion is much enhanced by the way in which Schelling reveals without gush that he knows that there is more to the value of life and the horror of death than economics is going to catch. "I doubt whether this kind of population economics is worth all the arithmetic," he writes. "At best it is the way a family will deal with the loss of a cow, not the loss of a collie. Though children are not pets, in the United States they are more like pets than like livestock, and it is doubtful whether the interests of any consumers are represented in a calculation that treats a child like an unfinished building or some expensive goods in process." He displays an unsentimental tact which affects the content and the tone of his discussions. If a salary earner dies, "we should distinguish . . . between his life and his livelihood. His family will miss him, and it will miss his earnings. We do not know which of the two in the end it will miss most, and if he died recently this is a disagreeable time to inquire."

There are some subjects on which Schelling still seems to me more surprised than he should be. He is puzzled by the fact that a person sometimes behaves and feels like two people, giving commands and making resolutions which are often ignored or have to be enforced with external help. Though Schelling gives many striking examples and evidently knows how common such things are, he seems taken aback by the discovery of them. He is certainly puzzled, as many philosophers have been from Plato and Aristotle onwards, about how best to describe such cases, but here his puzzlement does not seem to find a sharp enough focus: in particular, despite sophisticated recent discussion by Jon Elster (to whom he refers) and others, he remains too attached to a simple version of the two-person model, and some of his speculations, for instance on ways in which the law might conceivably reinforce the prudent and respectable motivations, involve taking the model too seriously.

The book is subtitled *Perspectives of an Errant Economist*. As I have already implied, these essays are free from kinds of reductionism which non-economists often find a galling feature of economists' reflections on policy—galling, that is to say, when the economist claims or does not deny that it is policy he or she is discussing in these terms rather than economic aspects of policy. Schelling can press economic formulations in uncomfortable ways, but he knows where and why they are uncomfortable. A theme he comes back to more than once concerns the rights or wrongs of running aircraft, ships and so on with lower safety standards for customers who do not want or cannot afford a better and more expensive service. He knows that this may be found a rather distasteful proposal, but reasonably asks why. At the same time, he recognizes that the success of organized society depends on traditions, attitudes, beliefs and rules that may appear extravagant or sentimental to a confirmed materialist (if there is one). The sinking of the *Titanic* illustrates the point. There were enough lifeboats for first class; steerage was expected to go down with the ship. We do not tolerate that any more. Those who want to risk their lives at sea and cannot afford a safe ship should perhaps not be denied the opportunity to entrust themselves to a cheaper ship without lifeboats; but if some people cannot afford the price of passage with lifeboats, and some people can, they should not travel on the same ship.

It is all the more interesting that there are some points at which reductionism still gets in his way. It particularly shows itself in the opening essay, "Economic Reasoning and the Ethics of Policy," a fairly recent piece, where there are strong traces of two basic types of reductionism, both very typical of economic writing about ethical issues in policy making. One of them is more expressive of moralism than of materialism (though those two things were of course made for each other). This is the idea that the only ethical outlook relevant to policy is the attitude of being disinterested or impartial. "The ethics of policy," Schelling writes, "is the relevant ethics when we try to think disinterestedly about rent control [etc.] . . . I want to define the ethics of policy as what we try to bring to bear on those issues in which we do not have a personal stake. It is hard to find issues that are absolutely unsoiled with personal interest. On abortion and capital punishment our personal ethics usually dominate." (Schelling's emphasis.)

But he cannot think, and surely does not mean, that on those issues our personal interests are usually involved. What he means is that people have ethical opinions on these subjects which they care about and which are not simply a reflection of how they see everyone's interests. Schelling's own understanding, shown in many other places, is that people do have such attitudes, and it would have to be a very crass confusion of personal attitude and personal self-interest that would make one deny that those were ethical attitudes. Indeed, Schelling does not deny that they are—he merely says that they are personal ethical attitudes. But then it is not clear why they cannot be brought to bear on policy issues. The claim that they cannot needs more than a blank appeal to the ethical as impartiality. It needs a very particular account of the nature of the state.

Sometimes, Schelling goes in the other direction, and seems to suggest that the process of thinking impartially and in economic terms about policy eliminates the need for the ethical. If we think about rent control or gasoline vouchers, medical facilities or safety equipment, in the spirit of asking what we would hope to get if we were a recipient and what we would be prepared to give as a taxpayer, we may come to agreement: "And it would not strike us as an ethical issue." But it would be an ethical issue, and there is no reason why it would not strike us as one. The economic and contractualist formulations (those are not of course necessarily the same thing) do not eliminate ethical thought: they offer one way of thinking about (some) ethical issues.

These ways of thinking, moreover, as Schelling applies them, do involve another kind of reductionism. He is committed to thinking that when there is a question of distributing or providing certain goods, it must help to get things straight if one thinks in terms of turning those goods into money. On airport safety, once more, there is an ingenious discussion on what happens if we agree that you should get some of the tax money needed to buy airport lights, and you are left free not to buy airport lights with it. But the assumptions of substitutability that run through these discussions deny something that elsewhere Schelling willingly admits, that we think of some goods—life, safety, public health and order—as not simply goods that one is free to buy or not to buy. It follows that if people are thought to have a right or claim to them, which policy should honor, what has to be honored is an interest in those goods, not an interest in money which, if it is not spent on something else, might buy them. Indeed, there is something near to a contradiction in these arguments. Some important lack or need is identified in a section of society, for education, health, safety or whatever; when the question is raised of providing for this need, it is said that it would serve both efficiency and freedom better if the people involved were given money with which, if so disposed (and, one may add, sufficiently organized and so on), they can choose to provide for the need themselves. But those who make this argument have no brief for economic equality as such, and if the disadvantaged people had merely pointed out that they had less money than the others, there would have been no suggestion that they should therefore be given more. It is only because they were asking for those things that the discussion got going in the first place, and the idea came up that anyone should give them anything.

The reductivist economic argument neglects the ethical and, indeed, anthropological truths that not all social goods mean the same thing, and that they do not all mean the same as money: a truth well stressed by Michael

Walzer in his recent *Spheres of Justice*, and (as I have already said) well known to Schelling, at least when he is not discussing this kind of argument. It also neglects, or prefers to forget, a political truth, that when the original claim is turned into a claim for money, it is less likely to be honored. This is hardly surprising: if it had originally been a claim for more money, it would not have been listened to, except by egalitarians. In what Schelling calls difficult times ("it is the problems, not the times, that are hard"), one very important effect of seeing all social goods as money is that they can all with less difficulty be cut. Particularly when Schelling is talking about what he is doing, he tends to admit a reductionism about economic motivation and a restricted view of what is involved in living in an ethical community, which turn against the admirable concessions to human reality which he makes at other places.

Indeed, there is a question whether his concessions should not carry him further than he has gone at any point in this book. As the opening piece rightly implies by its position, a good deal of the economic analysis is related ultimately to policy: the idea at the back of the discussions, naturally enough, is that these ways of looking at transport safety, risk estimation or whatever, should be carried into practices for our society. They are indeed used in our society, and those ways of thinking, or very much crasser versions of them, standardly figure in social practice and political rhetoric at the present time. But the point Schelling so admirably made about the *Titanic* must apply more widely. Perhaps some people should be allowed to pay for better health care, while others with less money should not be denied the opportunity to entrust themselves to worse standards of medicine. But then they should not travel in the same society—or, perhaps, on the same planet.[2]

Notes

1. *Choice and Consequence*, by Thomas C. Schelling (Harvard University Press, 1984).

2. Originally published in *Economics and Philosophy*, 1985, © Cambridge University Press. Reprinted with permission.

48

Privacy: Studies in Social and Cultural History, by Barrington Moore, Jr.

The more time that citizens spend thinking about public matters, Rousseau said, and the less about their own private affairs, the better a society is. One good test of political sentiments is whether you find this thought invigorating or repellent. Either reaction to it, however, implies that you have an understanding of the contrast, some conception of the private.

Barrington Moore's book raises the very interesting question of what that conception may be.[1] His approach is to consider the quite different ideas of privacy and different attitudes toward it that are to be found in various cultures, thus bringing out the complexities of our own ideas of privacy. There are the privacies of intimacy, such as sexual privacy, which seem, except in ritual and other special practices, to be observed in a very wide range of cultures. ("The preference for seclusion appears to be overwhelming," as Moore puts it.) Much less widely observed is privacy for defecating and urinating, and among those functions male urination tends to make the lightest demands on privacy, something that used to be illustrated in the streets of Paris by a sparsely enclosed urinal, the *vespasienne*. (That revealing device has now been replaced by a strange, enclosed structure that is divided equally between the sexes and conceals its purpose so discreetly as to seem thoroughly suspicious.)

For an activity to be private in these ways, it needs only to be hidden; the concealment, as in the *vespasienne*, can be quite local: other people may readily know what someone, in private, is doing. Other kinds of privacy involve secrecy, as with the undisclosed transactions that take place in a family or among friends. Often, of course, as with other secrets, they are not so much undisclosed as unacknowledged, and what is indecent or embarrassing is to show that one knows. In Eskimo life, about which Moore gives some information, the cramped conditions of the igloo make heavy demands on this kind of convention.

In still other cases, experience is private because it is free from demands or obligations imposed by others. One is free to read, or to go to the movies, or to travel where one wants. This need not have anything specially to do with hiddenness or secrecy; it is merely accepted that at certain times one may do what one wants rather than what one is required to do. Moore particularly stresses this idea, and it is perhaps his central conception of privacy. But it immediately raises several questions. When the private is contrasted with public life or public concerns, as it is by Rousseau's remark, the world of the private does not have to be understood as one in which there are no obligations—rather, it is one in which there are no *public* obligations. Within my private life, I may be under an obligation to visit my mother; but if I am obliged, for example, to take part in political meetings, work on civic projects, participate in public ceremonies, or serve in the army, those obligations reduce the sphere of private life.

When we think about it in this way, the idea of the public seemingly comes first, and the private has to be understood as what, in time or space or feeling or social situation, is exempted from it. That idea takes a special form when, further, people claim a right not to be constrained by certain public demands. Any such right defines a kind of activity which is, in a way, private—expressing opinions, for instance, or publishing what one wants, or carrying on business. But we are now a long way from our starting point, and what is private in one sense may be public in another. Publication and free speech are both the opposites of secret, and these "private" activities can in their own way be contrasted with the privacies of hiddenness or intimacy.

How are these different aspects of privacy related to one another? Do they go together in various cultures? How far, starting from the narrowest concept of physical privacy, should one go to defend a substantial private life against public demands, resisting Rousseau and the claims of communal consciousness?

Barrington Moore asks these questions and encourages one to think about them, but he does not offer much help in answering them. He has produced a collection of materials rather than a book, and a collection, moreover, with some eccentric features. It is arranged on a comparative scheme, telling us about four different kinds of society and inviting us to consider them together with our own. He starts with one or two very simple traditional societies, each of them more or less lacking a formal authority. These primitive communities characteristically lack any developed contrast between public and private, but one of several interesting points is that even at these very basic levels of organized life some societies encourage people to be more reticent or self-contained than others do—differences partly (but only partly) related to their various styles of hunting or food gathering.

Many of the anthropological reports that Moore quotes are well worth reading. They should be studied by anyone (if there still is anyone) who entertains fantasies of the noble savage and the satisfying wholeness of the primitive life. One tribe in particular, the Siriono Indians of South America, is, as Moore describes it, startlingly horrible. The Siriono ceaselessly fight among themselves, hide food from one another, pay no attention to cripples, have a sense neither of privacy nor of common interests. The Jívaro Indians of Ecuador sound not much more amiable; about them Moore, no friend of Christianity, cheerfully remarks that as a whole, their "society and culture recall the Western European world of Gregory of Tours." To read some of the material in these early sections requires a strong stomach. One description of "penis bleeding" during a male initiation rite in the New Guinea highlands is so appalling that one wonders what anyone could learn about privacy from being forced to read it, beyond the generally useful reminder that even when privacy takes its most solitary and anomic modern urban forms, there are vivid styles of community life that are worse.

Moore next pursues the theme of privacy in classical Athens, emphasizing the peculiar relations between private initiative and public expectation that were held to produce good results for the general public in that society. Rich men were expected to pay for the choruses for the dramatic festivals, for instance, or for the triremes of the navy, as matters of individual public service. Going through, somewhat discursively, many aspects of Athenian social history, Moore shows how the Athenians tended to think that a fully developed life for someone who was adult, male, and a citizen involved public, indeed political, activity. The Greek term for a private person, he observes, is the direct ancestor of the word "idiot."

The private life that men (but not women) were expected to transcend was the domestic life, and they were expected to act to an important degree outside the home, in public places and in the presence of others. However, this distinction between the public and the domestic was not simply the distinction between what was displayed and what was hidden from the neighbor's attention. Domestic disorder and sexual irregularities were both acknowledged as being of strong public interest, and were subject to various restrictions. Yet the first democracy was already able to formulate a conception of the tyranny of public opinion; in a remarkable passage, which I did not find in Moore's book, Thucydides presents Pericles as saying:

> The freedom that we enjoy in our government extends to our everyday relations to each other. There, far from exercising a jealous surveillance over each other, we do not feel called upon to be angry

with our neighbour for doing what he likes, or even to indulge in those injurious looks which cannot fail to be offensive although they inflict no positive penalty.

Moore does not go very far or very professionally into the scholarship of these matters, quoting for the most part from what must have been a punishingly copious reading of Demosthenes and one or two other writers. When he gets beyond the Greeks, he relies even less on historical research, and confines himself in each case to taking points from one or two literary sources. The subject that follows the Greeks is not pre-Christian Jewish society, but the Old Testament ("the Revised Standard Version," he unnervingly remarks in a note, "is presumably more accurate"), and he seems not particularly vexed by questions of what sort of document, or set of documents, it is; even the claim that Solomon had 700 wives and 300 concubines he apparently takes to be a historical fact. He clearly has a personal distaste for Yahweh, and tends to find the Hebrews a tiresome and fanatical crew, regretting that they did not produce a more powerfully secular and analytic historian of themselves: "If a Hebrew Thucydides had been possible," he remarks—a wonderful possibility indeed—"our conception of that society might be quite a different one."

If he finds the Old Testament irritating, the classical Chinese writers who provide his last body of evidence seem to have proved rather wearying, and nothing very interesting comes from his reports of them. His attempt to base his account on comparative social history, after its opening movements, seems to have failed him. I wish in fact that he had laid aside some of the Athenian orators and the selections from translated Chinese sages, so that he could tell us how he sees the differing aspects of privacy as fitting together in the modern world, a question he interestingly raises in his closing pages.

There is a "modern pathology" of privacy, he remarks, meaning by that the defensive solitude, the unwillingness to get involved or come to the help of others, that are notorious in the modern city. It is perhaps wrong to see such behavior as simply an exaggeration of positive values that people have conferred on privacy in modern times. It can be seen as something quite different from those values and even opposed to them, since it is based on fear and indifference. A genuine recognition of others' privacy need not be based on those reactions, it could be argued, but can come from a respect for other people rather than from a lack of interest in them. There is something in this argument, but we also have some reason to be grateful that it often does not apply to the lives we lead. If one is not simply condemned to solitude, but actively wants privacy in order to protect one's happiness or to deal with one's unhappiness, one may be pleased that those around, rather than respecting one's rights with concern and restraint, simply do not give a damn.

One of the historical achievements of bourgeois culture has been the development of private life. Some features of that culture, including those that have most notably provided the makings of the novel, are falling victim to further developments of individual freedom itself. As Moore says, the special intensities of romantic love probably flourish most against a background of publicly supported conventions. He does not mean simply sexual conventions and the obstacles that they can provide. There also needs to be a convincing world of social rules and understandings that surrounds and conditions such a relationship. The rattle of Woody Allen's ironies, like the bleaker Bloomsbury memoirs and correspondence, reminds us that if all that is interesting to lovers is each other, there may not be much of interest.

I do not see how our societies can be kept going unless people are willing to acknowledge in some way the idea of a public order that means more than simply what is "out there." This would mean seeing others as citizens and not just as residents or wanderers on the same patch of ground. But the sense of shared citizenship that we need does not exclude or even weaken individual rights, such as the rights to privacy. On the contrary, it requires them. We have a sense of citizenship only if we think that others are like us, and one way in which we know that they are like us is that they need to be protected, as we want to be, from destructive and unpredictable intrusions, whether by the state or by other agencies.

The right to privacy, in its more intimate senses, is closely connected with the capacity to form close personal and family relationships, which must involve a circle of information and experience from which others are excluded.[2] (Edmund Leach, when he lambasted the institution of the family in his Reith Lectures, *A Runaway World*, particularly deplored its "squalid secrets.") Various reformers, revolutionaries, and social theorists who have stressed the values of community and citizenship have wanted to counteract the influences of personal and family loyalties, seeing them as potentially divisive and disloyal when they are exercised in their usual place. Rousseau was only one of many who have hoped to dissolve the private into the public. It is not merely Robespierrean champions of the virtuous republic who have done this, or Hitlerian embodiments of the less virtuous nation. Even some Fabians, too, in less oppressive style, have been suspicious of private life as a self-indulgence, and have despised what they have seen as its triviality and its lack of public commitment—the lack memorably expressed by Wilde in his remark that socialism would take too many evenings.

There are no psychological reasons at all to trust the policy of trying to affirm a useful sense of citizenship by destroying the private or by compulsorily extending it (which comes to the same thing); and there are many historical reasons for fearing it. A modern program to extend the sense of sharing in a community has to start from justice rather than fraternity, and has to recognize that social justice means something only if it acknowledges individual lives that have their own loyalties and are not entirely shaped to its demands. Rousseau's dismissal of private life in the interests of community was not only wrong and harmful; it was self-defeating, and a deeper understanding of privacy will help to show us why.

Notes

1. *Privacy: Studies in Social and Cultural History*, by Barrington Moore, Jr. (M. E. Sharpe, 1984).

2. The connection is well explained by James Rachels in an article called "Why Privacy Is Important," which is reprinted in *Philosophical Dimensions of Privacy*, edited by Ferdinand D. Schoeman (Cambridge University Press, 1984).

49

Ordinary Vices, by Judith Shklar; *Immorality,* by Ronald Milo

Judith Shklar's *Ordinary Vices* is a wise, clever, thoughtful book about the danger and the value of various personal vices—cruelty, hypocrisy, snobbery and others.[1] Professor Shklar asks how important they are; which are worse than others; what they can positively do for society, and how their meanings differ from one society to another. She uses a wide range of writers, but her book gives far more than a well-written set of reflections on what has been thought about these bad characteristics. It also explains and (in a fairly unassertive style) defends a certain view of society and politics, a liberal view, in terms of which these vices can be ordered and understood. The connection works in the other direction, too: if you think that cruelty, for instance, is more important than other vices, that will already lead you in certain political directions. Judith Shklar, like her heroes Montaigne and Montesquieu, thinks that cruelty is more important than anything—that it *comes first*, as she puts it.

She is good at detecting cruelty. She finds it, for instance, in the heart of some philanthropy, but unlike others who have made that discovery, she does not give up hating it. Moreover, unlike some others who hate cruelty, she is alert to the dangers of that hatred: in particular, its ready decline into a desolating misanthropy which can itself be a source of cruelty. It is essential to hold back misanthropy, which can destroy almost any virtue. What holds it back is not merely benevolence, or any other virtue; for Montaigne, it was uniquely friendship that 'resists that avalanche of disgust which can at any moment overwhelm anyone'.

Because she puts cruelty first and fears misanthropy, she distrusts the special hatred that much modern feeling reserves for hypocrisy. She quotes a long passage from the 'stunning scene' in which Uriah Heep— 'looking flabby and lead-coloured in the moonlight'—explains to David Copperfield the experiences that showed him the value of being 'umble. 'Dickens was a great connoisseur of hypocrisy,' she writes, 'yet he was not obsessive about it . . . Why has his sense of humanity been so rare? Why are people so overwhelmed by loathing for hypocrisy?' In answering her question, she explores, as Hegel did, the modern virtue of sincerity: in particular, a sincerity which, in the absence of agreed ethical standards, may dangerously take on the role of providing the ethical standard all by itself. She points out that those who denounced the insincerities of Victorian capitalism probably did less, in doing that, to alleviate its horrors than the liberal reformers who had their own styles of insincerity. She reasonably reminds us that in many circumstances, especially extreme ones, it may not matter very much what people's motivations are, and a nice concern that they should match what people say can wait for less demanding times.

All this is finely done, but she gives most of her attention to self-conscious hypocrites, or at least to those who do not have to look very far to detect their own dishonesty. One of her favourite authors, Molière, provides a gross instance, Tartuffe, and an example also of the destructive hatred of hypocrisy, in Alceste, the misanthrope, with his fear of being deceived. But that fear, which is indeed a powerful political and ethical force, is not directed only against self-conscious deceivers. Those who have been called the three great unmaskers in modern thought, Marx, Nietzsche, Freud, all alert us to forms of deceit that do not merely overlay personal or social motivations, but help to constitute those motivations. In the spirit that these writers helped to create, those nowadays who are concerned with truth at all are often worried that they may be living a false life or in a false world. The impulse to uncover these false-hoods may very often leave us only in a state of unfocused, debilitating and resentful suspicion, but the impulse itself, and the desire to live truth-fully, are not merely superficial features of the modern world—least of all as that world is conceived by liberalism—nor are they merely the legacy of a self-destructive Protestant Christianity (though, as Nietzsche said, they are certainly that as well).

Judith Shklar encourages us to accept a fair measure of evasion and bogusness, and so far as personal relations are concerned, she gives some good reasons for adding this to the platform of the campaign against mis-anthropy. But I doubt that it will be enough to stop her liberals being nagged by the need for truthfulness, or even being overcome, on a bad day, by disgust at the complacent, evasive and self-serving rubbish that piles up in our channels of communication. The aspiration for a society and a life that understand themselves, or at any rate can reasonably think that they are not based on deceit, goes deep with us: indeed, the appeal of her own text has a lot to do with that aspiration. Her book must be read in the tradition of those who force us to become undeceived about the humbug which has helped to make people too keen on killing one another.

Snobbery comes next in her catalogue after hypocrisy, and she thinks that they are connected: 'the link,' she writes, 'is obvious enough: both are false claims to merit; both are expressions of utter insincerity.' I can-not understand this, any more than her definition of snobbery as 'the habit of making inequality hurt'. It seems to me that people can be great snobs who are entirely sincere and who also think that it would be either bad form or a waste of time to hurt those they see as their inferiors. At one point I wondered whether Judith Shklar's account suffered from the archetypal snobbish error about snobbery—that it can afflict only those who are not actually in a superior position. But I think that the thinness of this section, the weakest in the book, comes rather from two other causes. In the first place, and very much so, she is American, and while, as she makes very clear, there is a great deal of American snobbery, it tends to be rather simple: uncomplicatedly unpalatable, like some kinds of American food. Again, snobbery, like insomnia, is something that you really find interesting only if you suffer from it. Both reasons taken to-gether suggest that to write well on snobbery one had better be English (for instance) and a snob: Harold Nicolson, whom she quotes, did better on this tiresome subject than she does.

She scores some good hits, for all that. She points out that 'two of Eu-rope's main racist theorists, Gobineau and Lapouge, were bogus counts. Snobbery and racism, in fact, belong to the same family: cousins.' She ruthlessly nails the dangers of the radical snobbery that can lead to dazzling political ambitions in academics. She is rather too kind about this phenomenon in Britain, but she thinks that it creates 'political expectations and daily manners that are useless and indeed self-defeating in America. The most recent public display of these illusory hopes was by the servile and fantasy-ridden court that gathered around President Kennedy.' There is a remark about university snobbery itself, as seen in her own institution, that leaves it wonderfully unclear whether her characteristic irony is or is not in play: 'it is a snobbery that does not follow from the recognised fact that Harvard is indeed a very great university, perhaps the greatest, but from the fancy that it is the only one that matters.'

Judith Shklar sees her book as belonging to political theory, and that is an important fact about it, particularly because some of it does not seem like that, looking rather as if its reflections lay in the ethics of individual life. But it is precisely their relations to personal morality and to individual character that define the concerns of her political theory. In one section, her excellent discussion of betrayal, her concern is directly to bring the domestic and the political together, to remind us, for one thing, how unspecial the circumstances of political treachery may be. 'Some people are so passive and so unaware of the character and activities of their friends that they virtually collaborate in their own betrayals. The complaisant husband used to be such a figure; but a careless, class-bound intelligence service, such as the British, is no different.' She has an outstanding section on 'My Country or My Friends', which is the best thing I have ever read about E. M. Forster's famous remark to the effect that if it came to it, he hoped that he would have the courage to betray the first rather than the second. 'Even without its heroics,' she starts, 'this is not an intelligent statement,' and it is hard to see how anyone, two pages later, could disagree.

In her last chapter, Judith Shklar describes her book as 'a tour of perplexities, not a guide for the perplexed'. In that chapter she delicately nudges our perplexities about the relations in a modern liberal state between personal character, both of citizens and rulers, and the state's impersonal system of law and administration. There is more connection between them, she concludes, than the founders of liberalism hoped, but less, much less, than is demanded by those who see it as the business of the state to make men good. She embraces in this what she calls a 'liberalism of fear', and agrees with Montesquieu that 'the real point . . . is not to paint the free citizen as a virtuous person, but to insist that without freedom everyone is intolerably paralysed or demeaned.' To put cruelty first is to acknowledge that 'one fears nothing more than fear,' and the political consequences of acknowledging it, she rightly claims, are enormous. Many have felt, in the past, and once again now, that it is impossible to reconcile, to the extent that liberalism needs, a state seen merely as impersonal regulation, and an ethical life understood in terms of personal character and sentiment. She does not claim to tell us how to do it, and she may possibly underestimate its difficulty: but she rightly makes this question central, and she leads us in a compelling way to some of its deepest implications.

In allocating her work to 'political theory', Judith Shklar implies that it is not, or not simply, philosophy. Ronald Milo's book illustrates in this respect, as in others, her wisdom.[2] *Immorality* is a competently argued, and hence all the more depressing, example of Anglo-American moral philosophy at its most arid. As is often the case in this subject, it argues for something that no sane person ever denied except in philosophy: that there are many different ways in which people may come to do the wrong thing—through having the wrong moral ideas, for instance, or having the right ones but being too weak or negligent to act on them, or simply not caring what morality says. These and other possibilities are distinguished and sensibly defended against implausible and very abstract philosophical arguments claiming that they are impossible. But the discussion is oppressively controlled by these arguments themselves, so that most of it is very thin controversy and little of it realistic moral psychology. It suffers, too, from a standard deformation of the genre, which consists in subscribing to the unity of the philosophical profession through the ages. The people referred to are those who turn up in philosophy courses: this practice excludes all great writers with three or four exceptions, and also unblinkingly brackets together geniuses of philosophy, authors of half-forgotten textbooks, and the author's colleagues, so there is a good deal of, as it were, 'this view is held by Aristotle, Trubshaw and, in his earlier article, Birnbacher.'

The most important weakness of Milo's discussion, however, comes from its exclusive attachment to the notion of morality. This has two results, which together more or less kill off the inquiry before it starts. The agent who is considering what to do is represented as thinking that a certain action is 'morally wrong' or 'morally right', and the question of how his actions are related to that thought is then discussed. But this is at best a very special case. We can understand our capacity to behave badly only if we start from the obvious fact that we think most of the time in much more specific ethical terms. When we go wrong, it is often because we think, for instance, that a piece of cruelty is just, or an injustice is helpful, or that to avoid some brutal act would be cowardly. The space in which those self-deceptions can occur is the same as that occupied by sounder thoughts, and it is much larger, and provides many more hiding places, than the area provided simply by 'right' and 'wrong'. The influence of the morality system shows up, too, in what is said about our own or others' reproaches. The only question for Milo seems to be whether one is blamed or excused, as though we were dealing with some transcendental penal system. In fact, our ethical life is made of many more reactions than those, and they play a large part in the account of how we may live well or badly. How does 'morality' deal with the many reasons for behaving badly that lie in the desire to be loved? As another of its 'temptations', no doubt, like a craving for marmalade.

That her book is about political theory means for Judith Shklar that it is in good part about history, and one of the things that she understands historically is the abstract morality system itself, and the problems that it has generated since it came into being. This history is our history, and her book is specially rich because its psychological understanding is rooted in history; for the same reason, the historical materials she gives us are unfailingly interesting. Unlike a lot of what is called 'moral philosophy', her admirable book is not all about books, and when it is about books, it is about good ones, of many different kinds.

Notes

1. *Ordinary Vices*, by Judith Shklar (Harvard University Press, 1984).
2. *Immorality*, by Ronald Milo (Princeton University Press, 1984).

50

The Right to Know: The Inside Story of the Belgrano Affair, by Clive Ponting; *The Price of Freedom,* by Judith Cook

Two months ago I was in a country where, in a dreadful economic situation, surrounded by memories of a recent and very nasty tyranny, and conscious that the forces that had sustained the tyranny had not simply disappeared, people close to the government were discussing in a very concerned and scrupulous way the limits of free speech; the independence of the judiciary; the extent to which justice requires the law to be definite and not to rely on vague and catch-all phrases; how far it is an adequate defence of what public servants may do that they are obeying orders or carrying out the policies of government. Lawyers, philosophers, administrators in that country are struggling to place a democracy securely on ground that for the past fifty years has not been at all receptive to it, and they are trying to do so in a way that makes intellectual sense.

That country is Argentina, and it is one of several deep ironies that surround Britain's relations to it that the new democratic government there should be seriously concerned with a correct understanding of these questions of individual rights, while the British government tries to discipline its public servants with a vague law that no one with any respect for rights can accept, and British judges are prepared to interpret that law with formulae that would certainly, now, be unacceptable in Argentina. It is a further irony that the most recent and dramatic case in which that law was brought to bear, the prosecution of Clive Ponting, was concerned with the conduct of the war to which, together with the junta's own folly, the present Argentinian government owes its existence.

Argentina's democratic government is probably Mrs Thatcher's finest achievement. She does not seem to value that achievement, as opposed to having won a war "against Argentina"; if she did, she would allow the diplomats to be a little more flexible in their formulations about the future—the distant future—of the Falklands, as it is rumoured that they would like to be. There are virtually no Argentinians who doubt that the islands belong to Argentina, and while the subject is not at the top of any agenda, it might be important to the Argentinian government that it could show some progress on the question. At the moment the democratic government still has breathing-space, because the military are discredited and anti-democratic opponents are tainted by association with them. But it needs all the help it can get, and it might help if it could point to a trace of a hope of future negotiation. If British policy insists on being as obstinate with the democracy as with the junta, it neglects the only good thing that the war achieved.

Members of the junta are now on trial, before a civilian court. The government has been accused of insufficient zeal in pursuing the crimes of the previous régime; while I was in Buenos Aires, a party of Socialist members of the European Parliament arrived to give the Argentinians the benefit of their disapproval on this subject. The complaints are that the authorities have taken too long and that they are not prosecuting enough people. There was a purpose behind the delay. For both constitutional and political reasons, the military had first to be given the option of dealing with the crimes in a military court. They had a predictable difficulty in either accepting or refusing, and did nothing. When the time-limit expired, the cases came to a civilian court, a procedure which also brings with it television coverage, which has been giving the Argentinian people a sustained and painful history of the junta's activities.

The question of how many should be prosecuted, and how far down the line punishment should travel, raises the issue of the "Nuremberg principle", whether acting under military orders can count as a defence for acts that would otherwise be criminal. It also raises questions of policy. An indefinite campaign to pursue everyone who has committed brutal acts under the previous régime may not be the best way to reconcile the better elements of the military to a democratic government, or to help people to take the existence of that government as an irreversible fact.

The questions of principle that interest the thoughtful people close to President Alfonsín run in the other direction as well. How far should those in command be held responsible for brutalities if they did not authorize or know about them? In practice, however, a lot of evidence at the trial suggests that these were not commanders whose behaviour need raise any very refined questions of this kind. A notorious instance quoted to us was the matter of the undertakers of Córdoba, who wrote to the then President (not Galtieri) to seek compensation for the extra work generated by the large detention centre in that city: the President replied that they had a case, but their submission should properly be made to the governor of the province.

Another, perhaps more typical, example came up at the trial on the afternoon we had the opportunity to visit it. A young woman appeared, a schoolteacher, who had been associated with the trade union. Her evidence was that one evening she had been picked up, thrown into one of the famous Ford Falcons, taken to a detention centre, and tortured. Later, her blindfold was removed, and she was confronted by an imposing military figure. "You know who I am?" he said; it was Galtieri. "You know that I have the power of life and death over you?" She accepted it. "What is your name?" She told him. "It is the name of my daughter. You may live."

Granted a recent history of such crude and melodramatic tyranny, the concern shown by the present decent and determined government for human rights and for their detailed interpretation may seem to some heroic or even quixotic. To the people we talked to who were associated with government it seemed, simply, essential; if they did not do everything they could to stick to the rules and to develop respect for them, their government was nothing and there was no reason why they should be in power rather than someone else. Many British people, I suspect, may cheerfully agree with them to the extent of thinking that such practices may well be a good thing *for Argentina*. It is a typical British reaction to think that an insistence on formulating individual rights may be needed in a country that lacks a democratic tradition, a history of orderly change and citizenly good sense—it is part of the price one pays for an unhappy history: in a country such as ours, however, where a better past has left us with a shared sense of what counts as fair and reasonable behaviour, such obsessions are irrelevant and probably damaging.

Clive Ponting's book, *The Right to Know*, is important not just for what it tells about the history of the sinking of the Argentinian ship General Belgrano, but because it shows particularly clearly that these complacent assumptions about British life and the justice of our arrangements will not do.[1] On the history itself, only an expert in the complex subject that Tam Dalyell calls "Belgrano studies" could say whether all the details are correct. Even those who know about these events only by following the newspapers will recognize that there is at least one matter—his delay in owning up—that Ponting passes over. Occasionally it is less than clear what is report and what is speculation—on the question, for instance, whether the commander of HMS Conqueror, the submarine that sank the Belgrano, sought confirmation of the order to do so. But in general it is a well-told, unpretentious and impressive tale. It is forgivable, I think, that Ponting should emphasize the respects in which Dalyell was right in his dogged pursuit of the government, and should say little about the wilder suggestions which may have done something to leave the impression that this is a crank's and bore's subject raising no very substantial issues. It is certainly not that. Beyond the immediate issues, which are important enough, of how this government behaved, the affair raises central questions about our political culture.

The circumstances surrounding the decisions that empowered the Navy to sink the Belgrano on May 2, 1982, when it had been sailing away from the Task Force for eleven hours, are very clearly set out, so far as they are known: in a few important respects, they remain obscure. Ponting does not press any charges against the government in the matter of the sinking itself or the motives for authorizing it. His accusations are aimed at the subsequent cover-up. This started from Mr Nott's statement to the House of Commons on May 4 which contained three major errors of fact, when correct information had been available for thirty-six hours. False or misleading statements were included in the White Paper and the Official Dispatch which were published in December 1982, while various prevaricating answers were given in Parliament to the tireless Dalyell. Ponting gives a summary of six falsehoods that were several times repeated about the position and course of the Belgrano when it was sunk, the time of the order to attack it, and other matters. By March 1984, the Government was under increasing political pressure about its story, and Ponting, as a senior official at the Ministry of Defence, was asked to write a paper giving a detailed chronology of the events leading to the attack: this was the paper that came to be called "The Crown Jewels".

Ponting gives a very interesting account of some ministerial discussions about what should be done with this material. Heseltine was at first in favour of giving more information, but backed away from this, and in fact admitted to the Foreign Affairs Select Committee on November 7, 1984, that his objection to telling some of the truth had been that he might have to tell more of it. Evasions continued, in reply to letters from Dalyell and from Denzil Davies, in answer to Parliamentary questions, and in preparing answers for the Select Committee. In all this, there was one Minister who, according to Ponting, always recommended as strongly as he could that they should tell a simple lie, that all the relevant information was classified: this was John Stanley, who is still, as he was then, a junior Defence Minister. It was when the Select Committee had been deceived that Ponting blew the whistle, revealed the relevant facts to Dalyell and was eventually prosecuted under Section 2 of the Official Secrets Act.

The questions of principle raised by Ponting's account are closely connected with that very bad law. Section 2 of it is concerned with what is called "the unauthorised communication of official information by a Crown servant". "Official information" means any information (secret or not) that a government servant acquires in the way of duty: it thus means virtually anything. An "unauthorised communication" is said to be a communication to someone other than a person to whom the public servant is authorized to communicate it, or to whom it is in the interests of the state that he or she should communicate it. Ponting's case is not only the most recent and one of the most dramatic cases brought under this section; it also elicited from the judge, Mr Justice McCowan, an interpretation of this provision which managed to shock even *The Times* and which, with any luck, will help in the long run to bring it about that the Act, already discredited, will be seen to be indefensible and will be repealed, as the Franks Committee indeed recommended in 1972 that it should be. What McCowan was reported as saying was that the policies of the State had to be understood as the policies of the government in power. As an interpretation of the Act, this is in fact very peculiar, since the Act refers not to the policies of the State, but to its *interests*. Even McCowan, presumably, if he thought about it, would find it hard to claim that the interests of the State were identical with those of the party in power, so it is actually obscure what he thought he was saying, except that Ponting should be convicted, a proposal which the jury laudably resisted.

It is not a good idea to have an Act—any Act, but particularly one covering matters so closely connected with the public interest—that has such vague and threatening scope. It is also not a good idea to have judges who do not care, or who are unable to think, what the principles underlying such a law might reasonably be; and one of several important lessons of Ponting's case is that we have good reason to distrust a legal culture which does not train judges to reflect in any coherent way about the point and the limits of the law.

We certainly need new provisions to secure freedom of information, and another important lesson of this case is not merely that this is so, but that a standard line of argument used against such proposals is worthless. Ponting quotes Mrs Thatcher, who in 1984 argued against the Freedom of Information Campaign with the usual claim that freedom of information would diminish Parliament and reduce Ministers' answerability to it.

As a reply to the issues raised by this case and by the Belgrano affair, this entirely misses the point. It was only because Ministers had been misleading Parliament—individual Members and a Select Committee alike—and intended to go on doing so, that Ponting acted as he did. Perhaps there was a time when conventions of ministerial behaviour were strong enough to make it safe to rely on the pressures that Parliament can apply. If there was such a time, it was those conventions, and not just Parliament, that were protecting us; in any case, if there was such a time, it has gone. In this respect, as in others, we have to recognize that the tacit understandings which used to make Britain a relatively liberal country have lost their power, and we must develop a more explicit style of political culture, based on new institutions to guarantee stated and enforceable rights.

Any legislation designed to increase the information available in society, and make us less liable than Britain notably is to deceit and mystification, has to be based on careful thought about the point of our having access to various kinds of information. There is no general "right to know", in the sense that if you would merely like to know a certain thing, then people, unless there are very special reasons, are obliged to let you know it. The mere fact that members of the public are interested in certain information, or a journalist thinks that they will be, does not give them, or him, a right to that information. What is true is that there are vital interests, individual and collective, that can be safeguarded only granted access to relevant information.

The actions and policies of government are not the only areas in which our vital interests require knowledge to be available. Judith Cook's crisp and densely informed book, *The Price of Freedom*, which offers a forceful argument as well as a compelling collection of horror stories about the British reliance on secrecy, touches a number of such areas, including nuclear power policy and medical research.[2] She also discusses the different kind of case in which an individual has a special right to know certain information because that information is about him or her. But the business of government must be a special case, because it affects so many vital interests, and because of what democracy is supposed to be. Granted certain obvious exceptions, of which the genuine concerns of national security are indeed one, the assumption should be that what government is up to is in all senses the public's business.

We urgently need institutions to put that assumption into practice. I am not saying that the Ford Falcons, or their British equivalent, are an imminent threat; it is a mistake, the same old British mistake, to think that it is only in those circumstances that they are necessary. We need them also to provide some protection against prejudiced, lazy and poorly argued decisions, which at the moment are hidden within the circular wall of Whitehall's typical assumption that since the administration knows more than other people, interventions by those people can only be poorly informed and useless, so there is no point in giving out more information.

Freedom of information has a lot to do with avoiding oppressive government, corruption and complacent inefficiency, but it is not simply to be seen as a means. It is more intimately involved than that in the proper relations between government and people in a democratic and liberal state. Suppression of public information not only may lead to tyranny—in its own way, it is tyranny. The friends of liberty in Argentina understand that, and we should do so as well.

Notes

1. *The Right to Know: The Inside Story of the Belgrano Affair*, by Clive Ponting (Sphere Books, 1985).

2. *The Price of Freedom*, by Judith Cook (New English Library, 1985).

51

Taking Sides: The Education of a Militant Mind, by Michael Harrington

Michael Harrington started in literature. As he says in the introduction to this collection of his essays, his mentor was T. S. Eliot, "a self-proclaimed monarchist and classicist."[1] But he came to be a liberal journalist, a theorist of democratic Socialism, and, above all, a political activist, and this book, collected from the writings of more than 30 years, consists for the most part of reports from the front, bearing the occasional reactions, self-accusations and justifications of someone who has constantly sought to explain himself, his changing commitments and alliances, to himself and to the world.

There are not only reports, but reflections. The book, divided by subject as well as by time, sets out his thoughts on a range of things from the politics of the Peace Movement to the political novel and the lessons that Disney World has for Socialists (a splendid piece). Some of the material comes from a long way away, or will now seem so to those younger or from a different place. Just occasionally the controversies of the day before yesterday become inaudible under coverings of discretion: "For Mr. F., C. H., and others, there is a counterposition between political freedom and economic and social freedom. As Mr. F. writes . . ."

Sometimes Mr. Harrington writes in his own defense, but self-justification is by no means the prevailing tone. He has written a new introduction to each section, which gives his sometimes rueful assessment of his essays and of the situations to which they responded. He writes with more realism than some old campaigners ever achieve, and with a commendable honesty: "I was, after all, a young and enthusiastic man under the spell of a soaring theory and that often leads to over-arching generalizations that do not exactly hold up. So even though I find much of what I said valuable and true, my prediction was simply wrong."

He honestly brings out his conflicts of the 1960's, when an admiration and sympathy for student radicals was at the same time checked by a sharp dislike of what he calls "youthful middle-class petulance and self-indulgence." There are a few false notes in all this, some hollow heroics and also moments of self-abasement; but from these fraught documents, crumpled papers from a time of deep conflict and a personal breakdown that occurred in 1965, he comes out as having sturdily declined to join those of the older left who immolated themselves in guilt and envy at the greening of America. He reminded impatient middle-class radical grandees of the interests of working people; insisted that the aim of protesting the Vietnam War was to stop it; and at the same time held the corner for democratic legalism and the First Amendment, partly for the very sound reason that the suppression of speech is agreeable to the right, and there are more of them.

Mr. Harrington calls himself a "social democrat." His democracy—in the sense of protected rights, not of mere populism—is impeccable. Dissociating himself from the illiberal enthusiasms of some young radicals, as he also does when attacking the Stalinists, he was concerned not to let himself become a professional anti-Communist. Giving the American

Committee for Cultural Freedom a working-over in 1955, he shrewdly remarks: "The *kind* of anti-Stalinism which follows from supporting the Smith Act [to outlaw the Communist Party], or even from supporting it with numerous qualifications as Sidney Hook does, is fundamentally different from that which follows from condemning the Smith Act."

What about the social, or Socialist, part of his social democracy? The organization with which he has been associated is called "Dee-Sock," the Democratic Socialist Organizing Committee. He engagingly describes it as being on the "Left wing of the possible." Its aim is to take Socialism from the margin of American society, to help Socialist ideas contribute in the next move to the left in American society, which he predicts will occur some time between 1986 and 1992.

In Britain, we have a political party called the Social Democratic Party. It split off originally from the Labor Party and now runs in an electoral alliance with the Liberal Party (which is not exclusively liberal in an American sense). A few of Britain's Social Democrats might call themselves Socialists; most, though they entertain some radical aspirations, would probably now not do so. That title would still find its natural home in the Labor Party. Although Mr. Harrington, so far as I can see, never mentions the Labor Party, he describes his relations with various other European parties of similar outlook in a way suggesting that his sympathies would be with the central, non-Marxist traditions of the Labor Party.

But the Labor Party, both electorally and ideologically, is a declining force. It may possibly revive enough to benefit from the rejection of Margaret Thatcher's Conservative Government, which even the most pessimistic suppose must come about one day. But it has few new ideas, and those that it does have fit together badly with its old ones. At one point Mr. Harrington identifies the aims of his Socialism, very much in the Labor Party's terms, as the redistribution of wealth, government intervention on behalf of disadvantaged people and the extension of public ownership. In another piece, he is more cautious about the last; like his friends in European politics, he has also become more cautious about the power of public ownership in itself to increase either justice or efficiency.

In some respects he has moved away from the traditional European Socialist conceptions of centralized economic management to ideas of participation (which, in British politics, are put forward with particular enthusiasm by the Social Democrats' allies the Liberals). He stresses the importance of workers' control and, more generally, decentralized decision making. He even suggests that critical minorities should be provided with resources by the management to help them in criticizing management. These proposals are not very practical, and they are certainly not very economical; although Mr. Harrington, as the structure of his book shows, is good at moving on from outdated ideas, he seems to find it hard to abandon altogether the 60's notion that the task for radicalism is to plan a society with limitless resources.

Apart from questions of cost, a prime question about the proposals for participation and workers' control is how they are supposed to hang together with the old Socialist objectives of the redistribution of wealth and the use of government power to benefit the disadvantaged. The aim of the left is to make economic power more responsive to popular needs, more just in its distribution and effects and less subject to the vagaries of private greed. What the European left is facing is that, far from reinforcing one another, these objectives in many ways conflict. It used to be thought that public ownership was the means to all these objectives, but few except the most conservative (strongly represented in the British Labor Party) now believe that.

Many have come to see that there is no reason to expect that if power is decentralized among local or factory groups, this will generate decisions in favor of social justice on a national scale. What about regional policy, for instance, or the related problems of declining industries? Why should those few holding on to jobs in the rust belt—in the northern part of Britain, for instance, now an industrial desert—vote for anything except support of them?

Why should those in more hopeful spots want the limited resources to go in that direction? What can possibly resolve those deep conflicts of interest except very powerful central governments, which at the end of the line must be resistant to many local demands?

These are the problems of the Socialist inheritance now, and Mr. Harrington has not fully faced them. The same problems are even more obvious on the international level. There is no reason to expect that decisions democratically made on a national scale will help justice between countries or regions of the world, and when Mr. Harrington says that Socialism will provide the solution to the energy crisis and famine, his attitude must seem a monument to the triumph of hope over experience.

In 1981 a Socialist Government was elected in France. It has not been a great success, and it has been forced to abandon many of its distinctively Socialist initiatives. Mr. Harrington honestly chronicles this, and says, bravely, that he is not discouraged by it. But perhaps he should be, and by the many other circumstances that are now causing those in Europe who have their heart on the same side as Mr. Harrington to rethink anxiously their political objectives and to wonder how far in the present world they are compatible with one another.

Socialist ideas are still a significant source for a critique of social justice—perhaps more so in America than elsewhere, just because in America Socialist ideas have been so much at a discount. Mr. Harrington has certainly been a tireless champion of that critique. But he, like the rest of us, must face the fact that the picture of what it would be like for those ideas to succeed is less distinct and vivid than it once seemed.

Note

1. *Taking Sides: The Education of a Militant Mind*, by Michael Harrington (Holt, Rinehart & Winston, 1985).

52

A Matter of Principle, by Ronald Dworkin

When I took part—as it seems, many years ago—in a Committee to recommend reforms in the obscenity laws, we received evidence from an American constitutional lawyer who happened to be in England, was an expert on the subject, and agreed to come and talk to us about it. He explained the complex constraints exercised by the First Amendment to the US Constitution, which says that no law shall be made to abridge the freedom of speech. He rehearsed various devices that lawyers and legislators had used to try to get round these constraints in order to control pornography, including the argument that pornography was not, constitutionally speaking, 'speech'. When he had gone out, one of the lawyers on our committee, Brian Simpson, said: 'I think I should explain something to the Committee. Americans believe in rights.'

Ronald Dworkin is also an American lawyer; he is Professor of Jurisprudence at Oxford and much of the time resident in England. He assuredly believes in rights, and his first and now very well-known volume of papers has the title *Taking Rights Seriously*. He is, as well as a lawyer, a philosopher (in the technical or academic sense, not merely at the breakfast table), who addresses himself to questions of political and moral philosophy as well as to the nature of law. This spread of interest is well illustrated in the present collection of essays, which range from the political and moral basis of law to the ethics of reverse discrimination, questions of civil disobedience, and the rights, indeed, of free expression.[1]

Some of the pieces are a bit slight, constrained by the occasions that gave rise to them, but there is no reason to regret the inclusion of any of them. It would be a pity to miss the 12 pages of forensic argument (originally presented at the Metropolitan Museum) from which Dworkin concludes that a liberal state can support the arts, consistently with egalitarian principle and without either 'paternalism' or 'élitism', so long at least as it does not support one kind of aesthetic endeavour as being more excellent than another. I am hoping that, for his next act, he will show how to administer this policy.

This and other pieces rest on Dworkin's egalitarian conception of social justice, and it is a pity that his arguments for that conception are not more strongly represented here. He has written two very substantial articles favouring equality of resources as a political ideal rather than equality of welfare. The central idea, roughly speaking, is that equality should be determined in terms of what is distributed rather than in terms of the satisfaction of wants or preferences of the recipients. He favours this not only for philosophical reasons—the measurement of welfare or utility has always been a suspect activity—but also for more than one moral reason. The appeal to utility seems often to give the wrong answer, as when those with greedy or over-fastidious tastes come out with a right to more. A basis in resources, moreover, leaves more elbow-room for the recipients' freedom.

These articles, which have already started a controversy among economists, are for some reason not reprinted here, and these important interests are represented only by a brief piece against utilitarian supplysiders, and his review of Michael Walzer's book *Spheres of Justice*, in which Dworkin rather loftily denounces a theory which in fact has more to offer on these problems of equality than he allows—in particular, by allowing more room for the historical peculiarities of a given society than Dworkin's conceptions do. Dworkin looks to a timeless moral framework in matters of justice, and when he is talking about legal adjudication rather than political equality, and so is manifestly confronted with the special practices and institutions of a particular place, one of his major preoccupations is to explain how judgments which have to be determined by the traditions of a given body of law can nevertheless be regulated, as he supposes they should be, by the timeless moral framework.

The range of Dworkin's interests, the connections he naturally sees between the law, politics and general ethical principles, are not a purely individual matter, though he displays very great individual brilliance, ingenuity and intellectual power in discussing them. American lawyers tend generally to be interested and involved in more than the law: or rather, the law and lawyers turn up in more places than those reserved to the law in other countries. Everyone knows of Americans' legendary litigiousness, but besides lawyers who chase ambulances or take an action against the bus company when someone's grandmother has had a heart attack at the sound of a horn, there are others who, for instance, virtually run corporations, playing much the same role in making American business flourish as accountants do in ruining ours.

Then there are those that change their country's history. In 1954 the Supreme Court, deciding *Brown v. Board of Education*, ruled that racially-segregated schooling was unconstitutional, and thereby brought about very large changes in American society. Even those who wonder whether a constitutional court is in general the best engine of social change cannot fail to be moved by this extraordinary image of a nation under law, where a few men in black gowns can decide under the constraints of argument that an historically entrenched practice is illegal, and the power of the state is then deployed to stop it.

Dworkin does not say much here about the difficulties that are to be found in such a system, such as its sensitivity to the political and ideological composition of the Court. When he is considering the decision of particular cases, as in his discussion of the Bakke case (which raised questions of principle about reverse discrimination), he is very much aware of these political matters: but when he is thinking at a more general level, he tends to be concerned with questions of philosophy and morality rather than with political or sociological explanation. He powerfully criticises those who interpret the decisions of judges in terms of political or economic interests, and, equally, criticises those judgments that give colour to such interpretations; and he eloquently argues for an alternative and more principled account of what they should be doing. But there must be a question whether political and economic motives can be kept out of judicial decisions if judicial decisions are asked to do as much for the society as they are in the United States.

Dworkin's views, quite appropriately, tend to start within the theory of legal adjudication, and to be generalised from there to issues of political theory. In saying how legal judgment should go, and also more generally, Dworkin appeals to a basic distinction between 'principle' and 'policy', where—roughly speaking—principle appeals to rights, and policy appeals to consequences. As Brian Barry pointed out in a sceptical review of this book in the *Times Literary Supplement* (25 October 1985), this choice of terms is itself a bit tendentious, since it suggests that, unless an argument is couched in terms of rights, it must fall below the level of principle and be a matter of opportunistic politics. This suggestion makes it a bit easier than it should be to agree with Dworkin that the best way of thinking in a principled way about political issues is always to think about them in terms of rights.

Because he starts from the law, and because, as I have already said, he does not display much interest in the sociology of political institutions, Dworkin does tend to assume the American model of a constitutional court as the instrument that not only guards but advances people's rights. But even if we agree with him that judges should think in terms of rights rather than consequences, and also agree (with rather more hesitation, I hope) that thinking in terms of rights is always the best way of deciding matters of political principle, there is still room for discussion of what institutions will be best (in a given place, with a given history) for making those decisions. Are we bound to agree that the best way of getting such matters decided is to have them decided by judges? It is an important question, and for Britain a very real one. Many of us in recent years have come to think more favourably than we used to of a charter of rights, in the light of the unprincipled activities of the British executive. But we are bound to be doubtful of the consequence that large-scale issues of principle are to be decided by British judges. The most encouraging thought in that direction is that the institutions of a Supreme Court might themselves bring about an improvement in the clarity and imagination of legal and political thought on large issues.

What Dworkin wants of principled political argument is well brought out in his fair and carefully argued criticism, reprinted here, of the Report of that Committee on obscenity that I mentioned earlier. It is called, revealingly, 'Do we have a right to pornography?' The criticism is very detailed, but it has a central target, which Dworkin calls the 'Williams strategy'—that of considering primarily whether laws directed against pornography are likely to curb any harm which it is the business of the law to curb. Against this strategy, which thinks in terms of consequences, Dworkin urges an argument in terms of rights.

In fact, the Report's argument is not entirely in terms of consequences. It claims that there is a strong presumption in favour of freedom of speech and publication, a presumption which comes to much the same as a right. What the Report does try to do is to give some reasons in favour of admitting that presumption, and those reasons are partly in terms of consequences. Dworkin should not really object to this, since his own rights are not simply plucked out of the sky: he gives a schematic account of how to derive them. However, there is something odd about that derivation. Dworkin shows the value of rights by pointing out how awful the consequences of unrestrained Utilitarianism would be. Indeed they would be, but why should anyone suppose that we have to start from there? It seems more reasonable to start, as the Report tried to start in this matter of freedom of expression, by considering how human beings might lead a worthwhile life under the conditions of ignorance and conflict that they actually face.

The Report recommended banning only a limited range of pornography, and a system of restriction for the rest. The basis of that system was the offence caused by pornography to the average citizen if it is publicly displayed. Dworkin is very suspicious of this argument. However, it should be said at once, he does not reject the practical conclusion that there should be a system of regulation, and thinks that he would recommend something very similar himself. It is the reason given for it that he does not like. His reason is that people's offence in face of the public display of pornography is likely to be 'morally freighted', dependent to an indeterminate extent on moral opinions; and it is unsound to restrict some people's activities simply because some other people morally disapprove of them.

But if those two things are both true, then Dworkin seems to have landed us with a clear and nasty choice: either there should be no legislation restricting pornography (and, equally, public sexual activity and so on), or else there may be such legislation, but it should not be based on people's objections to those things. Dworkin in fact escapes from this dilemma, because he does not think that people's moral opinions, and the reactions freighted with those opinions, should never figure in arguments for legislation. He thinks they may come into the argument, but only if the argument is conducted in terms of rights. He introduces a 'right of moral independence', and argues that just because people's reactions of offence are (to some indeterminate degree) morally freighted, there is a case for saying that their right to develop morally in their own autonomous way is infringed by the display of pornography. At the same time, of course, the right to moral development of those who want pornography will be violated by its suppression. So the scheme of regulation can be justified as a compromise between two conflicting applications of one and the same right.

I confess that I do not find this argument more convincing or more principled than that of the Report, but I shall not try to take it any further here: those with an interest in such matters should read Dworkin and see. What is more widely interesting is the style of his approach—in particular, that so much should be made to turn on a very refined discrimination of two styles of political argument. In one way, this is encouraging and reassuring, as is the power of the Supreme Court: getting it intellectually right can make a difference. On the other hand, there is something perverse in the demand to force all principled political argument into this one mould, and to ignore the wider range of conceptions that certainly have power in our political discourse. Perverse, and perhaps dangerous: if all important matters of public morality have to turn on what is effectively very refined legal reasoning, all discussion of them may be met by something to which Dworkin's own passionate and impressive counterarguments bear witness—the wide and deep public scepticism about legal reasoning.

Note

1. *A Matter of Principle*, by Ronald Dworkin (Harvard University Press, 1985).

53

The View from Nowhere, by Thomas Nagel

'It seems to me that nothing approaching the truth has yet been said on this subject,' Thomas Nagel says in the middle of this complex, wide-ranging and very interesting book; and he says it at the end of a chapter (on the freedom of the will) not, as some other philosophers might, at the beginning.[1] The book argues in a determined way about the largest philosophical questions: the nature of reality, the possibility of knowledge, freedom, morality, the meaning of life. It offers, not answers to those questions, but a distinctive and unified approach to them. In that sense, the book is very ambitious. Yet one of its most notable features is its modesty. Nagel regards the problems he has chosen to discuss as more compelling than his own contribution to them, and he is always willing to say that he does not know the answer to a difficulty. His discussions are informed by a sense that what he is saying may be overthrown or overtaken by other views. It is a great relief from the remorselessly demonstrative tone that grips the work of analytical philosophers, including some of us who in principle know better.

The unifying theme, as Nagel puts it at the beginning, is the problem of 'how to combine the perspective of a particular person inside the world with an objective view of that same world, the person and his viewpoint included. It is a problem that faces every creature with the impulse and the capacity to transcend its particular point of view and to conceive of the world as a whole.' The problem comes in many different forms. One, very basic version concerns the place of experience in the world. We have perceptions, pains, feelings, and we naturally say that these are events. In our own case, we have an understanding of these events from the inside. In the case of other creatures we believe that analogous events take place, though we do not understand in the same way what they are like. In a famous article, Nagel earlier considered what it was like to be a bat: in the present book, he touches on the daunting question of how scrambled eggs taste to a cockroach. But whether we can imaginatively represent the content of the experience to ourselves, as most of us can with the smell (to humans) of vinegar, or, as in the case of the cockroach, we cannot, the problem remains of how to regard the experiences as events, standing in relation to other events, such as physical changes in the organism.

That is one of the difficulties of combining the subjective and the objective, the inside with the outside view. Nagel thinks that an objective view cannot include everything, and will always be incomplete. He also makes a claim about what is real, when he says 'reality is not just objective reality.' It is not clear, however, how this represents his thought. For him, objectivity does not apply, at least in any direct way, to things: it is not a way in which some (but not all) things exist. It is, rather, a style of understanding, one that tries to describe any kind of experience or thought from the outside, to include it in a wider account of things in which that experience or thought occupies no privileged position. The experience or thought is had from a certain point of view: the objective account is an account *of* that point of view which is not itself given *from* that point of view.

When Nagel says that reality is not just objective reality, he means, I think, not just that a wider account could always be given, but that there are some things an objective account can never capture: some things will have been left out *within* the account. Yet it is not clear what, exactly, he thinks will have been left out. Sometimes the objective account seems to be equated with a scientific account, and then the point is that some aspects of certain events, how they seem to subjects who have experiences, will not appear in such an account at all. Some things, or at least some aspects of some things, will be missing from any scientific description of the world.

But does that mean that no objective account at all could include them—which is surely what is implied by saying that reality is not just objective reality? The objective view was not originally defined as a specifically scientific view, but only as an external and inclusive view. There seems to be no reason why that has to leave out the subjective aspects of experiences. It can perfectly properly refer to 'the way vinegar smells to Jones' or 'the way eggs taste to cockroaches'. Those are, of course, very unspecific descriptions of these features of reality: they might be said, still, to leave something out. But might they not be made more specific? Here Nagel's point seems sometimes to be that, as in the second case, we have no idea how to make them more specific, though we believe that we are talking about *something*; sometimes—as in the first case—that we can make them more specific, but that in doing so our understanding essentially depends on taking up, in imagination, the subjective point of view in question. Those are significant points, but I do not think Nagel has made quite clear how they bear on questions about what exists or is included in reality.

As I said earlier, Nagel does not claim to solve all these problems. In fact, he may not think they can be solved; early in the book he says, 'certain forms of perplexity—for example, about freedom, knowledge, and the meaning of life—seem to me to embody more insight than any of the supposed solutions to those problems,' and I doubt whether he means only the solutions that have been offered so far. It is all the more important, then, for him to make clear to us the perplexity that is generated by reflection, the tension implicit in our views of the world. He is often very successful in this: he brings out well, for instance, a sense of the puzzling inaccessibility to us of whatever it is that is going on in the cat's 'furry little mind', and he is good at setting out the classical tensions of scepticism, where the sane conviction that the world exists independently of our thoughts can lead rapidly to the idea that we have no reason to suppose that our conceptions of it are true—indeed, can leave us wondering what it is for any thoughts of ours to be conceptions of such a world at all. Nagel attaches himself firmly to the 'realist' side of this tension, and rightly resists the idealist tendencies that he identifies in much recent philosophy, which suggest in one way or another that the nature of our thought determines what the world can possibly contain. Some critics will feel that Nagel has taken this line in a heroically strong form, and has left too little space between realistic modesty—'the world may be very different from what we take it to be'—and incurable scepticism: 'the world may be totally different from anything we could ever take it to be.' But the opportunity that he has left for such critics comes from the impressively strong style in which he has presented a natural and basic perplexity.

What one finds naturally perplexing, however, is not just a matter of whether one has a philosophically disposed nature. It is also a matter of what sort of philosophy one's nature is disposed to, and there are some other cases in which a reader, open enough to being perplexed, may wonder whether some problem, which Nagel powerfully feels and has vividly expressed, is quite as deeply intractable as he suggests. There is, for instance, this problem: given various actual people—TN, BW and so on—what is it for one of those people to be *me*? The fact that I am BW certainly goes beyond the mere fact that there is such a person as BW, but how does it go beyond it? What more is involved? Nagel will, I think, convince anyone disposed to such thoughts that there is a problem here, but I am less sure that he will convince all of them that it is a very deep problem: or rather, that there is a further deep problem over and above the deep problem which he has presented already, that the world contains centres of consciousness. This is one point at which a more sharply technical discussion is needed, to show that the difficulties come from structural problems in understanding ourselves objectively, and do not consist merely in a soluble semantic tangle.

In one section, it is just because Nagel's own sense of the problem is so powerful that he has not done enough to explain it to readers who may be, variously, constitutionally un-worried by it, immunised to some strains of it by previous philosophy, or else troubled by something other than its traditional form. This is the question about which Nagel said that he thought nothing satisfactory had been said, the question of free will, and his discussion of it provides what seems to me the least satisfactory part of his book. This problem looks like a paradigm of what he is concerned with—the tension between the inner perspective and the other, objective view. Here the tension lies in the relations between the inner view taken by an agent, the engaged perspective of someone forming and carrying out intentions, and, on the other hand, an outside explanatory view of that agent and his intentions. To the outside view he and they seem part (many, Nagel included, are fond of saying 'merely part') of a causal network that reaches outside him. This tension has seemed to many to be plain inconsistency: they think that if this causal network exists, there is no such thing as genuinely intentional action. There is, it is true, a tension, but there are good arguments to suggest that it is not an inconsistency. Rather, it comes from the fact that one cannot think in two modes at once, practically as an agent, and as the explanatory observer of those very aspects of one's own action. These arguments may be inadequate, but Nagel should pay them more attention; this is one point where he seems to be transfixed by his problem at the expense of possible solutions to it.

The problem of free will has two parts. One part is the question just mentioned, whether there can be genuine, intentional, chosen action if the agent's doings are located in a causal network that reaches beyond him. The second part concerns the relations of all that to certain moral notions—in particular, responsibility and blame. Do these notions make sense in the light of our understanding of people and their actions? It is important that the answer to the first question may be, reassuringly, 'yes', even though the second question deserves a much more sceptical answer. Our conceptions of blame may never have made much sense; they have stood up poorly to reflection based on quite ordinary unsuperstitious human observation, and do not need elaborate causal theories to make them look fairly seedy. Nagel, perhaps because he is so impressed by the analogy of these questions to his central theme, does not go far into this aspect, and this is rather odd, because in earlier writings he has himself implacably taken apart some of the assumptions implicit in common notions of moral responsibility.

In the case of free will, Nagel's application of his central theme does not provide a very interesting pattern for his discussion, but when in the later part of the book he gets to general questions of moral philosophy, it once again does. Here the tension takes the form of a contrast between the engaged perspective of the agent, living a life and expressing his projects in action, and an impartial moral view of his life which the agent, as much as others, may take. In an earlier book, *The Possibility of Altruism*, Nagel was disposed to think that if someone has a reason to get rid of a pain in his foot, this is because it is, simply, a bad thing that there should be such a pain; and if this is so, then everyone else may equally have some reason to end that bad state of affairs. This pattern applies generally, so that all individual action, if rational and morally correct, is directed to embodying what is good or bad from everyone's—or rather, no one's—point of view. He has modified that view, and there are very interesting and detailed discussions here of the complex relations, as Nagel sees them, between particular personal interests, impersonal value, and individual action.

Nagel now fully admits a distinction between those aims of an agent that make some moral claim on others' co-operation and those that do not. If someone is in severe pain, then that does make some claim on the concern and time of other appropriately placed people (however ambitiously or defensively 'appropriately placed' may be construed), but they are under no obligation at all to assist his passionate ambition to build a monument to his own god. What explains this difference? Nagel says: 'the more a desire has as its object the quality of the subject's experience, and the more immediate and independent of his other values it is, the more it will tend to generate impersonal . . . reasons'—that is to say, reasons for other people to do things. This seems to imply that a passionate and selfish hedonist, concentrated specially on the improvement of his pleasures, would have a special claim on our assistance, and I doubt whether this is what we want to conclude. More generally, I doubt whether the distinction can be fastened, as Nagel tries to fasten it, simply to differences in the structural or experiential nature of various projects that agents may have. It is likely to depend, more than he allows, on social conceptions of what counts as a basic need as opposed to a mere want or taste.

Debussy said of Maeterlinck that he had a 'passion for the beyond', and while Nagel's work has no religious or manifestly mystical tinge, such a passion does touch his relations to the view from nowhere. The modesty I mentioned is not merely a personal matter: repeatedly in this book, he reminds human beings that they have a very limited grasp of the physical universe, and of the truth about values which he believes objectively to exist. This is not, like Montaigne's, a humility grounded in permanent scepticism: he looks to unimaginable degrees of progress, notably in our moral existence. Nor is it a Platonic contempt for the human and the contingent in the face of the universal and impersonal. But a sense of the universal, an implied view of all activities from outside, does shape the argument. Nagel does not think that we can coherently achieve such a view, still less that we should stay with it, but as a limiting idea, it conditions his view of everything. That is why he can ask, for instance, whether we are all equally important or all equally unimportant. For many of us the question is not whether the truth lies with one of those options (or, as Nagel rather strangely puts it, 'somewhere in between'), but whether those options mean anything at all, if we are not talking about our importance to each other.

The passion for the beyond, and its synoptic ambitions, make this in some ways an untypical work of contemporary philosophy. Although it is deeply and expertly involved in contemporary discussions, it aspires, in some part, to an earlier style of high philosophical reflection. But, in the spirit of its own thesis, at the same time it knows where it is. The ongoing tension between the universal and the local is also a tension within the book between abstract metaphysical argument and the vividly immediate, which occasionally displays itself: in the unforgettable story, for instance, of a spider who lived in a urinal at Princeton.

Note

1. *The View from Nowhere*, by Thomas Nagel (Oxford University Press, 1986).

54

What Hope for the Humanities?

1   The Present Situation

It will be no news that Humanities departments in UK universities are suffering from lack of morale, lack of recruitment, and from the pressures exerted by cuts in the past and more, it seems, to come.

In this they do not of course differ from departments in other areas of academic and research activity, including those that one would suppose most relevant to technical and hence economic success. The recent report of the Royal Society for the Advisory Board on the Research Councils has pointed out that we spend less on basic science per head of population than the USA, France, West Germany, or, indeed, The Netherlands. This is *not* because we spend disproportionately much on the Humanities. It is interesting in this connection to note the following statistic: seven UK organisations are members of the European Science Foundation— the five Research Councils, the Royal Society, and the British Academy (representing the Humanities); the subscription is divided in proportion to the budgets of these organisations, and the British Academy's share is ·48 of one per cent. Scientific research is of course a great deal more expensive than Humanities research, but certainly the Humanities have a considerable interest in conferences, and another notable statistic is that the Royal Society is able to devote fifteen times as much money to funding conferences as the British Academy can.

The point of these comparisons is, emphatically, not to suggest that funds should be diverted from the Natural Sciences to the Humanities. It has not been England's characteristic problem that too much attention has been paid to the Natural and Applied Sciences, or that they bulk too large in the preferences of school leavers. There are two points in these comparisons. The first is that the Humanities are, along with the rest of the academic enterprise, under-funded. One effect of that is the unchanging department, which generates the *long-stay boarding house effect*: everyone has already said many times anything that they could possibly say in reply to anything that anyone else might say. The DES [Department of Education and Science] and the UGC [University Grants Committee] recognised this, if reluctantly, by extending to Humanities departments the system of 'new blood' appointments. The extent of these was small, and the scheme also confused two different problems, of recruiting new people and of developing new subjects; they are not the same problem, since the most urgent problem is often to recruit people to teach the established subjects. (As the philosopher David Wiggins put it, the scheme confused new blood and new bottles.)

The second point arising from these comparisons lies in the very small figures involved relatively to other activities. The pressures on universities, on research, and on the Humanities, are not solely matters of Government priorities and Government preferences: any Government will be faced with a shortage of resources to deal with these and many other problems. But it must be significant, when considering priorities, to think how much in these fields might be done for comparatively how little.

2 A 'Civilised Society'

The Humanities are under-supported, and they need defending. There are several vital questions about the terms in which they should be defended. In fact, not even all academics are clear that the Humanities should be defended, except out of a spirit of collegial loyalty and the feeling that it is better for subjects to stick together when the university is under attack. Moreover, the case for the Humanities may not be too obvious when subjects more manifestly relevant to economic problems are themselves so seriously under-supported. More generally, there is a question of the Humanities' significance in the changed intellectual social circumstances of the modern world.

One form taken by attacks on Humanities is the suggestion that the Humanities are a luxury article, and that in these hard times we cannot afford much of them. One style of defence of the Humanities says, "the Humanities are cultivated in a civilised society". This defence is put forward for a variety of motives, many of them excellent; and what it says is also, as a matter of fact, true. The trouble is that it can be too easily associated with some views that are very bad defences, because they effectively accept the luxury status of the Humanities. These assimilate the Humanities to aspects of expensively cultivated life, to such things as select outings with a well-behaved company and an adequate aesthetic content. One might call this the 'Harrods Leather Blotter' view. In the coarsest versions of this outlook, the Humanities are regarded simply as a preparation for such a life. To call it the 'Leather Blotter' view does perhaps imply one version of it rather than another, the more conspicuous consumption version. There are more highbrow versions of the same thing, which focus less on conspicuous consumption and more on the cultivation of good taste. But any view that simply associates the Humanities with a class of high-grade luxuries or indeed the graces of life, will not do, and can very easily destroy what it is seeking to defend.

There is another defensive line, which sees itself as quite the opposite of the Leather Blotter view. This is a much more Puritan view. I shall call it—with some unfairness—but not much—'the F. R. Leavis view'. This view does see the Humanities as a necessity, and to that extent it does better than the view of them as a luxury. But it does not manage to show that much of them are necessary, and it is pretty confused about what is supposed to be necessary to whom. Oddly enough, it has more in common with the Leather Blotter view than it supposes. Dr Leavis, himself, first of all, was not even in a position to defend all the major studies of the Humanities. His was a defence of the study of literature, and it explicitly rejected from its own orbit of interest philosophy and, implicitly, history. What, on this view, was the study of literature necessary for? It was necessary for the formation of an educated, cultivated and mature person; and it is particularly necessary for that, because it was associated with certain central and stern virtues, of sensibility, honesty and truthfulness.

If that claim is applied directly to individual people, it seems that good readers and sensitive critics will be noticeably better people than a lot of other people, and that is extremely hard to believe. But more important than that is the point that even if the claim were true, it would still say nothing about the relation of such persons to the rest of society. It is also very important that such a view cannot give any account of the significance of *research* in the Humanities. More generally, it is not well-designed to draw any consequences about who should be doing what in relation to the Humanities.

The fact that the Leavis view does not face such issues can be put by saying that it lacks a politics; and that is something that it shares with its apparent opposite, the Leather Blotter view. In Leavis's own case, the lack of a politics took the extreme form of rejecting most of the modern world altogether. In this respect, it was just an example of that deepest of British neuroses, the Pandaemonium complex,[1] the hatred of the Industrial Revolution. This perhaps can be represented in psychoanalytical terms as a desire to destroy one's own child, which is fantasied as having been conceived by rape. That feature is in fact very important for the understanding of the Humanities in Britain, but I shall not take it any further here. There is a more general point that is more central to the question.

Both these views fail because they try to justify a study of the Humanities just in terms of desirable qualities of cultivated individuals. That is quite a good thing to try to do, but one can't do it *first*. What has to be discussed first is *the pursuit of certain subjects*—the organised, funded, necessarily institutional pursuit of certain subjects, of certain kinds of knowledge.

We can, after that, ask questions about the distribution of that knowledge: what is the role of the expert, what is the value of a smattering, what indeed a smattering is—to know some of a subject, or to know something about it? In short, we can ask how many people who are never going to be experts should be taught how much of such subjects. Obviously, these are very important questions, and they are the ones that involve us directly in matters of university funding and so forth. They are questions about the politics of distribution of knowledge of the Humanities. But you can answer such questions only in the light of a more fundamental question, about the value of the Humanities as on-going subjects, an understanding of what they are and what they do.

3   Humanities and Social Understanding

In Boston, there is a rather grand and mysterious painting by Gauguin called *Where do we Come From? . . . What are we? . . . Where are we Going?* Everyone always has difficulty with the last question, whether they are an oracle, a politician or a business analyst. What is certain, I take it, is that there is no hope for answering the last question unless we have some ideas for answering the first two; even if we conclude that we can never answer the last question, that will only be because we have some insight into answers to the first two. The most basic justification of the Humanities as on-going subjects is that our insights into the first two questions essentially involve grasp of humane studies, in particular because the second question involves the first. Any understanding of social reality must be based in understanding its history, and you cannot read its history without insight into its cultural products and those of other times.

There are various different ways of conceptualising that necessity. Some may particularly emphasise the kind of social self-consciousness that is made possible by literacy. Others, again, may emphasise the further elaborated self-consciousness of distinctively *modern* societies, which are peculiarly reflective about themselves. Indeed, the question whether the modern world is different in quite fundamental respects from earlier forms of society, is itself a matter for the enquiries of the Humanities, such as history and philosophy. It is obviously not a matter only for them, but also for what are conventionally called the Social Sciences, but it certainly calls on the Humanities as well. One reason, indeed, that I personally prefer the term 'the Humanities' to the familiar organisational title 'the Arts' is that it reminds us of the connections embodied in another phrase, 'the Human Sciences'.

It is not just a matter of philosophy and history. We have literatures of the past, and their criticism and their interpretation are not simply matters of historical recovery—or if they are matters of historical recovery, it is not simply so. What a text means, now, cannot by the merest necessities of historical change simply be a matter of what it meant then, and the commitment to understanding must be a commitment equally to reinterpretation.

4   Kinds of Knowledge?

There is a tradition that suggests that if one says, as I am saying, that history and more generally the disciplines of the Humanities play a vital role in understanding social reality—'What we are'—this implies a very fundamental split between human and scientific knowledge: some contrast between 'intuitive' and 'discursive' understanding, between 'empathetic' and 'objective' knowledge (or in the German tradition, between *Verstand* and *Vernunft*). This may raise the question, again, whether some of the social sciences may not be on the other side of this fence from the Humanities; some, such as social anthropology, certainly will not be, but it may be thought that others will, and (more aggressively) that the Humanities may not play such a basic role as I am suggesting.

My belief is that these divisions are very importantly being overcome by developments in the Humanities and in some of the social sciences themselves. There are different styles of social investigation and understanding that can be roughly assigned to the opposite sides of these contrasts, but it is absolutely certain that we need both of them. The quantitative or, again, formal social sciences on the one hand, and humanistic, historical or hermeneutic disciplines on the other, stand in manifest need of each other. Tendencies in history, such as the history of *mentalités* and its relation to economic interpretations, are illustrations of this. A particularly interesting example on the other side is the formal theory of iterated games, which provably have multiple equilibria and yield no absolutely determinate 'rational' solution. This importantly means that in empirical applications, choice of a strategy will depend on notions of culture or shared understanding. These and similar results show, I think, that rational decision theory and similar procedures cannot solve all our problems, and that this conclusion can be shown by the methods of rational decision theory itself. Moreover, what is essential in arriving at social understandings or rational strategies in determinate social situations is an understanding of those situations that very frequently involve the kind of knowledge with which the Humanities, notably history, are concerned.

5 The Humanities and Social Criticism

It is the connection between the Humanities and social understanding that justifies the Humanities as *subjects*, and on-going research into them as forms of knowledge. I suggested that there was a further question, the politics of their distribution: what follows from all this for who should be taught how much of the Humanities? To answer this further question requires us, as I have said, to understand the points of these subjects themselves, but it requires some more as well. It requires some views about how such knowledge should properly be used and applied in political structures of the modern world, and that involves some connection between social understanding and the possibility of social criticism. That there should be any connection between the Humanities and social criticism may seem surprising to some, since an emphasis on the Humanities, certainly as against some of the social sciences, is conventionally often seen as itself conservative. But this perception, of the Humanities as of the social sciences, is merely convention, and at best represents a few local social facts, perhaps of the kind that feed the Leather Blotter and related views. In fact, emphasis on the study of the Humanities and their importance is in itself neither conservative nor radical. What it implies is rather something about the level of reflectiveness at which either conservative or radical opinions are held. Some people believe, of course, that if an outlook on society is reflective enough, it must be radical—and that belief itself can be held either optimistically by radicals, or pessimistically by conservatives. But any such beliefs lie further ahead. The present point is simply that the Humanities, in their heartland, should, and do, encourage reflection.

I have deliberately made no reference so far to the now archaic controversy between Lord Snow and Dr Leavis about the 'two cultures', in particular because it was conducted very much in terms of the cultivation of the individual. If we are to think in the terms set up by that controversy, there is perhaps one contrast that can be drawn between the formations offered by these two cultures. It is at least possible to be an absolutely outstanding and original scientist but at the same time be an unthinking conservative, while it is not possible to be an absolutely outstanding and original worker in the Humanities and be at least an *unthinking* conservative. (I recognise that this contrast is to some extent idealized.) The classic error of thoughtless conservatism is to forget that what is old is merely what used to be new. One form it can take is to invest the traditional with a sacred quality; another, and at the present time more destructive form, is to forget that anything has any history at all, and to suppose that the social world simply consists of a set of given objects to be manipulated by go-getting common sense. No such views are likely to survive unchanged by the enquiries of a truthful and imaginative history. These and other humane studies are unlikely to leave room, then, simply for thoughtless conservatism. It may well, of course, leave room for other kinds of conservatism. There are conservative views which very well recognise that social reality does not always mean what it superficially appears to mean, but thinks that things go better, on the whole, if that understanding is not too widely spread. Such a view rejects an aspiration which many modern societies have tried to adopt, and in varying degrees have succeeded in adopting, the aspiration that society should be so far as possible *transparent* in its workings, and should not depend for its operation on its citizens not understanding how it operates.

Most societies in the past, and very many today, are certainly not 'transparent' in this sense; in the past, at least, they have managed also to be innocent, possessing an elite or hierarchy which could be accepted fairly contentedly and in not too coercive a spirit. In the past, Britain may to some extent have been a society of this sort. But in the modern world, it is increasingly difficult to run a society which fails even to try to be transparent, and yet is at the same time innocent. While in many cultural respects modern societies may be coarser and cruder than their predecessors, in their understanding of large-scale organisations and in their distribution of information, they are at the same time vastly more sophisticated, and attempts to keep their political and social processes at a level at which they are simply taken for granted and fail to be the subject of question are likely to be increasingly unsuccessful and, therefore, increasingly more coercive.

It is in this area that one must look for an answer to the question of the politics of the distribution of the Humanities. If it is right that the Humanities as subjects make an essential contribution to the understanding of society and that the understanding of society is essentially connected to ways in which we can reflect on it, question it, and hence try to change it: then questions of who should be taught how much of the Humanities are essentially connected with questions of how open or transparent society should seek to be. If an elite were to run society in a relatively unquestioned way, then only an elite would need to have much insight into what it is and where it has come from. But if we believe that in the modern world, at least, that cannot indefinitely work, then the conclusion is not only that it is vital that the Humanities should be pursued as on-going subjects but that access to them, and some kind of knowledge of them, are things that should be as widely spread as they can be.

Conclusion

In the temper of the present times, and in the short term, this may seem a slightly quixotic way to defend the Humanities. To associate them, as I have done, with certain areas of the social sciences, and also with possibilities of social criticism, may seem counter-productive at a time when nei-ther of these things is perhaps outstandingly popular in this country. It may seem safer simply to stick to some version of the Leather Blotter view, and to associate the Humanities with objects of cultivated con-sumption. In the present dust storm, it may seem safer to shelter down-wind from the extension to the Royal Opera House. But this would be a short-sighted policy. The Humanities are concerned with a truthful understanding of what we are and where we have come from, and they, above all, demand a truthful understanding of themselves, and hence a truthful justification of their value. Moreover, society itself and those who are trying to run it also need those understandings. For it is only those understandings that can issue in reasoned demands for change, and the alternative to reasoned change is, as always, not no change, but unreasoned change, which will destroy not only the Humanities but the society that forgets about them.

Note

1. See the collection of texts made by Humphrey Jennings (1985) *Pandaemonium: the coming of the machine as seen by contemporary observers* (Ed. by Mary-Lou Jennings & Charles Madge) (London).

55

The Society of Mind, by Marvin Minsky

Psychologists make models of the mind in order to explain what we say and do. Some particularly want to explain our abilities: how do we build a tower from toy blocks, or recognize a goldfinch? How do we manage to get across a room without hitting the furniture? Like many naive ques-tions that lead to science, these do not have a meaning that is entirely fixed before people start to answer them. The questions seem, rather vaguely, in place when we reflect that we must learn to do these various things, that characteristic mistakes are made in trying to do them, and that our abilities to do them can be impaired through illness, injury, or age.

Yet at the outset, it is not very clear what you are asking when you ask exactly how we do such things: Is there a *way* in which you pick up a brick? The models of the mind that are designed to answer such questions also help to set them up, by defining what a "way" of doing something will be. They provide a topography of the mind's functions, according to which our skills in perception, movement, or thought can be analyzed. We shall have come to understand how we do one of these familiar tasks when we see what must go on within the mind, so described, if we are to do it.

That bland and general description, however, conceals a difficulty—one large enough to make some people think that no explanation in such terms could ultimately succeed. How are we to describe what goes on in the mind? If we say that elements in the mind are able to do various relevant things—that one element recognizes a brick, for instance, and another sends the arm off to reach for it—we have only moved the problem back, from a familiar agent (the person) to a less familiar agent, the departmental chief in the mind. We shall have fallen into the homunculus fallacy, the old mistake of explaining a person's actions in terms of actions by another (perhaps more specialized) person inside him.

If the aim is to provide a model by which all basic psychological skills can be explained, there is only one way out of this difficulty: the analysis must be carried to a level at which the mental elements themselves have no psychological capacities at all. Each of these ultimate mental items must be the kind of agent that simply, when it receives an input, sends off some output, which typically triggers other elements. The model-builder, aiming to display the structure of the mind of an agent who does have psychological abilities, will construct hierarchies and systems of such elements, specialized in the information that can affect them and in the changes that they can initiate.

It is a system of this kind that Marvin Minsky discusses in his book—or, rather, the possibility of such a system, or speculations around that possibility, since the book is ruminative and discursive, presents no detailed theory, and is not tied down to technicalities.[1] It is large in format, and full of simple diagrams, and every section is presented on a separate page. It is the model-builder's thought-book, designed to encourage you to wander around in it and go off in interesting directions. I think that Minsky conceives of it as rather like a mental model itself, an application of its own theory. Its reader is in somewhat the situation of the explorer in a recent *Doonesbury* strip, clambering around inside Reagan's brain; and as that adventure itself suggests, he or she will find much of it fairly easy going.

Minsky's model involves numerous "agents" organized hierarchically into "agencies." An agent is merely a switch that turns on something else when it itself is turned on, and an agency is an organized set of switches. They are linked by complex lines of communication, called "K-lines," which are set up and modified by what happens to the system (by experience, as one might say). The organization of the agencies is explicitly bureaucratic, and this is one of two analogies that helps to guide this model of the mind. It is a very old analogy, that of the Leviathan. The organization of agencies is the "Society" of the book's title, but the society in question is conceived not as a political community, but as a rigidly stratified corporation. The other analogy that guides the model is that of a computer, an information-processing device, and here the similarity is thought to go beyond an analogy: the mind, for Minsky, *is* such a device, and the project of discovering its architecture constitutes a well-known research program, that of psychology as cognitive science.

This is closely related to the subject called "Artificial Intelligence" of which Minsky has been for many years a leader, having set up in 1959, with John McCarthy, the Artificial Intelligence Laboratory at MIT. "Cognitive science" is now the usual name for the subject that tries to explain human psychological capacities in these terms; "artificial intelligence" particularly emphasizes the project of simulating thought processes, which is not necessarily at the heart of the matter. Although computer programs controlling robot devices have played a big part in the development of cognitive science, that science is not committed to thinking that one could simulate much of what a human being can do on the kinds of computer we are familiar with. Minsky freely admits that the brain does not work like such machines, and that moreover we know little of how it does work. The models of various agencies with their linking connections are not meant to relate directly to structures in the brain but rather suggest the structure of the work the brain does. It could perhaps be misleading that some of the diagrams, with their interweaving cords, look rather as though they were intended as neurology.

The idea of cognitive science is that the description of the mind should correspond not to a wiring diagram but to a computer program. In the case of a machine, it is not hard to identify the program, since someone wrote it (or, in some cases, wrote another program that wrote it). In the case of human beings and other animals, however, the Divine Hacker who wrote the system has provided no manual to it, and we have to discover the program by scientific inquiry. That inquiry is constrained by what we know or believe about the nervous system, but within those constraints, there is a vast range of possibilities for what such a program might be. Granted there is no manual or directly identifiable software, what counts as the mind's actual program? What does it mean to say that a given structure is *in fact* part of it? Presumably it means that a theory including that structure provides the best fit to the psychological data, such as the mistakes that people typically make, and also fits our understanding of evolutionary history. Thus it is a plus for a particular theory of vision expressed in these terms (derived from the work of the late David Marr) that it helps us to grasp how our visual system can be an elaborate descendant of more primitive visual systems.

Some who criticize the research program of cognitive science think that they can show that in principle it could not work. Some suggest that if it escapes the homunculus fallacy, it will merely land on the other horn of a dilemma: how could an arrangement of elements that do not understand anything issue in a system (as Minsky puts it, a society) that does understand something?[2] This Catch-22 style of argument is too quick to be convincing, and like some other arguments in the history of philosophy designed to show that a particular scientific advance is impossible, can be accused of begging the question: what is at issue in this research, in part, is precisely whether intelligent systems can be compounded of unintelligent parts.

Other critics are merely empirical and skeptical, and say that there is no reason to think that a program of this kind must work, and that the rate of progress achieved after a great deal of labor provides not much reason to think that it is going to do so. This is a weighty objection, and what has been achieved is disappointing, particularly when measured against the large promises still made by some of the apologists of artificial intelligence. In this book, Minsky does not do much to reassure the skeptics, but I do not think that he is trying to. Except in passing, he does not report results, nor does he set out to justify the entire enterprise. He merely sets out various ideas and models, and invites us to consider what might be done with them.

Two authorities quoted on the back of the jacket refer to the "theory" of the mind that the book offers, but I do not see any such theory. A theory would have actually to explain something, and to explain anything, especially in this kind of field, involves explaining a lot. As Noam Chomsky has always emphasized in linguistics, it is not hard to think up some model or principle that will fit a few cases—the difficulties break out when it is confronted with a wider range of phenomena. To get to a point at which anything was actually explained, and there was really an effective theory, the notions sketched in this book would have to be given a demanding application. It may be that existing work in cognitive science has succeeded, to some extent, in giving them such an application, but if so, it is not displayed here, and Minsky, as I read him, does not suppose that it is. His aim is rather to get the reader used to the notions.

Minsky introduces a good many new technical terms, but (despite his dismissing old terms as vague or being attached to discredited theories) the new terms are sometimes just ways of labeling well-tried conceptions. A "polyneme," for instance, is an old friend from empiricist philosophy, the *complex idea* (without the demand, made by some empiricist philosophers, that it should present itself as an image). Just as a word was supposed, by that old philosophy, to have its meaning in virtue of a complex idea compounded of simple ideas, so exactly the polyneme associated with the word "apple" "sets your agencies for color, shape, and size into unrelated states that represent the independent properties of being red, round, and 'apple-sized.'" (The word should strictly speaking be "polymneme," since its suffix is said to indicate a connection with memory; it is not clear whether etymology has been overridden or overlooked.)

Polynemes are connected, indirectly, to items in the mind Minsky calls frames, which are, effectively, sentence-forms. A frame embodies the structure of a certain kind of situation. A kind of frame that Minsky finds particularly important is the "*Trans*-frame," which relates two items by some kind of trans-action, as when one causes another, or information is passed from one to another, or a spatial movement occurs. Thus there are "travel-frames," containing blanks or "pronomes" for each of a number of elements including Actor-Origin-Trajectory-Destination-Vehicle. A particular value of such a frame would be a sentence such as "Jack drove from Boston to New York on the turnpike with Mary." When you think of this sentence, and you think of the destination of the trip, you think of New York, and this is because

> the polyneme for New York is attached to an AND-agent with two inputs; one of them represents the arousal of the travel-frame itself, and the other represents the arousal of the *Destination* pronome.

In these connections, Minsky emphasizes the role of "stereotypes" or "default assumptions." A frame embodies a standardized situation. Given the sentence about Jack's travel, we assume, unless there is an indication to the contrary, that it was a car that he drove, that the car had no more than four wheels, that Mary was with him in it rather than in another car, and so on. There can be little doubt that a structure of stereotypes or presumptions does underlie our linguistic and other capacities, and to this extent the view that Minsky uses is shared by much contemporary philosophy of mind and language.

Just as there are traditional elements in the account, however, so there are traditional problems, which Minsky seems not to recognize. One problem concerns "frames," and the ways in which they are linked to language. It is easy to postulate a frame corresponding to a sentence about travel, with appropriate "pronomes": it is simply read off from the structure of an English sentence. But what is the psychological status of this frame? Do we come to acquire it because we have been exposed to English sentences, and have in effect abstracted it from them? How could we do that unless we already understood them? And how could we understand them, at least on Minsky's account of the matter, unless we already possessed the frame?

If we are to get out of this circle, it looks as though we must suppose that there is an innate structure, a basic architecture of the mind, that is brought into action by learning a given language and by other kinds of experience. But then it is surely quite naive to suppose that this structure should stand in simple correspondence to the surface structure of English sentences. Minsky himself makes the point that a small child can easily acquire any human language. (He also offers the very ingenious, if not quite convincing, hypothesis that this ability decays before the time of puberty—as indeed it does—in order that parents should not acquire imperfect speech habits from their children.) Real work in comparative linguistics is needed if we are to know what structures of the mind underlie this ability. The point is not that, in absence of such work, Minsky's models provide too narrow an explanation of understanding, one that may need generalization in the light of other languages. Rather, without such work there is no psychological explanation at all—for all we know Minsky may merely be rewriting English in psychologese.

Minsky well brings out the enormous complexity of simple tasks, such as picking something up or putting one thing on another. We certainly know, in part from the hard and often disappointing work of AI investigators, that whatever processes underlie the capacities to do such things, they are very subtle and complex. But having started off admirably by making us look again at what we take for granted, he is disposed to move to another thought, that what we regularly think of as deep or difficult is merely complicated, and probably no more complicated than what we ordinarily think of as simple.

This step has rather less admirable results. It rests on the assumption that all complexity, cultural or personal, is of the same type, and this assumption leads Minsky to occasional outbreaks of reductivism, particularly near the beginning of the book, that are always unnecessary and sometimes astonishing. Thus he writes that "Selves" are not, as some "ordinary views" are alleged to hold, "magic, self-indulgent luxuries that enable our minds to break the bonds of natural cause and law. Instead, those Selves are practical necessities." Their function is to enable us to carry out our plans. Without Selves, "we'd never get much done because we could never depend on ourselves"; as he also puts it, "*One function of the Self is to keep us from changing too rapidly.*" Too rapidly for whom? How can there be plans for the future to worry about, without already a self that has a future and whose plans they are.

In supposing that "we" can adopt ingenious schemes to bring ourselves into existence, as also when he tries to answer the baffling question, "How do we control our minds?" Minsky seems to have been driven to absurdity by a desire to represent the noninstrumental as instrumental. This emphasis does not necessarily follow from taking cognitive science seriously as a research program; but I think that it is a very natural result of exaggerating what it might achieve. Because it basically tries to find out *how* we do things, it naturally represents what we do in terms of problems and tasks, success and failure, and this, of course, presupposes that we have ends in view. With many of our activities, such as picking up a brick, the end is obvious, and at the same time the question of *how*, as Minsky emphasizes, is not trivial. But when we get away from these immediate or obvious kinds of ends, it may be less easy to see our projects or concerns in the light of problem-solving, and so less rewarding to try to apply the cognitive science repertoire, at this level, to what we do and experience.

One aspect of our activities to which this obviously applies is what is called "creativity." Minsky, like other writers in these subjects, discusses this as a matter of problem-solving, considering such things as programs that "try out" strategies that may have been, in part, randomly generated. Such strategies may do for chess; but for most creativity in the arts and, indeed, the sciences, such an account is misconceived. To make a creative step is not simply to produce something new or unpredictable, but to produce something new that we find interesting or significant; and the fact that we do see some innovation in that light is, first of all, a cultural and not merely a psychological matter, and, inasmuch as it is a psychological matter, it is not in the first place a question of the heuristics of problem-solving.

The right conclusion from this is not that cognitive science is a dead duck, but that it should stick to trying to solve the kinds of problems it is adapted to solving, which, as it reminds us itself, are hard enough.[3] When it goes beyond those problems into larger ambitions of explaining human life, it can fall into a stupid and shallow reductivism that is not essential to it. It does this because it has to look for elementary and obvious ends that are supposedly served by more complex and culturally elaborated activities. A particular, and notably ideological, version of this is that in which the "success" that is introduced by the very idea of problem-solving is identified simply with Success: career advancement, fame, and competitive victory are assumed to be the ends of human activity. There is a strain of this in Minsky's book, minor but, when it appears, quite dramatic. "Consider," he says, "an example from everyday life":

> I was trying to concentrate on a certain problem but was getting bored and sleepy. Then I imagined that one of my competitors, Professor Challenger, was about to solve the same problem. An angry wish to frustrate Challenger then kept me working on the problem for a while. The strange thing was, this problem was not of the sort that ever interested Challenger.

Well, there's one strange thing. Another is that this is an example from everyday life. Yet another is that this is the example from everyday life that would first occur to one in thinking about the self's construction of itself.

It would be wrong, however, to suggest that this represents the limits of Minsky's view of things, or even a major part of it. His book is full of other kinds of thoughts, including numerous quotations from religious, philosophical, and literary writers, from Proust to the Buddha to what seem to be calendar mottoes. A few seem to me intolerably cute and corny; others are marvelous, and some of them come from a quite different kind of life, casting a great and revealing shadow over the book. So Dr. Johnson:

> And while it shall please thee to continue me in this world, where there is much to be done and little to be known, teach me, by thy Holy Spirit, to withdraw my mind from unprofitable and dangerous enquiries, from difficulties vainly curious, and doubts impossible to be solved.

It is certainly no complaint that the quotations are a mixed bag. Going through Minsky's book is a bit like going around his house, and he has a perfect right to put up on its walls what he finds familiar, helpful, interesting, or attractive. It is perhaps rather more disappointing that these thoughts are merely stuck on the wall. If he takes seriously some of the things he quotes, it is hard to see how he can say some of the things he says.

For another kind of reason, too, it is hard to see how he can say some of them. At various points in the book, statements turn up that should not be there, not because they are theoretically shaky or deeply misconceived, but merely because they are, in the most immediate and everyday sense, not true. Minsky says:

> When Jack says, "Mary knows geometry," this indicates to us that Jack would probably be satisfied by Mary's answers to the questions about geometry that he would be disposed to ask.

It does not indicate this, unless we know something special about Jack, for instance, that he is Mary's teacher: on the contrary, a centrally important occasion of Jack's saying "she knows geometry" is that on which he might add ". . . but I don't." Again, Minsky points out that we might say, "I just heard a pin drop," but not "I hear a pin dropping"; and he says that this is because a pin takes so short a time to drop that we cannot get the sentence out. But we could not say it even if the pin were dropping from the top of the Empire State Building. The explanation might rather be that a pin dropping *makes no sound*.

In both these cases, and others, we might repeat what A. E. Housman said about an evident but neglected principle of classical scholarship: "Three minutes' thought would suffice to find this out; but thought is irksome and three minutes is a long time." Does it matter if Minsky, economizing on time, cannot spare a second to turn up the corner of a sentence he has just written? There are circumstances in which it may help inquiry not to fuss with exactitude. But it is very doubtful that cognitive science is in those circumstances, and granted that it is struggling with the complexities of our thought about the everyday, it will do best if it listens carefully to its own words.

I think that many people will enjoy Minsky's book. It brings in a lot of ideas and gives a suggestive sketch of a certain kind of psychological model. In addition, it has a kind of disheveled, undemanding, personal quality that contrasts amiably with the aggressive scientistic display that characterizes some of cognitive science and, still more, the philosophical propaganda for it. It is written in an easy and unintimidating manner. It is intriguingly concerned with skills of an everyday kind. But it is sometimes inattentive to everyday truths, and it cannot afford to be: no inquiry that is going to help us understand ourselves can do without that kind of truthfulness, an acute and wary sense of the ordinary.

Notes

1. *The Society of Mind*, by Marvin Minsky (Simon and Schuster, 1986).

2. This is one possible reading of John Searle's well-known "Chinese Room" argument: see, for instance, *Minds, Brains, and Science* (Harvard University Press, 1985). On another reading, Searle's point is simply that we cannot say that a system understands a language unless it has some way of showing that it understands what things in the world the terms of the language refer to: this is certainly true.

3. As Charles Taylor has rightly stressed; see in particular his essay "Peaceful Coexistence in Psychology" (1973), reprinted in *Human Agency and Language* (Cambridge University Press, 1985).

56

Whose Justice? Which Rationality?
by Alasdair MacIntyre

In a previous book, *After Justice*, which came out in 1981, Alasdair Mac-
Intyre claimed that the ideas of justice available in the modern world are
like a pile of ruins, historical fragments that can make no coherent sense.
Politicians, reformers, administrators, appeal in a haphazard way to items
in this deposit. Philosophers and social theorists toil away trying to make
sense of it, but they cannot possibly succeed. The ruins are not even the
ruins of one building, but the disordered remains of various ethical conceptions. These were, in their time, coherent: they belonged to various
traditions. But now we have no coherent conceptions, and because we
are trying to solve our social problems with those fragmentary ideas, we
are doomed to endlessly inconclusive and conflicting arguments about
questions of justice.

   With regard to distributive justice, for instance—the questions of how
goods should rightfully be distributed in society—some conceptions insist on our asking whether it is fair that some people should enjoy markedly more advantages than others. Those ideas dispute the ground, not
just in the journals but in politics, with the presently more successful notion that you are entitled to what you have got or can get, so long as you
rightfully acquired it: where 'rightfully' often means not much more than
'without breaking the law', if that. Some philosophers see the disputes
between such ideas as embodying two different views of society, which
genuinely compete with each other and mobilise different ethical conceptions of property, justice and a social order. Those philosophers are also
disposed to think that philosophical discussion, together with empirical
knowledge, will contribute to making clear those views of society and
help us to see how far they make sense. For MacIntyre, however, these
discussions are simply a waste of time, since we have no tradition or coherent set of ethical conceptions by which they might be decided or even
advanced. All we have is endless disagreement and the sway of power and
political fortune. This hopeless lack of intellectual and ethical resources
applies not only to questions about inequality of property, income and

power, but just as much to other issues that touch on justice, such as the death penalty, abortion or affirmative action.

His new book sustains the same theme.[1] It is not a work of political philosophy, and indeed contains little philosophy of any kind. It is rather a study in intellectual history, exploring what MacIntyre sees as three different traditions of Western ethical thought: one running from Homer to Aristotle and passing through Arab and Jewish writers to St Thomas Aquinas; another, Biblical, tradition that came to Aquinas from St Augustine; and a third that informed Scottish thought in the 17th and 18th centuries. The studies of these various traditions fill out his general thesis with historical detail. The thesis has also become more ambitious than it was before. It is not only justice, but conceptions of practical reason itself—that is to say, of the processes by which, socially or personally, we work out what to do—that are relative to a tradition. There are, in MacIntyre's view, no ideas of justice or practical reason that are not relative to some tradition or other, and the attempt to identify and use such ideas independently of any tradition at all is precisely the main cause of our modern confusions, expressed in the ruinous outlook of liberalism. Although he admits that liberalism had some historical precursors, MacIntyre sees it basically as starting in the Enlightenment, a development that produced, as he puts it, 'a new social and cultural artifact, the individual'.

MacIntyre as intellectual historian is very widely informed and his story of developments in the traditions that he identifies is learned, interesting and notably well-written. He is also extremely and idiosyncratically selective. Any historical treatment of Western ethical ideas that rests a lot on there being divergent traditions is bound to play up some similarities and differences at the expense of others, and anyone who takes up this book should expect MacIntyre to be making a case, laying out a particular story without much qualification. There is one central matter, however, in which it is not even clear what case he is making, because the most important part of the story is simply missing. This is the example of the Scottish tradition leading up to the Enlightenment, which gets the most detailed treatment of all his examples, perhaps because it is the least familiar subject. This tradition was rooted in both Christianity and the practice of the law, and it offered, according to MacIntyre, a distinctively Scottish contribution to discussions about the basis of law in God and human nature. The hero of the story is a figure barely known except to specialists, a judge named Sir James Dalrymple of Stair, who argued, as against what was to be the dominant English view in the 18th century, that property rights could properly be limited in various cases. The work in which Stair set out his opinions, *The Institutions of the Law of Scotland* (1681), is an instructive example of the development of a tradition.

This tradition, however, even if its formation were historically interesting, is further from having a claim on our current attention than the other Christian traditions that MacIntyre discusses: if anything can lead us out of our modern fractured state, it is not likely to be a 17th-century Scottish combination of Calvinism and Roman Law. Its special interest for us must surely lie in its relation to the Scottish Enlightenment. But about this MacIntyre tells us very little: the only relevant relation of this tradition to the Enlightenment seems to be that of being its victim. Its fate was for it to be destroyed, like the Scotland in which it flourished, by the English. It was subverted from within by a disloyal Scot, David Hume, the first of two chapters on whom is indeed called 'Hume's Anglicising Subversion'.

Hume is conventionally regarded not only as the greatest of British philosophers but also as one of the most amiable and personally admirable, but MacIntyre, striking out, as often, by himself, seems fairly obviously to detest him: for his Toryism, for his desertion of Scotland and toadying to the English, for his insincerity in seeking academic appointments for which a profession of Calvinist Christianity was necessary, and—perhaps more than anything else—for his rejection of that Christianity and his hatred of 'the monkish virtues'.

MacIntyre has some interesting things to say about Hume, particularly on his similarities to Aristotle and the role of social assumptions in his account of practical reason. But in pursuing Hume to England, and taking up some peculiarities of Hume's thought, he seems to lose hold on the story he was developing about Scotland. It is one of the oddest features of his account that, although he gives us more detail about Lord Stair and more aspersions on Hume than either deserves, he then explicitly declines to say anything further about the Enlightenment in Scotland. In particular, virtually nothing is said about Adam Smith. Smith, who must be counted one of the most significant influences on the world of liberal individualism, has been the subject of important recent work, which has brought out the extent to which his ethical outlook reached beyond the division of labour and egoistic commercialism. His inclusion would have brought the story to a more helpful conclusion and also, surely, have changed some of its lessons.

MacIntyre has more general problems with the Enlightenment and with its offspring, liberal individualism. Like all who see modern life in terms of the collapse of a previous order or orders, MacIntyre tends to exaggerate both the coherence of the past and the incoherence of the present, to a point at which the outlooks of modernity come out as almost formless. 'Liberal individualism' is barely identified at all, except as the utilitarian philosophy of a consumer society. He does, rather contemptuously, admit that we might recognise, by now, another tradition, that of liberalism itself, but he sees this as little more than a tradition of endless disagreement, a self-congratulatory inconclusiveness. You would scarcely gather that there are liberal traditions that have tried to make ethical sense of modern society in terms of rights and other notions that go a long way beyond consumerism.

MacIntyre's central criticism of the Enlightenment, and of its legacy to liberalism, is that it set out to free political and social consciousness from any allegiance to tradition, and from any overarching conception of human good, and to substitute simply a framework within which individuals could pursue their own conceptions of the good. He claims that this had to fail, and that it yielded simply another tradition and another conception of the good, both inadequate. Other people have said this, and they may be right. But MacIntyre is peculiar in thinking that this is just about all that needs to be said about liberalism. What this line of criticism shows is that liberalism has failed to understand itself: but that, on MacIntyre's own admissions, is true of all the other traditions he discusses as well. If liberalism is indeed another tradition, then it should be treated like the others, and given the benefit of the methods for trying to bring different traditions into coherent relation with one another that MacIntyre sketches towards the end of the book. But then, on MacIntyre's own account of a tradition, there may be more intellectual hope than he allows for the liberals, or at least for those (and there are some) who have noticed that it is no longer 1789 or 1913. They recognise that the self-description of liberalism that it inherited from the Enlightenment was basically flawed, but hope to find a sounder understanding of it, which may help to preserve the more humane institutions of the modern world.

There is more than one reason, I think, why MacIntyre is likely to resist this consequence of his discovery that liberalism itself constitutes a tradition. One is a strong distaste for liberalism. (On page five of the book, already, there is a reference to that part of the readership of the *New York Times* 'which shares the presuppositions of those who write that parish magazine of affluent and self-congratulatory liberal enlightenment', a jibe they collect because of their contempt for evangelical fundamentalism.) A more philosophical reason is that MacIntyre thinks that liberalism, unlike other traditions, is peculiarly disqualified from thinking constructively about justice because it has such an impoverished idea of practical reason itself, denying in particular the truth that conceptions of practical reason are relative to a tradition.

In fact, it is not even clear that this supposed neglect on liberalism's part would necessarily make it less competent at helping us to think about conflicting conceptions of justice in our present situation. Even if the liberal were as incurably self-deceived as MacIntyre believes, liberal fantasies of impartiality and neutrality would perhaps serve the discourse between traditions better than the manifest and equally fantastic partiality to be found in other places. But in any case the claim that notions of practical reason are relative to traditions is poorly made out, and the least convincing element in the book is MacIntyre's account of the ways in which practical reason has supposedly been quite differently understood in different historical periods. Right at the beginning he gives some examples of the differences between various conceptions of practical reason: a calculation of egoistic costs and benefits, for instance, as contrasted with a concern for impartial constraints, or the objective of aiming at true and ultimate human good. These are indeed different ways of thinking about what you and others should do, and of course there are other ways of doing that, other styles of prudential or political thought, as well. But the question is whether they represent basically different forms of practical reasoning, or whether, on the other hand, it is possible to find a more general account of practical reasoning, within which these different kinds of consideration and ways of thinking can be understood as variants. Not every disagreement between two people about what counts as a good reason—a disagreement, for instance, about the merits of patriotism— should lead us to say that they disagree about the very nature of practical reason. Are there disagreements that must lead us to say that? Are there any that could?

This is a very important question, which links ethical and political issues to questions in philosophical anthropology: for how can we even understand other people—in other traditions, for instance—unless we start by ascribing to them some standards of rationality that they share with us? There has been a lot of discussion of these matters, but MacIntyre does not confront those discussions, or offer the philosophical arguments needed to show that the historical differences he brings out cannot be understood at a deeper level in terms of differences of content within a common human capacity to reason practically. It would certainly need a lot of philosophy to convince me of some things that he says: for instance, that it is a peculiarity of the modern world that an agent can count as a reason for doing something (a reason which may, of course, be outweighed by other reasons) the fact that, simply, he wants to do it. Indeed, MacIntyre himself has made it clear earlier in the book that the ancient Greeks, not surprisingly, well understood this basic kind of reason.

A less relativist and more realistic view of practical reason might make it easier than MacIntyre allows to achieve a more substantive understanding of justice, starting from our present position. MacIntyre does not rule out in his last pages the possibility of some such development, but he sees it in terms of turning our back on the ruined landscape of liberalism and seeking to carry on some one of the traditions he has identified, one that will have been modified by what it has learned from others. I suggested earlier that the despised tradition of liberalism might itself be in better shape to carry on these tasks than MacIntyre supposes, but he demands some more drastic and definitive turn away from the modern world. In his earlier book, only some millennial disaster seemed able to clear away the rubbish of modern incoherence. Here, he seems to relent a little and looks rather towards Thomism as a tradition that might still have some power to save us.

This might seem at first sight rather more optimistic, though it is bound to be better news to someone who professes himself an Augustinian Christian, as MacIntyre does, than to sceptical liberals or, come to that, evangelical fundamentalists. But it may in any case be less optimistic than it looks. His own searching and sympathetic accounts bring out the many ways in which the Thomist tradition involves at the deepest level belief in the Christian God and in a cosmic order very different from that of modernity; and it is precisely his point to insist on the ways in which Thomistic ideas of justice and of practical reason are implicated in that view of the world. To get back to some version of it from our modern or post-modern condition—and on MacIntyre's account of Enlightenment, it would indeed have to be *back*—might, after all, require some vast disaster.

Note

1. *Whose Justice? Which Rationality?* by Alasdair MacIntyre (Duckworth, 1988).

57

Intellectuals, by Paul Johnson

Paul Johnson is a prolific British writer who has produced histories of the Jews, Christianity, the modern world, and the English people. He is, I believe, a Catholic (if so, it commendably did not discourage him, in his substantial and very readable history of Christianity, from admitting that the religion, to all intents and purposes, was founded by Saint

Paul). Between 1955 and 1970 he worked on the left-wing journal *The New Statesman*, and for six years was its editor, with more success than anyone has achieved since. He is now firmly entrenched on the right, and is a fierce critic of left intellectuals.

The background to his new book is the rise and influence of secular intellectuals as moral and political guides, a development which he interprets as an unsuccessful replacement for clerical authority.[1] This general theme is only the background to the book—indeed, it might be called the excuse for it—and not its subject, since Johnson does not discuss the role of the intellectual in general terms, nor does he consider the difference between secular and religious intellectuals or ask whether they have a more significant part in some societies than in others. In fact, he does not pretend that the book is anything more than it is, a series of unflattering short biographies of people identified as secular intellectuals. They are an odd assortment, ranging from Rousseau and Shelley to Kenneth Tynan and Lillian Hellman, by way of Marx, Tolstoy, and Hemingway, among others. He describes them all so as to bring out their bad behavior. According to Johnson, they all—this seems to be their defining characteristic—"preferred ideas to people." Ruthless or exploitative personal relations are particularly emphasized: the well-known histories of Rousseau's treatment of his children, for instance, and Tolstoy's relations to his wife are rehearsed.

The chosen intellectuals are also represented as characteristically, if not universally, very unscrupulous about the truth, though this charge takes different forms, not always very carefully distinguished. Sometimes, as in the case of Russell and Sartre, it means that they made reckless and irresponsible political statements. With others, particularly Marx, it means that they would not admit it when proved wrong. With many, it means that they lied to their wives or their creditors. In the case of the left-wing British publisher Victor Gollancz, who is particularly picked on for sins against veracity, it paradoxically means, in several instances, that he stated with extreme frankness to authors that he would not publish material with which he did not agree.

One or two intellectuals are rather heartlessly mocked for practical incompetence: the aged Sartre became confused at a meeting; Bertrand Russell was unable to bring a kettle to the boil or adjust his hearing aid. A long paragraph devoted to the accidents in which Ernest Hemingway was involved makes a blackly comical catalog, but hardly a surprising one, granted the feats he was always attempting and the fact, firmly emphasized by Johnson, that much of the time he was drunk.

Above all, the writers in *Intellectuals* are shown as sexually unscrupulous and in many cases insatiable—and in almost every chapter (Ibsen is resistant to the treatment) there is a detailed rehearsal of the subject's adulteries, infidelities, and general sexual disorder. All the subjects but one are men; in the case of the exception, Lillian Hellman, Johnson is not content with the material he has about her sexual adventures and throws in a good deal more about those of Dashiell Hammett. The censorious and distinctly prurient tone of all this suggests that the Church's revenge on the secular intellectual has been shaped by the more dubious aspects of the confessional.

Much, then, is said about the less intellectual activities of the intellectuals. Not much is said about their ideas. The account of Marx is a standard caricature; the remarks about Rousseau's political theories would not pass a first-year exam. The little that is said about the technical work of Russell, Sartre, and Chomsky would have been better left out. The creative writers Johnson discusses he in fact admires, but he has nothing interesting to say about them. All the unlovely chatter about writers leaves in the end some sense of respect for only two of them: Ibsen and—interestingly—Brecht, who is represented as so unrelievedly and chillingly horrible that even an author who is prepared to patronize Marx and sneer at Tolstoy seems rather awed by him.

So the whole enterprise is quite useless. But it does raise two questions, at least. One is why an intelligent and hardworking writer with a sense of the past should have thought it worth doing. I have no idea. The other is the question of whether there was a subject to be written about, if Johnson had chosen to pursue it seriously. Is there anything interesting to be said about "intellectuals" as such? Who are they? What authority, if any, do their pronouncements have? It is these questions, particularly the last, that Johnson's book might have addressed, and perhaps was originally intended to address.

If there is a question worth addressing, certainly one would have to start with a less eccentric selection of intellectuals. One elementary improvement would be that they should not be selected just for being badly behaved. Johnson himself, as a matter of fact, undermines any general lesson to be drawn from his selection by several times mentioning other people who were nicer than his subjects, were exploited by them or at least were there to pick up the pieces, and yet had as good a claim to be secular intellectuals as the subjects had. In the tale of Tolstoy, there is Turgenev. Near Sartre at one time, there is Camus—though Johnson says he is not an intellectual, on the simplistic ground that he did not hold ideas to be more important than people. Above all, as friend and victim of the wretched Rousseau, there is Diderot. Diderot was an extremely sympathetic human being who was interested in a vast range of ideas and experience and as an organizer, an editor, and a writer of the great

Encyclopedia did as much as any other single person, perhaps more, to form modern consciousness. If Diderot was not a secular intellectual, then there is no such person.

Johnson's principles of selection are partly formed by the notion, explicitly applied to Camus, that exploitation of other people is a defining mark of an intellectual, or at least of a secular one. This is an uninteresting conception and begs all the questions. But in addition to this, and indeed contrary to it, Johnson may have another idea. It may be that he is not claiming to produce a generalization about all secular intellectuals (the language of "typically," "characteristically," and so forth makes it hard to tell), but is rather saying that these examples serve in themselves as a demonstration of the truth he wants to bring home: that possession of the sorts of characteristics by which intellectuals are distinguished—an interest in ideas, perhaps, and a disposition to see the world, particularly the world of politics, in abstract and general terms—carries no guarantee at all of moral reliability or good judgment. So why should the intellectuals have any authority? Why should anyone take any notice of them?

If this is Johnson's question, as I think it is, his principles of selection still are inadequate. For one thing, there are still questions to be answered about nonsecular intellectuals. Why should anyone have listened to them, either—to T. S. Eliot, for instance, or to Paul Claudel? He says nothing at all about this, but it is possible to imagine what his answer might be. From two very brief passages about the replacement of clerical authority by that of the secular intellectual, one might infer the opinion that if Christian intellectuals (in particular) are to be listened to, it is because they are Christian, not just because they are intellectuals. Or, rather differently: it may be they should be listened to because they are intellectuals, and their abstract and general formulations are what attract intellectual interest, but any authority they have is the authority of their Christian beliefs and derived from their religious tradition, and does not simply come from their status as intellectuals. With secular intellectuals, on the other hand, there is nothing to commend their views to people's attention beyond the fact that they are intellectuals.

This is some sort of an answer, but a very incomplete one. Many secular intellectuals do attach themselves to a tradition, as many among those reviewed in *Intellectuals* have attached themselves to Marxist traditions. Johnson thinks those traditions false and pernicious, and indeed sometimes proceeds in a peremptorily right-wing way (he counts the judgments of *Commentary* magazine as authoritative without further argument, and a statement about Sartre by the extreme right paper *L'Aurore* is unquestioningly accepted, although it is at the same time described as a sneer). But that should not be the point. Even if Johnson does not like the tradition in question, it will still be true that the authority that is claimed for these intellectuals' judgments does not derive from a pure act of personality, but is attached to traditions of discourse that stand behind the thoughts of particular people, as the works of Hegel, Saint-Simon, Ricardo, and Feuerbach, to name only a few, stand behind the ideas of Marx.

Equally, it would be a great mistake to suppose that the authority of Christian intellectuals is just the authority of the Church. Their role as such intellectuals is not that of a priest; moreover they have in fact often been heretics. Nor are their characteristics as intellectuals at all simply related to their Christian belief, or to the Church, and there is much to be said about the questions of how much help or harm may be done to the Christian life by its expression in abstract terms and in connection with a wider range of ideas. "What is the authority of an intellectual?" is as good a question about a Christian intellectual as about a secular one, and has been recognized to be so by Christians: by Newman, for instance, to take one notable example about whom Johnson certainly knows a good deal.

There is another, quite different, respect in which Johnson's list of examples needs to be reconsidered if the right question is to be isolated. It is necessary to separate from the supposed authority of the intellectual something else, the authority of the artist. By including Shelley, Tolstoy, and others who were creative writers Johnson confuses the issue in several ways. One is that the self-centeredness, the exploitation of others, what he calls the "monumental egotism" of these people, tells us nothing special about intellectuals. It simply reflects the well-known fact that some creative people make ruthless demands on those around them. It is another, and in fact totally useless, question whether those people's achievements "excuse" their behavior. Their neglected children, abused wives, abandoned mistresses, unpaid creditors, and other victims needed an answer to that question, perhaps, and they can hardly be blamed if their answer was negative. But we scarcely need an answer to it. Moreover, this entire theme has very little to do with the authority of intellectuals. The authority of these artists lies in their works, not in the characteristics typical of intellectuals.

Johnson strangely neglects this point. He admires most of the artists he discusses—in the case of Shelley, perhaps too indiscriminately. (Is it because he does not admire his work that he did not take up Wagner, an artist who, one would think, was from all points of view ideally suited to his style of treatment?) But he does not try to understand, or relate to his theme, the hardly unfamiliar fact that work displaying great insight can go with a heartless life and ridiculous pronouncements. In one case he runs into critical trouble, since he both regards Tolstoy as "perhaps the greatest of all novelists" and yet claims to find in the novels what he finds in Tolstoy's life, an inability to sympathize with other human beings.

It is true that the respect awarded to artists because of their works may get extended, in the case of some of them, into a regard for, or at least an interest in, their pronouncements on political and other subjects. This may not be entirely rational, any more than it is when the same thing happens with scientists or entertainers. But it is hardly surprising: such people may well be remarkable, singular, interesting, with a talent for powerfully expressing feelings. In any case, this is not an issue of the authority of the intellectual. The intellectual, in Johnson's sense of a distinguished or well-known person, is someone who has a disposition and capacity to discuss and think in an informed way about ideas, and is thought to have some authority to speak about questions of immediate public concern, particularly about politics, in virtue of that capacity.

In some cases, the distinction between the authority of the intellectual and that of the artist is of course blurred. This is particularly so with the theater and with film, and there has been the tiresome phenomenon, for instance, of writers such as John Osborne or Arnold Wesker, whose awkward plays were thought better than they were because they expressed political ideas, which in their turn were better regarded than they should have been because they were expressed on the stage. But in the end, the authority of the intellectual, if there is such a thing, should be a purely intellectual authority. It is more than an expertise or scholarship, because it is applied outside the sphere of experts and scholars. It is the authority of a person to speak about the particular issues, above all political issues, derived from that person's capacity to handle ideas. Can there be such a thing?

The first requirement is that ideas should have something to do with politics. It is of course possible to pretend that they do not, and the present British government is a sustained exercise in pretending they do not. Its well-known anti-intellectual position of course includes its being against intellectuals, but that is only a small part of what it includes, since there are not many intellectuals to be against: intellectuals, as opposed to men of letters or academics, have never been a very common phenomenon in Britain. Moreover, a good number of those that there are find themselves somewhere on the left, and the government has good reason to be against them anyway.

But it is not much more encouraging to right-wing intellectuals. An example is to be found in a recent article in the London *Times* by Roger Scruton, certainly a right-wing intellectual, written to mark Isaiah Berlin's eightieth birthday and mostly devoted to an attack on him. The attack itself has no substance—it merely applies to one of the least appropriate targets conceivable the old line about liberals committed to free speech being soft on communism—but it does offer a glimpse of Scruton's own location on the right, when he says that he senses in Berlin "a dearth of those experiences in which the suspicion of the liberal idea is rooted: experiences of the sacred and the erotic, of mourning and holy dread." What this might have to do with any politics now accessible to anyone is a question for Scruton, but, as he is well aware, it certainly has nothing at all to do with the politics of Mrs. Thatcher.

In one way, that is undeniably reassuring. On the other hand, the fact that Scruton's rhetoric, vapid as it is, has no conceivable relation to current political speech is an illustration of something more general and less welcome, that current speech has no room for any exercise of the imagination. In fact, although they are anti-intellectual, Thatcherian politics are deeply involved in ideas. They are, with their fixation on the competitive market and contempt for public assistance to the noncompetitive, more intensely ideological, as has often been noticed, than is usual in Britain. It is not that they have no ideas, but that they lack imagination, and those who develop the ideas are public accountants, publicists, and blinkered theorists of the market, rather than anyone who reflects more imaginatively on anything else. Certainly they are not intellectuals.

It is the intellectual imagination that gives intellectuals whatever authority they have. Of course it is true that the particular judgments of intellectuals may be impractical or poorly related to a given situation. But they are not meant to govern: that is the business of government, and to say that no one should comment on government except those in government is to say that there should be no comment. Of course, some intellectuals may be vain, self-important, and mendacious: that merely suggests that there should be more intellectuals who do not have such characteristics. Of course, the interest attached to the pronouncements of intellectuals may, in some cultures, be exaggerated. It is hard to deny that that used to be true in France, or at least in Paris; it is remarkable what intense scrutiny used to be applied to every shift of position, every analysis and rationalization, of certain Parisian thinkers who had never demonstrably shown good sense about anything.

But even such distortions raise questions that need answers. At the end of his chapter on Sartre, Johnson reports, in a bewildered tone, his funeral:

> Over 50,000 people, most of them young, followed his body into Montparnasse Cemetery. To get a better view, some climbed into the trees. . . . To what cause had they come to do honour? What

faith, what luminous truth about humanity, were they asserting by their mass presence? We may well ask.

If we may well ask, we should do well to answer. We need not suppose that the reputation of Sartre was entirely well-founded to acknowledge the truths to which it spoke: that politics necessarily involves ideas, and particularly so when it denies this; that political ideas need the surroundings, the criticism, and the life provided by other ideas; and that some people are able to bring those ideas imaginatively into the thoughts of those who are going to live under that politics. There is such a thing as the authority of the intellectual, and it is to be found in that capacity—an authority which, like that of the artist and unlike that of the clergy, depends on the uncommanded response of those it affects.

Note

1. *Intellectuals*, by Paul Johnson (Harper & Row, 1988).

58

Contingency, Irony and Solidarity, by Richard Rorty

An energetic thinker with some original ideas may understandably rebel against the oppressive demand to get it right, especially when the demand comes, as it often does, from cautious and conventional colleagues. In responsible subjects such as the natural sciences, such people rebel against the demand only at their peril—or rather, their ideas will succeed only if the demand is, in the end, obeyed, and the colleagues turn out merely to have been too cautious. In philosophy, however, the bets are less clearly drawn: the very idea of getting it right is more problematic. The innovator may see the demand as not just cautious, but in itself restrictive and conventional, asking for correctness, in terms which the new ideas are

designed to overthrow. He may be tempted to reject the demand altogether. This reaction is naturally self-fuelling; the further one goes, the
more irrelevant the demand may seem.

However, the demand to get it right has great survival value. All the
philosophers who have been found interesting for more than a very brief
period of fashion have been driven by a need to get it right in some terms
or other. Even Nietzsche, the thinker who most self-consciously constructed himself in a new style, and most radically mistreated received
standards of relevance and correctness, frequently reminded himself and
any readers he might have that he was originally a philologist and had
derived from that a respect for the decencies of exactness. Nietzsche's
very extreme case shows something true more generally: that there is no
one style in philosophy that displays the need to get it right. If one believes that careful treatises in a semi-scientific style are appropriate to
philosophy, then some plain virtues of that sort may meet the need. More
Nietzschean pretensions make more Nietzschean demands. But some
acknowledgment of the need is required, some concern for truthfulness
that goes beyond the disposition to put next what occurs next. Otherwise, what is conceived of as a radical philosophy will unsurprisingly
turn out to be just like conventional work which equally lacks intensity.
It will be predictably edifying, or perhaps predictably unedifying: in any
case, predictable.

Richard Rorty is a philosopher for whom the standards and the point
of getting it right have become very problematic, not only in philosophy
but quite generally. In his influential and interesting book, *Philosophy
and the Mirror of Nature*, published in 1979, he claimed that we should
give up the idea of language and thought mirroring or representing an external reality, and think in terms of 'metaphors' or 'vocabularies' striving
with each other. We invent descriptions ('of the world', as we mislead-
ingly put it), and some of them catch on, while others do not. This general line of thought does not exclude the notion of getting things right,
but it does raise doubts about what it may be to do so. It also gives a hard
time to some standard ways of construing that idea (those familiar to
structural engineers and archival historians, for instance). In that book,
the doubts about getting it right had only to a limited extent affected the
book itself; a good deal of it sounded like a philosopher arguing carefully
for one position and against another, distinguishing views, scrupulously
expounding the work of others. In his new book, however, there are dis-
tressing signs that Rorty has slackened his grip on conventional notions
of getting it right without yet forcing us to accept any others.[1]

In part, this may be because the book is rather untidily derived from
two sets of lectures (one set, the Northcliffe Lectures at University College London, appeared in an earlier version in these pages). The themes

announced in the title are not very firmly related to one another, and there is the phenomenon, familiar in lectures, that important matters are repeatedly introduced as asides. But that is not the most basic problem. Nor is it a problem, in itself, that Rorty moves freely between philosophical exposition and history of ideas and mild forays into literary criticism (particularly on Proust, Nabokov and Orwell): a lack of concern for frontiers is one of the most engaging things about the book. The reason the book is unsatisfying is that Rorty has seemingly lost the sense of a difficulty, of anything that needs to be got right.

This loss is illustrated by Rorty's account of his basic metaphysical view. Rorty would in fact prefer his outlook to be called 'post-metaphysical', since, like Wittgenstein and (I am told) Heidegger, he hopes to have moved away from the old claims and counter-claims of philosophy into a territory where his utterances do not claim to tell you how it is with these matters, but rather get you to see them differently. But Wittgenstein and (doubtless) Heidegger, and before them Nietzsche, went to great lengths to establish ways in which they could be understood like this, to find a space in which what they said would not simply count as another move in an old metaphysical game. One cannot simply say that one possesses this space—one has to change by intellectual and imaginative force the terms in which one is heard. Rorty himself insists on this, but he has not done it. He just tells us that things are thus and so with language and the world: for instance, that 'truths are made rather than found,' or that there are 'no truths independent of language'. These can be taken as innocuous platitudes; that is what they are if they say no more than, as Rorty also puts it, that language is a human invention. Indeed, nothing can be said without a means of saying it.

But Rorty wants more than these platitudes, and says things that go far beyond them. It does not follow from those platitudes, for instance, that there is no such thing as a scientific discovery of how things are (of how they would have been anyway, even if we had not discovered them), but this is what Rorty seems to say. He thinks that scientific theories are simply clusters of metaphors which 'happen to' have caught on. He writes: 'We need to see the constellations of causal forces which produced talk of DNA or of the Big Bang as of a piece with the causal forces which produced talk of "secularisation" or of "late capitalism". These various constellations are the random factors which have made some things subjects of conversation for us and others not, have made some projects and not others possible and important.'

But he has not done enough to make us take this as a serious statement of anything. What is excluded, if anything, by that boneless phrase 'of a piece'? What are the causal forces, and how mobilised, that indeed make DNA for the first time 'a subject of conversation'? (Might Crick and

Watson have economised on all that trouble with the X-ray photographs — there's a causal story for you—and just spread some gossip about the helix, as they did occasionally about their rivals?) What, above all, makes a project 'possible' for us? Should the unhappy discoverers of cold fusion, as they still may take themselves to be, strengthen their position by a course in persuasion? Rorty has not brought it about, as on his own account he has to do, that those questions and many others equally banal simply lapse. He will not bring it about by sentences such as those. Faced with the great power, technical and intellectual, of modern science, Richard Rorty, on his own view of things, must Try Harder.

Rorty himself, I think, does not recognise what he does face. In a revealing passage, he says: '. . . the sciences are no longer the most interesting or promising or exciting area of culture.' What he means by this comes out in a contrast a few lines later with 'the areas which *are* [his emphasis] at the forefront of culture, those which excite the imagination of the young . . .'; and they are identified as art and utopian politics. This identification itself seems at this present moment rather strange, but even apart from that, it is clear that whether or not the sciences do or do not excite the young has very little to do with how things stand with them — for instance, with whether they are indeed 'promising' (or, come to that, threatening), whether they will continue to advance in what they take to be knowledge and to affect our world. The definition of a cultural agenda which is as careless as this is not going to reveal how that agenda stands in relation to the sciences and the sciences' own conceptions of discovery.

At the heart of his enterprise Rorty has a very important question — about the ways in which liberalism should now understand itself. He mentions the claims made by some of the Frankfurt School (and taken up with enthusiasm in May 1968), to the effect that the Enlightenment and its child liberalism have turned into instruments of technological and scientistic oppression, and must now be rejected. He rightly replies that no set of ideas should be identified with the first ways they find of describing themselves. If the Enlightenment tended to see the paradigm of understanding as scientific knowledge, and society as a machine — in fact, it did not uniformly do either—we do not have to follow it in that. There may be other and more serviceable ways of describing liberalism and helping to save it.

Rorty's own way of approaching this very real problem takes the cavalier form of trying to do without the peculiar concerns of truth at all, scientific or any other. He also expresses his aim in terms of exchanging for the 'rationalisation' of society its 'poeticisation': a form of self-consciousness about the contingency of its guiding metaphors. To help us understand these ideas, Rorty turns to some works of literature. His engagements with them are a mixed success. His brief treatment of Proust, in particular, who turns up in a chapter in the surely uncongenial company of Nietzsche and Heidegger, fails, not because (as Rorty hints in the preface) it is too bold or unsupported, but because it does not take the first step of questioning the relations between the author and the narrator. He thinks that he has said something about the novel by saying that the collection of people Proust 'redescribed' in it is 'just a collection, just the people Proust happened to bump into' (and the confusions of fiction and reality are not helped when Comte Robert de Montesquiou, a source for the figure of Charlus, turns up as 'Montesquieu'). Nabokov is more interestingly considered, on the subject of cruelty: more interestingly, because there is here, more than in other parts of the book, a sense of felt resistance, of Rorty's having to find his way into an understanding of this notably sly writer. I am not sure whether he has found the right way, but his care in trying to do so is both noticeable and agreeable.

Granted that the physical world is for Rorty just a matter of our vocabularies, it is not surprising that everything else is as well. Human beings are entirely the products of culture: 'there is nothing to people except what has been socialised into them,' as he puts it, and what this may be is a matter of contingency. This might seem to be an extremely bold claim in the human sciences, solving at a stroke a large number of scientific questions about the genetic and the environmental. But I do not think it is meant in that way. It is rather a large (and uninviting) metaphysical conclusion, that since everything is a matter of vocabulary, vocabularies must certainly be a matter of vocabularies. We, like everything else, are our words—or something like that.

However, this account of the matter, which is about all that Rorty gives us, is rather ruffled by the fact that there seems to be an exception to the principle. The capacity to feel pain and to be humiliated is said to be universal: human beings will be open to pain and humiliation however they are acculturated, and pain and humiliation are the only things of which this is true. However, the *badness* of pain and humiliation are by no means independent of culture. Indeed the liberal ironist who is Rorty's hero is one who is against pain and humiliation (and against them more than he is against anything else), but recognises at the same time that he cannot demonstrate their badness, that it is as culturally grounded as anything else. The liberal ironist commits himself to things while knowing that that is all he is doing; he believes in things while knowing, in a sense, that there is nothing to believe in.

Rorty suggests in passing that he may be able to do this because he has been incompletely socialised: but I suspect that this is an unconscious recurrence of Mannheim's self-congratulatory conception of the intellectual as a 'free-swimming intelligence' who can move between ideologies.

Why should the liberal ironist not be, rather, someone who has been thoroughly socialised in a certain kind of liberal culture?

Ironists realise, most basically, that 'anything can be made to look good or bad by being redescribed.' This is a point at which it becomes very clear that a more urgent commitment to getting it right is, as it always is, an ethical matter. Of course, there is a boring sense in which what the ironist is said to believe is true: we can find some way of telling you about a terrible thing which is marginal or vague enough to conceal its terribleness. The recent Bay Area earthquake was, without doubt, an event that brought neighbourhoods together and gave employment to the plywood industry. But the ironist must have recognised something more challenging than this, surely? Does he think that a terrible thing can be redescribed so as to look good, even though the redescription reveals just those things that made it look terrible? Can the redescription make it look good to those very people who thought that it was terrible—us, for example? Why should we believe this? Why should Rorty believe it, since, on his own view, we are who we are and not someone else? Then the redescription will make it look good to someone else—someone who will rejoice at, say, accurate descriptions of Auschwitz? But then Rorty must say what, on his view, makes them descriptions, and accurate descriptions, of the same thing: of Auschwitz.

Rorty cannot get rid of the truth as lightly as he pretends. In his discussion of Orwell, Rorty very properly confronts the saying of Winston in *1984*: 'Freedom is the freedom to say that two plus two makes four. If that is granted, all else follows.' Rorty says 'it does not matter whether "two plus two is four" is true . . . all that matters is that if you believe it, you can say it without getting hurt . . . If we take care of freedom, truth can look after itself.' Earlier he says a similar thing, that it is not that truth will win in a free and open encounter, but that freedom is to be fostered for its own sake. 'A liberal society is one which is content to call "true" whatever the upshot of such encounters turns out to be.' But there is an important reservation: 'It is central to the idea of a liberal society that, in respect to words as opposed to deeds, persuasion as opposed to force, anything goes.' The reservation is not only important but conventional. But why should Rorty believe that these liberal distinctions can be defended or even understood if we do not take seriously the idea of telling the truth? Is the idea of persuasion itself, as opposed to mere force, independent of notions of the truth?

It is not merely because they ban singing or telling stories, and not merely because they beat people up, that authoritarian regimes are hated, but because they conceal the truth, tell lies, try to prevent people from knowing how things are. Nothing that Rorty says in this book, in his confrontation with Orwell or elsewhere, helps us to rethink in new terms the relation of a liberal society to truthfulness, or to our commitments (of science, but by no means only of science) to respecting how things actually are. Rorty has an immensely important project, to give liberalism a better understanding of itself than it has been left by previous philosophy. This book offers not much more than a benign celebration of the task. A closer focus, more patience, more strength, are needed in order to get on with it.

Note

1. *Contingency, Irony and Solidarity*, by Richard Rorty (Cambridge University Press, 1989).

59

Sources of the Self: The Making of the Modern Identity, by Charles Taylor

Charles Taylor is concerned with the ways in which we can and should think of ourselves as people who have—or lack—a sense of what is important to us, of what we most care about, and of what is valuable. This sense of our moral identity, for most of us, is not fully explicit, and does not consist of a set of formulated beliefs. It may look sometimes as though our sense of what is valuable is described by a set of beliefs, when a system of moral philosophy or a political creed seems to sum up our outlook; but as Taylor brilliantly shows in several different connections, it is typical of such formulations that they fail to explain their own appeal.[1]

Take, for instance, the general idea that it is a better world in which as many people as possible, whoever they may be, are happy rather than not. Utilitarian philosophies find in this idea, the idea of impartial benevolence, the basis of all value. And the same idea has a hold on our sentiments so firm that it may seem odd even to challenge it. But what is the appeal of impartiality and benevolence themselves? Where does that appeal—we might ask—come from? Again, the idea of modern man, lonely and unsupported by metaphysical comforts, braving an infinite and unfriendly universe, has played a large part in the rhetoric of secularism; but how do we account for the value of the qualities of heroism and solitude to which that rhetoric appeals? It is because he had no answer to that question, and barely saw the need to ask it, that some of Bertrand Russell's writings evoking the heroism of the lonely modern, such as *A Free Man's Worship*, are so disastrously sentimental.

If we ask where the appeal of such values, their pull on us, "comes from," we are likely to be met with familiar philosophical questions. What does "come from" mean? If it is a matter of philosophical explanation, showing how some values depend on others, then perhaps there is no value more basic than impartial benevolence; but (it will be said) why should there be a more basic value than that? In the well-tried phrase, we have to stop somewhere. If, on the other hand, we are concerned with psychological or historical explanations, these will not give any further insight into the value of anything, but merely tell us how our values came about. Taylor exposes and rejects the assumptions that sustain this kind of defensive analysis, in particular its uncritical trust in a distinction between fact and value.

What we value is, unsurprisingly, connected with what we believe about human beings and the world. If we have a faith in the value of impartial benevolence, for instance, this implies some pictures rather than others of what human beings are. Such a faith may go with a secular picture of human beings craving satisfaction, or, again, with certain religious images of God's equal concern for his creatures. There are other accounts of human nature, however, both secular and religious, that cannot encourage the belief in impartial benevolence as the supreme value. One of Taylor's aims is to look behind our values for the images of humanity that naturally support or encourage them.

These images, moreover, change over time, and the attitudes we think of as typical of modern life have a history: to trace their sources is also to trace their history. Most of Taylor's book consists of history: the history of philosophy, of ideas, of literature and, to a lesser extent, of other arts in the West, and their various contributions to modern ways of thinking. The history starts with Plato and ends with Derrida, but large tracts of time are left out: in particular, thinkers and artists of later antiquity and the Middle Ages fail to appear altogether, except for Augustine. This gap is standard for secular courses on the history of Western philosophy, and comes naturally to those of us who, however much we may be rightly told about the medieval origins of Renaissance and early modern ideas, still determinedly think of the Middle Ages as resembling a historical parenthesis. But it is odd for Taylor to proceed in this way, for he is a Catholic, and his book is, to a significant degree, a Catholic tale: indeed, it is a more distinctively Catholic tale, I am going to suggest, than Taylor wants it to be.

Sources of the Self is in every sense a large book: in length and in the range of what it covers, but above all in the generosity and breadth of its sympathies and its interest in humanity. In taking modern moral identity as its subject, it also considers the familiar suggestion that there is no such thing; and Taylor has a certain amount to say, particularly in the opening chapters, about alienation, rootlessness, a loss of the sense of self in the emptiness of modernity, and so forth. But temperamentally—one might say, ethically—*Sources of the Self* is a world away from the denunciations of modern thought and of the calamitous effects of liberal Enlightenment that are familiar from neo-Hegelians, right-wing Wittgensteinians, left-wing cultural critics, followers of Leo Strauss, and other reactionaries. Taylor, it is true, strongly attacks the standard modern approaches to self-understanding, such as those offered by Kantian or utilitarian theory, but his aim throughout is to suggest that we have more moral resources than we have thought, and to help us to understand how we have come by them, and hence—by implication—how we might better make use of them.

Taylor's first big book was on Hegel, but he has never been a Hegelian. He has not accepted that history has a purpose, that the dreadfulness of the past can be redeemed, or that categories can be drawn from the philosophical sciences that will serve to describe everything. But he does believe with Hegel that we can understand human affairs only according to their history, and history only according to our best understanding of human affairs. He also agrees with Hegel that hectoring the world has not much to do with either changing it or understanding it: if some idea or practice or attitude has come to be part of human life and helps to keep it going, then it cannot simply be a mistake; there must be something to be learned from it more interesting than that human beings are foolish or wicked. While his book contains many moral perceptions, and finds many things not to like about the world, and expresses distinct ethical assumptions, it is wonderfully unpreachy. Its religious themes are not sanctimonious, and its considerable ambitions are very unpretentious. Few large books on such large subjects are so engaging.

Deconstructive critics will have a hard time eliminating the author from these pages, an author who is a distinctive and a trustworthy human being. The sense of an unassuming presence is even enhanced, up to a point, by the book's rather improvisatory air. It seems to have missed some stage of editing, as though the manuscript had been put into shoe boxes and sent to the printer. Some of this is merely tiresome, such as the festoons of misprints: the odds are fifty-fifty, for instance, whether both the "o"s in "philosophical" will appear.[2] The formalities and informalities of the lecture room combine awkwardly: we seem to be getting both the notes and a recording. Some lists of points are desultorily numbered, while metaphors get amiably mixed and the prose wanders in and out of the chatty, for instance in the exposition of Locke:

> The ideal would be a much higher and better and ultimately even more advantageous way to be. But we can't somehow get it together. This is where God comes in.

Yet the air of informality and disorder has some rewards—even its own authority. As a stiffly presented treatise, the book would have had not merely less appeal, but less force. It has demanding things to say, but it is itself in the best sense undemanding. By avoiding the cute obscurities of one kind of philosophical writing, and the coercive argumentativeness of another, it speaks in a voice appropriate to what it is trying to say.

The historical part of the book is divided into four sections. The first concerns "inwardness," and discusses a traditionally Hegelian topic, the ways in which during the modern period people acquired a new and more deeply subjective sense of themselves. Modernity has no definite beginning and, as Taylor's treatment itself implies, some of its features may be traced to nineteenth-century industrialism, some to the Enlightenment, some to the Reformation, and so on. It was at the Renaissance, Taylor believes, that subjectivity took a distinctive turn. As he writes about Montaigne:

> We seek self-knowledge, but this can no longer mean just impersonal lore about human nature, as it could for Plato. . . . We are not looking for the universal nature; we each look for our own being. Montaigne therefore inaugurates a new kind of reflection which is intensely individual, a self-explanation, the aim of which is to reach self-knowledge by coming to see through the screens of self-delusion which passion or spiritual pride have erected.

The second historical section, called "The Affirmation of Ordinary Life," deals centrally with the Protestant trust that secular activities such as daily work or raising a family were expressive of a religious life, and considers various ways by which this Protestant outlook affected the development of a modern identity both in itself and through its offspring, not only rationalized Christianity but also Deism. The Deist view, for example, that God created the world and its natural laws and that these laws can be understood through reason, helped bring about a greater feeling for nature and a heightened awareness of personal sensibilities.

Taylor then turns to Romantic ideas of expression of various kinds, about which he shrewdly remarks that so far from being wholly opposed to scientific materialism, as many have believed (including many of the

Romantics themselves), those ideas are in some ways closely allied to it, for example, in the idea that nature is the source of human understanding and fulfillment. Finally Taylor gives an account of "our Victorian contemporaries" and their belief in science and progress and in the notion of universal justice, and a survey of various styles of modernism, particularly "epiphanic" art. He considers, for example, how the conceptions of subjectivity and of experience in such modernist writers as Musil, Proust, and Joyce challenged common-sense notions of a single, unified identity in linear time.

The arrangement of the subjects treated in the historical section is rather awkwardly made to coincide with a chronological progression. The first of them, on subjectivity, gets us only as far as Locke, and this has some real costs. For example, Diderot's *Neveu de Rameau*, a famous text for this question, is not considered, and more generally the arrangement seriously limits Taylor's discussion of the very interesting and difficult question, central to his theme, of what exactly does distinguish modern conceptions of the inner life from various ideas of self-consciousness that earlier times did, after all, possess.

The discussion in the different parts varies a good deal in ambition, and also in success. The treatment of Protestantism is admirable: sympathetic and discriminating, it draws on some splendid writing, especially from Puritan sources, such as a passage from Joseph Hall from which Taylor quotes for the title of a chapter:

> The homeliest service that we doe in an honest calling, though it be but to plow, or digge, if done in obedience, and conscience of God's Commandement, is crowned with an ample reward; whereas the best workes for their kinde (preaching, praying, offering Evangeli- call sacrifices) if without respect of God's injunction and glory, are loaded with curses. God loveth adverbs; and cares not how good, but how well.

Elsewhere, however, Taylor seems less intensely engaged with the writers he deals with, and on some topics—the English Romantic poets are one example, and Impressionist painting another—he presents a dutiful or breathless survey that might recall introductory courses in the "humanities." Even when he is more engaged, as he clearly is with some modernist works, there is a question about the style of his readings, the spirit in which he is speaking to us.

He is too good a reader, and also too good a historian of ideas, to try to use literary texts merely as illustrations of intellectual themes, in the flattening style familiar a generation ago from volumes devoted to the "intellectual background" of various centuries. He needs some critical position toward the texts, some way of reading them that will give them a place in his historical story. But it is not clear to me what he takes his position to be: how much he is doing for our understanding of *Prufrock*, for instance, when he says about its opening lines that "we triangulate to the meaning through the images." The few words given to the "refusal of depth" in D. H. Lawrence, supported by a short quotation from *Kangaroo*, left me asking for either more or less: there is not enough weight in this commentary to make Lawrence into a distinctive presence, or to move any pieces in the account of modernism.

The discussions of literature (those of painting are much fewer, and fainter) can of course be read in the friendly light shed by the whole book, simply as remarks on interesting books made by someone one wants to listen to. Taylor's unpretentiousness and lack of critical jargon, his gift for striking quotation, and his sharp observations do much to earn him that response, but there are several reasons why the response cannot disperse all doubts. One is that Taylor simply cannot dispense with some critical position if we are to relate his readings to his philosophical account in any clear way; another is the contrasting intensity that Taylor himself displays elsewhere.

In using these literary texts and his other more philosophical sources, Taylor is not trying to give us the causes of our modern outlook. In a sensitive chapter on historical explanation, he makes it clear that he does not suppose that our ideas will have been caused just by ideas. But any causal account will have to make sense of those ideas while explaining them, and relate them intelligibly to the ideas of the past: Taylor quotes approvingly Max Weber's view that an explanation in sociology has to be "adequate as to meaning":

> All historiography (and social science as well) relies on a (largely implicit) understanding of human motivation: how people respond, what they generally aspire to, the relative importance of given ends and the like.

Making sense of our ideas, and relating them to our past, is what he intends his historical story to do: this is the way in which it will contribute to a causal story.

The most characteristic feature of the modern outlook, as Taylor expresses it, is that we "feel particularly strongly the demand for universal justice and beneficence, are particularly sensitive to the claims of equality, feel the demands to freedom and self-rule as axiomatically justified, and put a very high priority on the avoidance of death and suffering." He is well aware that these ideals are not universally respected, let alone observed; but he is surely right to say that liberalism of this kind is typical of modern attitudes. These are the moral claims we need to understand, and, according to Taylor's account of how they came to be so, they have three sources. One "centers on a naturalism of disengaged reason," and makes use of the conception that people should, if rational, seek to understand the world and themselves as objectively as possible; this line of thought in our day often uses language that sounds characteristic of science, but it is not essentially tied to programs of modern science.

The second formative set of views finds its sources in the Romantic tradition, in notions, for example, of personal self-expression, expression of national and cultural identity, and of human self-discovery through art. Some of these notions, such as the formalistic and classicizing tendencies in modernism, arise precisely through an opposition to typically Romantic views. And the third source—in Taylor's order of exposition, the first—is none other than the Judeo-Christian tradition, "the original theistic grounding for these standards." Or, as Taylor also puts it, what we rather have is "a space in which one can move in three directions. There are the two independent frontiers and the original theistic foundation." The two modern directions, disengaged reason and expressivism, are called "frontiers" because they are inherently open to question and contestable. They not only conflict with each other, but it can be constantly asked how they are related to our moral life, and in what ways.

> The question is whether, even granted we fully recognize the dignity of disengaged reason, or the goodness of nature, this is in fact enough to justify the importance we put upon it, the moral store we set by it, the ideals we erect on it.

With these conceptions, then, though certainly they sustain our sense of value, there is always a question of whether they should do so, and of how much they can provide.

So what about the "original theistic foundation" itself? Here we meet a basic assumption of Taylor's: that theism is, from this point of view, in a different situation from any secular outlook, at least of a modern kind.

> Theism is, of course, contested as to its truth. Opponents may judge it harshly and think that it would be degrading and unfortunate for humans if it were true. *But no one doubts that those who embrace it will find a fully adequate moral source in it.* [my emphasis]

But in this remark there is a crucial ambiguity, which winds its way through much of Taylor's argument. The remark may mean merely that, as we all understand, each person who has a theistic belief can find in that belief some account that will justify valuing the things he or she most deeply values. I doubt that even this is unqualifiedly true: some people who have had such a belief seem to have felt there was a discrepancy between it and their values. But it is quite reasonable to say that we expect religious people to make some connection between their values and their religious beliefs. It is quite a different claim, however, and a much less reasonable one, to say that someone—in particular, a religious skeptic—who is trying to understand those values historically must simply accept the religious belief as their ultimate source, and agree that no further explanation is necessary or possible. To suppose that an unbeliever should think in these terms about religious values runs against a simple and powerful principle, which we might call "Feuerbach's axiom": if religion is false, it ultimately explains nothing, and it itself needs to be explained.

Of course, the unbeliever accepts that religious institutions and religious power, indeed religious ideas, can explain a lot. But if God does not exist, he has no control over anything, and what happens in his name must have a naturalistic explanation, because there is no other. This is not just an abstract and general principle. If religious beliefs are fantasies, how likely is it that they will determine to a very high degree the social or ethical developments that happen in their name? Sometimes they do so, but more generally it is quite obvious that religious beliefs themselves are modified by other forces such as political and economic interests or popular superstitions and mores. It is not merely that, as a matter of principle, a false religion cannot explain its own existence; more concretely, it cannot explain all that much.

Taylor tells a story according to which important elements of the modern liberal outlook were formed in the Christian consciousness. He tells less of a story about the ways in which such developments have been resisted by the Christian consciousness. That story is there to be told, as Taylor well knows, but he has no reason, for his purposes, to tell it. He should keep it in mind, however, as a reflective believer who is trying to give an account of the moral sources of liberalism: in particular, an account that does not presuppose (and he is very insistent that it does not) the truth of theism. Does he have that point firmly enough in mind when he says "the original root of the demand that we seek universal justice and well-being is of course our Judaeo-Christian religious tradition. In broad terms, this is obvious . . ."?

The only obvious thing is that, as he shows us, those demands developed within the Judeo-Christian tradition and were often expressed in Judeo-Christian terms. But we need more than that if we are to speak, as Taylor does, of a source, or a root, or a foundation. A source or root does not have to be the cause of a change, but it needs to provide more than a way of describing changes when they happen. A good example is provided by one of the earlier manifestations of a movement in the direction of universal justice, the disappearance of ancient slavery. It has been known for a long time that Christianity, though it became the official religion of the Roman Empire in the fourth century, played no distinctive or early part in this development. Such facts (it has many modern counterparts) must surely have some bearing on the claim that Taylor finds obvious. To the naturalistic and skeptical eye, they have a rather direct bearing: they make the claim seem either not obvious at all, or else so weak that it does not offer much to the self-understanding of modern liberalism.

The outcome of Taylor's inquiry, that theism turns out to play a large (and itself unexplained) role in our moral consciousness, is interestingly prefigured in the way he introduces that consciousness and its demands in the philosophical section at the very beginning of the book. There he argues that we can make no sense of our moral world, cannot situate ourselves in it, unless we make "strong evaluations" of "right and wrong, better or worse, higher or lower": we must regard some of our preferences as not just stronger, but as more worthwhile, more important, more admirable than others. Such evaluations tie in with our aspirations for ourselves, and embody an image of a person we would wish to be; in this way, they serve to give a structure, not only to a field of preferences, but to a field of obligations as well.

Connected with these features of our moral experience is another, that we cannot coherently regard our moral outlook or principles as freely invented; the idea that moral distinctions are invented "out of whole cloth" is, as Taylor brilliantly puts it, "equivalent to the notion that we invent the questions as well as the answers," and we cannot see our moral experience as factitious in that way—or, if we do, it is because it has ceased to have any hold on us at all.

Though there is room to disagree about the ways in which Taylor ties these various ideas together, much of what he says about the character of our moral experience seems to me, up to this point, importantly true, and any adequate account of morality must try to explain it. From this strong base in experience, however, Taylor very rapidly moves uphill, metaphysically speaking. First, he says that the character of our experience means that we have a craving for the good, and wish to be "rightly placed in relation to it"; two pages later, we have a sense of "the incomparably higher," and this, we soon learn, we conceive of as "infinitely valuable." By this stage, the pale Galilean, in some generic, Platonic form—or, rather the yearning for him—has definitely arrived.

Two problems press on this account of our moral consciousness. The first is that it goes a long way beyond what, in its first steps, it rightly said was necessary to any moral consciousness at all. Many people in antiquity, many people now, no doubt a few in the times in between, have lived with a sense that nothing they know of is incomparably higher than other things or infinitely valuable: they have often lived precisely with the pathos of caring for the finite and the comparable. To move as determinedly as Taylor does to the transcendental level is to freight the moral consciousness with demands that it not only can live without, but has lived without quite successfully. Furthermore, so far as these higher aspirations of morality are concerned (and this may of course be true of some of its less ambitious claims as well), a version of Feuerbach's axiom applies again: if there is no higher condition to aspire to, then this consciousness cannot mean what it seems to mean, and it demands another kind of account altogether: one that does not suggest that these aspirations might, as they present themselves, be satisfied.

Taylor, if I understand him, believes two things about this: that the aspiration for something transcending our finite wants, needs, and attitudes is not baseless or delusive, even if God does not exist; but that if God does exist, then it is he that satisfies it. Though this is a version of a very traditional position, it is a rather unstable one. If this aspiration does have this relation to any God there may be, can it really be immune to damage if we come to believe there is no God? Nietzsche thought not, and supposed that the beliefs in God, and in a Platonic good, and in many other ideals that morality has at various times collected, demand to be understood in terms that make it clear that those beliefs *could* not be satisfied: that they are not and cannot be what they seem.

Taylor mentions Nietzsche quite often, and almost always with respect, but he gives a reductive and limited account of what he was trying to do. In particular, he thinks that Nietzsche is relevant to the inquiry principally because he presents the radical option of giving up on the liberal ideals altogether. But that is not his main importance, which lies rather in pressing all the way the thought that if our moral aspirations do not, cannot, mean everything that they seem to mean, then they cannot come from where they seem to come from, and another kind of inquiry will be needed to understand their hold on us.

Nietzsche indeed thought that such an inquiry would also do away with liberalism (or rather, make it clear why history was going to do away with liberalism), but that is another, and subsequent, question. The first question is the question that Taylor indeed pursues, of how we are to understand the moral hold of liberalism. One thing to be learned from Nietzsche is that Taylor's own explanation, which depends on the theistic tradition, cannot be as neutral as he hopes, for the fundamental reason that the explanation would not go deep enough unless theism itself were true.

Some years ago, Alasdair MacIntyre published a book that said our choices lay, broadly, between Aristotle and Nietzsche.[3] Taylor and MacIntyre have some things in common. Both are Catholic; both think most modern accounts of moral experience are quite inadequate; both find importance in the ethical and explanatory powers of tradition. But they also profoundly differ, since MacIntyre, very roughly speaking, thinks that liberalism and the Enlightenment are disasters, and if we can get away from them without complete catastrophe we shall be lucky. Taylor in this book expresses wonderfully well why he resists that view, and lays out in a generous, illuminating, and convincing way the human value that is to be found in these distinctively modern ideals, even if the account their defenders give of them is defective. But as one who agrees with Taylor about the Enlightenment, and disagrees both with him and with Mac-Intyre about God, I think that Taylor, in his search for the sources of value, seems not to have taken seriously enough Nietzsche's thought that if there is, not only no God, but no metaphysical order of any kind, then this imposes quite new demands on our self-understanding. Though Taylor inhabits, unlike many philosophers, what is clearly and vigorously planet Earth and relishes its human history, his calculations still leave it being pulled out of orbit by an invisible Being.

Notes

1. *Sources of the Self: The Making of the Modern Identity*, by Charles Taylor (Harvard University Press, 1989).

2. Connoisseurs of textual criticism will enjoy the appearance on p. 66 of the Greek word for contemplation as "*thewria.*"

3. *After Virtue* (University of Notre Dame Press, 1981). A later book, *Whose Justice? Which Rationality?* (University of Notre Dame Press, 1988), rather modifies the position, roughly in the interests of Saint Thomas.

60

The Need to Be Sceptical

"Linguistic analysis", that now distant philosophical style, used to attract particular odium for its attitude towards ethics. In every area, the charge against it was that it neglected the traditional serious issues of philosophy; in ethical matters there was added to this the idea that the traditional concerns of philosophy were not only philosophically serious, but serious, so linguistic moral philosophy was perceived by its enemies as humanly frivolous as well as intellectually empty. The general charge was always uninteresting, but the charge in the field of ethics did have some force. The aim, which much of that philosophy cultivated, of being entirely higher-order, and concerned only with the form of moral thought and not with its content, was doomed to failure; it also laid itself open to the charge of obstructing real moral discussion, because substantive moral assumptions were hidden by the methodology.

Moral philosophy now is particularly concerned to avoid that charge, and substantive ethical discussion is in full fashion. Some of it deals with very general theoretical questions, some of it with specific ethical and legal issues of abortion, for instance, or affirmative action, or the proper treatment of animals. The more specific discussions often take the form (not, I myself think, a very helpful form) of trying to derive an answer from some general ethical theory: this is why these issues are often said to belong to a subject called "applied ethics".

The ethical theories themselves take the form, typically, of very general principles or, again, abstract patterns of moral argument, which are supposed to guide one's judgments about specific issues. Applied ethics, in the form that directly corresponds to its name, takes up the task of arriving at those judgments. It operates, of course, still at the level of principle: it concerns itself with the rights and wrongs of abortion, for instance, not of Susan's abortion. But at the end of the line, the general theories are supposed to guide, so far as we are rational, our judgments and decisions about quite particular issues.

Much current work in moral philosophy consists of articulating, refining, qualifying and defending such theories (as well, of course, as criticizing others). A characteristic concern is to ask whether the theory will accommodate some everyday moral belief: if so, on what terms; if not, whether that is bad news for the theory or, on the contrary, bad news for the everyday judgment, which will have been shown to be irrational. Utilitarianism, the ethical theory that finds all value in (very roughly) the satisfaction of as many desires or preferences as possible, is particularly adept, from long practice, at this exercise. Utilitarians are still, for instance, discussing with their critics, in a more sophisticated style and with rather less ideologically objectionable examples, a problem left to them by one of their ancestors, William Godwin. Godwin claimed that the rational Utilitarian person would clearly save from a fire, if the choice had to be made, the intellectual luminary Fénelon rather than the chambermaid's baby; and that it would be irrational to depart from this conclusion because the baby was also, as it happened, one's own. What is the moral power, Godwin asked, of that little word, *my*? Utilitarians still wonder whether they should agree with him.

The reactions of Utilitarians when their doctrine, strictly applied, diverges from unreconstructed moral sentiment, have always taken two different forms, the intransigent and the accommodating. Both parties have their present representatives. The intransigent (to whom Godwin of course belonged, as Bentham did) understand Utilitarianism to be a revolutionary instrument of reform, and denounce recalcitrant sentiments as irrational or prejudiced or self-serving. Intransigent Utilitarians will claim, for instance, that starvation and suffering in the Third World make as urgent a moral demand on one as suffering on one's own doorstep; some claim that buying a luxury instead of giving the money to Oxfam is the moral equivalent of murder. Another current concern is that for other species. The issue of "animal rights", as it is often called (though not very happily for Utilitarians, who have traditionally denied that there are such things as rights), has been advanced by philosophers who are not Utilitarians, but many of the prominent advocates, such as Peter Singer, do take a Utilitarian position.

Utilitarians of the more accommodating persuasion may take radical attitudes to some issues, but they have less confidence than the intransigents that the whole structure of our moral sentiments can or should be moved directly by the one lever of the Greatest Happiness Principle (or its modern, more technically sophisticated, descendants). They hope, rather, to explain our sentiments, even if they are apparently at one level not Utilitarian, in terms of the utility of a state of affairs in which people have sentiments of that kind: not every piece of promise-keeping increases general utility, but the general disposition to keep promises without calculating utilities too closely, even if it sacrifices some utility in the short term, will increase utility on the whole. The classical Utilitarian of this "two-level" kind was Henry Sidgwick; the most notable representative of the position now is R. M. Hare, who is unusual in still believing also that his ethical theory can be derived from the nature of moral language.

"Our": this powerful little word, applied to our ethical beliefs, gives philosophy many of its problems. Who, relevantly, are "we"? Members of this society or community? Representatives of all humanity? Just some sentient creatures among others, whose concerns should be directed to all of them? Utilitarianism assumes the last answer. At the opposite extreme is a kind of view that takes the community, the particular social space to which one belongs, as the centre of one's ethical experience. It has been a recurrent theme of modern moral philosophy, a problem perhaps first explicitly set by Hegel, to try to bring into some comprehensible relationship two different kinds of pull: on the one hand, that of local practices and understandings which provide, or have provided in the past, much of the weight of ethical life, and, on the other, claims of abstract rationality and universality, which are likely to condemn as irrational or parochial practices which cannot be justified within some very general framework of thought, a framework that could in principle be applied to any set of people anywhere.

There is one style in recent moral philosophy, influenced by the later work of Wittgenstein, that particularly emphasizes concrete practices and shared understandings as against abstract ethical theory, and indeed has not time for that sort of theorizing. Unlike some other critics of ethical theory, this view arrives at its opposition to it not in the first instance by reflection on ethical or social issues, but from considerations about meaning. This is one kind of moral philosophy that has continued to put at the front of its interests, as linguistic analysis did, questions about the meaning of ethical expressions and the ways in which we understand them, but its conclusions are the opposite of those typical of linguistic analysis. It rejects any sharp distinction between fact and value, and also any view which claims that values are merely attached to, read into, or projected on to a world that is in itself the inert subject of scientific inquiry—an empiricist theory which was influentially advocated in the more recent past by the late John Mackie.

The attack on the empiricist view takes from Wittgenstein a basic idea that all our understanding of language is a matter of children picking up practices, being inducted into a "form of life"; nowhere is it a matter of applying abstractly formulated rules. This is true even of mathematics—Wittgenstein emphasized that even with a mathematical rule one needs a shared understanding of what counts as applying it, and this cannot be supplied by some further rule. The use of ethical language, equally, depends on a shared form of life and the practices of a community within which we pick up the terms of our ethical experience. One thing that has been usefully brought out by these philosophers (John Macdowell, now at Pittsburgh, and Susan Hurley at Oxford are leading representatives of this style of thought) is the importance of "thick" ethical concepts, such as *treachery* or *lie* or *cowardice*, as contrasted with thin and general terms such as *good* and *right*; it is the thin terms, by contrast, that exclusively interest the ethical theorists.

The difficulty is to know, in the ethical case, who "we" are, whose practices and form of life are in question. When Wittgenstein spoke of mathematics resting, in the end, not on any absolute foundations, but only on how "we" go on, the "we" would seem naturally to embrace all those who share an understanding of mathematics. But "thick" ethical concepts are not typically shared by everyone; and the concepts belonging to other cultures that we (that is to say, we here) may come to understand, we by no means necessarily share with them. If the "we" to which the Wittgensteinian account speaks includes all humanity, then it still needs to explain how it is that some of us structure our ethical life with concepts that are unknown, strange or even repellent to others. If, on the other hand, the "we" that is relevant is that of a real community, a set of people whose ethical language and practices have a genuine social identity, then this philosophy still has to tell us how we can pick up and understand the ethical concepts of others (as to some extent we clearly can) and yet reject those concepts.

Equally it has to tell us how we can come to embrace new ethical concepts. A philosophical account that considers only the concepts that we pick up from our local community will find it hard to explain the criticism and alteration of ethical practices. It runs the risk of sharing with a certain kind of Right Hegelianism (though without Hegelianism's confidence in history) a cultivation of an inarticulate conservatism of the folk-ways. It is natural that people who are anyway drawn to a Right Hegelian enthusiasm for the folk-ways (or rather, as is their habit, for a condescending fantasy about the folk-ways) often welcome the Wittgensteinian line, interpreted in this way. They see it as the continuation of Hegelian conservatism by other means.

However, there is also, or at least there should be, a Wittgensteinian analogue to Left Hegelianism: this will be a view that accepts the insights about the thickness of our primary ethical understanding and its relation to social practices, but leaves room for a radical critique in the name of interests not adequately expressed in the folk-ways. Richard Rorty (though his widely discussed work does not bear very directly on moral philosophy) might seem to occupy such a position, but it is not clear that he does; he is perhaps tuned in, rather, to the sounds that can still distantly be heard from a particular set of folk-ways, those of American New Deal liberalism. Rorty's enthusiasm for assimilating the philosophies of Wittgenstein and also of Dewey to that of Heidegger causes uneasiness in those suspicious of the folk-ways, and his claim that Heidegger's unrepentant Nazism was simply personal aberration does not reassure them.

Moral philosophy naturally stands close to political and legal philosophy, and in political and legal connections an emphasis on community and social solidarity has, in the United States, given rise to what has rather vaguely been called a "communitarian" stance, as against the emphasis on individual rights and opportunities that has been prominent in the liberal tradition, notably as it was expressed in *A Theory of Justice* by John Rawls, published twenty years ago and continuously a focus of discussion ever since. Particularly in constitutional connections, communitarians are often identified as conservatives, who are more reluctant than liberals to interpret the provisions of the constitution in such a way as to advance general objectives of social justice. But others who have been classed as communitarians, such as Michael Walzer, would want to claim more radical positions.

In this debate the central issue is not, as in the discussion with the Wittgensteinians, the nature of ethical understanding itself, but rather the wider question of the extent to which the State and major social institutions should be committed to some rather than other "conceptions of the good", that is to say, ideas of what is a worthwhile human life. Should modern societies favour particular conceptions of how people may best live? Should they rather continue the liberal tradition of accepting that modern States are essentially pluralistic in this respect, and should be understood rather as giving their citizens equal opportunities and equal protection in pursuing whatever the citizens may, individually or in more local communities, conceive of as a good life? Rawls himself, whose views have continued to develop since his book was published, sees this pluralism as the central issue for a modern political philosophy; and he now considers his theory of justice as a solution to a modern political problem, rather than as a timeless interpretation of the values of social justice.

In taking this turn, Rawls's thought has become more directly historical than it used to be. In *A Theory of Justice*, the theory emerged as the result of a thought-experiment (roughly, that of considering what social system you would rationally choose if you did not know what position you were to occupy in it) which, it was supposed, might in principle be conducted by any rational agent at any time; equally, the thought-experiment yielded results that were supposed to be universal in their application. Rawls now sees the task more in terms of answering some distinctive questions of modern life, questions closely connected with the legitimacy of the modern State. This raises the issue for other outlooks in moral philosophy as well, of how historically self-conscious they need to be, and whether they are not still too hopeful of developing moral conclusions which will transcend their own circumstances.

Some other writers have insisted on a more detailed historical understanding of modernity and the special problems it presents to ethical life and understanding: Charles Taylor, for instance, whose ambitious *Sources of the Self* speaks to some of these issues. Alasdair MacIntyre, in his *After Virtue*, argued for an ethics that would concentrate on the traditional idea of the virtues, as contrasted with more distinctively modern concepts, such as individual rights and the maximization of satisfaction. Unlike some others who have taken up the tradition of the virtues, MacIntyre has a historical sense, and this leads him to see that it would be rather improbable if the late twentieth century, as it actually is, needed the same account of desirable human characteristics as recommended itself to Aristotle or Aquinas. However, this acknowledgement does not take him very far, since he thoroughly rejects the late twentieth century as it actually is, and he sees not much hope for the moral incoherences of the post-Enlightenment world. Taylor, on the other hand, though he rejects many of the characteristic formulations of modern liberalism such as those offered by Rawls, is much more sympathetic to the positive achievements of the Enlightenment.

The work of Rawls and of his major critics has to be understood in relation to the constitutional system of the United States, which is very good at raising issues of public principle, even if it has the disadvantage of turning every such issue into a question of law. Taylor's work, again, is involved with a critique of Habermas, a thinker whose understanding of modern society is closely connected with an interpretation of the history of Germany. In Britain, any such philosophy has been modest in extent and in quality, and this is no doubt connected with the traditional unreflectiveness of British politics. However, after a decade of government which invokes the folk-ways only in the interests of respectability and acknowledges individual rights only in the interests of business, which denies society when it is a question of welfare and asserts it when it is a matter of control, it may be that our benign toleration of incoherence will finally give up, and we shall feel the same need of political thought as others do.

What is surprisingly lacking from all the philosophical undertakings I have mentioned is the voice of a genuinely disturbing scepticism. A purely analytical or epistemological scepticism about moral judgments, such as was put forward by the positivists (who construed those judgments basically as expressions of feeling), or again the more recent empiricist scepticism of Mackie, are no longer very much to the fore. Moreover, that scepticism, just because it was purely analytical and based on very general considerations about knowledge or language, tended to leave moral questions very much where they were. It is the same with scepticism in ethics as it is with scepticism elsewhere, that the more general it is, the more harmless. The overall sceptical argument that we know nothing at all about other people's minds, for instance, is painless, because it is totally theoretical; it is more disturbing to consider that perhaps we know something about other people, but a lot less than we suppose. Similarly, more is to be feared and learned from a partial scepticism in ethics, one that casts suspicion on tracts of our moral sentiments and opinions, because of their psychological origins or our actual historical situation. Some of our moral ideas may no longer do what they once did for us; some of them may not, in honest reflection, now be credible.

The voice of a scepticism that is both psychological and historically situated is above all that of Nietzsche. He has had little evident influence on most Anglo-American philosophy, and where he has it has largely been in varyingly different relations to Foucault's historical work; to Heidegger; or to Derridean literary theory, a deeply Alexandrian and academic enterprise which to some people has appeared, amazingly, as an instrument of political power. But Nietzsche has a much more direct relation to all this work in moral philosophy, in that he makes it hard to take at their face value many of the sorts of moral assurances which almost all the work, whether in ethical theory or otherwise, still takes for granted.

Whatever its other differences, the recent work tends not to ask very searching questions about values that have been the staple of moral reflection for a long time. Intransigent Utilitarians reject some of our conventional beliefs, but on the basis of an unquestioned belief in impartial benevolence which is itself traditional, and also a miracle of moral and theoretical over-confidence. Nietzschean suspiciousness, which has done only too well in some historical and literary studies, still needs to take a black look at the received pieties of much moral philosophy.

It may seem a paradox to combine this suggestion with my earlier encouragements to liberal political theory; why should Nietzsche's black look do anything but destroy it, as he supposed it would? In part it is a paradox, but it is our paradox, that of people who need a theory of individual rights, but have lost some of the traditional reasons for asserting them. But at the same time, it is not altogether a paradox. We need a politics that makes ethical sense of individual lives, and we need it to be psychologically and socially realistic. It remains a major task for moral philosophy to meet these two needs together, and some of Nietzsche's ideas, notwithstanding his own politics, will most certainly help.

61

The Saturated Self: Dilemmas of Identity in Contemporary Life, by Kenneth J. Gergen

This is not a book about alcoholism. For Kenneth J. Gergen, a professor of psychology at Swarthmore College, the self is saturated, rather, with ideas, images, experiences, possibilities, and has lost its center in the rootless and superficial variety of post-modern life.[1] The expansion of media

technology and of travel, the decay of traditional loyalties and identifi-
cations, the disappearance of the face-to-face society, together with the
developments in culture that go with these changes, all contribute to a
world in which the self is fractured and dispersed and lacks any stable
identity. We have no real sense of ourselves and can become, temporarily,
almost anything we like.

You may think you have heard all this before, and you have. "The Saturated Self" is yet another exercise in cultural nostalgia, and is not much
different from most of the others. Toward its end, the book is mildly
more positive about contemporary chaos, suggesting very tentatively one
or two things that might be said for pluralism, relativism and the loss
of traditional dogma. But if it is less extreme in this respect than many
books of its type, it is at the same time even more shamelessly superficial,
secondhand and ill informed. If post-modern culture is a pile of fragments tossed around by commerce and inattentive frivolity, this book is
a symptom of it, not a diagnosis.

One trouble is that Mr. Gergen has badly misunderstood the term
"post-modern" itself. He thinks that it means post-*modernist*, and this
is one thing that it indeed does mean, particularly in connection with
architecture and music, where a post-modern style represents a rejection
of the formal austerities of the modern movement in favor, roughly, of
eclecticism, historical reference and greater jollity. In other connections,
however, and above all in relation to politics, post-modernism hopes to
overcome *modernity*, which is a phenomenon, and a spirit, identified
with such things as the Enlightenment and the ambitions of 19th-century
political theory.

Since modernity set in not later than the 18th century, and modernism,
flourishing in the first half of this century, rejected many of its most typical products, such as naturalism and romanticism, Mr. Gergen's confla-
tion of the two conceptions produces an epic degree of historical confusion. In one of his breathless surveys of popular culture, he cites as typical
expressions of *recent* post-modernism the anti-naturalist theater devices
that were modernist commonplaces (in Pirandello, for instance) in the
1920's and 30's. But a displacement of 60 years or so is fairly minor. Mr.
Gergen also tells us that 20th-century physics rediscovered the atom as
an irreducible particle; in fact, it was the 17th century that rediscovered it
and the 20th century that, so to speak, undiscovered it. To write a book
about 20th-century culture that understands neither modern art nor the
atomic bomb is quite a feat.

It is a historical commonplace that modernity displaced traditional
face-to-face forms of community. It has never been easy to locate this
process, and the nostalgia that makes a lot of such a transformation can
find itself wandering uneasily anywhere between the Reformation and

the early 20th century looking for the site of the Fall from the integrated community and its assurances. Mr. Gergen, given his problems with the identity of the modern, is even more insecure than most in locating this Golden Age, as well as exceptionally sentimental about what it was like. He seems to think that until 1900 or so almost everyone lived in a village and hardly ever left.

The many serious questions about people's sense of themselves and of their relations to others in the present world are not revealed, let alone addressed, by this empty, ignorant book.

Note

1. *The Saturated Self: Dilemmas of Identity in Contemporary Life*, by Kenneth J. Gergen (Basic Books, 1991).

62

Realism with a Human Face, by Hilary Putnam

There is a wonderful passage in Nietzsche's *Daybreak*, about the ageing philosopher. 'Subject to the illusion of a great moral renewal and rebirth, he passes judgment on the work and course of his life, as though it were only now that he had been endowed with clear sight.' He 'considers himself permitted to take things easier and to promulgate decrees rather than demonstrate'; and the inspiration of 'this feeling of well-being and these confident judgments is not wisdom but *weariness*'.

The American philosopher Hilary Putnam, now in his sixties and with a lot of important and influential philosophy to his credit, shows in this collection of essays and occasional pieces that he is for the most part creditably resistant to the seductions of maturity.[1] He does tell us occasionally about his place in the history of recent philosophy, but it is in a chatty and unpretentious style, which is present in most of the book. Many of the papers were clearly talks, and the cheery scattering of exclamation marks and amiable references to his colleagues give it the air of some personal and informal communication—letters home from a very bright pupil at a very philosophical school, perhaps—and not the self-congratulatory musings of late career.

Certainly it does not torment him, as it did Nietzsche's ripe sage, that 'he cannot be the last thinker.' The sense is present all the time that philosophy and other creative activities continue, that nothing will look the same in a while, that none of us has the final word about anything. Decrees are, admirably, not promulgated from certainty. However, it must be said that they are sometimes promulgated from briskness, and some things go by a good deal too fast, particularly when Putnam calls on his authority in the philosophy of physics and mathematics. At one point an argument zooms through which is supposed to show that it makes a difference to the question of free will that physics is now indeterministic, the difference being that (after all) we are free. It is a version of a very old argument, and on the face of it no less awful than the other versions, but Putnam does not stay around to make it any more convincing; he seems, as he does on a number of large subjects, to be just visiting.

The collection covers a wide range, including the history of recent philosophy, the interpretation of literary texts, and a few political thoughts. There is a lot of overlap, and some areas are visited so briefly that even Putnam's snaps have not come out too well. But most of the book is concerned with one very basic and important set of questions concerning the world, knowledge and values. The choice of the title, with its echo, perhaps shows less than total sensitivity to a painful history which, granted Putnam's own political past, has some claims on his consideration: but it does well express the central subject of the book.

We have the idea that we live in a world that exists independently of us and our thoughts. This idea may be called realism. Almost everyone shares it, and even those whose philosophies seemingly deny it really accept it in some form—some literary theorists, for instance, who say that we can never compare our texts to 'the world' but only to other texts. (As a colleague in Berkeley said to me: tell that to the Veterans of Foreign Texts.) The question is, how much can be made of realism? How much theoretical weight can it be given?

Putnam thinks that it comes in just two basic forms. 'Metaphysical realism' is the view that we can conceive of the world in some way quite independent of our own theories and the terms in which we describe it, and raise the question whether our descriptions fit its real character—whether our descriptions correspond to the way it really is, the way it was before we got to it. This version of realism is indeed theoretically ambitious, but it is false or unintelligible. It suggests that we can, so to speak, get round behind our descriptions and see how they fit the world, and this makes no sense at all: any conception of the world we can use at all is one that is already expressed in terms that we understand, our terms. The world cannot describe itself for us.

So what is the idea of realism that, this side of insanity, we all share? Putnam calls it 'internal realism', and this, he says, while it is true and sensible, is entirely trivial. It yields such truths as that before there were human beings there were trees and rocks; that the English phrase 'the sun' refers to a certain star; that our theory that we live on a planet in the galactic system is true because we live on such a planet. Such formulae can express our scientific and other knowledge, but they give no general philosophical understanding of how our thoughts and words latch on to the world. As expressions of the idea that the world is independent of our thought, they exclude nothing except what the ordinary non-philosophical understanding would regard as mad—for instance, that there was no planet or sun until there were human beings to describe them.

'Internal realism' does not say much. All the same, there are, according to Putnam, some philosophical advantages in insisting on it. One is that it resists a certain kind of relativism, the theory that we cannot properly say 'the sun is a star,' but only 'according to our way of looking at things, the sun is a star.' Putnam conclusively disposes of this line, pressing the objection that if this is all we could say, we could not identify what it is that, according to our way of looking at things, we take to be true. He also shows, equally conclusively, that formulations in this relativistic style that have been popularised by Richard Rorty, in particular, simply tear themselves apart. If, as Rorty is fond of putting it, the correct description of the world (for us) is a matter of what we find it convenient to say, and if, as Rorty admits, we find it convenient to say that science discovers a world that is already there, there is simply no perspective from which Rorty can say, as he also does, that science does not really discover a world that is already there, but (more or less) invents it. These are excellent points: but when we look more closely at Putnam's contrast between 'metaphysical' and 'internal' realism, we may begin to wonder how deeply he has assimilated them himself.

What exactly, first of all, have we rejected in rejecting metaphysical realism? Internal realism, after all, is not confined to banal remarks about banal objects. It can license banal remarks about less banal objects: if we believe that matter consists of certain types of particle, for instance, then we can say that what makes this true is that matter does consist of such particles, and that such particles are among the things that were there anyway, before our investigations. Metaphysical realism seems now to have added to all these acceptable banalities only a picture: a less acceptable picture, presumably, but also a very elusive one.

The issues become sharper, if we bring into the discussion a further idea: that some of our descriptions of the world are more local, or perspectival, or anthropocentric, than others. On the face of it, there should be something in this idea. I can say of the moon that it is a body of a certain shape with irregularities on its surface some of which, when illuminated by the sun, reflect more light than others. I can say that when so illuminated, it looks like a man's face. I can say that it looks like your Uncle Henry, indeed (icing this stale bun) that it looks amusingly, or strangely, or evocatively like him. These are all human descriptions of the same thing, but the understandings they call upon are increasingly parochial. On a larger scale, when Pascal said of the spaces of the universe that they were immense, that they were silent, and that they were terrifying, he spoke from an increasingly local perspective.

Applying the idea of such comparisons between the materials used in various descriptions, I brought into the discussion of these matters some years ago the notion of an account of the world that would be maximally independent of human peculiarities, the ideal of a description that could be used by any observer, even a non-human one, who was capable of investigating the world. I suggested that such a description might be said to express an 'absolute conception' of the world; and that it was such a conception that, as an ideal, science sought to achieve. The whole point of this was not to fall back into 'metaphysical realism', insofar as we can identify that illusion. If we use Putnam's contrast, this idea belongs with 'internal realism'. At the same time, however, it does not regard all the descriptions offered by humans as being on the same level. We can, I suggested, by a reflection within the resources of our human understanding, identify among our various descriptions of one and the same world some that, in order to be understood, make more demands on experience that is peculiarly human, and others that make less.

Putnam will have none of this, and in one piece in this book he works himself up into a state of extreme (though, happily, temporary) state of fury about these notions. His criticisms are a very ill-assorted lot. My view of them is doubtless skewed, but they all seem to me either to miss the point or at least to require more care in showing how they hit it. One uses a consideration which Putnam deploys in several places against various kinds of 'realism', that the world contains no fixed number of objects: asked whether a grove of five trees is one object, five, six, or what, there is no answer. But all this shows is the exceedingly well-known point that 'object' is not a concept under which you can count: there are, for instance, five *trees*. At a different level, he invokes conventional aspects of scientific description, or the relations of observers and observed in quantum theory: but he does not show how these aspects make the descriptions given by one kind of observer (in particular, human ones) local or perspectival in the relevant sense. If quantum mechanics presents these features, then it presents them to observers using a similar theory elsewhere in the universe. The 'absolute conception' is one that abstracts to the maximum degree from the *peculiarities* of any set of observers.

Of course, if extraterrestrial observers are doing well without any such theory, that raises another set of questions, about what we should think of quantum theory, as compared to their theory. Can we explain their theory in principle, or they ours? If so, we can understand, in terms of our conception of what science is, what is going on; if not, we shall be puzzled (we must remember that we have already made a lot of assumptions in supposing that these others are inquiring into the world, and successfully so). But on Putnam's view of things, it looks as though there is no reason for puzzlement at all. Everything we say is equally what *we* say; his 'internal' realism has a distinctively human face. It looks as though there would be no more, and no less, reason to be puzzled if extraterrestrial physics were quite different from ours than if extraterrestrial fashions or food are.

It may be that Putnam can show that the idea of an 'absolute conception' is, as he claims, incoherent, but his breathless assault has not yet done so. I suspect that he is hostile to it because he wrongly thinks that it represents the return from the grave (just when you thought you were safe) of Metaphysical Realism. But to the extent that this horror can be clearly identified at all, this is a mistake. I did say that the idea of the 'absolute conception' could be used to give a sense to the contrast between 'the world as it is in itself' and 'the world as it seems to us'. This, I believe, is a contrast that we need—in particular, when we explain the ambitions of science; and my aim was to explain what we might mean by this contrast, not from outside our conceptions, but in terms of reflections we can conduct within human life, the only place (needless to say) in which we can conduct them.

Putnam seems to say—though he does not address the question directly—that there is no sense in any such contrast at all, and, moreover, that science is not committed to it. He cheerfully says that it is mere dogmatism to suppose that even human scientific investigation will continue to converge on an agreed picture of the world; and he does not mean (as many might agree) that it is dogmatic to think that science will necessarily continue to succeed. He means that it might continue to succeed, but not by converging, or feeling the need to converge, on an agreed picture of the world. This seems to me a misunderstanding of what the scientific enterprise takes itself to be, precisely because it does not leave science with the conception that it is trying to tell us what the world is like.

Another thing that Putnam dislikes, and perhaps dislikes more than anything else, is a further suggestion, which I have also made, that there is an asymmetry in these respects between scientific and ethical thought. His aim on anything I have said in this area is even shakier: he goes on, a lot of the time, as though I aimed to distinguish facts from values as such (a traditional project which I explicitly reject), and as though I had to be a relativist (a necessity which I explicitly deny). Never mind. There are, Putnam and I agree, two important questions about these topics. First, do humans' basic thoughts about our relation to the world—a world where we find ourselves, in the banal sense, and which we do not make—bear the same basic relations to that human endeavour which is scientific enquiry as they do to our ethical life? Second, does an understanding of scientific enquiry as finding out what the world is really like call on vacuous or false metaphysical images which modern philosophy should finally have left behind?

The message of Putnam's book is that he says 'yes' to both these questions. The first affirmation may seem reassuring; rather less so, perhaps, when one reflects on the heroic paradox of the second. Whatever we eventually say about the first question (and it still seems to me that there are quite straightforward reasons for thinking that the relation of ethics to the world is very different from that of science), we should surely try to get rid of the paradoxical idea that we can only avoid metaphysical delusion by denying altogether that science is interested in what the world is really like (as opposed to the way it seems to us). Putnam is forced to this paradox, it seems to me, because of the very way in which he sets up his two kinds of realism in the first place.

In calling the acceptable and banal kind of realism 'internal', Putnam implies that the vital contrast is between a standpoint inside human experience, and one outside it. The outside standpoint is that which metaphysical realism tries to take. We cannot actually understand what the outside standpoint would be, and as a result, we find it hard to say what metaphysical realism would imply. We seem to have a boundary, but no conceivable idea of anything outside it. If we put it like this, however, and insist that the only standpoint is 'inside' human experience, we are still, in fact, using the idea of the boundary: we are claiming that there is a boundary, and that everything intelligible is on this side of it. Once we are stuck in that formulation, people who say such sensible things as that the world has certain characteristics which affect our experience—help to form our science, for instance—are read as trying to push the world and its characteristics back to the outside of this boundary.

But as Wittgenstein insisted, there is no such boundary—the very idea of it is unintelligible. Putnam says he agrees with Wittgenstein in this, and indeed Rorty says the same: but like Rorty, if less blatantly, Putnam is still guided by the ghosts that have supposedly been banished. An *internal* realism must be inside something, but what we have learned is that there is nothing for it to be inside. A distinction between metaphysical and internal realism makes sense only in terms of a diagram drawn by metaphysical realism itself. Once this lesson is properly learned, perhaps philosophers will be less anxious about saying what most people say, that the aim of science is to tell us what the world is like, as opposed to ways in which it seems (peculiarly) to us. Some may also think—it is certainly a separate question—that this is one of many ways in which science is different from ethics.

Note

1. *Realism with a Human Face*, by Hilary Putnam (Harvard University Press, 1990).

63

Political Liberalism, by John Rawls

It is over twenty years since John Rawls's *A Theory of Justice* was published. It was recognised at once as an immensely significant contribution to modern political philosophy, and its reputation has only grown since. There are many questions, about social justice, toleration and the stability of a modern state, that can scarcely be discussed unless one starts from ideas that have been shaped by Rawls.

The author himself has not been idle in these years. Unlike some who have made large contributions to philosophy, he has not been content to act as the janitor of his system, stopping leaks, explaining it to visitors, and replacing some of the wiring to meet improved modern standards. On the contrary, he has in certain respects basically rethought it. Rather than merely fiddling with the details in order to answer his critics and to provide new applications, while keeping all the central emphases the same, Rawls has done almost the opposite. He has preserved nearly all the structure, including most of the detail, but has given a new account of what it is about, the purpose that it primarily serves. He has provided what is almost a new interpretation of his own ideas.

He has done this over the years in a series of published lectures, which *Political Liberalism* now brings together.[1] They are still called lectures, and they still display marks of the form. Some of them have been rewritten or edited more than others, and there is a good deal of repetition; the last two pieces in the book particularly, 'The Basic Liberties and their Priority' and 'The Basic Structure as Subject', start from the foundations of the system—which, by this stage, is hardly necessary. The book does not try to be independent of *A Theory of Justice*, and no one will get much from it who does not know that work quite well. A good deal of it (especially in the very helpful and instructive footnotes) is concerned with detail, and with Rawls's discussions with his critics, discussions that are unfailingly courteous, concessive to the furthest limits that reason, honesty and good will can reach, and marked throughout by a most distinctive quality—a straightforward and unfeigned gratitude for being helped to see things more clearly. In many respects this book is a commentary on the earlier work, but above all, among its detailed developments and concessions, it offers a new conception of what Rawls is at.

Theory, as Rawls calls the earlier book (and we might as well follow him), offered a reasoned basis for thinking about social justice in the form of a fundamentally very simple thought-experiment. Those who are going to share life in a society are represented, in this fiction, by people in an 'Original Position' who are instructed to choose the structure and fundamental principles of a social system without knowing what role in it each person will play. The question of what people would choose if they did not know how they would benefit from the arrangements (if they were behind a 'veil of ignorance', in Rawls's famous phrase) is used to model what would be a *fair* arrangement for people in ordinary life, rather as you may get a fair division of a cake by asking someone to cut it who does not know which piece he will get. Behind the veil of ignorance, the parties choose 'rationally', as Rawls puts it, which means on the basis of intelligent self-interest. However, behind the veil, they do not know what their particular interests are, so everyone's self-interest has to be stylised in terms of a set of all-purpose or 'primary' goods—notably, liberty, money and self-respect—which it is assumed are valued by any human being, or at least any human being who is a candidate for living in a modern society. Under these assumptions, Rawls argued, people would choose a rather specific set of provisions to shape their society, including a priority for liberty over other goods, and also a principle of distributive justice, called 'the Difference Principle', which says that any departures from equality can be justified only if they benefit the worst-off. This principle can be expected to have a notably redistributive effect.

Although in the Original Position the choice is made in terms of rational self-interest, Rawls did not suppose that social justice could be based solely on self-interest. To suppose that this was the idea is to leave out the device of the Original Position itself. A self-interested person is not bound by what he would choose if he did not know who he was or what his advantages were. The whole point of the model is that a person who is willing to think in these terms, to imagine himself into the Original Position, is someone prepared to consider what is fair; he is a person who, as well as being merely rational, is 'reasonable', as Rawls says, and is willing to live on reasonable terms of co-operation with others. This point, central to *Theory*, was made entirely clear there, and Rawls has shown a saintly degree of patience with the remarkable number of critics who have not understood it.

The conception of justice that emerged from *Theory* was called Justice as Fairness. Some of its principles invited interpretation as constitutional features of the society; others, and in particular the Difference Principle, looked more like determinants of a desirable policy. It was itself a moral theory, which applied moral criteria to a political subject matter, saying what, from that moral point of view, a just society would be like. It seemed, moreover, to represent an ideal for any society anywhere, or at any rate for any society secure and developed enough for such aspirations to social justice to become real possibilities for reflection and for action.

The radical change in Rawls's position is that he now sees Justice as Fairness as a distinctively *political* conception. This means that he wants to distinguish it from any comprehensive moral doctrine among the many that claim to tell human beings how to live. It is both more and less than any such doctrine. It is less, because it does not claim to determine important metaphysical and moral questions that are vital to a view of life—religious issues, for instance, or questions of what sort of individual life is most worth living. It is also more than any overall moral outlook because, just in virtue of its minimalism, it can serve a purpose that no such comprehensive doctrine could serve—that of providing a decent shared framework within which people with different outlooks can share a social life.

The importance of this purpose is intimately connected to another change in the interpretation of Justice as Fairness: that it no longer offers a universal theory of justice. As, now, a political theory, it offers a solution to what Rawls sees as a distinctively modern political problem: how to settle the structure and principles of a society that contains a variety of groups with differing comprehensive outlooks or creeds—a society that is, and is going to remain, as Rawls supposes, pluralist. Justice as Fairness is seen as providing a central structure, a set of principles, on which the differing groups can agree as a basis for society as a system of ordered and principled cooperation, despite the fact that the groups disagree on many matters of great ethical importance. Its spirit, therefore, is very closely associated with the idea of toleration, and indeed Rawls often mentions the ideas of toleration that emerged from the wars of religion as a historical precursor of the ideas he is exploring.

That case, as Rawls points out, is not a perfect example of what he has in mind. For one thing, the arrangements were felt by many, at least at first, to constitute merely a *modus vivendi*, the best that could be achieved granted that no one could win and most people had tired of violence. Rawls insists very strongly that his pluralist society is not based merely on such a compromise. His principles of justice are more than devices to get people to live together as an alternative to their dying together. Life in accordance with the principles of justice, the life of toleration and fair cooperation under ideological difference, itself represents a higher human capacity for reasonableness and intelligent moderation. At some points Rawls salutes this capacity as among the most valuable human characteristics. Since it is distinctively elicited by the circumstances of pluralism, it should follow that the condition of pluralism itself is not just a special feature of modern societies (still less, as cultural conservatives would have it, a deplorable feature), but a particularly valuable historical development, an expression of progress. Rawls comes close to saying this, without quite doing so. At certain moments he acknowledges that while the values of liberalism are those particularly developed by modernity, there are other human possibilities, certainly valuable, which liberalism has ruled out.

Religious toleration has both encouraged and been helped by religious scepticism; sensible people, faced with the clash of fanaticisms, can reasonably wonder whether any of these positions can be known to be true—whether indeed they may not all be untrue—and their enthusiasm for any of them declines. Rawls certainly rejects fanaticism from his reasonable republic, but equally he does not want scepticism and indifference to overcome the outlooks that coexist in it. People must live by some conception of the good. Rawls hopes that in the pluralist state such conceptions will be strong and will give distinctive meaning to the lives of those who follow them, but at the same time he needs the conceptions to be peaceable and reasonable enough for them to coexist amiably within the shared framework of justice. Indeed, the shared framework itself needs the various conceptions of the good to flourish. In giving a detailed account of the way in which the institutions of justice can be grounded in, and can hold together, what he calls the 'overlapping consensus' among the various ethical conceptions, he sees moral energy as passing in both directions, between the central values of justice and the various ideals. Scepticism and cynicism about the various overall ethical outlooks can only serve to weaken the liberal structure of Justice as Fairness at the same time.

It is often asked whether the ideals of liberalism are robust or substantial enough to provide a focus of loyalty or aspiration. To this question, in this form, Rawls gives careful and reassuring answers, articulating the values and aspirations that go with Justice as Fairness, and explaining how it can coexist with a range of other, more comprehensive outlooks. The difficulty for him comes rather when one asks the converse question: how robust and distinctive can the various views be that coherently coexist under liberalism? It is not all that clear, first of all, what sort of thing they are. Sometimes Rawls seems to have in mind certain philosophical moral theories, such as Utilitarianism; but it will be no great political feat, obviously, to get such typical products of modernity (Mill and Kant, for instance) to coexist under liberalism. Sometimes he has in mind various religions, but in order to form part of the overlapping consensus, they and their followers have to be reasonable, and the demands of Rawls's reasonableness are strong enough to make one suspect that only domesticated and already liberal forms of religion will count. Rawls's state has no way of including militant Hinduism or Islam, for instance, or the most fanatical variants of Orthodox Judaism, and no doubt it is not sensible to expect that it should, but Rawls would help us to understand better how wide his state could go if he said more about that frequent condition of mankind, violent and enthusiastic unreasonableness. Its forces look as though they may be making more rather than fewer demands on liberalism in the near future.

Even within his state, the space that Rawls leaves for the operations of the various outlooks is quite constrained. The desirable rules of public speech require politicians (at least with regard to important and national matters) to lay aside appeals to the distinctive beliefs about the good that they and their group may hold, and to move rather at a level of the shared structure and the common good. One is not even supposed, ideally, to vote (at the national level) with the motive of expressing one's distinctive views of what kind of life is worth living, or any other such sectarian outlook. As an account of how one's strongest convictions and values should be related to politics, this seems to leave a very narrow space between there being either no politics or no convictions. It is significant that when Rawls addresses the one issue in current American politics that is acknowledged to carry a powerful religious and ethical charge, abortion, Justice as Fairness itself delivers one answer rather than the other: the right to abortion should be constitutionally protected.

Rawls's theory is obviously grounded very deeply in the American constitutional experience, which he salutes, while at the same time he freely admits the many ways in which the American system has fallen short of its own best aspirations. Despite his admissions, however, his account even of America, the heartland of his conception, sometimes seems disembodied and idealistic. It is not that he mistakes abstract moral theory for concrete political reflection; he is very good on the role of abstract thought in politics, and he has many sensible reflections on the psychological and political effects of adopting one or another attitude to social justice. What is lacking, rather, is the dimension of what might be called the sociological imagination, a sense that the peculiarities (including the peculiar successes, to date) of American constitutionalism may depend on features of American society which are grounded neither in its political organisation nor in its ideals, but in such things as the history of its immigration and its dedication to the aims of commercial society. Without some discussion of the peculiarities of America, it is very hard to do what Rawls wants us to do, which is to agree that a system based on America's experience (though it registers some limitations of that experience) can serve as the basis for reconciling, in order and decency, conflicting moral or religious claims as they occur in very different sorts of society.

When *Theory* first presented the theory, one thing that attracted particular attention was the strongly redistributive implications of the Difference Principle. It seemed a theory especially addressed to defining economic and social justice. Now that it has taken on its new aspect of a political theory of the tolerant liberal state, the Difference Principle has come to play a distinctly secondary role compared to the elements that help to define a constitutional structure within which the debates of politics can go on. Rawls indeed explains with some care why the Difference Principle cannot enjoy the same kind of status as other principles generated by the theory; cannot, in other words, provide the central constitutional structure. The main reason is that anything as obviously a matter of contested politics as redistributive taxation cannot expect the support of the overlapping consensus. But this is a strange reason. The argument for the Difference Principle is as strong as any other in the theory, and if people can be expected to reject it, despite those arguments, because of their conflicting political commitments, it is not clear why that should not apply to the more constitutional provisions as well.

Rawls's movement from a near-universal moral theory of social and economic justice to a political theory of the modern liberal state, with its pluralism and its toleration, is a remarkable, impressive and compelling transformation. Anyone concerned with these questions and familiar with *Theory*'s original formulations will want to follow the arguments that Rawls offers here in support of that transformation and for its consequences. As we follow them, we shall be bound to ask: how much room does Rawls's liberalism really leave for radically various moral conceptions of human beings and of society? What place does it find, in its new incarnation, for one of its own most distinct conclusions, the demand for a thoroughgoing redistribution of advantage? It is characteristic of Rawls's achievement that these are questions that in one form or another we shall have to confront anyway.

Note

1. *Political Liberalism*, by John Rawls (Columbia University Press, 1993).

64

Inequality Reexamined, by Amartya Sen

Every modern state and every modern political philosophy believes in equality of something. As Amartya Sen points out in this book, even libertarians, who think that there should be no politically imposed limits on what people may retain of what they gain without force or fraud, believe in the equal right to exert oneself in the market and not to be taxed.[1] Those who think that more effortful or productive or responsible work deserves higher rewards think that this principle should be applied equally to all citizens. The important issue, then, as Sen has helpfully insisted over many years, is not whether we are in favour of equality, but rather: equality of what?

Even if all modern outlooks accept some kind of equality, many of them do not list it among their political ideals. There is a question, then, about what it is that makes some conceptions of equality rather than others into the focus of political programmes that aim to increase equality; programmes, for instance, which stand in the tradition of linking equality with liberty and fraternity. There is a question, too, of why it is that all modern states do profess some conception of equality. It is not enough to reply that they have to do so, because equality is (even now) a leading catchword of modern politics: this merely raises the question again, in a more cynical tone of voice. The answer seems to be that in the modern world, which has largely rejected mythical or merely traditional sources of authority, only some conception of equal consideration for each citizen can form the basis of uncoerced and informed allegiance to a government.

Not so many governments at the present time can be said without any hesitation or qualification to live up to the promise offered by that formula, and that fact itself leads back to the problem of defining equality as a political ideal, rather than as a mere assumption. The point of articulating and pursuing a political ideal of equality is not to indulge resentment or a managerial passion for uniformity, even though both have no doubt played some part in the history of egalitarianism. The basic aim, now more important than ever, is to find a practical conception of equality that can give people a genuine sense that they receive equal consideration from society and so have a stake in it. Only this has any hope of giving people a reason why they should obey and co-operate. Without such a reason, there are only coercion, mystification, habit, and the hope that people will be content with making the best of where they find themselves. The sort of equality that contains no aspiration and can be comfortably announced as being already here, such as an equal legal right to become a millionaire, is quite obviously not enough. It is extraordinary that anyone can have thought, as some followers of Lady Thatcher have thought and perhaps in a few cases still do think, that mere equality in the face of the market could realise enough of an idea of equal citizenship to make anything work, including the market itself.

Sen's theory of equality does yield an aspiration that can speak to the problems of the modern state, although he does not himself discuss the most basic and general reasons for which a modern society might be interested in ideals of equality. He concentrates rather on what such an ideal should be. He properly reminds us that if we are going to develop ideas of equality, we had better have some notion of their purpose, and that for different purposes we may want to use different ideas of equality. For some purposes of economic understanding, inequality of income may be the relevant measure, but for broader political and social aims we need richer ideas. Sen is extremely aware of political issues, such as poverty, deprivation and injustice to women, but this book is not a work of political theory, and it does not start from the political questions that themselves create the demand for an understanding of equality. Sen is both an economist and a moral philosopher, but he approaches the problems of equality by a route that runs from economic theory.

The issue, as I said at the start, is, equality of what? Or as Sen also puts it, in the language of mathematical economists, in what space do we want equality to obtain? It is a fundamental point that equality in one space can, in virtue of the very same facts, mean inequality in another. To take one of Sen's favourite examples, people have different needs with respect to food, because of their body weight, their age, their state of health, and so on. To give them all the same food will not generate the same degree of nutrition in each; equality in the space of food provision means inequality in the space of nutrition. Similarly, equality of money or other such resources does not mean equality in terms of what people can achieve: for many different reasons, people are not the same in their capacity to convert resources into worthwhile or satisfying activity.

Welfare economists have made this point in terms of what was traditionally their favourite measure, 'utility'—which means roughly the degree to which someone is satisfied with a given outcome or gets what he wants. An addition of the same resource does not yield the same increase in utility, either between different people, or indeed for the same person in different contexts. One application of this point is the familiar 'diminishing marginal utility of money', by which an additional hundred pounds means more to someone who has a little than to someone who has a lot. Sen, however, has been a powerful and influential critic of those who overestimate the usefulness and, beyond a certain point, the coherence of the concept of utility, and for many reasons (not for the most part stated here, but referred to as appearing elsewhere) he rejects utility as the measure of what he calls 'basal equality'.

He also rejects as the measure of equality the 'primary goods' that John Rawls has specified as the objects of distribution in his political theory. Rawls described these as multi-purpose goods that any reasonable human being in most social circumstances would want: they include money and 'the means to self-respect'. Sen's own proposal is that the space in which the most basic equality is to be established is that of freedom itself. Rawls's primary goods, he claims, represent means rather than ends: the only point of money as a primary good is its power to increase one's freedom to choose. The criticism should, perhaps, rather be that the description of the primary goods that Rawls gave in *A Theory of Justice* was misleading. One of Rawls's primary goods was freedom itself, and Sen's criticism, that the primary goods are only means to freedom, can hardly apply to that; but then Rawls's description of a primary good does not apply to it very neatly, either.

If we can make freedom equal between different people, then we shall make equal the range of choices they have, and, with that, the range of 'capabilities' they possess for different kinds of human 'functioning'. If we bring it about that disabled people get more resources, we increase the range of things that they can choose to do, and this is the sense in which we increase their freedom. In explaining these ideas, Sen makes a number of careful and important distinctions. In many cases, having a range of alternatives from which to choose is an instrumental good, in the sense that it enables one to find the most satisfactory option. This is so in the standard type of economic model centred on utility, in which the desired outcome is merely identified with the item one picks, and the range of choice one had serves only as the basket out of which one picks it. Sen points out, however, that in many connections, choosing is itself important. It often makes a difference whether one chose a certain outcome, or the outcome was simply delivered to one, even though the outcome is just as good in itself. Sen thus wants to give choice and action a real place in the theory of equality, and not leave them as merely the routes that lead to desirable outcomes, as they standardly have been left, not only in theory, but, too often, in the practice of the welfare state, which has tended to regard the disabled as beneficiaries rather than as people who want the chance to make their own choices.

If equality is basically to be understood as equality of freedom, then the supposed clash between equality and freedom, so famous from confrontations between Left and Right, must in some way be ill-defined. Sen indeed says that to put the problem in these terms reflects a category mistake. 'They are not alternatives. Liberty is among the possible *fields of application* of equality, and equality is among the possible *patterns* of distribution of liberty' (his emphasis). Sen does not go as far as Rousseau and some other philosophers who say that there cannot be a conflict between liberty and equality at all, on the ground that nothing which conflicts with equality can be genuine liberty, and nothing that conflicts with liberty can be genuine equality. To the extent that equality at the most basic level is being extended, it must indeed be true in Sen's view that someone's freedom (of some kind) is being increased, since freedom is what is being more equally distributed. However, this does not mean that we can think solely in terms of an increase in freedom, and forget about conflicts between freedom and equality.

Suppose that the freedom of some poor and disabled people to get around is increased by special provision, and this is paid for by an increase in redistributive taxation. (Given present attitudes in Britain, the example is distinctly utopian, but that does not affect the argument.) As a result of the tax increase some higher tax-payers' range of choices, and hence, in Sen's sense, their freedom, is diminished: they can no longer afford both the Bentley and Gstaad this year. Now what is being bought with this bit of their freedom is an increase in someone else's freedom. However, it is not necessary to Sen's argument that the increase in the disabled person's freedom would be greater than the rich person's loss of freedom. One person's freedom is being set against another's, because freedom is the currency of equality, but it is not necessarily the case, merely in terms of freedom, that one person's gain will more than cancel out the other's loss: all that is necessary is that at the end we should be nearer to equality. In such a case there can be a real conflict between freedom and equality — even though the equality is itself equality of freedom.

Sen recognises that in such transactions there is a danger, as with equality over other spaces, of 'levelling down', but argues that there are other values to be taken into consideration. He accepts, for instance, that it would not be sensible to use large resources in order to increase marginally the capabilities of disadvantaged people, if the cost of this were to reduce severely the productivity of advantaged people; that would be an unacceptable loss in efficiency. He does not say much about values other than economic efficiency in their relation to equality of freedom. Thus he does not say much about the situation just discussed, in which the loss is of freedom. Again, he does not say very much about fairness, for instance in relation to questions of giving people who are more skilled better rewarded positions. He discusses this in terms of incentives and efficiency, but many people think that it is not merely inefficient, but actually unfair, not to give some such rewards (though Rawls dissents on the ground that no one deserves their talents, which is true but doubtfully relevant). It would be interesting to see how Sen would bring together freedom, the basic currency of equality, with desert and similar differential ideas of fairness; outside the area of punishment, does anyone *deserve* more freedom than another?

Determinations of equality and inequality in the space of freedom demand, as the examples show, some ways of 'measuring' increases or decreases in freedom. No sensible person should demand highly determinate or quantitative measures, and Sen has for many years been a leader in trying to persuade his fellow economists that some reasonable comparisons in the actual world are worth a great deal more than highly sophisticated operations on quantities that exist only in mathematical models. In the matter of counting or weighing freedoms or capabilities, however, we do need some guidance, and it can be fairly complained that Sen does not give us very much. It is an obvious point that one can count capabilities, choices, and so forth in any way one likes. To use an example I have put to Sen before, someone who introduces a new washing powder introduces also indefinitely many new choices (such as choosing between buying some arbitrary other good and buying this washing powder) and at the same time takes others away (such as the chance of making an informed choice of washing powder without worrying about this one). Counting, clearly, will get us nowhere. To this line of questioning Sen gives a robust reply to the general effect that any criterion can give rise to some such difficulties, and you just have to use good judgment in the face of actual circumstances.

The considerations one uses in actual circumstances rely, unsurprisingly, not on numbers, but on weight: some capabilities (or freedoms or possibilities of choice) are more important than others. In very many cases, however, the importance of the freedom is directly related to the importance of the functioning in question. The capacity to walk is important in the first instance because walking is important. If I can walk, there are many more things that I can do, and choices come with this, of where and when to walk. But if there is a real question that centres on the choices—a question whether I can walk where and when I choose—this is naturally understood as a further matter, one that comes up only if I can walk. To put both questions under the language of freedom runs the risk of mixing together two different kinds of political concern: it is one thing to able to walk (not to be paralysed, for instance), and another to be free (e.g. from police interference) to walk where and when I want.

There are other cases in which Sen's emphasis on freedom seems to pick on a consequence, rather than the centre, of some undesirable state. Stressing, as Franklin Roosevelt did, the importance of 'freedom from' such things as malaria, he lays the weight on counterfactual choice, the kinds of life people could choose to lead if they did not have malaria. It is importantly true that malaria is not just unpleasant but disabling. On the other hand, does that fact in itself pick out what is so obviously bad about it? 'If only I had not been . . . I could have chosen a richer life than the one I have' can be truly filled in many different ways, and not all the fillings have anything like the same political or social significance.

In many of Sen's examples, there is no doubt at all that the state of disadvantaged people would be improved if resources could be devoted to relieving their disadvantage: malnutrition, disease, ignorance, insecurity. Equality would be advanced if their state were better. But—as Sen himself admirably brings out in some of his technical discussions of comparabilities—you can arrive at this conclusion on almost any account of equality. With regard to these disadvantages, any reasonable story about the way human beings should live will deliver much the same result, and the special emphasis on freedom seems unnecessary, and in some cases, as I have already suggested, secondary. In other cases, on the other hand, the emphasis on freedom makes a considerable difference, but its results are also contestable. This is true with Sen's admirable discussion of gender discrimination in various parts of the world. Many of the statistics about women's disadvantage refer, once more, to such uncontroversial evils as malnutrition and early death, but others, relating to women's levels of education and chances of employment, raise ideologically disputed questions of what capabilities should be developed by women.

It is no criticism of Sen that he should take a stand in favour of women's rights to self-development. What is unclear, rather, is the extent to which he thinks that these dimensions of freedom and capability can themselves be theoretically derived. Does his theory say only that freedom and capability are the proper basis of claims to equality? Or does the theory deliver also the conclusion that the demand for equality of educational opportunity for women follows from any adequate account of human capabilities and potentialities? I should not be surprised or disappointed if he wanted to say the second. But then his theory will need to be supplemented by materials which at the moment it does not offer or even promise, in particular a theory of false consciousness which will explain why many women have failed to understand their own capabilities.

As it is, Sen's theory does stand rather oddly to the politics with which he is so evidently concerned. Much of the disadvantage that he mentions, which a move to greater equality would hope to reduce, is so uncontroversially awful that the refined arguments about the primacy of freedom seem unnecessary: whatever space you are working in—whether it is that of utility, resources, primary goods or freedom—you will get the same answer. In other cases, the results of the approach are much more controversial, at least in terms of local cultural problems, and then one must ask how far Sen's theory licenses us politically to treat such cases as being just like the uncontroversial cases (which is what, in terms of his theory, they are: all the cases equally involve the restriction of basic freedoms). But that needs a further political dimension of the theory: a dimension in which we can understand such things as false consciousness and the ideological misrepresentation of basic human capacities, and which will help us to discuss (among other things) the relation of Western agencies to people who do not necessarily share Western views.

In his work on many topics, notably famine, and also on several subjects discussed in this book, such as the definition of poverty, Sen's acute analysis and his remarkable powers of making subtle and relevant distinctions combine with his astonishing range of information to make instruments suitable for immediate political application. The theory of equality as the equality of freedom does not seem quite to do this. Its distinctions seem to yield either more than we need for political purposes, or less. Perhaps this is only to say that we need more weapons than this compelling and elegantly argued book can offer. Granted the depth and the growth of inequality in this country, to look no farther, it is hardly surprising.

Note

1. *Inequality Reexamined*, by Amartya Sen (Clarendon Press, 1992).

65

The Therapy of Desire: Theory and Practice in Hellenistic Ethics, by Martha Nussbaum

This is a book about therapeutic philosophy, the philosopher as doctor.[1] It is a historical work, concerned with the schools of philosophy that developed in the Hellenistic period, the period in which, after the death of Alexander the Great in 323 BC, Greek culture adapted itself to existing in the large and loosely organised states that took the place of the independent city-states in which most Greek life had gone on in the Classical period. These schools continued to develop and to have influence in the Roman world, and indeed some of the principal sources on which Martha Nussbaum draws in her rich and interesting book were written in Latin. It is a work of scholarship, with many references and exegetical notes, but Nussbaum makes it very clear throughout that she regards the issues raised by these ancient styles of philosophy as urgent for us, and she sets out her claim for this in a fluent, unpedantic, and sometimes emotionally urgent style which invites us to get close to what these long dead teachers may have had at heart.

Hellenistic philosophy is often called 'post-Aristotelian' philosophy, and Nussbaum takes Aristotle (who died a year after Alexander) as the starting-point, setting out his ethical outlook as a kind of bench-mark. She claims for him, as she has in many other writings, a rather more open-minded and exploratory humanism than some people find in him; and she gives reasons for starting from him rather than from what one might have thought the more obvious choice of Plato, the true parent of therapeutic philosophy. She then leads us through the arguments, aims and procedures of the Epicureans, the Sceptics and the Stoics. It is rather sad, as Nussbaum herself says, that she has not given us the Cynics, a movement (if it amounted even to that) of ill-behaved malcontents, represented by the famous figure of Diogenes, who is said to have lived in a barrel and to have told Alexander to get out of his light. She may be right in saying that we know too little for them to fit into her plan.

Nussbaum introduces a character who is imagined as moving between the various schools of philosophy, a young woman named Nikidion whom Nussbaum has retrieved from an ancient source in which she is mentioned as one of several courtesans with whom Epicurus was said by an enemy to have had a relationship. Despite this promising start, it must be said that Nikidion is a slightly creaky device who barely earns her keep in the narrative, since there is not much that can be kept constant about her as she takes up one course of therapy after another over the centuries. (At the beginning, when she is in Aristotle's school, she has to be a man, since he made his views about women as thinkers excessively clear.)

Nikidion takes part in the educational procedures of each school, always being offered one or another philosophical therapy for her passions, her fear of death, her trivial attachments, or (in the case of the Sceptics) her mere desire to know anything at all. What exactly has to be cured is somewhat different in each case, and Nussbaum skilfully brings out ways in which the concerns of each school define both a distinctive mode of treatment and a distinctive conception of what needs treating. In all the schools, however, what the pupil is thought to need and is taken to be seeking is peace: *ataraxia*, as it was called, freedom from emotional disturbance. This objective itself Nussbaum, not surprisingly, finds problematic. Equally problematic is the idea that it can be pursued by philosophical means.

Nussbaum's account is given largely in terms of philosophies: most of the material consists of reconstructions of what was taught by teachers who had these various allegiances. The reconstruction is itself a very difficult undertaking. No work by any of the leading figures survives except in fragments, and we rely on reports or on works which may be complete—and indeed, in the case of Lucretius' poem, which is a main source for Epicureanism, outstanding—but which are not direct products of the schools. Moreover, the 'schools' themselves are to some extent the construct of people, in the ancient world and more recently, discussing views which were handed on, modified and mixed together over long periods of time. These technical problems are well-known, and Nussbaum both points them out and addresses them resourcefully, even if the result is perhaps to make contrasts between the different approaches rather starker than they should be.

This problem, of reconstructing the philosophies, is the same for everyone concerned with these subjects. However, Nussbaum has another problem which is specially severe for her, since she wants to emphasise the work of the various teachers as a therapeutic practice, and this raises the question of how the philosophy when it has been reconstructed—the typical questions, doctrines and arguments that these various groups or traditions elaborated—might at any given time be related to such a practice. In part, this is a question of how the teachers conducted themselves, of how and under what conditions someone seeking such a therapy might be treated. Nussbaum does tell us a little, where there is something to be told, of how the fictional pupil Nikidion might be received and addressed, but most of this has to be constructed from the evidence for the philosophies themselves, and there is hardly any social or cultural material in her book to give us a sense of people who really might have sought a therapy from such teachers, or of what they might have had in mind.

The Therapy of Desire does not aim to give, and granted its scope and its plan, it could not have given, the kind of picture that Peter Brown has given, in his life of Augustine and other books about early Christianity, of what it was like to be someone at a certain date in Alexandria or in Carthage, wondering what to believe. It is not, in that sense, a work of history, as distinct from the history of philosophy, and it is no reproach to it that it is not. However, this does mean that great weight is thrown on the account of the philosophies to make it clear what therapeutic needs they might be thought to meet; and this is not a weight the account can always bear.

In these respects, the most successful treatment is that of Epicureanism. Here, there is some evidence, if indistinct, of a 'therapeutic community' which an aspirant might join. It sounds rather familiar in some ways, with advertisements (perhaps) and an exaggerated respect for the master. Equally, of course, there will have been many people who were interested in Epicureanism and influenced by it without belonging to any such group. In this case, too, it is clearer than in any other case what exactly philosophy, as such, was supposed to do for the patient. Nussbaum reminds us that if it is to be distinctively philosophical, a therapy needs to give an important place to rigorous argument and intellectual analysis. The Epicureans do well in this regard, because they thought that our fears and our obsessions were grounded in false beliefs, about death, the gods, and our relations to our and others' bodies, and that philosophy could defeat those beliefs, by showing clearly that religion was an illusion and death nothing to be feared. Nussbaum works well with these arguments, and in the most brilliant chapter in the book, gives a compelling reading of Lucretius' extraordinary treatment of sex, a reading which at once assembles an argument, shows why the argument is relevant, and allows the poetic voice its role in delivering the treatment.

Things go less easily with the Sceptics. There are some historical complexities which Nussbaum has reasonably left to one side, and she concentrates on the extreme or 'Pyrrhonian' scepticism which is presented in the works of Sextus Empiricus. Sextus has had an immense influence in delivering some of the thoughts of ancient Scepticism to the modern world. However, his work is an assemblage of very varied material, some parts of it more philosophically interesting than others. Moreover, it is not clear how exactly his books are related to teaching or to any therapeutic practice.

Indeed, there is a well-known problem of what, in any case, a practice of Sceptical teaching could coherently embrace. Pyrrhonians thought (more or less) that the aim of *ataraxia* would be reached by not assenting to anything, including that claim itself, and its tradition, reported by Sextus, includes the famous images that were supposed to capture this paradoxical outlook, such as that of the purgative that purges everything from the body including the purgative itself, and the story of the painter Apelles who, despairing of capturing the effect of a horse's breath, threw his sponge in irritation at the picture, thus getting that very effect.

Nussbaum relentlessly forces the Sceptics into admitting that if they are in the business of therapy (and she shows that some, at least, did think of themselves in such terms), then the one belief they cannot avoid is that the Sceptical method will favour *ataraxia*. She expresses some concern that they were willing, in order to encourage unbelief, to use some very bad arguments. She quotes a passage from Sextus (who was himself probably a doctor) called 'Why the Sceptic sometimes deliberately puts forward arguments which are weak in persuasive power', in which he proposes that, just as the doctor will not give a patient an overdose but the weakest remedy that will meet the condition, so the teacher will give the pupil the weakest argumentative remedy that will knock out the obstacles to unbelief and hence to peace. But the assumptions behind this argument are extraordinary. 'Strong' medicine is dangerous medicine, treatment which may have bad side-effects. If arguments are medicine, strong arguments—that is, sound ones—are not strong medicine, in this sense, but good medicine, and it is the weak arguments that are likely to make people ill. Of course, the Sceptic might say that the illness is belief, and strong arguments induce more belief than weak ones. But even if that were true, which it is not, it would merely underscore the point that the whole idea of using arguments as a Sceptical therapy for belief is ineliminably paradoxical; and by now, I think it must be admitted, rather tediously so.

If someone really did think that inner peace was the overriding imperative, and that it could be reached only through giving up the desire to know—to know anything at all—he would not try, much of the time, to get his pupil into the desired state by arguments, or if he did, it would be clear that they were used only to bewilder. His way would be more like that of a Zen master. Nussbaum has some such thought to hand when she appropriately mentions those in the late Sixties who indeed wanted to drop out of belief, but it raises a question for her procedure. She very much wants us to take each of her therapists seriously, and she very much does so herself, but it is hard now to take ancient Scepticism seriously as a therapeutic enterprise, even if its puzzles (which Descartes already called 'yesterday's cabbage') can still reasonably provide material for an academic and non-sceptical activity, the theory of knowledge, which is not the stuff of therapy.

The Stoics should be the most heavyweight of the three schools. Stoicism lasted in many variants over a very long time, it had substantial public expressions, and it passed on an extensive legacy, good and bad, to the modern world, in such forms as a gritty moralism of inner intention and a belief in human equality. Yet as it emerges here, it is also hard to take seriously, at least as a therapy. It is not that, like Scepticism, it should have given up on philosophy altogether if it was aiming to be a therapy, but rather that one is left unclear what philosophy it invites one to accept. The Stoics thought that the passions should be extirpated altogether. At the end of her account, however, though Nussbaum writes well about their complex theories of the emotions, we are not finally enlightened about why they thought this, or quite what it was supposed to involve. This is because there is no coherent account of the value of the things that typically arouse the passions. The Stoics held that everything except virtue and reason was *adiaphoron*, 'indifferent'. Nussbaum tries to argue that this need not mean that those other things have no value at all, but she finally admits defeat. Without some credible account of this, Stoicism seems attached to a lethal high-mindedness which we can hardly recognise as the materials or the goal of a therapy.

There remain some problems, as well, about the way in which Stoicism saw rigorous philosophy. These emerge as rather more severe than they need because Nussbaum puts closely together doctrines from Greek and Roman Stoicism and lays particular emphasis on Seneca (who tried to inculcate virtue in Nero and paid for his failure with his life). Besides being a very strenuous attempt to make Seneca seem both more coherent and more appealing than perhaps he altogether was, this does leave us with an unclear idea of how Stoicism typically understood the relations of theoretical philosophy to the therapeutic enterprise, given that Seneca shared the widespread Roman impatience and incapacity with abstract subjects. On one page, Nussbaum says of Chrysippus (the real founder of Stoicism) that he 'clearly was one of the greatest logicians in the history of the subject', and on the next, she tells us about Seneca's endless abuse of logic as a waste of time. If we are to pay as much attention to Seneca as she would like, it is not clear where this leaves us.

Wittgenstein sometimes spoke of philosophy as though it were a therapy, but in his case the therapy was primarily against the need to do philosophy. Philosophical therapy was, in Karl Kraus's famous phrase about psychoanalysis, the disease for which it was itself the cure. This conception indeed raised a problem of what philosophy might be like if it were to serve such a purpose. How could anything which was continuous with the practice of traditional philosophy assist the therapy of its own elimination? In fact, even in Wittgenstein himself, therapeutic philosophy looks quite a lot like other philosophy, in its concerns if not altogether in its style of presentation, and it is not surprising that Wittgensteinian themes are now developed in the usual academic manner, with no connection to any conception of therapy. There is not much alternative to this, if philosophy is to be a subject that is taught. If you really thought that philosophy was a therapy, and one that operated just against philosophy, why should you encourage anyone in the first place to acquire the disease? Inoculation is a useful technique only because it injects into the body a harmless version of a harmful bacillus which otherwise might attack one. The philosophical vaccine, by contrast, seems to inject at full strength a disease you are unlikely to catch otherwise. The Wittgensteinian may think that you might catch philosophy anyway, but even if there is such a risk, the best way to head it off is surely not to introduce the philosophical condition into people, but to encourage them (as Wittgenstein often did) to do something else.

The philosophical therapies with which Nussbaum is concerned raise quite different problems. The ills that they seek to cure are not philosophy itself or the products of philosophy, but universal human ills—despair, frustration, anxiety. Moreover, Nussbaum insists that the therapy should consist at heart of orthodox philosophy, with a proper place for rigorous argument (even if, as she also insists, it should pay serious attention to the rhetoric of its presentation). She is severe with the Epicureans for taking too instrumental a view of philosophy, and with the Sceptics, as I have said, for using bad arguments. In this insistence on the integrity of philosophy she distinguishes her own approach to these thinkers from Foucault's, who saw them only in terms of techniques directed to the *souci du soi*.

But can we really believe that philosophy, properly understood in terms of rigorous argument, could be so directly related to curing real human misery, the kind of suffering that priests and doctors and—indeed—therapists address? How deep an insight do we have into a culture in which this could be believed? How many people can really have believed it? At the end of her long, intriguing, inventive book, she has left me, for one, feeling how strange it might be to see rigorous philosophy (Chrysippus's logic, for instance) exclusively or mainly in this light, and also how great a distance separates these thinkers, inasmuch as they did believe this, from the modern world. Despite all the subtlety and insight that she finds in them, despite the fact that the Stoics, in particular, recognised unconscious operations of the mind that were unknown to earlier philosophy, we are surely bound to find the Epicureans too rationalistic, the Sceptics too procedurally self-obsessed, the Stoics (at least in their Roman incarnation) too unyieldingly pompous for us to take entirely seriously, not just their therapies, but the idea of them as philosophical therapists. Nussbaum indeed alleviates the formal implications of their use of philosophy by reminding us, often and well, of the literary dimensions of some philosophy, notably in the case of Lucretius. But this still does not locate the activity where we need it to be, since the relation of writer to reader is not for us, any more than that of teacher to pupil, the relation of therapist to patient.

Standing on the other side of so much history, above all of Christianity and Romanticism, we are bound to find these therapists very strange, in their aims, their tone and their methods: stranger, as it seems to me, than some thinkers who went before them, such as Thucydides or indeed Plato. Just because she has not sought to include any of that history, and has simply tried to bring these Hellenistic philosophers as close to us as she can while acknowledging their differences from us, Martha Nussbaum has given us a vivid sense of that strangeness. She may not perhaps have succeeded as much as she hoped in bringing them close to our concerns, but she has certainly redeemed them from celebratory entombment in the history of philosophy.

Note

1. *The Therapy of Desire: Theory and Practice in Hellenistic Ethics*, by Martha Nussbaum (Princeton University Press, 1994).

66

Only Words, by Catharine MacKinnon

Best known as an eloquent campaigner against pornography, Catharine MacKinnon is a lawyer—a Professor of Law at the University of Michigan Law School. Not all of this book (based on talks given at Princeton) sounds much like legal argument, and particularly when she is talking about pornography she gives a rhetorical display which may well have been breathtaking in the lecture hall.[1] But the book does in fact offer a legal argument, one which is interesting, and also deeply American, in the sense that MacKinnon discusses the problems raised by pornography and also by speech that constitutes sexual or racial harassment in terms of American law and the American Constitution. MacKinnon herself does not accept those terms as presently defined, and her book is an eloquent plea to Americans to move beyond what she sees as the prejudiced limitations of current doctrine, in particular of current liberal doctrine. As a plea to Americans, it takes for granted several aspects of American discussions. Some of this a British reader may find rather bewildering.

The First Amendment to the US Constitution protects 'freedom of speech'; this has been interpreted in a robust way that makes it quite difficult to ban anything. There are some provisions to restrict pornography, in particular to make child pornography illegal, but hard work has gone into generating the rather shaky formulae that support the restrictions. Some of those who do not want pornography to be Constitutionally protected have tried to argue that it does not count for the purposes of the Constitution as 'speech'. This is not because it now more often consists of pictures than words—a great deal of Constitutionally recognised 'speech' is not verbal. The claim is, roughly, that pornography is not 'speech' because it does not convey ideas: it is designed to produce erections rather than opinions. But this line has not found much favour, particularly with liberals. While most pornography conveys no ideas, some expressions that convey ideas may be thought pornographic (a mild case is a jacket of the Vietnam War era, often mentioned in the literature, which said 'Fuck the Draft'). More generally, it is hard to draw a line between different types of expression, with respect to their form, or their intentions, or their effects, and proclaim that some and not others count as the 'speech' which the First Amendment protects.

This is a point, then, at which liberals do not want to draw a line, and in order to understand some of what MacKinnon says, in particular some of her more vituperative asides, one has to see that she is attacking them on this score. MacKinnon does want to draw a line here. Since she wants the law to suppress pornography (or at least to provide remedies to those who have complaints against pornography), but does not want to suppress political argument on sexual subjects, she needs a distinction between more and less argumentative forms of expression.

While liberals are not keen to draw a line by distinguishing a kind of expression that is (so to speak) less than speech, they do need to distinguish what is 'merely' speech from what is more than speech—that is to say, from action. The First Amendment protects speech, argument, the exchange of ideas, and that includes obnoxious ideas, for instance of a racist character; but it does not protect hostile actions designed to intimidate people of another race. The extremely obvious problem is that some speech acts just are intimidating acts of that sort; or, to put it the other way round, some acts of an intimidating kind take the form of 'mere' speech, produced in some specific circumstances to a specific audience. In the case of political speech or anything that might conceivably be construed as political speech, the prevailing interpretations of the First Amendment go to remarkable lengths to protect the speaker, rather than the people whom the speech is intended to insult. In 1978, the American Nazi Party proposed to hold a march in Skokie, Illinois, a site chosen because many Jewish Holocaust survivors lived there. This demonstration was legally held to be protected speech, a decision upheld by the Supreme Court (Justice Blackmun dissenting).

This line of interpretation seems particularly perverse in light of the fact that in other connections, especially in relation to conditions of employment, American law is keen on the idea that speech or other forms of expression can constitute action. Under the Fourteenth Amendment, which guarantees 'equal protection' to all citizens, legal action can be taken against sexual and racial discrimination, which may include verbal and related kinds of harassment. Attempts have been made, with some success, to extend such provisions from the work-place to university campuses, in the form of 'speech-codes'. This has given rise to some argument, because of supposed difficulties in distinguishing between loutish insults, on the one hand, and, on the other, academic arguments or other material which a woman or a member of a minority might find contributed to a 'threatening environment'. In the work-place, however, various forms of speech and other kinds of expression, such as pornographic photographs, have been held to contribute to discrimination and inequality.

Taken together, all this leads to the result that American law can restrain locker-room crudities or dirty photographs in the factory, but neo-Nazi thugs shouting threats and racial insults at elderly Jews in a Chicago suburb are protected by the police. To some, particularly Europeans, this seems quite extraordinary. Catharine MacKinnon writes: 'It is my observation that anyone who attended primary school anywhere but in the United States tends to regard this approach, and the passion with which it is defended, as an American cultural peculiarity or fetish to be tolerated.' She is right. Perceptions differ in the other direction as well. A few months ago I expressed a few reservations on these lines to some liberal friends in New York, and later heard that after I had left it was found amazing that this reasonable Englishman should be, on questions of free speech, the next thing to a fascist.

However, it is not simply a question of cultural peculiarities. All democracies have problems about the relations of free speech to other political values, but the United States has problems which are severe and not always adequately acknowledged. I do not think that MacKinnon exaggerates when she says that 'the law of equality and the law of freedom of speech are on a collision course in this country.' MacKinnon herself tends to be on the side of control, of affirming equality by punishing speech, but you do not have to go all the way with her on that to acknowledge the problem.

The present liberal position requires one to hold three views at once. The first: there is no safe or clear line between speech and other forms of expression less than speech. The second: there is a clear and enforceable line between speech and action that is more than speech. The third: there is an effective line between insults directed to particular people in work-places and insults directed to classes of people in public space. The third view means, in effect, that there is a kind of speech that is, in a very broad sense indeed, political or public, and this is protected by the First Amendment, as opposed to speech which is (let us say) 'non-political', which is not protected. In particular, 'political' speech cannot be constrained by any provision that favours one side of an argument over the other, so racist speech must be tolerated. Racial discrimination in action, however, is forbidden, so at this point one has to rely—when in a 'political' context—on the distinction between speech and action (the second of the three views). In a 'non-political' context, however, it is accepted that speech can be action, and it can be legally restrained. But where can we find a distinction between the 'political' and the 'non-political' strong enough to support these two different ways of treating speech?

The first of the three liberal views is based on the idea that all sorts of behaviour of an expressive kind can contribute one way or another to the moral and political environment: if we are to protect the 'political', this view says, we must protect much more than public political argument. But then, why are offensive acts or displays in the work-place not protected, since they also presumably contribute fairly generously to the moral environment? Conversely, if it is right to defend racial equality by controlling speech in the work-place, why is it not right to control the speech of racist groups in public places chosen in order that the speech shall harass—which one might think was a more spectacular form of harassment?

These problems are under discussion in America, and liberals are anxious to find legal formulations that will distinguish what I have called the 'political' and the 'non-political'. But there is a real conflict between ideals here, and its resolution is likely to require a rethink, not simply cleverer distinctions. The United States claims to be dedicated to affirming racial equality; the Fourteenth Amendment is mobilised to express this; its writ allows the possibility of much intrusive legal activity. When it comes to matters that involve the First Amendment, there is an enormous strain in combining this with what MacKinnon calls 'the studied inability to tell the difference between oppressor and oppressed that passes for principled neutrality in this area'. The strain is yet more severe when one must say that speech which is action in a 'non-political' area is not action in a 'political' area; and when, moreover, what counts as speech in the 'political' area is construed so broadly that it is unclear why there is a 'non-political' area.

MacKinnon has strong arguments, it seems to me, to show that in these ways American liberal opinion is in a tight corner. However, there is more than one reason why the reader might not immediately see what these arguments are. One is that, as I said earlier, she takes for granted or mentions only obliquely what she is attacking, and British readers, in particular, may not only fail to recognise the target, but may wonder why the detailed hagiography of the First Amendment matters to them. (There is an answer to that: we deeply need something like the First Amendment, as we need affirmations of other basic rights, and should be warned of problems that can come with them.)

There is another reason, however, why any reader might find it hard to follow her argument. The reason is that it is associated with a polemic about pornography that often conceals the argument and for some people is likely to discredit it altogether. On the strength of its first chapter and its closing pages, you might say that the book is actually about pornography, and that the arguments about the First Amendment are mobilised only as a weapon in that cause, but I do not read it in that way. It seems to me a book about the law and politics of equality and free speech, overlaid by an oration about pornography which is rhetorically spectacular and in that line sometimes quite enjoyable, but which systematically runs together most of the distinctions that are needed if one is going to make sense of the problems of controlling pornography. Indeed, they are distinctions that are needed if MacKinnon is to make sense of her central argument.

Two assumptions are made throughout the oration, both of them untrue. The first is that all pornography is both heterosexual and sadistic. Pornography is solely a matter of the abuse of women by men, and gay pornography, or pornography which is erotic rather than aggressive in effect, simply disappear from the discussion altogether. The second false assumption is that it is straightforwardly known, scientifically established, proved beyond doubt etc, that pornography 'causes', 'is responsible for', 'is the agent of' rape, sexual abuse, sexual murder and so forth.

Beyond wearily noting that this is no better known now than it ever has been, and that MacKinnon offers no evidence for it, I shall leave aside this kind of claim—which is anyway not as distinctive a part of MacKinnon's case as two other assertions she continually (and it is clear, intentionally) runs together with it. One is that crimes are sometimes committed in the course of making pornography. This is certainly true, and any sensible scheme of regulation will seek to ban pornography which can be supposed to involve such crimes. (The Committee on Obscenity and Film Censorship which I chaired in the late Seventies recommended this as the one ground for banning pornographic materials, as opposed to restricting them to adults who choose to view them.) American law bans child pornography under this principle. MacKinnon approves of this ban, but finds American practice inconsistent in not extending it to other cases. However, she does not tell us how far she would extend it. If there are 'snuff' movies, or movies that make us suspect that real torture or coercion was involved in making them, many would agree that there is reason not just to pursue those crimes, but to suppress the movie. How much further does MacKinnon want to go? Sometimes she seems to think that no woman would appear in a porno movie unless she was coerced by a man, so the mere existence of a porno movie shows that a crime was committed in making it.

The other distinctive idea that MacKinnon appeals to here is that there is no relevant distinction between doing it in a movie and doing it. This is not the idea that pornography causes rapes, nor the idea that some pornography may be made by bringing about a rape. This is the idea that a pornographic representation of a rape just is rape. It is the most extreme version of the idea that speech is action.

It is true that photographic pornography is, as it might be grandly put, 'auto-iconic': so far as basic sexual activity is concerned, at least in the hardcore case, the participants are doing what they are represented as doing. But this, platitudinously, does not extend to everything that they are represented as doing; for instance, to leave aside simulated violence for the moment, they may be represented as having just cheerfully got together on a bicycling holiday, when they have in fact wearily started on the fourth day of filming sex in an LA cellar. Similarly, the reactions of people watching the movie are not necessarily the same as if they were watching everything represented in the movie. It is because these truths are so obvious, presumably, that MacKinnon devotes her advocacy so single-mindedly to obscuring them. 'In terms of what the men are doing sexually,' she writes, 'an audience watching a gang rape in a movie is no different from an audience watching a gang rape that is re-enacting a gang rape from a movie, or an audience watching any gang rape.' That weasel qualification, 'in terms of what the men are doing sexually', has to do a lot of work to stop that from being, to put it plainly, a lie.

MacKinnon deliberately enacts an indifference to almost every distinction that might be thought relevant to this subject: between what actually happens and what is represented as happening; between reality and fantasy; between crimes possibly caused by the film and crimes actually committed on the set; between pornography that shows women being humiliated and dismembered and pornography that represents them as active and enterprising sexual participants. This indifference does not come, I am certain, from intellectual confusion, but from a deliberate policy. It is part of a strategy to obliterate the liberals' usual hiding places, to deny them their lines of intellectual communication. In the open spaces that will be left when the usual distinctions have been blown away, the liberals will be seen for what they are, the guerrilla forces of male power.

Like other strategies of the same kind, this has considerable political and human costs. One victim of MacKinnon's tactic is her responsibility to the law. It is quite unclear what her proposals about pornography would in fact catch. She and Andrea Dworkin designed a Model Ordinance making pornography actionable as a civil rights violation; it was declared unconstitutional in the United States, though a version of it has had more success, with rather dubious results, in Canada. It is drawn in terms that leave it very unclear what it might be taken to cover. Again— besides the distinction between what is and what is not political argument, which I have already mentioned—MacKinnon also needs the law to distinguish between mere pornography and works of art or radical expression which (just once and very briefly) she admits should be defended. But there is no reason to think that this can be done, and in the Report of the Committee on Obscenity and Film Censorship we argued, I still think correctly, that the whole idea of legal protection for creative works, entrenched in English law in the form of the 'Public Good Defence' under the Obscene Publications Act, is misguided in principle.

What is clear is that MacKinnon, at least at this stage of her campaign, does not mind about any of this. There is a rather alarming note of angry, moralistic, populist impatience with these legal quibbles. This is not suitable to someone who is presumably committed to the integrity of the law. It is also not necessarily very clever politics. It is a tone more familiar, in these subjects, from the Right, and MacKinnon should reflect—as feminists have often been asked to reflect—who are her real allies; who would use the vague and moralistic laws she wishes to introduce, and to do what? She will be lucky if they are the friends of women's freedom.

MacKinnon claims, imperiously and without any questions, to speak for women. But many women may not want to be spoken for in such tones. It is not only that they may take a more positive view of some pornography than MacKinnon allows (as Linda Williams, for one, does in her book *Hardcore*). They may wonder whether pornography can be quite the all-consuming, omnipresent and supremely important threat to their freedom and autonomy that MacKinnon makes out. She quotes her friend Andrea Dworkin as saying 'pornography is the law for women.' This seems to me an insult to women, who have more to fear from the law, and more to hope from it, than this would allow.

Slogans of this kind also obscure the force of MacKinnon's more general arguments. She has laid bare significant weak spots in the modern liberal doctrine of free speech, particularly in the United States; but many people, including many women, will fail to take her seriously on this if they have no alternative to crouching together with American liberals under the indiscriminate onslaught which she aims at all consecutive thought about pornography.

Note

1. *Only Words*, by Catharine MacKinnon (HarperCollins, 1994).

67

The Limits of Interpretation, Interpretation and Overinterpretation, Six Walks in the Fictional Woods, Apocalypse Postponed, Misreadings, and How to Travel with a Salmon & Other Essays, by Umberto Eco

At the beginning of Umberto Eco's novel *Foucault's Pendulum*, there are two epigraphs. Every chapter of this book also has an epigraph, so these are particularly prominent—they come before everything else. One is a quotation from an occultist writer, Heinrich Cornelius Agrippa von Nettesheim. The other is from a contemporary logician, Raymond Smullyan: "Superstition brings bad luck." The quotations bring together two obsessions in which much of Eco's work is involved, one with logical paradox, the other with obscure facts about Hermetic traditions, magical riddles, prophecies, the cabbala, and interpretations of history and nature according to complex, hidden, and often conspiratorial patterns.

As its many readers know, such things are themselves the subject of *Foucault's Pendulum*. At its center is the idea of a vast trans-historical Plan, initiated by the Knights Templar and involving the Holy Grail, the Society of the Rosy Cross, numerological ratios, the Great Pyramid, Freemasons, the Seven Dwarfs, and the Protocols of the Elders of Zion. In the novel, the contemporary characters, Milanese publishers who get sucked into the world of this conspiracy, turn out to have been deluded; "the interpretative frenzy of my monomaniacs," as Eco calls it in *Interpretation and Overinterpretation*, is checked when a young woman, more sensible than her friends, plausibly conjectures that the central document is a "laundry list," as it is from then on unquestioningly called: though while it is a list, it does not seem to be a list of laundry.

However, even if the Plan turns out in the book, as in history, to be a myth, Eco does not think that nothing is left over from it. We are invited into the "excess of wonder" that leads the Hermetic interpreter on, and at the end of the novel there are some strange events to wonder at. Moreover, we are invited, by the existence of the novel and the material that Eco assembled in it, to wonder at the strange processes of "Hermetic semiosis" itself.

Eco sees quite clearly what is wrong with the principles of interpretation (mainly of texts, but also of events) that lead to the paranoid belief in the Plan. They permit everything, because any similarity or association, of the many different kinds that were exploited, as Eco explains, by the Renaissance "art of memory," is enough to get them going; the plant called orchis can stand for the testicles (by similarity of shape), or the crow for the Ethiopians (by similarity of color), or the ant for Providence (by a hieroglyphic relation), and since, as Eco says, "from a certain point of view, everything bears relationships of analogy, contiguity and similarity to everything else," by exploiting "a false transitivity" you can get anywhere from anywhere. As a result, there can be no final Hermetic secret:

> Every object . . . hides a secret . . . The ultimate secret of hermetic initiation is that everything is secret . . . Hermetic thought transforms the whole world theatre into a linguistic phenomenon and at the same time denies language any power of communication.

It is not merely that each thing means something, but that each thing means almost anything. As a character in *Foucault's Pendulum* says, "The more elusive and ambiguous a symbol is, the more it gains significance and power." What is wrong is well illustrated (though I do not know whether Eco has mentioned it) by the activity, once quite popular, of finding messages coded in Shakespeare's writings which revealed that they were written by Bacon. It seems to have stopped after researchers, using the same methods rather more elegantly, decoded messages to the effect that they were written by various other people, for instance by Shakespeare.

Just because these interpretative activities are unlimited, uncontrolled, indeterminate, they are quite specially and limitlessly boring. It does not follow that facts about the human appetite for this kind of interpretation are themselves boring. The discovery of those facts, after all, is not effortless or unconstrained, and the extraordinary range of information about such things that Eco mobilizes in *Foucault's Pendulum* and elsewhere must have cost him an immense amount of work. However, it is the point of the novel that one should not just learn about this interpretative frenzy but take pleasure in sharing it, and, for me at least, Eco's attempt to sustain one's interest in that world is not entirely successful. It is less successful than it is with the world, also very densely illustrated, of *The Name of the Rose*, and I was a bad candidate for that book, too, with its combination of two things neither of which has much charm for me, the English detective story and the Middle Ages.

The self-destruction of unconstrained interpretation concerns Eco, of course, not simply in the form of zealots tracing the tracks of the Templars across history. He is concerned with the directions taken by contemporary readers of literary texts, particularly of fiction, and several of the books under review address the question of how interpretation can be constrained, and of how reading, once it is freed from traditional (and poorly considered) conceptions of its limits, can be saved from falling into an indeterminacy as empty, and certainly as boring, as the fantasies of Rosicrucian paranoia.

Eco wants us to allow a play of many interpretations of fiction and poetry, and he often quotes Verlaine's saying that there is no one true sense of a poem; but some interpretations are definitely out. He would agree with the classical scholar I know who admitted, perhaps a shade reluctantly, that the free play of the signifier did not extend to the possibility that the word "album" in a poem of Horace could be taken to suggest a book of photographs. He notes approvingly that Geoffrey Hartman refrained from reading Wordsworth's line "A poet could not but be gay" in the sense that it might now suggest, and he remarks that this has something to do with knowing when it was written (a point which, I shall suggest, may go rather further than Eco wants).

Eco's desire to step back from uncontrolled interpretation is expressly encouraged by the thought that he may have done something to encourage it. In his book *Opera Aperta* of 1962,[1] he writes, he "advocated the active role of the interpreter . . . I have the impression that, in the course of the last decades, the rights of the interpreters have been overstressed." In his writings from that time on, Eco has taken part in developing, along with others such as Wolfgang Iser,[2] the concept of an implicit reader, now called by Eco "the Model Reader," who is the reader having the linguistic understanding, the empirical knowledge, and more generally the expectations (for instance, of a text of that form) which the text can be taken to assume. The Model Reader is "a sort of ideal type whom the text not only foresees as a collaborator but also tries to create."

Along with that, equally, can be constructed various notions of implied authors, among whom the narrator, as contrasted with the empirical author (the historical figure who wrote the book) is only the most familiar.[3] Some of the most interesting chapters in the attractive set of lectures *Six Walks in the Fictional Woods* are concerned with these themes, particularly in relation to a text that has fascinated Eco for a long time, Gérard de Nerval's tale *Sylvie*.[4] In this case, besides the empirical author (who was in fact called Gérard Labrunie, and hanged himself in 1855), there is a first-person narrator ("Je-rard"), and behind him, further, a model author, an impersonal voice which says everything that is said in the novella. Eco does ingenious work with these elements, as he also does with the temporal intricacies of the book, starting with the tense of the verbs in its first sentence and opening out into elaborate formalist analyses of flashback.

The Model Reader is, so to speak, the location of the constraints on interpretation. This does not mean that the idea provides a *criterion* for acceptable interpretation. Clearly it could not, since the Model Reader is himself or herself constructed only from the text itself; indeed, Eco is just as happy to express the limits of interpretation in terms of "the intention of the text." There is no criterion of acceptable reading, only plausible or implausible readings, and the idea of a Model Reader offers a focus or a frame for assembling the constraints that seem appropriate. Among the examples and explanations that he gives in *Interpretation and Overinterpretation* are some comments on his own novels, where, with scrupulous and winning denials of authorial privilege, he casts himself as a Model Reader and tells us, with perhaps a little help from his empirical memory, that the "Foucault" of *Foucault's Pendulum* of course has to have an echo of Michel Foucault, as well as of Léon Foucault (the one who invented the pendulum).[5] Eco wants the Model Reader to understand that the leading character called "Casaubon" was named after the Renaissance scholar Isaac Casaubon, not for Dorothea's husband in *Middlemarch* (so much the book indicates); but he also tells us, surprisingly, that it simply had not occurred to him that the work on which George Eliot's character was endlessly working was "A Key to All Mythologies." But: "As a Model Reader, I feel bound to accept that innuendo."

That surely is right: the "innuendo" is totally within the range of the associations that this book can appropriately invoke, and it could be helpfully put into the head of a reader who was being told what the book meant. According to Eco's own testimony, it was not part of the empirical author's intentions. This, for Eco as theorist, is of no interest, since the empirical author is the figure in this *galère* who gets, officially, the least attention, and is treated most of the time with contempt. "I'll tell you at once," Eco says early in *Six Walks*, "that I couldn't really care less about the empirical author of a narrative text (or, indeed, of any text)," and he goes on to say that knowing the author's age will not help you to judge whether *Le Diable au Corps* is a masterpiece, or tell you why Kant introduced twelve categories. This is indisputable, but not much of an argument: you might as well say against formalism that knowing the number of words to the page will not answer those questions either.

The questions are not only, or mainly, about a writer's intentions, though it is worth saying that Eco's objections to intentionalism, like many other people's, do seem to rely on a very crude notion of an intention. He sometimes gives the impression that on an intentionalist account an author would have to have in his head at each moment a cartoonist's balloon containing an expository paraphrase of what he was writing; but that is not a sensible account of doing *anything* intentionally. Quite apart from questions about intention, however, Eco's wholesale dismissal of the empirical author does seem a manifest case of repression. In fact—and it is hardly surprising—Eco keeps his interpretations under control, and supplies the Model Reader with what the Model Reader needs, by appealing all the time to facts about the empirical author: who he was, when he wrote, and, indeed, what sort of book he took himself to be writing—i.e., his intentions in a broad sense. He has an elaborate and quite enjoyable argument about street names in *The Three Musketeers* which turns on the date when Dumas wrote the book, the topography of Paris at the time, and what Dumas (the actual Dumas) might reasonably be expected to expect his reader to know.

Information about the empirical author is only one example of many things that it is, unsurprisingly, useful to know. In one of the essays in the collection called *The Limits of Interpretation*, Eco writes, in a discussion of Derrida:

> If it is true that a notion of literal meaning is highly problematic, it cannot be denied that in order to explore all the possibilities of a

text, even those that its author did not conceive of, the interpreter must first of all take for granted a zero-degree meaning, the one authorized by the dullest and simplest of the existing dictionaries, the one authorized by the state of a given language in a given historical moment, the one that every member of a community of healthy native speakers cannot deny.[6]

Moreover, when Eco refers to a dictionary, even a dull one, he follows much contemporary philosophy in not wanting to distinguish it in principle from an encyclopedia.

This much seems (if the word is not too dampening) sensible; and Eco's actual practice in bringing empirical information to bear on interpreting texts seems notably sensible, even if he sometimes permits himself a Derridean flourish which makes the actual world just another text: "In order to compare worlds," he says in *The Limits of Interpretation*, "one must take even the real or actual world as a cultural construct. The so-called actual world is the world to which we refer—rightly or wrongly—as the world described by the *Encyclopedia Britannica* or *Time* magazine. . . ." Here, particularly as we pass that sinister word "so-called," we seem to be on our way to one of those more maniacal post-structuralist views about which a friend once said to me: Tell that to the Veterans of Foreign Texts. But clearly Eco's heart is not in it; he is a respectable empiricist in these matters, who only looks as though he were taken with the suspect charms of Rien de Hors-Texte. Indeed, as soon as he has suggested his threat, he allows "rightly or wrongly" to take it away again, leaving us only with the alarming thought that the world could conceivably be as it is described by *Time* magazine.

Some of Eco's critics think that he is too sensible. In *Interpretation and Overinterpretation*, the same volume of Tanner Lectures in which Eco's essay appears, Jonathan Culler shrewdly remarks that "over-" begs some questions. "[L]ike most intellectual activities," he claims, "interpretation is interesting only when it is extreme." (The editor of the book, in his mildly condescending introduction, omits the word "intellectual" when he refers to this quotation, turning the contestable into the idiotic.) It depends, surely, on what interpretation is for. Culler is assuming, I take it, that what is at issue is the discussion of literature as such. In that connection he refers to a helpful distinction made by Wayne Booth between understanding a text and "overstanding" it, where the latter consists of "pursuing questions that the text does not pose to its model reader . . . it can be very important and productive to ask questions the text does *not* encourage one to ask about it." As Culler says, "One advantage of Booth's opposition over Eco's is that it makes it easier to see the role and importance of overstanding than when this sort of practice is tendentiously called over-interpretation." "Overstanding" is needed to correct overly respectful readings. Culler quotes Barthes to the effect that those who do not re-read condemn themselves to read the same story everywhere: "They recognize what they already think or know."

That certainly is one reason for overstanding imaginative texts, for moving beyond the horizons of the Model Reader. Even with literature, however, it is not a reason for always overstanding them, for instance when they are being introduced to students who have never read them before. The teachers are indeed re-reading them, and have entirely intelligible reasons (as well as those of finding a market niche) for wanting to make something new of them, but their students (if they are going to read these texts at all, which is another matter) need in the first place to have something old made of them, to be shown how to be Model Readers.

But there is a quite different and more important reason for guarding against the idea that interpretation should always try to be extreme, or that it should constantly aspire, in Culler's term, to be interesting. Eco's history of paranoid fantasy, which culminates in the Protocols of the Elders of Zion and their offspring, reminds us that interpretation is an urgently political matter, and not just in the sense in which the Secret Agents of literature departments take a re-reading of *Heart of Darkness* to be a political matter. Records are being interpreted when the Holocaust is denied, and then what is required of interpretation is not interesting extremity, but, to put it baldly, truth.

Because Eco is aware that the vicissitudes of interpretation can be seriously political, his novels speak to political issues, even if one does not go all the way with the suggestion Robert Lumley mentions in his informative introduction to *Apocalypse Postponed*, that they are "political allegories."[7] This introduction tells one a certain amount about Eco's rather ambivalent relations over the years to Italian politics, particularly to movements of the left. (I also learned from Lumley that Eco is the author of the standard Italian work on how to write a doctoral thesis: *Come si fa una tesi di laurea*, a title in which the reflexive voice makes the task sound, at least to an imperfectly Italianate ear, agreeably easier than it is.) The book itself addresses politics, but they are almost entirely the politics of culture. It is not altogether a satisfactory collection. There are translations from a book published in 1964, *Apocalittici e Integrati*, followed by an assortment of pieces on popular culture and cultural politics, some of which are very dated (Italian events in the 1960s; Orwell in 1984; rather painfully, the Royal Wedding).

"Apocalyptic" and "integrated" intellectuals are distinguished by their attitudes to popular culture, and, as that choice of labels makes heavily obvious, Eco sides unequivocally with the latter, those who wish to make something of it, while the apocalyptics see in TV and "mass culture" the end of civilization. Eco salutes the apocalyptics, and indeed dedicates the book to them, but he thinks that their formulas—in particular the term "mass culture" itself—are fetishes, that their view of the past as contrasted with the present is unhistorical, and, most basically, that they snobbishly withhold themselves from manifestations that can be enjoyable, interesting, and rich with semiotic extravagance.

The apocalyptics whom Eco was addressing when he wrote these essays came supposedly from the left, even if (as in the case of Adorno) this represented a choice of rhetoric rather than anything else. But those at the present time who are drawn to American Straussianism or other versions of cultural pessimism will find themselves challenged by Eco, for instance in the short essay "The Future of Literacy," to reflect on what exactly it is that they deplore and how exactly it differs from what it was in the past. In particular, he is good on showing the implications of simple McLuhanite assumptions about the image and the word. As he points out, in the Middle Ages visual communication was more important than writing. "Cathedrals were the TV of their times, and the difference with our TV was that the directors of medieval TV read good books, had a lot of imagination, and worked for the public good." Admittedly, this takes us only as far as asking some better and harder questions about literacy, and Eco, at least in these pages, does not help us much in answering them. In this respect, the category of the "integrated" intellectual is something of a delusion. It registers, as contrasted with rejection, only the point that some intellectuals have absorbed popular culture to the point where they can sing along with it, as Eco does in his essay on Charlie Brown and Krazy Kat. In itself, it offers no hope that some intellectuals might be integrated into popular culture and have some influence on it, as Eco would clearly like to be the case when he compares the management of RAI unfavorably to the designers of Chartres.

In fact, Eco has been involved in TV, in publishing, and in journalism as well as being a professor. Many of the essays on cultural politics are reprinted from newspapers. However, besides these familiar activities of the academic critic, he has written a lot in lighter styles. Starting in 1959, he wrote for a literary magazine a monthly column called *Diario Minimo*, and *Misreadings* offers a selection of translated pieces from that column.[8] They take the form of parodies—of Nabokov, Robbe-Grillet, Adorno, and Anglo-American anthropology, among other targets. They have come a long way by now, from originals in English, French, or other languages to Italian to English, and despite the linguistic skills of Eco and his translator, the parodic impulse that set them off has not always survived to the present volume. The other little book in Eco's lighter manner, *How to Travel with a Salmon*, represents a translated selection of items from a second *Diario Minimo*, in this case put into a drawer as they were written and published later.[9] These are comic numbers, on "How to Be a TV Host," "How to Eat in Flight," and so forth. One of them contains a genuine narratological discovery, which reappears in *Six Walks*: a sure way of telling whether a film is pornographic is that it contains many scenes in which the protagonists travel in a car, enter or leave buildings, pour drinks, and engage in other everyday activities, all of which are displayed *in real time* and take just as long as they would take in life (it is a device for separating the sex scenes without having to invent any plot). One piece about the gadgets advertised in airline magazines, is to me, at least, very funny:

> LeafScoop is a glove that transforms your hands into those of a palmiped born, through radioactive mutation, from the cross-breeding of a duck with a pterodactyl via Dr. Quatermass. It is used in the collection of fallen leaves in your eighty-thousand acre park. Spending a mere $12.50, you save the salary of a gardener and a gamekeeper (we recommend it to Lord Chatterley's attention). TieSaver covers your neckties with a protective oily film so that, Chez Maxim, you can eat tomato sandwiches without then appearing at the Board of Directors meeting looking like Dr. Barnard after a difficult transplant. Only fifteen dollars. Ideal for those who still use brilliantine. You can wipe your forehead with the tie.

Others, such as a laborious working out of Borges's famous idea of a map on the scale of 1 to 1, seem to me notably unfunny, sometimes to a degree that I find almost bewildering.

Perhaps there is nothing to this except the usual vicissitudes of humorous writing — different times, different cultures, different temperaments, the joke that does not travel. But I suspect that there is something deeper involved. It relates to a characteristic that Eco does share with many of his academic colleagues in literature, particularly those more dedicated than he is to literary theory. He is much more learned, steadier, more humorous, and when in the presence of solid fact more sensible than many of them, but he does share an affliction with them. This is paradoxic bulimia, an ungoverned appetite for seemingly contradictory conundrums. Its symptoms drive philosophers to fury, and the difference between the two parties in this respect marks, more than anything else, the contemporary front line in the age-old war between the troops of philosophy and the troops of literature.

Faced with an apparent contradiction, philosophers, the friends of consistency, want to resolve it. Logicians such as Raymond Smullyan (whose good joke, quoted by Eco, I mentioned at the beginning) love paradoxes, but want to explain them. The other party, the friends of the conundrum, move in the opposite direction: given a boring fact, they do the best they can to represent it as a contradiction. Many years ago I read a little book called *Zen and the Art of Archery*, which tried to illustrate Zen teaching by telling you, for instance, that in archery one should aim by not aiming. This meant simply that if you were to hit the target you needed to get into a state of mind in which you were no longer consciously trying to do so. But this is true of most such activities. I remember clearly the irritation I felt, as a hardcore member of the consistency party, at what seemed an entirely gratuitous mystification.

That case was, in fact, doubly bad, since the truth wrapped up in the contradiction was an obvious one, and the only point in wrapping it up, the Zen point, lay in a practice of meditation and discipline which no book was going to impart. Of course, in many other cases the party of consistency is rightly seen as consisting of clumsy wreckers, who feel threatened by the first sight of contradiction and reach for their rationalizing tool kit. They—that is to say, we—always run the risk of forgetting that the first sight of something worth understanding may take the form of a contradiction. The best way there may be of putting something worth saying may take that form, and, in personal life at least, it may sometimes be best to leave it that way, since the roots of the contradiction can sometimes only be found by digging up the plant. But if that is so, there is at any rate a consistent explanation of why it is so. Contradictions in themselves do not make life more abundant. They do not even, much of the time, make it more interesting, and this is for the same reason that the search for the Hermetic secret is so boring, that in themselves they leave you with something indeterminate and limitless, a world in which nothing is impossible and everything is the same. Hence one's (literally) desperate weariness as the more mechanical forms of deconstruction grind out their paradoxes.

Eco is never boring in such a way or, most of the time, in any other. Yet he seems to have a serious problem, as they say in the eating disorder clinic, with paradox, and I think that this is why his jokes seem so uneven, since a shared sense of humor rests heavily on a common sense of what is paradoxical, and Eco is prepared to find amusingly paradoxical what some of his readers may see as merely elaborate or forced. He seeks out formulations that trip themselves up, ways of putting things that might be taken, at a pinch, to undo what they say. His sympathy with people who love contradictions is hard, at points, to distinguish from a sympathy with contradictions, and he occasionally stuns the principles of logic with a shot of cultural relativism, as when he refers in the Tanner

Lectures to "the typical pattern of thinking of Western rationalism, the *modus ponens*: 'if p then q; but p: therefore q.'" How far east do you have to go for that to stop being valid?

In *Foucault's Pendulum*, they say to the narrator:

> "You can always tell a genuine Piedmontese immediately by his skepticism."
> "I'm a skeptic."
> "No, you're only incredulous, a doubter, and that's different."

A little later the narrator goes on:

> Not that the incredulous person doesn't believe in anything. It's just that he doesn't believe in everything. Or he believes in one thing at a time. He believes a second thing only if it somehow follows from the first thing. He is nearsighted and methodical, avoiding wide horizons. If two things don't fit, but you believe both of them, thinking that somewhere, hidden, there must be a third thing that connects them, that's credulity.
> Incredulity doesn't kill curiosity; it encourages it.

Umberto Eco, in his dealings with interpretation, is to a wonderful degree what the subject needs, someone who is incredulous without being a paralyzing skeptic. He is incredulous about skepticism itself: about the limitless space of unconstrained semiosis. At the same time he is incredulous concerning traditional assumptions about the author and the extent to which meaning can be determinately recovered. But in all his inventive dealings with these questions he shows, as well as vast learning and a high sense of fun, a robust belief in the obstinacy of fact, a historical past that can be recovered, if not as a large-scale story, at least as an assemblage of undeniable bits and pieces. It is only from time to time, in his dealings with logic, when he reveals a taste for paradox that is more unconstrained than he allows interpretation to be, that he seems to flirt with deep skepticism. But this may, finally, only be one of his games, for it is very clear that he recognizes that good sense and an understanding of the past, including the lunacies of its interpretations, are sustained in fact by a vigorous belief that one thing follows from another, and that wishful interpreters can no more empower contradictions than they can prove the existence of the Templars' conspiracy.

Notes

1. Translated as *The Open Work* (Harvard University Press, 1989).
2. *Der Implizite Leser* (Munich: Fink, 1972); English translation, *The Implied Reader* (Johns Hopkins University Press, 1974). *Der Akt des Lesens* (Munich:

Fink, 1976); English translation, *The Act of Reading* (Johns Hopkins University Press, 1978).

3. Eco gives some history of these ideas in "Intentio Lectoris," one of the articles collected in *The Limits of Interpretation*; he particularly picks out Wayne Booth's conception of an "implied author," which was first published in 1961.

4. *Six Walks in the Fictional Woods*, by Umberto Eco, Charles Eliot Norton Lectures (Harvard University Press, 1994).

5. *Interpretation and Overinterpretation*, by Umberto Eco, with Richard Rorty, Jonathan Culler, and Christine Brooke-Rose, edited by Stefan Collini, Tanner Lectures in Human Values (Cambridge University Press, 1992).

6. *The Limits of Interpretation*, by Umberto Eco (Indiana University Press, 1994).

7. *Apocalypse Postponed*, by Umberto Eco, translated and edited by Robert Lumley (Indiana University Press/British Film Institute, 1994).

8. *Misreadings*, by Umberto Eco, translated by William Weaver (Harcourt Brace, 1993).

9. *How to Travel with a Salmon & Other Essays*, by Umberto Eco, translated by William Weaver (Harcourt Brace, 1994).

68

On Hating and Despising Philosophy

As long as there has been such a subject as philosophy, there have been people who hated and despised it.

I do not want to exaggerate, in a self-pitying or self-dramatising way, the present extent or intensity of this dislike. I am not thinking of the philosopher as emblematically represented by the figure of Socrates, the martyr to free thought who reaches what the pious or conventional regard as the wrong answer. Nor do I suppose that philosophers are often seen as politicians are in Australia, where that profession (I was once told) is regarded as much like that of night-soil workers. Still less are they like American lawyers, notoriously considered powerful, ubiquitous and horrible.

Few people, after all, think about philosophers much, and some of those who do may well regard them with a mildly bemused respect. But the subject does collect a familiar style of complaint: that philosophy gets no answers, or no answers to any question that any grown-up person would worry about, or no answer which would be worth worrying about, even if the question were. The complaint is, basically, that philosophy is useless: either intrinsically useless, or useless in the form in which it is usually done, a professional or academic form. It is this second view, that philosophy is useless but ought not to be, that is likely to add dislike to mere contempt.

In asking many of their questions—what doing an action is, for instance, or how by making noises we can make sense to each other, if indeed we can—philosophers are motivated by curiosity. But that is not their only motive, and particularly in asking political and ethical questions, about justice, the rightful use of power, and what sorts of life might be worth living, they have wanted to be helpful. They have even hoped, some of them, to redeem or transform humanity.

Of course, not every such question is philosophical. Politics itself, and religion, and people in the bar discuss these things, and they are not all doing philosophy. Philosophy comes into it when the discussion becomes more reflective or theoretical or systematic, and it is typical of philosophy that its discussions of ethics and politics have some connection with those other more theoretical questions, about knowledge, action and psychology. Arguments for political toleration have often been linked to the idea that no one has a monopoly of moral truth. The idea that all human beings share moral freedom has been offered as a basis of liberalism. These examples are modern, but philosophy in the past had similar interests, and equally it was capable of attracting some rather special styles of dislike.

The most radical form of the complaint against philosophy is that it is *as such* irredeemably useless: that all of it is empty, pointless, word-spinning which wastes time and distracts people from worthwhile work. This style of objection came, once upon a time, from certain religious outlooks: Tertullian, for example, said that he agreed that Christianity was absurd, and that was why he believed it. Other pious people have thought that philosophical reflection was a distraction from the religious life and an evasion from it, putting aridly clever arguments in place of an honest view of life's commitments. That complaint was directed as much to religious philosophy as to any other: in fact, theology was seen as in some ways the worst kind of philosophy, being a parody of religion as it should really be.

These days, most of those who take this kind of attitude to philosophy are not religious, but scientists, or—more typically—fellow-travellers of science, and they take it not in the name of religion but in the interest of an anti-philosophical and confidently puritanical view of science. Just as the religious haters of philosophy most hated religious philosophy, so these complainers may particularly dislike the philosophy that is nearest to science, such as that which considers the relations between thinking and the brain. The scientific critics are disposed to see this as a lazy substitute for work in the lab.

These complainers have a problem, which is similar to one that their religious forebears had: they cannot hope to justify their story that science is useful and philosophy is useless simply by doing science—in order to justify it, they will have to do philosophy. Their best strategy, then, is not to try to justify their complaint, or even to mention it, but to ignore philosophy and, if they are scientists, get on with science.

A different view is that philosophy does not have to be useless, but that in its present forms it mostly is. On this account, there is something that philosophy could do, indeed used to do, but which it has now forsaken. It could and should help us, but instead of doing so, philosophers spend their time in academic exercises which are technical and inaccessible. This is the sort of attitude which was expressed in a recent review by Roger Scruton,[1] who is, among other things, a philosopher, and certainly does not think that he despises philosophy as such. He claimed that philosophy should 'say something useful to the ordinary person', and should give him 'help in confronting the moral morass which surrounds him'. The complaint here is that philosophy is too technical and abstract to be available and helpful to people who lack the appropriate training. In a formal and unappealing way, it is too *hard*, and in being too hard, it has betrayed its promise of human helpfulness.

This, too, is an old complaint, which goes back at least to Plato's time, and in that fact there is a considerable irony. Plato is a hero of those who claim the human importance of philosophy, and rightly so; indeed, if he does not speak (rightly or wrongly) to our most basic concerns, it is hard to see which philosopher does. Yet those who in Plato's time complained that philosophy was becoming technical and inaccessible—concerned, worthy, pompous, in some cases merely opportunistic, citizens—had Plato as their enemy. We are told that at the door of Plato's Academy there was a sign that read 'Let no one enter who knows no geometry,' and the studies that went on inside it were very hard. Plato thought, with increasing sternness as he got older, that philosophy could not help anyone unless it was true to itself. Its truthfulness meant, too, that it could not tell in advance what would help; and since that was so, it could not hope to find things that would help if it thought that it knew in advance what kinds of thing they would be.

As Plato knew, the road to something helpful is not only hard, but unpredictable, and the motives that keep people moving down it don't necessarily have to do with the desire to help. They include that other motive of philosophy, curiosity. In fact, the two motives cannot really be taken apart; the philosophy that is concerned to be helpful cannot be separated from philosophy that aims to help us to understand.

There is an illustration of this in a question which is certainly a philosophical question, and at the same time politically important: the question of the value of free speech. What is this value? What are the most basic reasons for it? Is it just an example of the value of freedom, the freedom to do anything at all? Or is it particularly connected with a democratic value, the freedom to participate politically? Or, again, is it connected with the importance of truth—specially, perhaps, truth as involved in a political and social critique? Different practical consequences will follow from these various answers. The first approach merely encourages as much speech as possible, or as much as people like, but it does not suggest why speech is more important than anything else, and in face of the fact that all freedoms need curtailing sometimes, offers speech no special protection. The second does privilege political speech, however distracting or irrelevant, but leaves a nasty problem about the boundaries of political speech. If truth, lastly, is the aim of the exercise, it is far from clear that the confused din of unhampered speech is the best way of its being either found or heard.

But perhaps, quite apart from politics and the need to expose deliberate untruth, there is a deeper connection between freedom and looking for the truth. Primo Levi tells in his autobiography how he found a refuge from Fascism's suffocating and poisonous lies in his work on chemistry. His idea was that the pursuit of objective scientific truth itself expressed freedom, because what one did was not under the control of other human beings, but was governed by the structure of the world as it is independently of human will. Levi's vision has a good deal to do with political freedom and the value of free speech, but if we are to share it, it will be important to know whether science can reasonably be expected to achieve objective truth, and to understand what types of human research, if any, can lead to results that are independent of human will.

So in the end the question of free speech, one of the most practical questions of political value, leads, if one takes it seriously, to basic issues in the philosophy of science and metaphysics. Those issues simply are hard, technical, and not immediately helpful. Those who work at them may well not have a hand free to stretch out to the ordinary person, to help him confront the moral morass. Plato's answer, that serious philosophy is (or very rapidly becomes) unobvious, remains in place.

The general complaints, then, that philosophy is inherently useless, or that it has betrayed its destiny just by being hard and unobvious, are as baseless now as they were two thousand years ago. But there is certainly room for complaint, and it would be a bad friend of philosophy who did not admit that there is quite a lot of philosophical work that is unrewarding by any standard: unhelpful, boring, sterile. The awful fact is that some of it hardly tries to be anything else. It consists of exercises that are necessary for the structure of philosophy as providing an academic career. The professionalisation of philosophy has been going on for more than a century (or longer, if you count the Middle Ages), but it is now at an unprecedented level. It undeniably brings its own deformations, and the question that Stravinsky used to ask disobligingly about much contemporary music, 'Who needs it?', can press hard on some philosophical production.

There is another worry that goes beyond the numbing presence of too many professional exercises. Analytical philosophy has, correctly, held onto the idea that there must be something in philosophy that counts as 'getting it right'. In this, it properly rejects Richard Rorty's model for the future of philosophy (or rather, as he sees it, of what used to be philosophy), the model of a conversation. Unless a conversation is very relentless—for instance, one between philosophers—it will not be held together by 'so' or 'therefore' or 'but', but rather by 'well then' and 'that reminds me' and 'come to think of it', and it is simply unclear who will stay around for it, and why. In fact, it is tempting to think that the conversation model is secretly an ally of professionalisation: the only people who will take part in such a conversation are those who are paid to do so.

If philosophy, or anything like it, is to have a point, the idea of 'getting it right' must be in place, and so must clarity and precision. But there is more than one kind of all these things. It is hard to deny that over too much of the subject, the idea of getting it right which has gone into the self-image of analytic philosophy, and which has supported some of its exclusions, is one drawn from the natural sciences; and that the effects of this can be unhappy.

There is a lot of philosophy that lives closely with science. Some philosophical subjects have scientific neighbours, to such an extent that there may be no clear boundaries between them. This is true for the philosophy of quantum mechanics, for the philosophy of mathematics, for some philosophy of language and some philosophy of mind. But even in areas where its practices are most relevant, science can be a bad model for philosophy.

There are several features of natural science which, applied to philosophy, may have a baleful effect on it. One is that science does not really need to know about its own history. It is no doubt desirable that scientists should know something about their science's history, but it is not essential to their enquiries. A parallel conclusion has been drawn by some philosophers: in one prestigious American department a senior figure had a notice on his door that read JUST SAY NO TO THE HISTORY OF PHILOSOPHY. In one or two areas philosophy may be near enough to science for this attitude to be justified. But if so, they are an exception. In general, one must take extremely seriously Santayana's warning that those who are ignorant of the history of philosophy are doomed to recapitulate it.

A second point is that science really does have an effective division of labour. It is of course true that great breakthroughs have been achieved by the transfer of skills between scientific fields: for instance, by John Maynard Smith, trained as an engineer, turning his attention to biology. But in everyday practice there are perfectly well established methods of getting local results, and even if the results are not very exciting, they are results. It follows from this that professional training exercises, however run-of-the-mill, make a contribution not just to education but to the subject itself, but as we have already sadly noted, this is not necessarily true of philosophy.

Last, there is a question of style. Science of course displays imagination, but when it does, it tends to be creative rather than expressive. It leads to the discovery or theory, and does not necessarily emerge in the way in which the result is expressed. Scientific writing should be clear and effective, and it can be stylish, but the question of whether scientists have got it right or not is not much affected by the expressive power of their writing. It is not necessarily so with philosophy. The traditions of the plain style that are familiar in analytic philosophy have much to be said for them, but they can become a dead weight under the influence of the scientific model. One should not approach philosophical writing in the spirit of the analytic philosopher who (in actual fact) said to another when they were trying to write a book together: 'Let's get it right first and you can put the style in afterwards.'

Why do we assume that it should be like this? When we turn, in particular, to moral and political philosophy, and we look at the canon of past philosophy that even analytical philosophy agrees on, does it look like this? Plato, Hobbes, Hume, Rousseau, indeed John Stuart Mill, not to go into more disputed territory: do we really suppose that their contributions to the subject are independent of the imaginative and expressive powers of their work? There is indeed the extraordinary and unparalleled case of Aristotle, who has had an immense influence on the analytic tradition's conception of what it is to get it right. But why should we even assume that these affectless treatises represent his own voice? To the extent that they do, what does the tone mean? The pictures that Aristotle gives or implies of the society he lived in are to a notable degree fictional: perhaps we should recognise the colourlessness, the lack of history, the technicality, as themselves an evasion? In any case, why should we want to sound like that? Most philosophers do not deserve their historical legacy: Plato did not deserve most sorts of Platonist, and even Hegel did not deserve many Hegelians, but Aristotle, perhaps uniquely, deserved what he got—he invented scholasticism.

As those other authors (and many others) remind us, moral and political philosophy demand more than such a style. They may need to give us their picture of life and society and the individual. Moreover, a philosopher may need not merely to give us such a picture, but to give it in a way that integrates it with what he or she cares about. If a philosophical writer does not solve or, as in many cases, does not even face the problems of how to express those concerns adequately, he or she will have failed to carry reflection far enough. So the demand that moral and political philosophy should sound right, should speak in a real voice, is not something arbitrarily imposed by those with a taste for literature, or for history, or for excitement. It follows from philosophy's ideal of reflectiveness, an ideal acknowledged in the subject's most central traditions.

There are, undeniably, problems associated with philosophy's becoming a profession—problems shared, to some extent, by all the humanities—but they do not show that there is something wrong with the idea of philosophy as a discipline. The hopes that still exist for philosophy as an enlightening and constructive discipline are threatened by its being made into an academic routine, just as they are by its being advertised as offering instantly accessible help. In both cases, what philosophy loses is a quality which is essential to it, whatever questions it is addressing: an intense attention to what it is saying, and to the question whether what it is saying is not only true, but rings true. In this sense, good philosophy (or, at least, very good philosophy) on any theme will display some kind of urgency or intensity, and routine philosophy will lack it.

However, these kinds of urgency or intensity come about (remember Plato) only by philosophy's taking itself seriously as a hard discipline. Philosophy does not acquire these qualities, as many of philosophy's critics suppose, by instantly addressing the urgent and the deep. There is much cultural criticism and supposed philosophy which sounds, superficially, very urgent, only too heart-breakingly involved in the end of humankind or the horrors of the 20th century. It offers an easily accessible and instantly impressive eschatology, and it is this that some critics hold up as a model of seriousness. But these writings, just because of their message that what is really important is instantly awesome, are on the wrong side from philosophy—on the wrong side, not between literature and philosophy (which is another story), nor between rhetoric and plain statement, but between kitsch, on the one hand, and truthfulness, on the other. In philosophy, at least, a truthful style is not likely to make it immediately obvious what the work has to do with our most urgent concerns, because its interest is in the less obvious roots and consequences of our concerns.

This is not true of every kind of writing. Philosophy has its own responsibilities and limitations, and fiction or drama or reporting may be able to speak directly to suffering, in ways that are not open to philosophy. But they, and all other kinds of serious writing, do face together with philosophy some common demands of truthfulness, which each must acknowledge in its own style. (Perhaps these common demands show how philosophy, too, can be a form of *imaginative* writing.) Nothing, in any of these forms, will be helpful or enlightening if the writer thinks first about being helpful, rather than about getting it right. In the case of philosophy, 'getting it right' may involve exploring paths that seem fairly dank and unrewarding.

There is another demand of truthfulness. Even in everyday conversation, being helpful does not necessarily involve being comforting. Still less is this going to be so with a truthful philosophy, and the ways in which a serious philosophy might prove, in the end, helpful may well not be those that bring, even in the end, comfort. It will not, either, bring comfort by the way in which it refuses comfort; it will reject those familiar assurances of a rhetorical and immediately recognisable despair.

If there could be what serious philosophers dream of, a philosophy at once thoroughly truthful and honestly helpful, it would still be hard, unaccommodating and unobvious. For those reasons, it would doubtless be disliked by those who dislike philosophy as it is. But it might, more encouragingly, succeed in recruiting some new enemies as well, who would do it the credit of hating it for what it said and not just for what it was.

Note

1. *Times* (21 September 1995). He was reviewing (as it happens) a collection of essays by myself, *Making Sense of Humanity*.

69

The Last Word, by Thomas Nagel

1

> This discussion will be concerned with an issue that runs through
> practically every area of inquiry and that has even invaded the gen-
> eral culture—the issue of where understanding and justification
> come to an end. Do they come to an end with objective principles
> whose validity is independent of our point of view, or do they
> come to an end within our point of view—individual or shared—
> so that ultimately, even the most apparently objective and universal
> principles derive their validity or authority from the perspective
> and practice of those who follow them?[1]

This is the question Thomas Nagel raises in *The Last Word,* and the
answer he gives in his subtle, compact, and forceful book is firmly and
eloquently of the first kind—a "rationalist" answer, as against answers
that he variously calls "subjectivist," "relativist," and "naturalist." We,
most of us, have a moral outlook which is (very broadly speaking) liberal:
we support universal human rights and are in favor of toleration. Others, elsewhere, do not have that outlook, and neither did most people in
the past. We favor the medicine of medical practice over the medicine of
medicine men, and think that we have scientific reasons to do so; medicine men have a different view. Nagel wants to vindicate our rationality,
and the justifications that we offer for our beliefs, against people who
say that these ways of thinking are simply the ones that we are culturally
used to and happen to favor.

Some people who say this, Nagel's relativists, just leave it at that: "This
is our way, but who are we to say that those others are wrong?" The
subjectivists among us go a little further, and say that those who disagree
with us are wrong, but they are very impressed by the thought that there
is no objective point from which the disagreement can be resolved. Others, more skeptical still, pretend that we can do without "true," "wrong,"
and so on altogether, except as decoration or rhetoric, and urge us to
see these disagreements and arguments as simply one or another sort of
politics.

Nagel wants to show, against all these parties, that "understanding and
justification come to an end ... with objective principles whose validity

is independent of our point of view." By this he means that if the argument between conflicting positions or interpretations were pursued far enough, and if the parties were fully rational, they would have to accept one resolution of the debate or another, or at least agree with each other that for mutually intelligible reasons it could not be resolved. They could not retreat to merely explaining each other's outlook in psychological, social, or political terms.

In putting forward these ideas, Nagel sees himself as addressing a currently important intellectual and cultural question, and indeed he is. But it should be said at once that *The Last Word* is a work of philosophical reflection, not a polemic. The book is a significant contribution to the culture wars of our time, particularly to the recurrent and untidy disputes over the extent to which objective understanding and argument can be saved from skeptical suspicion (which claims that a sophisticated thinker should believe virtually nothing), and, equally, from a promiscuous relativism (which allows one to believe just about anything one likes). But there is not much in Nagel's text to show how it relates to any particular controversy. Almost the only examples that he gives of what is at stake are an obligingly self-refuting quotation from Richard Rorty (which I shall come to) and, in the matter of ethics, some opinions of mine. Readers who hoped to see their enemies or their friends skewered will be disappointed.

Who, in these discussions, are "we"? Is every claim to the effect that our understandings are relative to "us" equally threatening? When we reflect on what "we" believe, particularly in cultural and ethical matters, we often have in mind (as the relativists do) ourselves as members of modern industrial societies, or of some yet more restricted group, as contrasted with other human beings at other times or places. Such a "we" is, as linguists put it, "contrastive"—it picks out "us" as opposed to others. But "we" can be understood inclusively, to embrace anyone who does, or who might, share in the business of investigating the world. Some philosophers have suggested that in our thought there is always an implied "we" of this inclusive kind; according to them, when cosmologists make claims about what the universe is like "in itself," they are not abstracting from possible experience altogether, but are implicitly talking about the way things would seem to investigators who were at least enough like us for us to recognize them, in principle, as investigators.

Whether those philosophers are right in thinking that all our conceptions are relative to "us" understood in this abstractly inclusive way is certainly an important question in metaphysics. But does it matter to the culture wars and to the disputes about relativism and subjectivism that are Nagel's real concern? Nagel says that what he is attacking is the idea that we cannot ultimately get beyond a conception of the world as it seems to us. What is really disturbing, however, about the relativists and subjectivists is surely not this idea in itself, but rather their insistence on understanding "us" in such a very local and parochial way. Their suggestions—suggestions made at least by the most extreme among them—that all our ideas, including our theories in cosmology, are simply local cultural formations, and that there is no "truth of the matter" about such things as history, are indeed unnerving, and they have deep cultural implications, because they suggest that there are no shared standards on the basis of which we as human beings can understand each other—that there is no inclusive, but only a contrastive, "we."

These problems about the reach of human understanding, like many others in modern philosophy, go back to Kant. Kant was rightly impressed by the thought that if we ask whether we have a correct conception of the world, we cannot step entirely outside our actual conceptions and theories so as to compare them with a world that is not conceptualized at all, a bare "whatever there is." He concluded that we cannot get beyond thinking of the world as it might appear to creatures who resemble us at least to the extent of being intelligent observers, and so belong in the ultimately inclusive "us." With moral thought, however, Kant supposed that the situation was different. Kant did not take morality to be a matter of knowledge. It was concerned, rather, with practical principles which bind any rational person in dealing with other rational persons, and this leads to the result, at first sight surprising, that for Kant morality is less relativized to the ways in which the world affects us than science is. Kant's morality applies to us just because we are rational creatures. The "we" of morality is potentially broader than the group that could share science.

Nagel is sympathetic to Kant's unregenerately rationalist view of ethics, but he thinks that Kant's revolution in the understanding of science and of our everyday knowledge of the world was the beginning of the rot.[2] Kant, as much as anybody, is the "modern" in "postmodern," and there is a long story (though Nagel does not tell it here) of how, after Kant, critical reflection on our relations to the world went on to sweep away Kant's own assurances about what we can know and what we ought to do. Moral claims, the humane disciplines of history and criticism, and natural science itself have come to seem to some critics not to command the reasonable assent of all human beings. They are seen rather as the products of groups within humanity, expressing the perspectives of those groups. Some see the authority of supposedly rational discourse as itself barely authority, but rather a construct of social forces.

In a further turn, reflection on this situation itself can lead to a relativism which steps back from all perspectives and sees them all at the

same distance—all true, none true, each of them true for its own parti-
sans. Eventually we reach the kind of incantation produced by someone
quoted by Alan Sokal at a meeting in New York about his hoax, to the
effect that there is no fact of the matter as to whether Native Americans
originally arrived on the continent across the Bering Strait, or by ascent
from the center of the earth; both accounts are true (for someone: or
something like that).

This is the kind of jetsam to be found on the further shores of what
Nagel is against, but he is equally against everything on the way to
those shores: anything, that is to say, that represents beliefs or statements which should be understood to be straightforwardly about the
way things are as statements that depend on "us"—whether "us" means
humans and anyone humans could understand, as in Kant's case; or humans; or us here and now; or maybe some of us here and now, as in
various postmodern constructions. Nagel is not very interested in the
differences between wider and narrower understandings of "we," just
as he is not interested in identifying particular theorists of the relativist
and subjectivist tendency. He wants to get rid of the idea that seemingly
objective truths depend in any sense on "us." He believes that he has an
entirely general, abstract set of considerations which will do this, and
which will persuade us that reason and objectivity should have the "Last
Word" that appears in his title.

2

Nagel's basic idea is that whatever kind of claim is said to be only lo-
cally valid and to be the product of particular social forces—whether it
is morality that is being criticized in this way, or history, or science—the
relativist or subjectivist who offers this critique will have to make some
other claim, which itself has to be understood as not merely local but
objectively valid. Moreover, in all the cases that matter, this further claim
will have to be of the same type as those that are being criticized: the
relativists' critique of morality must commit them to claims of objective
morality, their attempts to show that science consists of local prejudice
must appeal to objective science, and so on.

We shall come back to some details of Nagel's basic idea, and to how
it works out in practice. First, however, there are some questions about
his approach, and the very general style of argument that he uses. If he
is right in this approach, he can stop the subjectivist and relativist attack before it gets very close to any particular target. This has the same
advantage as the proposed Star Wars defense system, that if it works, the
explosions occur in the stratosphere and nothing one cares about gets
damaged. It has the same disadvantage, that if it does not work and there

is no guaranteed interception, you have no way of telling how much of what you care about may survive.

This is one reason why the strategy seems to me misconceived: not everything that is threatened by subjectivism, or relativism, or naturalism is in the same situation. Some of the types of thought that have been questioned in these ways are in worse shape to face the attack than others. Parts of our morality, for instance, or our longer-haul historical narratives, or our models of personal self-understanding, are more open to suspicion, more liable to be shown in an unsettling way to depend on a narrow and parochial "us," than our science or our logic are. If so, this cannot be for entirely general reasons that apply equally to them and to those other types of thought. It will be for reasons special to them. Moreover, it may be for reasons special to them at this time: as with other illnesses, no diagnosis that ignores their history is likely to succeed.

In addition, they are our own illnesses. Another reason why, as it seems to me, Nagel's strategy is misguided is that it installs a long-distance, high-powered, all-purpose defense system to fight what is in fact a guerrilla war. The irrationalists or relativists or skeptics are among us. I do not mean the *Invasion of the Body Snatchers* situation suggested by some conservative fantasists of the academy, who seem to think that pods delivered secretly to departments of literature have yielded creatures that take over the scholars. I mean that the seeds of skepticism are there to germinate in anyone who thinks seriously about our intellectual and cultural situation as it is now. Nagel is quite right in saying that these kinds of skepticism cannot become total, this side of insanity. If we are to think at all; we cannot regard logic, or science, or history, as just local fancies. But the hard question is how far skepticism or relativism can go while remaining on the right side of insanity, and (to change the military metaphor) Nagel's policy of *they shall not pass!* does not seem to me to give enough help in answering it.

Nagel puts his basic idea by saying that there are some thoughts "we cannot get outside of." To understand ourselves, and more particularly to arrive at the conclusion that some of our thoughts or beliefs or experiences are merely "appearances," a function of how we are rather than of how things are, there are other judgments which we must think "straight" — that is to say, in a way that commits us to the objective truth of those judgments. If we can relegate some of our thoughts to being mere appearances, this implies that we have an objective view of a world—a world that is really there—to which we, and those appearances, belong. Insofar as it depends on taking an "external view of oneself," the "discrediting of universal claims of reason as merely subjective or relative has inescapable built-in limits." There are, Nagel says, some types of thoughts that we cannot avoid simply *having*—that it is strictly impossible to consider merely from the outside, because they enter inevitably and directly into any process of considering ourselves from the outside, allowing us to construct the conception of a world in which, as a matter of objective fact, we and our subjective impressions are contained. [Nagel's emphasis]

There are, Nagel insists, limits to the extent to which we can criticize our thoughts from a disengaged standpoint. We may indeed come to the conclusion that some of our apparently objective beliefs are an expression of some local peculiarity:

Someone who has been brought up to believe that it is wrong for women to expose their breasts can come to realize at a certain point that this is a convention of his culture, and not an unqualified moral truth. Of course, he *might* continue to insist, after examining the anthropological, historical, and sociological evidence, that it is wrong in itself for women to expose their breasts. . . . But this response is unlikely to survive the confrontation; it just doesn't have enough behind it. . . . [Nagel's emphasis]

If the original belief disappears in such a case, the change will have been produced through *other* moral argument. So reflection in this style could not possibly reduce *all* moral belief and argument to sets of local peculiarities. The same applies, Nagel believes, to all the fields of thought that he considers. One cannot ultimately get outside these styles of thought. *One has to go on in the same way.* In the end, anyone who tries to make the case against objectivity in a certain field will be involved in making claims in that field which, once again, have to be understood as objective.

A case that illustrates the merits of Nagel's idea, but also the limitations of his totally general approach, is that of the objectivity of science. He puts this question as a matter of a choice between two equally abstract outlooks. One is the "realistic" attitude taken by most people, including most scientists, to the effect that there is a world which exists independently of us all, and which has a determinate character which scientists' theories try to capture. The other is the "attempt to reconstrue the ordered world picture as a projection of our minds." (This reconstruction, I assume, may or may not take a relativistic form, depending on how "our" is understood, but Nagel is not much concerned with relativism in this connection.) This second outlook, he argues,

founders on the need to place ourselves in the world so ordered. In trying to make sense of this relation, we are inevitably led to employ the same kind of reasoning, based on the search for order.

Even if we decide that some of our apprehensions of order are illusions or errors, that will be because a better theory, by the same
standards, can explain them away.

At this quite general level, Nagel must be right. It is impossible for anyone *totally* to get outside, or "place," or disown as parochial, realistic
thought about the world, or indeed attempts to understand it by some
principles of order. Those who try will, in order to make their point, have
to take up the commitments of thinking and talking in the ways that they
are trying to set on one side.

However, it is not clear how much this tells us. There have been many
things written about scientific realism and the alternatives to it. There
have been and no doubt still are some writers, for the most part ignorant
of science, who seem to think that science is merely invented, or determined by ideological forces. But very few who know anything about the
subject think this.[3] The point is, rather, that science is a complex social
activity, and the fact that some branch of science at a given time settles on
certain theories or models rather than others is not an outcome straightforwardly determined by perception of the world, but rather by scientists' habits and practices, including their ways of selecting and interpreting observations. This is not an abstract philosophical point; it is the
conclusion of detailed historical studies.[4]

Nagel himself, in fact, seems willing to accept this; he is not disposed
to think that the world, with a little experimental encouragement, in-
scribes itself into scientific journals. But he does not take up the question
of where exactly that leaves us. Within the limits of what Nagel claims
here, we could agree with Lichtenberg that "the lofty simplicity of nature all too often rests on the unlofty simplicity of the one who thinks
he sees it."[5] If this line of thought is correct, who or what, precisely, has
the "last word"? Our science certainly engages with the world, but that
leaves room for the reflection that nevertheless it is a function of "us" to
a greater extent than is naively supposed. As often with such issues—as
with our images of the past or our understanding of other people—the
question is not *whether* we grasp anything objectively, but *how much* we
grasp, and the answer to that may be obscure enough to leave us with
some of the unease which, I take it, Nagel's strategy is supposed to dispel.

However this may be, Nagel does show that no one can disown scientific
discourse altogether; if someone says, for instance, that science is just our
local mythology, he will need a picture of the world that contains people
and their mythologies, and if he is to sustain that picture, he will have to
address himself to science. Nagel also effectively exposes a familiar style
of attempt to disown a kind of discourse and at the same time to stay

within it. Richard Rorty is especially fond of this kind of statement. He writes, for example,

> What people like Kuhn, Derrida and I believe is that it is pointless to ask whether there really are mountains or whether it is merely convenient for us to talk about mountains. . . . Given that it pays to talk about mountains, as it certainly does, one of the obvious truths about mountains is that they were here before we talked about them. If you do not believe that, you probably do not know how to play the usual language-games which employ the word "mountain." But the utility of those language-games has nothing to do with the question of whether Reality as It Is In Itself, apart from the way it is handy for human beings to describe it, has mountains in it.[6]

Nagel rightly insists that Rorty and his friends had better come clean (cleaner than he does in that statement) about the mountains. No doubt it is handy for human beings to have words for mountains, but it is very hard to explain why this is so without mentioning the fact that there are mountains. It is revealing, too—and Nagel might have added this as an illustration of his general argument—that Rorty unquestioningly accepts that it pays to talk about mountains. He does not merely say that it pays to talk about its paying to talk about mountains.

Perhaps from the same fastidiousness that keeps him from citing much of what he opposes, Nagel stands at some distance from Rorty's arguments. He reproves his errors. But Rorty does not simply fall into error, he places himself there, and it is worth looking more closely at his rhetoric. The capital letters with which Rorty invests "Reality as It Is In Itself" suggest the metaphysical idea of a world not yet conceptualized at all, to which we are supposed to compare our concepts—the idea which Kant saw to be useless. But how is this metaphysical idea of Reality related to everyday, lower-case, reality, such as the mountains that there really are?

This is a question that has been addressed by much philosophy after Kant. Rorty, moving in and out of references to an upper-case Reality, declines to address that question, and this is the point: he wants, as he often says, to change the subject. Now Rorty is not wrong in thinking that philosophy moves on, more often than not, by changing the subject; as Bertrand Russell said about witchcraft, it was never disproved but merely ceased to be interesting. Rorty's mistake is to think that the way the subject changes is by someone's simply announcing that it has changed.

Rorty's rather lightheaded view of what is involved in the intellectual landscape changing—that is his problem. But equally there is a problem for Nagel. *Why*, on Nagel's view, have the outlooks of subjectivism and relativism and so forth got so much hold? Why are things as bad as he says they are? It is hard to find his answer in the book. He seems to think merely that from slackness and laziness and perhaps a desire for fame people do not think very well about these things. There is a hint of disappointed moralism in this, which sometimes lends a slightly Blimp-ish tone to his writing. He argues against his (mostly unidentified) op-ponents from where he is, rather than trying to see where such people might be going and what might be drawing them there. The danger in this is that he may not notice that the questions which he is addressing really have, in some degree, changed. Philosophy wants to make things clear. Unfortunately, few things that are really interesting are in the first place clear: what needs clarifying, this new thing, cannot usually be picked out using simply the categories available before it happened. This means that in order to locate what has to be understood, we need to ask how it came about, and this is one reason why philosophy needs history.

Nagel's approach is of course shaped by the history of philosophy, to a considerable extent the history of recent philosophy, but the way in which he sets out what needs to be discussed and explained is resolutely untouched by history. This is quite deeply connected with his own posi-tion, and with his very ambitious aim, which is really nothing less than to turn back the clock on the whole of modern philosophy. Nagel resists Kant's attempt to make philosophy start from a reflection on the powers and limitations of observers such as ourselves. When Kant introduced this philosophy, he called it the *critical* philosophy. The process of cri-tique that Kant initiated subsequently undid much of his own philoso-phy, and among the results of this process are the strategies and ideas of relativism and subjectivism now current which Nagel regards with alarm and distaste. It is hard to go on from here as though none of this had happened. We should not forget that the style of philosophy to which Kant self-consciously opposed his critique he called *dogmatic* philoso-phy, meaning that it took the supposed deliverances of reason at their face value, without asking how they were grounded in the structure of human thought and experience.

Nagel's philosophy is certainly not dogmatic in tone or intellectual manner: it is patient, honestly open-minded, attentive to argument, and willing to pursue the discussion with any moderately rational objectors. It is also not dogmatic in the sense that it invokes anyone else's dogma; his book is meant to be a defense of reason. Yet, in the spirit of Kant's distinction, it is dogmatic, because it is not interested enough in explana-tions. It draws, as it seems to me, arbitrary limits to the reflective ques-tions that philosophy is allowed to ask.

3

Let us go back to Nagel's principle that one cannot "get outside" various forms of thought and discourse. In the case of logic, the critic is bound to use logic even in putting a criticism; with natural science, as we have seen, the critic is committed to forms of inquiry which eventually lead him back to arguments which accept conclusions of natural science. These are very good cases, but we need to ask: What exactly, and how much, is shown by the fact that we cannot "get outside" a given kind of discourse or reasoning?

Suppose we consider a world which lacked human beings and their perceptions. Some of the descriptions which, as things are, we base on our perceptions we apply straightforwardly to such a world: we say that dinosaurs moved among green leaves, even if dinosaurs were themselves colorblind. We are probably less disposed to say that some laughable dinosaur misadventure was funny (really), though the humorless dinosaurs failed to notice it. We are more likely to say that some things are funny to us, but nothing was funny to a dinosaur. We more readily adopt the relativist tone when it comes to humor than we do with colors. It is very significant, however, that with regard to other human beings, this is not always how we speak even about humor. Many of Nagel's readers will think that much of what people found funny in the past, those jolly japes of humiliation and brutality, were not funny at all (really).

What is the basis of these differences, and how deep do they go? Our concepts of greenness and funniness are both, surely, rooted in our sensibility and in our ways of responding to the world. In neither case can we get rid of the idea altogether; we cannot say and think just what we do say and think about either greenness or funniness without using those concepts, or concepts like them. In that sense, it is true of both these cases that we must "go on in the same way": we can't stand entirely outside them. Yet that in itself seems not to tell us anything very deep about objectivity.

To the extent that he considers such cases, Nagel is primarily preoccupied with reduction—that is to say, with the question whether we can get rid of our familiar concepts altogether and replace them with concepts that lack the features typical of our experience. "Behavioristic reductions and their descendants," he writes,

> do not work in the philosophy of mind because the phenomenological and intentional features that are evident from inside the mind are never adequately accounted for from the purely external perspective that the reducing theories limit themselves to, under the mistaken impression that an external perspective alone is compatible with a scientific worldview.

We can agree with Nagel, against some scientistic programs in the philosophy of mind, that reduction in this strong form is not possible for any aspect of our experience that raises such questions. So the failure of reductionism in itself is not going to tell us whether some of these various kinds of experience are more "objective" than others. It is more helpful to think in terms of explanation rather than reduction. If we ask why almost all human beings find some things or other funny, though they do not all find the same things funny, we may have little idea of what the answer should be, but we are fairly certain that it will not involve describing things as funny before we get to them—funny, as one might say, anyway.

Nagel also puts a certain amount of weight on the issue of whether in fact we speak in a relativist way. But it is unclear how much follows from our speaking or not in a relativist way. The case of funniness suggests that if we, in some cases but not in others, prefer the language of objective fact and error to the language of relativism, this may say more about our attitudes than about what the world contains. (Perhaps after all there is something in Rorty's point, that it can be part of our language game to deny that it is a matter of our language game.) Similar reflections, if more complex, will be involved in thinking about aesthetic judgment, which Nagel, rather surprisingly, does not discuss.

When we recognize that our capacities to have various kinds of thought are to be explained in different ways, this can affect the ways in which we understand our disagreements with others. To the extent that our local disposition to find some things rather than others funny or hideous can be explained without (seriously) taking the world to contain things that are already funny or hideous, we may also be able to understand why other human beings do not necessarily find those same things funny or hideous. Of course, not everyone agrees about what counts as an explanation, or about what needs explaining. This is important, and I shall suggest that, particularly in the case of ethics, the striking fact that Nagel is so sure of his objectivities while others are so confirmed in their suspicions of them itself comes from a disagreement about what needs to be explained.

Sometimes Nagel's limited interest in explanations seems to leave him unnecessarily thinking that something is inexplicable. He has an intriguing section on our understanding of the infinite. "We seem to be left with a question," he writes, "that has no imaginable answer: How is it possible for finite beings like us to think infinite thoughts . . . ?" "If there is such a thing as reason, it is a local activity of finite creatures that somehow enables them to make contact with universal truths, often of infinite range": a simple example is our knowledge that there are infinitely many natural numbers. There is a reductivist temptation to deny that we grasp infinite truths, but reductivism will not do. "The idea of reducing the apparently infinite to the finite is therefore ruled out: Instead, the apparently finite must be explained in terms of the infinite."

Descartes used an argument rather like this to prove the existence of God. He reasoned: "I am a finite being, but I have the idea of an infinite Being. Such an idea could not have come from any finite source, such as myself. So it must have come from just such an infinite Being, and the fact that I have this idea shows that God exists." No one thinks that this is a very convincing argument. One reason is that it uses a very simple principle of explanation, to the effect that any thought with infinite content must have an infinite cause. It was for reasons similar to this principle (and which form part of its history) that Plato thought that if we reflect on our capacities for geometrical knowledge, we can recognize that it is not in utter nakedness that we come into this world: there is a realm of geometrical truth which we must have (so to speak) visited.

There is a hint of something like this in Nagel, too, in a revealing phrase that he uses in a passage I have already quoted: ". . . enables them to *make contact with* universal truths . . ." (my emphasis). Whatever explanations there may be of the human capacity to do mathematics, they are not going to involve mathematical truths in the extraterrestrial way that this phrase suggests. Can it really be that merely by thinking about the nature of mathematics, we can rule out in advance the prospect that there might be some, broadly speaking, biological explanations of our capacity to think mathematically? Though the subject of mathematics has, of course, a cultural history, the basic capacities involved must be the product of evolution by natural selection, or be the byproduct of some other capacity which has emerged in that way. (One thing that evolutionary explanations will have to do is to make clear what these capacities are.)

Nagel seems to deny, in effect, that there could be such an explanation: it is certainly not going to "explain the apparently finite in terms of the infinite," as he requires. He assumes, I think, that any scientific explanation of mathematical capacities would have to be reductive in the drastic sense that it would rob mathematical thoughts of their infinite content altogether, so that we would end up denying that every natural number has a successor and that there is no greatest prime.

Any explanation which had that consequence would certainly be a bad explanation. But nothing Nagel says shows that there could not be a better explanation linking mathematical capacities in an illuminating way with other characteristics that human beings have as a result of evolution. This would be a naturalist explanation, in a broader sense than Nagel, at least in this connection, acknowledges. What we want, here as elsewhere, is naturalism without reductionism. We want not to deny the capacities we undoubtedly have, but to explain them; the aim of explaining them is to make it intelligible that they can be the capacities of creatures like us, who have a certain evolutionary history and a very special ethology, one that involves culture and self-conscious history.

4

The question of how explanations of our thoughts might affect our understanding of them and of ourselves takes on a rather different, and particularly pressing, form when we get to ethics. Nagel allows in principle that there might be unflattering explanations of liberal ethical ideas:

> To take some crude but familiar examples, the only response possible to the charge that a morality of individual rights is nothing but a load of bourgeois ideology, or an instrument of male domination, or that the requirement to love your neighbor is really an expression of fear, hatred, and resentment of your neighbor, is to consider again, in the light of these suggestions, whether the reasons for respecting individual rights or caring about others can be sustained, or whether they disguise something that is not a reason at all. And this is a new moral question. One cannot just *exit* from the domain of moral reflection: It is simply there. All one can do is proceed with it in light of whatever new historical or psychological evidence may be offered. It's the same everywhere. Challenges to the objectivity of science can be met only by further scientific reasoning, challenges to the objectivity of history only by history, and so forth. [Nagel's emphasis]

This is the ethical version of the theme that one cannot get outside a type of thought, that we have to "go on in the same way." But it raises again the question of how much is settled by those formulae. For what is "the same way"? How various might "moral reasons" be? The relevance of cultural, psychological, or economic explanation to ethical values does not lie simply in its providing a challenge to them all collectively. Nagel's argument may deal effectively with that challenge, but in doing so it at most defeats ethical nihilism, and does not touch the concerns of the relativists and subjectivists. The cultural and other explanations of ethical beliefs help to remind us that those beliefs vary from place to place, and, further, that our own beliefs have a peculiar history and probably a peculiar psychology as well. Those considerations should make us think differently and more reflectively not only about the content of our beliefs but about the style in which we argue for them.

In particular, there is the matter of how we think of our ethical differences from other cultures, such as those of past people who did not share our liberalism; Nagel writes:

> Faced with the fact that [liberal] values have gained currency only recently and not universally, one still has to decide whether they are right—whether one ought to continue to hold them. . . . The question remains . . . whether I would have been in error if I had accepted as natural, and therefore as justified, the inequalities of a caste society. . . .

But how much do I *have* to decide? Here there is a crucial distinction. Nagel is absolutely right to say that the liberal, if he really is a liberal, must apply his liberalism to the world around him, and the knowledge that few people in the history of the world have been liberals is not itself a reason for his giving up being a liberal. If there are reasons for giving up liberalism, they will be the sorts of considerations which suggest that there is something better, more convincing, or more inspiring to believe instead. In this, I entirely agree with Nagel—though an interesting question is left, why people do tend to lose hold of their convictions in this way, and I shall come back to it.

So the liberal must take his ideas seriously as applying to the world. But to how much of the world? Does it follow, as Nagel puts it, that, "presented with the description of a traditional caste society, I have to ask myself whether its hereditary inequalities are justified . . ."? Most of us will agree that if we are presented in actual fact with such a society we have to ask ourselves some such question. But is this the case if we are presented with the *description* of such a society, one from long ago, let us suppose, belonging to the ancient world? Of course, thinking about this ancient society, I can ask myself Nagel's question, but is it true that the force of reason demands that I must do so, and what does the question mean? "Would I have been in error if I had accepted its inequalities as justified?"—Would *who* have been in error? Must I think of myself as visiting in judgment all the reaches of history? Of course, one can imagine oneself as Kant at the Court of King Arthur, disapproving of its injustices, but exactly what grip does this get on one's ethical thought?

In particular, is it really plausible that one makes this imaginary journey only with the minimal baggage of reason? Granted the notable fact that no one had the liberal world view then, the ethical time-traveler must take with him implicitly the historical experience which has made him the liberal he is, and that experience does not belong to the place he is visiting.

The basic idea that we see things as we do because of our historical situation has become over two hundred years so deeply embedded in our outlook that it is rather Nagel's universalistic assumption which may look strange, the idea that, self-evidently, moral judgment must take everyone everywhere as equally its object. It looks just as strange when we think of travel in the opposite direction. "To reason is to think systematically in ways anyone looking over my shoulder ought to be able to recognize as correct," Nagel says near the beginning of his book. *Anyone?* So I am reasoning, along with Nagel, in a liberal way, and Louis XIV is looking over our shoulder. He will not recognize our thoughts as correct. Ought he to?—or, more precisely, ought he to have done so when he was in his own world and not yet faced with the task of trying to make sense of ours?

We are brought back to the demand for explanations. If liberalism is correct and is based in universal human reason, as Nagel seemingly takes it to be, why is it that earlier times did not think of it or accept it? Kant had an answer in his theory of progress and enlightenment: human beings had grown up from a long period of tutelage, and for the first time could decide rationally how they should live. Hegel and Marx gave related, if more conflictual, answers, filled out in historical and economic terms.

Nagel suggests no answer and seems not to want one. I would say that Nagel lacks a "theory of error" for what he calls moral correctness, but whether we put it like that or not, he surely lacks an explanation of something that cries out for one. He cannot take it for granted that explanations of various ethical beliefs will at most modify their content, in the way illustrated by the anodyne example of bare breasts, which I mentioned earlier. If we come to understand historically and psychologically how our own and others' ethical thoughts came about, this can change the way we think about the status of our thoughts, and about their relation to other people's. To neglect this possibility does seem to me to constitute a form of dogmatism in Kant's sense, a refusal of the kind of critique that has made modern philosophy (including the deformations that Nagel rightly rejects) what it is.

Readers of Nagel's book will look for clues to the underlying outlook which sustains him in this approach. So far as ethics is concerned, I am struck by two assumptions that he makes. One is that if one does not think of one's morality as universally applicable to everyone, one cannot confidently apply it where one must indeed apply it, to the issues of one's own time. I said earlier that some people do seem to think that if liberalism is a recent idea and people in the past were not liberals, they themselves should lose confidence in liberalism as applied to the modern world. This is, as Nagel says, a mistake. But why does the unconfident liberal make it? I suspect that it is precisely because he agrees with Nagel's universalism: he thinks that if a morality is correct, it must apply to everyone. So if liberalism is correct, it must apply to all those past people who were not liberals.

Why did those people not think this themselves? Some say it was because they were collectively wicked and selfish: the unconfident liberal (rightly) thinks that that is a silly thing to say and explains nothing. Others, believers in enlightened progress, think it was because past people were poorly informed, superstitious, and so on. But the unconfident liberal has lost faith in the ideas of enlightened progress, and (very reasonably) cannot see how advances in science and technology have revealed the truth about liberalism. He becomes less sure that liberalism applies to those past people, after all. So, he begins to think, liberalism cannot be correct. That is not the conclusion he should draw; what he should do is give up the universalist belief he shares with Nagel. This does not mean that we must slide into a position of irony, holding to liberalism as liberals, but backing away from it as reflective critics. That position is itself still under the shadow of universalism. We only have to recognize that new times mean new needs and new powers. In many important respects, we are like no one else who has ever existed, and one of those respects is that we have liberal ideas, and ways of living to which they apply.

A second reason for Nagel's position in ethics is, I think, his rigid understanding of what it is to "go on in the same way." He does mention, at one point, the possibility that a whole activity or way of going on may be rationally rejected: he gives the almost defiantly trivial example of prediction by tea leaves. He presumably thinks that such things are properly rejected because they are primitive operations of thought in the same line of business as science, and science does better. But who said that this was the relevant line of business? As anthropologists remind us, there are other ways of looking at practices such as augury. What determines which of several different practices counts as the "same way of going on"? One thing is clear, that the practitioners cannot simply determine it themselves. The aged oracle among the Azande says: "This is what counts as being an oracle, and I don't count what these newcomers are doing as the same thing." But for all that, his customers may move to the new hospital.

So Nagel says: The content of my morality may be modified by new discoveries, but this way of arguing, this universalist, rational enterprise, just *is* what we count as morality. This determines what it is to go on in the same way. Then Nagel's opponents, the naturalists and disaffected inheritors of Kant's critique, reply: You cannot just determine what counts as the same. We say that your peculiar morality has purposes; not to mention the less friendly ones, it tries to help us to live together, to formulate pictures of a life worth living, to make sense of one's desires in relation to other people's desires and needs, and so on. There have been other ways of doing these things, and no doubt there will be others in the future. Understanding this, it is we who in a broader sense go on in the same way, living as best we can by what makes sense now, remembering that it has not always made sense, trying to pick up hints of new things that no one can yet understand. What you call "going on in the same way" represents just one style of ethical thought, one which, in particular, tries to forget that it has a history.

Of course, those of us who think in these terms cannot determine, any more than Nagel can, what counts—what will have counted—as going on in the same ethical way. Nothing can do that, finally, except the future itself. The Last Word, as always, will lie with what actually comes about.

Notes

1. *The Last Word*, by Thomas Nagel (Oxford University Press, 1997).

2. Nagel has a section (p. 92ff) on Kant's "transcendental idealism," claiming that it cannot escape being an (unbelievable) empirical theory. This is certainly contrary to Kant's intentions. Kant can be more sympathetically understood as not denying the thought that the world is, as he himself says, "empirically real," but rather inquiring what the content of that thought itself must be, and how we are able to think it.

3. For instance, even Barry Barnes, David Bloor, and John Henry, who are associated with the so-called "Strong Program" in the sociology of scientific knowledge, which stresses social factors in the formation and acceptance of theories, reject "idealism," and insist that a sociological account must presuppose the interactions of science and reality. See *Scientific Knowledge: A Sociological Analysis* (London: Athlone, 1906), pp. 1, 32.

4. Such as Andrew Pickering, *Constructing Quarks* (Edinburgh University Press, 1984). As his title leads one to expect, Pickering himself sometimes says such things as ". . . the reality of quarks was the upshot of particle physicists' practice . . . ," which is not a prudent way to put his conclusion (the 1970s is a bit late for quarks to appear in the universe), but should encourage one to think about how better to put it. (I am grateful here to Ian Hacking, who discusses these matters in his forthcoming book *The Social Construction of What?* (Harvard University Press, 1999).

5. Quoted by Pickering, p. 414.

6. Richard Rorty, "Does Academic Freedom Have Philosophical Presuppositions?" *Academe* (November–December 1994), pp. 56–57; quoted by Nagel, pp. 29–30.

70

Wagner and the Transcendence of Politics

1

How should we think about Wagner? Those who are troubled by that question, as I am, presumably think that as an artist he is worth being troubled about: that his works, or some of them, are demanding, inviting, seductive, powerful. Not everyone who cares about music need share that opinion. The relation of Wagner to the history of Western music and to the formation of a taste is not the same as that of, say, Bach or Mozart: he is not in the same way necessary. His works are indeed necessary to explaining its more recent history, very obviously so, but they are not in the same way a necessary part of a taste for Western music. Indeed, it is possible for a serious music lover to hate them—but that is not really the main point, since hatred can be a reaction to their power, in particular because of the peculiarities I shall be discussing. So Thomas Mann referred to Nietzsche's 'immortal critique of Wagner, which I have always taken to be a panegyric in reverse, another form of eulogy'.[1]

You can have a well-formed, deep relation to Western music while passing Wagner's works by, finding them boring or not to your taste. But it is clear, equally, that a passionate engagement with these works is not a mistake or a misunderstanding. They are amazing, and there is much to engage with. It is no accident not only that Wagner is voluminously discussed but that immense efforts, expenditure and imagination are still devoted to producing these pieces.

As well as the troubled and the bored and the revealingly hostile, there has notoriously been a further party, of the utterly devoted, and perhaps there still is. Being devoted does not necessarily mean being uncritical, but if the members of this party are critical, it is on the very local basis that the Master did not always live up to his own standards. This party has a question to answer. No-one can deny that some of Wagner's own attitudes are ethically and politically disturbing, some of them very deeply so. I mean that they are disturbing to us; and by that, I mean that they are rightly found disturbing by people who have seen the crimes and catastrophes of the twentieth century. We do certainly have to understand his attitudes in the context of his time, taking into account the options and ideological contrasts that were available then. We need to understand what his attitudes meant. But, equally, we have to take into account what they have come to mean.

When it is said that 'we have' to take such things into account, one thing this means is that we have no alternative if we are not to be misunderstood. In Shakespeare's *Much Ado about Nothing* (V.iv.38), Claudio says, 'I'll hold my mind [i.e. stick to my intention to marry her], were she an Ethiope.' In the Norton Shakespeare, the editor, Stephen Greenblatt, gives an explanation: 'In other words, black and therefore, according to the Elizabethan racist stereotype, ugly'.[2] A review in the London *Sunday Times* criticised him for this on grounds of excessive political correctness. But as Greenblatt reasonably said in an interview, would they have actually preferred it if he had said, 'black and therefore ugly'? In Wagner's case, 'we have no alternative' does mean this, but it means something else as well: that we have no alternative to taking into account his attitudes and what they have come to mean if we are to experience and reflect on these works at the depth they demand—more precisely, if we are to understand them at the level needed for them to become a significant part of our experience. (Indeed, so far as staging is concerned, we have to take these things into account if we are to put these works on at all, and this is a point I shall come back to.)

If we try to understand as a genuine historical question what range of opinions and attitudes was available in Wagner's world—'where he was' on various matters—we find that in some cases, he was already in a pretty bad place. Above all, and most notoriously, there is his anti-Semitism. His article 'Das Judentum in der Musik', attacking Meyerbeer and Mendelssohn and, generally, the artistic impotence of Jews, did not make a big stir when it was first published under a pseudonym in 1850. The document had considerably more effect when he reissued it under his own name in 1869, with additions in an even sharper tone and with more directly racist implications ('so far from getting rid of his errors,' Liszt said, 'he has made it worse'). The racist emphasis, influenced by Gobineau, was prominent in other publications of his last years. It has reasonably been claimed that Wagner by his own writings contributed to the resurgence of anti-Semitism in Germany in the 1880s, in particular by helping to make it culturally respectable.[3]

Moreover, it was not only during the Nazi time, through the friendship of Wagner's daughter-in-law Winifred with Hitler, that the Bayreuth Festival, which Wagner founded in 1876, became associated with the most repellent ideas. The house journal, the *Bayreuther Blätter*, was founded in 1878, when Wagner was still alive, by an acolyte, Hans von Wolzogen, who, as an historian of the festival has put it,

> used the journal as an ideological instrument to propagate a racist, anti-Semitic, chauvinistic, xenophobic and anti-democratic ideology. It would be difficult to find anywhere in the Western world in the late nineteenth century, even in the darkest corner

of the French right, a publication so poisonous, so hate-filled, so spiritually demented.[4]

In some other cases, the attitudes that Wagner held were capable of taking more benign forms, but Wagner's versions were not among them, This seems to be true of the particularly chauvinist form that he gave to the idea that there should be a German art.[5] Thomas Mann considered this in his famous essay (from which I have already quoted) 'The Sorrows and Grandeur of Richard Wagner,' which, given as a lecture in 1933, led directly to his exile from Germany, and which is, along with some of Nietzsche's thoughts, still the most helpful reflection that I know on these questions.[6] Mann pointed out, using a distinction made by a Swedish writer, that Wagner's aspiration was for a German art in the sense of *nationale Kunst* rather than *Volkskunst*—that is to say, the nationalism was a matter of the destiny and political significance of German art, not of its materials.

This in itself may seem an entirely intelligible, even innocent or laudable, nineteenth-century ambition. But then we have to recall that the problem of a distinctively German art, and its relation to a self-conscious artist working in a broader European tradition, had been a preoccupation of German thought since at least the late eighteenth century. Above all it had been a recurrent concern for Goethe, with regard to the German language, its traditions of writing, the public for that writing, the self-conscious cultivation or rejection of differences from the rest of Europe, the relation of German art to various possible political regimes in the German-speaking states, and so on. Indeed, in his writings on these subjects Wagner, unsurprisingly, praises Goethe and Schiller.

Now the German world in the 1860s was certainly a very different place from what it had been in 1800. Yet it is still relevant to point out that in Goethe's case the question of how to achieve a distinctively German art was a problem *for him*, a problem to which he responded in ways that honoured its complexity; whereas for Wagner it was, of course, a problem to which, at any given stage of his career, he knew the answer, as against the traitors and enemies who took a different view. This absence of the Goethean spirit, not just in a form anachronistic by the 1860s, but in any form at all, is something I shall come back to when we confront the impression, not lightly to be dismissed, that for all their wonders and power there is an all-consuming assertiveness in Wagner's works which can be disgusting.[7]

I have moved directly from talking about Wagner's personal attitudes, as expressed in his writings, to talking about the character of his work. That is not an oversight; the problem is that the two cannot entirely be separated. It is possible that artists with politically disturbing views could produce works that are not politically disturbing. There are without doubt several things wrong with Hans Pfitzner's remarkable opera *Palestrina* (first produced in 1917), such as its heavy-handed attempt to present the Council of Trent in the style of *Die Meistersinger*; but they do not express what was wrong with Pfitzner himself, whose conservative and nationalist views were congenial enough to the Nazis that (to his great resentment) he was required to undergo denazification after the Second World War. Wagner's relation to his works was not like this. That is obvious now and has been obvious since they were created, but we shall have to ask what it is about the works that makes this so.

What is troubling is that the problems raised by his repellent attitudes on the one hand and by the disturbing power of his work on the other cannot be solved by a distinction between 'the work' and 'the man'. Or rather, we cannot immediately call on that distinction to solve them. The problems that matter of course concern the work: it is only the fact that we want to take the work seriously that forces us to confront Wagner at all. But it does indeed force us to confront him, because Wagner's is a case in which, if we are to deal adequately with the work and its power, we have to take into account the attitudes of the man and what they have come to mean. I do not mean that his views, even his views of his own works, necessarily determine our interpretation of them. His works are independent, in varying degrees, from the outlook expressed in what he wrote around and about them, but we have to ask in every case how far they are independent of it, and in what ways. We need to understand, in particular, how far what moves us in the work may be connected with what frightens and repels us in his attitudes.

Some contemporary approaches to the work, though they are very vocal about Wagner's attitudes, fail to grasp that this is the question, and fall short of what we need in order to think about it. A lot of writing about Wagner since the 1970s conceives the problem as that of revealing a hidden scandal; the authors try to trace the ways in which the attitudes have marked the works.[8] These writers spend a lot of effort, for instance, in trying to find signs of anti-Semitism in the operas themselves, claiming that the representations of Mime, Klingsor, Beckmesser and other characters introduce Jewish stereotypes. I am not concerned with the question, still much disputed, of whether the attempts at decipherment of these characters are correct. Even if a nineteenth-century audience did not need as much help in recognising such stereotypes as, seemingly, we do; even if Wagner consciously intended them (for which there is no direct evidence); the point is that these supposed signs are too trivial to help with the only question that can reasonably concern us. The only reason for worrying about Wagner's works is that they are powerful and interesting. But if that is so, what difference would these signatures, these local coded messages, make?

In effect, these writers reduce the problem of Wagner's anti-Semitism (so far as the works are concerned) to these supposed traces, to the idea that, in one instance or another, Wagner is knowingly signalling it. This cannot help to deal with any deep anxieties caused by Wagner's works. In fact, it serves to reconcile these writers' admiration for them with their bad conscience about his attitudes, but at a painless and superficial level. They have externalised the problem, moving it from where it truly belongs.

We can take an analogy from a quite different work of Thomas Mann's, *Death in Venice*: these critics treat the threat, the dangerousness, of Wagner as if it were the outbreak of cholera, which with luck you can signal and confine by whitewashing and disinfecting the walls. But our, and their, real problem with Wagner is not like this at all—rather, it is like Aschenbach's problem with Tadzio. These critics do not accept at the right level the way in which Wagner is related to his works. They are saying, in effect, that there had *better* be something wrong with the works, and they have come up with a circumscribed and relatively painless way of identifying what this is.

In a well-known book Robert W. Gutman has written,

> Unhappily, a proto-Nazism, expressed mainly through an unextinguishable loathing of the Jews, was one of Wagner's principal leitmotifs, the venomous tendrils of anti-Semitism twining through his life and work. In his final years, his hatred reached out further to embrace those with black and yellow skins. This attitude cannot be shrugged off as an unfortunate whim or a minor flaw in a musical hero.

This underlines the point that the presence of some anti-Semitic signatures is not in itself enough: they are not going to show that anti-Semitism is 'one of [the] principal leitmotifs' of Wagner's work. The works will have to be more thoroughly polluted than that, and in his book Gutman gives interpretations to suggest that they are (though he does less to show that these interpretations are inescapable). But then he is thrown back to the question of why these thoroughly polluted works are supposed to be interesting or important to us. To this, his answer appeals simply to the music:

> Yet Wagner survives, and primarily because he was a great musician. His ripe late-romantic style retains much of its allure. . . . A music of almost unparalleled eloquence and intimacy keeps his works on the stage.[9]

This is not an answer at all. Having refused to separate the man and the work, Gutman tries to separate the work and its music, an aim which can be seen to be failing already in the use of words such as 'eloquence' and 'intimacy,' and which is anyway peculiarly hopeless in the case of Wagner, who took unprecedented steps to unify musical and dramatic expression. If we end up with such an evasion, it is clear that we must start again.

2

Some modern productions of Wagner's works have another way of trying to 'externalise' the problems. It is a significant fact that we have seen in the opera house in recent years the coexistence of two kinds of radicalism. In cases to which it is appropriate, there is an increasing 'authenticity' of orchestral and vocal performance, based on historical research; and at the same time there are productions and sets which display all degrees of rethinking and creativity up to the now notorious extremes of directorial whimsy—which themselves are more or less what has come to be expected.

These two developments might seem to go in opposite directions. It is true, of course, that they can conflict, as when the production makes it impossible for the singers to express what the music requires or invites them to express. (It is important that this should not be described as a conflict between music and drama; it is a conflict between the dramatic contribution of the music and the dramatic contribution of the staging.) But this is a matter of particular failures, not of what is intrinsic to the two kinds of radicalism. Even quite extreme versions of them, if they are put together in the right way, can produce a triumphant success (this was true of Peter Sellars's 1996 production at Glyndebourne of Handel's *Theodora*). They can combine to the same end. The musical performance tries to offer a closer approximation to the composer's means of expression; the production offers a version of what this drama, these emotional relations, can mean in terms that make sense to us now—it tries to find visual and dramatic equivalences, which work for us, to the expressive content both of the words and of the music as that music is now presented to us. No theatrical presentation of the drama that was simply determined by historical research could possibly do that.

In fact, the idea of a theatrical production of an opera which is 'authentic' in the sense in which musical performances can aim to be 'authentic' (and that itself, of course, raises large questions which are not the concern here) seems to be virtually nonsensical. Critics who attack what they see as the extreme innovations of recent directors and call for 'traditional' productions of the *Ring* cannot mean that we should be given what Wagner in 1876 in Bayreuth actually had—for one thing, we know what Wagner thought of what he got in 1876.[10] But quite apart from that, since the question is one for us, of what we should do, even the most devoted intentionalist will have to ask not what Wagner wanted granted the resources he had, but what he would have wanted if he had had our resources; and that means of course, also, resources to present his works to audiences who have seen what we have seen (and not only on the stage). We are back, unsurprisingly, where we started, with the problems of staging Wagner's works for us now. In pursuit of a truthful production, there is absolutely no alternative to re-creation.

The objection to some recent productions of Wagner is not that they are in a new idiom, but rather that they do not use that idiom to re-create. What some of them offer is mere comment. Unlike the decipherment of the supposed anti-Semitic signatures, which I have just considered, the ideologically critical treatment of the works in these productions is not minor or episodic. Their comments may be continuous, as when Wotan is throughout represented as a tycoon in the 2000 Bayreuth production of the *Ring*. The problem arises if they are no more than comments, external to any response to the content of the works; in that case, they are like the supposed decipherment of anti-Semitic messages.[11] Just as being given a decoding of Beckmesser's vocal style as Jewish, even if it were correct, would do very little to help one understand or shape one's reactions to *Die Meistersinger*, so a continuous subjoined ethical health warning added to the *Ring*—the mechanical injection into it of modern hate-figures, for instance—does not help one to face what the *Ring*, both for good and for bad, requires one to face.

We have to address the works and the problems they present on a larger scale. We have to ask: what general features of Wagner's style contribute to the problems? I should like to suggest three, all of them characteristics that were mentioned by Thomas Mann.

Wagner shared with other nineteenth-century artists, notably Ibsen, the aim of uniting the mythic and the psychological. One might even suggest—this is my suggestion, not Mann's—that in a certain sense Wagner is Ibsen inside out. Ibsen succeeded in some of his works in taking realistic bourgeois domestic drama and giving it the weight, the sense of necessity, that one can find in Sophocles; Wagner took myths and medieval epics and installed in them a psychology which is often that of bourgeois domestic drama. There is a basic problem with this enterprise, implicit in Walter Benjamin's observation that the heroes of ancient tragedy or epic lack an inner life in a modern sense: many, if not all, of those ancient works gravely express a necessity that transcends biographical particularity. To reconcile this fact with a drama for which intensity almost unavoidably means intense subjectivity is a hard undertaking, as many nineteenth- and twentieth-century artists have found.

In fact, there are three levels involved. Besides the mythical or medieval materials, and the explicit motivations and situations of bourgeois drama, Wagner engages in depth-psychological explorations which are expressed in words and music that go far beyond naturalistic drama. Wagner is most successful in reconciling the mythical and the psychological, so it seems to me, when it is this last element that prevails: when the subjective intensity is so extreme, solitary and unrelated to citizenly or domestic life that in its own way it takes on an authority which is perhaps analogous to that of ancient tragedy. This is notably so in *Parsifal* and in Act III of *Tristan*. Elsewhere he succeeds because he can sustain an analogy with domestic drama which does not need to apologise for itself: an obvious example is Act I of *Die Walküre*.

Sometimes the analogies are imperfectly negotiated, and even the 'arts of transition' of which Wagner was justly proud cannot hold the levels together. I personally think that this is true, at all three levels, of King Mark's recriminations in Act II of *Tristan*. There is the problem that the view of the lovers from an everyday social perspective is less interesting at this point than what we have just experienced inside the world of night that they have entered; and in addition, for all the references to heroes and courtly honour, it is hard to dissociate Mark's complaints from a bourgeois embarrassment, doubtless familiar to Wagner himself. In such cases there are problems for production, but with skill and luck they can be dealt with. However, there is one central case, the character of Siegfried, in which there is a real vacuum, a collapse at the heart of the work, and the very questionable conception of heroism which is associated with him has, I am going to suggest, a political significance.

Another, and very manifest, feature of the style is that Wagner really did break down in some ways the conventional distinction between the musical and the non-musical. As Mann put it, while the old criticism that Wagner's music is not really musical was absurd, nevertheless it was not entirely unintelligible: Wagner's work does in a way fuse the musical and the literary. Mann says about the E flat chord that starts *Das Rheingold*, 'It was an acoustic concept: the concept of the beginning of all things. Music has been here pressed into service in an imperiously dilettante fashion in order to represent a mythical concept.'[12] This implies that the 'deeds of music made manifest' which, as he was finishing the *Ring*, Wagner said were offered in his work,[13] and the psychological/ethical/political significance of the text (or rather, one should say, the action), can only be understood in terms of each other. It is no peculiarity of Wagner that what the work means is not given merely or primarily by the action: it is true of all opera, or at least of all great opera. But Wagner's style does make the dramatic relations between music and action at once more pervasive and emotionally more immediate. We have already seen one consequence of this, that one cannot adequately explain the power of Wagner by simply appealing to the music. There is another consequence, in (so to speak) the opposite direction: that if someone feels that there is something ethically or politically suspect about, in particular, the *Ring*, that feeling, whether it is correct or incorrect, is not going to be met simply by appealing to the action or, more narrowly, to the text.

It is a paradox that some defenders of Wagner, having elsewhere extolled the unity of music and text in his works, think it is enough to meet these ideological criticisms by pointing out that, according to the plot, oath-breaking and theft do not pay off. Whatever the hopes may be for recovering an overall sense of the end of the *Ring*, you are not going to find it in its closing words, and it is a significant point, a point which comes back again to the figure of Siegfried, that one of the most overwhelming and also, I am going to suggest, unnerving episodes of *Götterdämmerung*, the funeral music, has no words.

Wagner is, more than any other, a 'totalising' artist; in any given work, all the elements relate to one underlying conception or tone. Mann, once more, puts this very well, in terms which, from a technical point of view, are no doubt exaggerated, but which express something entirely recognisable:

> It is this infinite power of characterization that . . . separates the works from each other, and develops each of them from a basic sound which distinguishes it from all the others; so that inside the totality of the *oeuvre*, which itself constitutes a personal world, each individual work again forms a self-contained unity, like a star.

Nietzsche said that in any given work of Wagner's it is as though it were all presented by one impersonator with a very distinctive voice; and, since the biographical presence is also strong, this impersonator may easily be taken for the composer.[14] All doubt, duality or underdetermination is either internalised into the action (the characters are represented as undecided or in conflict), or it is externalised, existing outside the work altogether (the work stands against the rest of the world); doubt and duality do not exist at the level at which the work offers itself. The work itself voices or implies total unity and certainty. Because the voice of the work is so distinctive in Wagner's case, and, once again, the historical presence of the composer is close (for instance in suggesting what the whole enterprise stands against), the sense is not of a world assumed, but of an outlook asserted.

The extreme modernism of Wagner's later style implies that he is not taking for granted the ethical or social assurances which give structure to many other confident dramatic works of the nineteenth century, such as those of Verdi. But at the same time, though he represents ambivalent characters and actions that have ambiguous or perverse consequences, he was not disposed in the least to the typically modernist development by which ambivalence and indeterminacy become part of the fabric of the presentation itself, so that it is essential to the work that it does not finally tell its audience what to make of it. There are few operas, in fact, that have achieved this effect, but they include two of the greatest among twentieth-century operatic works, *Pelléas* and *Lulu*.

3

I come back to the absence of the Goethean spirit that I mentioned earlier in connection with *Die Meistersinger* and the project of founding a German art. Part of the suspect quality of Wagner lies in the fact that although he portrays conflicts and contradictions, such as Wotan's indecisions, his recognition that he cannot directly achieve what he wants, the tensions between power and love, and so on, Wagner's tone in presenting these things seems to have at each point an indomitable assurance. He is telling us what it all adds up to. This aspect of Wagner's style can produce fear and resentment; one can have the sense of being locked inside Wagner's head; and it can also give a sense of fraudulent manipulation. Moreover, as soon as Wagner's assurance—the feeling that he thinks he has a hold on what is unconditionally significant—encounters the political, particularly in his trying to transcend it, it can become deeply alarming.

These features and the reactions they arouse may mean that some of his devices simply do not work. But sometimes Wagner's inventions work when it seems that they should not, and then our resistance (and hence our conflicts) can be especially strong. More than one consideration that has already come up leads us to particular and very central examples of this, the funeral music in *Götterdämmerung*, the orchestral interlude between the scene of Siegfried's death and the final scene of the whole *Ring*. The funeral music is almost entirely retrospective in its effect, and it is essential to our experience of the *Ring* that this should be so. No-one, I think, could describe it as regretful, or melancholy, or resigned. It is manifestly triumphant. It is offered as the celebration of the life, just ended, of a great hero. Yet, as many critics have noticed, the subject of this shattering musical memorial scarcely exists as a person.

Siegfried is the least self-aware, in every sense of the word the least knowing, of Wagner's heroes. He does not know much about anything, least of all about himself, and a lot of what he does know he forgets for most of *Götterdämmerung*, under the influence of Hagen's drug. Although, in his dying moments, the memories of his love for Brünnhilde are restored to him, they do not bring with them any greater understanding, but only a return to a blissful past. In this, and in his relation to these magic drinks, he is quite unlike Tristan, who in his great monologue in the third act comes to see how everything that has happened flowed from himself. To Siegfried, on the other hand, the machinery of spells remains external, and represents nothing in his motivations or his wishes. If he had any character at all, it would be only a limitless—one might almost say clinical—guilelessness.

His encounter with Brünnhilde did teach him something, fear. This gave him, we are told, a new experience, but it is notable that we are not given much more than the telling of it. There is a good deal of psychological material in the last scene of *Siegfried* after Siegfried awakens Brünnhilde, and it is of course expressed in the music, but it almost entirely concerns Brünnhilde's transition from warrior to lover. Siegfried as lover gets new music, but very little of a new psychology. What he carries forward from the encounter is nothing but a blissful memory; and when he reasserts his individuality as a hero and returns to the world of action, there is no project for him except action itself. 'Zu neuen Taten!' ('New deeds!') is the first thing that Brünnhilde says to him in *Götterdämmerung*, and, if we take it for granted that he is to resume the only life he is able to live, there is nothing else for her to say. What matters is the absence of an inner life, not in itself the absence of intelligence. Parsifal is defined by a holy lack of intelligence, but in the course of the action he gains an inner life; the confrontation with memory and sexuality that is enacted in such extraordinary terms in the second act changes him completely, whereas to Siegfried nothing significant happens at all.

It is not impossible for a great hero to lack an inner life: as Walter Benjamin pointed out, the heroes of epic and ancient tragedy are often presented with a notably reticent indication of their subjectivity. But it is much harder to present as a great hero one who is simply naïve and unimaginative, and whose great deeds, the slaying of the dragon and the journey to Brünnhilde, are not so much emblems of courage as the products of an infantile fearlessness. This is no Achilles. He appears, moreover, in a drama in which subjectivity, self-consciousness, reflection, personal ambivalence and so on are pervasive, expressed in the artistic means themselves, and, above all, central to the existence of another character, Wotan, who has a better claim to be the hero.

Because the celebration represented by the funeral music is of the seemingly uncelebratable, there is a crisis of theatrical production at this point. Recently we have often been given an empty stage or Siegfried's body lying undisturbed. On the occasions I have seen them, these came out as lame or desperate devices; but it is not surprising that there is desperation. Critics complain of a wilful, contemptuous rejection of the heroic. But it is not the directors' fault that there is a failure of the heroic. They are reacting, if inadequately, to a feature of the work which, if it is allowed to emerge, is bound now to seem empty or potentially alarming.

Since there is this dramatic failure, it is a real question why the funeral music can indeed be effective, in fact overpowering; and it is not enough to say that it is an astonishing piece of music, since it is a piece of dramatic music in the deepest Wagnerian sense. I think that there is an answer to the question of how it can move us so much, and I shall come back to this. But the problem that comes first, one that is signalled by the directors' difficulties, is that of heading off a different kind of message—an implicitly political message—which can readily fill the gap left by Siegfried's absence as hero. I said that the funeral music, granted that absence, can be alarming. The reason for this lies in its relation to the political, or rather, unpolitical, aspects of the *Ring*.

The serene and reconciling motive that appears in the last moments of *Götterdämmerung* used to be called 'Redemption through Love'. None of these labels for the leitmotifs has any authority, but this was worse than most. For what, even in Wagner's overgenerous use of such words, has been redeemed? Brünnhilde of course sacrifices herself by riding into Siegfried's funeral pyre, but if this is to count as redemption, rather than suttee on horseback, it has to have some further result. She says, 'This fire, burning my frame, cleanses the curse from the ring.' Indeed, the gold is now purified, because it has been returned to the Rhine—the only place, as the Rhinemaidens sing at the end of *Rheingold*, for what is close and true: 'Traulich und treu ist's nur in der Tiefe.'[15] The gold has been redeemed, if one insists on the word. But there is no suggestion that the gold's return, or the deaths of Siegfried and Brünnhilde, have also redeemed the world, at least if that means that the world has become a better or freer place. The future of the world, at the end of *Götterdämmerung*, is plainly not a concern, while the gods have no future at all. This is an embarrassment to the familiar political interpretations of the *Ring*. They all begin with a great impetus from *Rheingold*, with its manifest images of expropriation, self-impoverishment and slavery, but even the most resourceful of them tend to peter out as the cycle proceeds, finding material at its end only for some vapid aspiration to a politics of innocence.

The problem with this is not that the *Ring*, as it proceeds, avoids politics. It is rather that the hope for a politics of innocence is one thing that it seems to reject. If one wants transportable lessons from the *Ring*, a conclusion to be drawn from the story of Wotan will be that there is no politics of innocence, because nothing worth achieving can be achieved in innocence. Only in the depths, where nothing has been imposed on Nature or wrested from it, is the tender and true. But the nobility and grandeur of the funeral music stand against this. Not because of what it says (it says nothing) but, all the more, because of what it does, it can carry the suggestion that perhaps there could be a world in which a politics of pure heroic action might succeed, uncluttered by Wotan's ruses or the need to make bargains with giants, where Nibelungs could be dealt with forever: a redemptive, transforming politics which transcended the political.

Such ideas had in Germany a long, complex and ultimately catastrophic history. Politics, or at least 'ordinary' politics, the politics of parties, power, bargaining and so on, was seen as something divisive, low, materialistic and superficial, in contrast to something else which was deep, spiritual and capable of bringing people together into a higher unity: something, moreover, which instead of peddling satisfactions, demanded renunciation and suffering. There were two main candidates for this higher thing, art and the nation, or, indeed, the two together.

Such ideals informed the influential conception of the *Sonderweg*, the idea of a special path that German development might follow, distinct from (in particular) Britain and France; and one expression of the difference lay in a supposed contrast between *Kultur*, which was German and deep, and *Zivilisation*, which was shallow and French. (Thomas Mann himself had supported such ideas during the First World War, and still in part sought to justify them in the diffuse work which he published in 1918, significantly called *Betrachtungen eines Unpolitischen* ('Reflections of a Non-Political Man').)[16] All the elements of this tradition were to be exploited in a desultory but ruthlessly opportunistic way by Hitler.[17] Hitler was far from unpolitical, but he pretended to be, and perhaps himself believed that in him the nation had transcended politics: that the politics which brought him to power and which, together with terror, kept him in it was indeed a politics of transcendence.

Wagner was certainly deeply committed to the nationalist ideals of the *Sonderweg*, but it is rare in his works (as opposed to his writings) that the will to transcend politics points in a distinctively political direction. *Die Meistersinger* certainly has political implications; as Nietzsche rightly said, it is against *Zivilisation*, German against French. Moreover, it invites questions, which it notably fails to answer, about the politics of art. Hans Sachs believes in the judgment of the *Volk*, and in the last scene the young knight Walther gets their enthusiastic approval, with a composition which, we are told, reconciles inspiration with tradition. Wagner no doubt thought that the same could truly be said of his act as a whole. But in fact nothing in this bland formula, or in the way it is worked out in *Die Meistersinger*, is going to close the gap between Wagner's intensely radical avant-garde experiments and music that could be straightforwardly popular as, for instance, Verdi's was.

The politics of art—the relations of Wagner, his music and the German people—remain at the end of the opera an unsolved question. But the relation of all this to politics in a narrower sense, the politics of government, is not even a question in *Die Meistersinger*. Although in the last moments of the work (in a notably obtrusive passage, which Wagner seems to have put in at Cosima's insistence) Wagner gets Sachs to declare the ideals of artistic nationalism, he is careful not to commit himself to what its political implications might be. Sachs's last words on the subject are 'Even if the Holy Roman Empire dissolved in mist, yet there would remain holy German art!' And this in its context can fairly be taken to say that the ideals of German art can survive, even if politics change radically or go badly wrong. This might be called the avoidance of politics.

With *Parsifal*, the one work that Wagner wrote after he had completed the *Ring*, the situation is different again. Nietzsche was clearly wrong when he said that Wagner had ended up by prostrating himself in front of the Christian cross. Wagner did nothing of the sort: roughly speaking, he took some coloured snapshots of the Eucharist and used them to illustrate his journey into the psychology of sex, guilt, memory and pain. (He thought that Nietzsche lacked a sense of humour, because he presented him with a copy of the *Parsifal* poem inscribed from 'Richard Wagner, Oberkirchenrat'—as it were, 'The Right Reverend Wagner'— and Nietzsche did not find it funny.) But the work does undoubtedly steal some of its resonance from Christian ritual and its associations, and in particular, Wagner's recurrent theme of a redeemer sustains in this case much of its familiar religious meaning. Indeed, in the magnificent climax to Act III, Gurnemanz, crowning Parsifal as king, uses language so dense with references to redemption and salvation that it has even been suggested that he is addressing not Parsifal but the Redeemer Himself.[18]

Although Parsifal becomes a king, he is not a king over any subjects. Nor does the opera suggest that mankind is reclaiming its identity from religion, as in the more Feuerbachian moments of the *Ring*. Here we can speak of a genuine absence of politics. What we have is the exploitation of religious remnants in the interests of a drama that operates almost entirely at the level of depth-psychology. This involves a kind of trick, because in places the work has to pretend that the whole of human life is transcended and justified by something higher (as it is represented in the final scene, indeed, literally higher), the Holy Spirit. But the psychological material is so powerful, the symbols of the wound and the spear are strong enough, and, above all, the musical invention is so compelling that Wagner's *Allmacht*, his capacities as a magical manipulator, enable him just about to get away with it. The director is left with some nasty problems, but we need not be, and certainly not any that have to do with politics.

It is not an objection to *Parsifal* that at the time of writing it Wagner wrote increasingly crazy articles tying its story together with themes of racial purity. It might be, for some people, an objection to going to see *Parsifal*: they might feel that they did not wish to be associated in any way with a work written by a man with such an outlook. That is, as people say, their privilege. But it has nothing at all to do with interpreting or responding to *Parsifal*, because whatever theories Wagner may have had, they do not structure the work, or surface in it, or demand our attention in experiencing it.

When Robert Gutman, for instance, says, 'Parsifal's sudden insight in the magic garden was the realization that by yielding to Kundry he would dilute his purebred strain', he is not reporting the plot, the text or any implication of the music's associations. He is simply saying how it might look to someone who thought about little but Wagner's racist writings. My point here is not to reinstate the distinction between the work and the man, which I have already said is not a helpful device in Wagner's case. The point is just that one cannot decide in advance, either positively or negatively, what facts about the man, his views and their history may be relevant to responding to a given work. In particular, if we acknowledge its power, it is a question of what it is in us that does so, and in the case of *Parsifal* we have a good enough idea of what that is to know that it has nothing essentially to do with Wagner's racist ravings.

In *Die Meistersinger*, politics is avoided, and from *Parsifal* it is merely absent, but with the *Ring*, neither of these is true. The cycle emphatically addresses issues of power, and if at its end it suggests that the world in which they arise is overcome, it is hard not to be left with the feeling that the questions of power and its uses have not so much been banished as raised to a level at which they demand some 'higher' kind of answer.

I said earlier that there is an explanation of why the funeral music can move us so much even when we recognise that the supposed object of its triumph does not exist. I suggest that it makes sense because we hear it as the celebration not of a man but of a process, of all that has gone before in the *Ring*. The *Ring* as it moves towards its end elicits a cumulative sense of its own complexity and power, and it is this that the funeral music celebrates. The music itself helps to bring this out, as motives associated with earlier parts of the story come to the surface. In celebrating its own fulfilment, the work can make us feel that the whole disaster-laden history has been worthwhile.

What this expresses is not—and it is very important that it is not—the idea that life is redeemed by art, the idea that real life, and real suffering, cruelty and humiliation, are justified because they can issue in great works of art. It is doubtful that Wagner believed this even about his own works. It is not that the splendours of the *Ring* can justify real life. Rather, the *Ring*'s celebration of what it has presented can symbolise for us ways in which life even in its disasters can seem to have been worthwhile. In these terms the *Ring* emerges as what it should be, an affirmative drama, and not in a way that invokes a hypothetical and deeply suspect politics of heroism and sacrifice.

The problem still remains, however, whether the part that Siegfried plays in the story can, on any adequate reading, bear the weight that it is required to bear. Some of the strains in the work come, without doubt, from the complex changes of mind that Wagner underwent as he wrote it. But the problem is not just that the work is imperfect. What really matters is a product of history, that the strains pull us towards a sense of the work in which the transcendence of politics tends to suggest not the absence of politics, but a higher, transcendental, politics, of a peculiarly threatening kind.

This is signalled by problems of theatrical production, and those problems remain even if we come to hear the funeral music as a tragic affirmation rather than the celebration of an embarrassingly non-existent hero. The questions that emerge concretely as problems for the theatrical director are in any case questions for all of us, if we do not allow Wagner's extraordinary ingenuity to deflect us from them. Particularly with regard to the *Ring*, but not only there, it may be impossible, even in our imagination, to re-create Wagner's works altogether adequately. It may be that the total unity of psychology, myth and morally redemptive significance to which Wagner aspired is an illusion, not just in the sense that it is unattainable—that is true of Beethoven's ideals of freedom—but because, as Nietzsche said, it is based in some part on a pretence that a set of theatrical, often grandiose, gestures can reveal the nature of the world. If that is so, then to that extent no honest treatment of it can make it work as a whole. We can do it justice—but then it comes out guilty of that pretence, and justly associated, for indelible historical reasons, with a politics that has since Wagner wrote moved into the gap left by that pretence. Or it can come out less guilty—but then theatrical re-creation will have negotiated this as an accommodation between historical memory, what Wagner tried to bring about, and what we can now, decently and (as we say) in all honesty, accept.

If, at least for some of Wagner's works, a production which 'did them justice' would find them guilty, this will constitute the historical vengeance of the ethical on an artist who uniquely raised the stakes high enough for such a vengeance to be even possible.

Notes

For other general essays on music see *On Opera*, by Bernard Williams (Yale University Press, 2006)

1. 'The Sorrows and Grandeur of Richard Wagner', in *Pro and contra Wagner*, trans. Allan Blunden (London, 1985), p. 100. (In quotations from Mann, I have sometimes modified the translation.) Nietzsche's attacks on Wagner certainly represent an ongoing deep fascination with him, but some of his remarks may also strike a

chord with those who are less involved: 'My objections to Wagner's music are physi-ological objections. What's the point of dressing them up in aesthetic formulae?'

2. New York and London, 1997.

3. This is argued by Jens Malte Fischer in a helpful and admirably balanced in-troduction to an edition of Wagner's pamphlet, *Richard Wagners 'Das Judentum in der Musik': Eine kritische Dokumentation* (Frankfurt am Main and Leipzig, 2000). For a review of Wagner's anti-Semitism, see the article by Dieter Borchmeyer in *A Wagner Handbook*, ed. Ulrich Müller and Peter Wapnewski, translation edited by John Deathridge (Cambridge, Mass., and London, 1992).

4. Frederic Spotts, *Bayreuth: A History of the Wagner Festival* (New Haven and London, 1994), p. 84. According to Cosima's diary, Wagner did once tell Wol-zogen that he wanted the journal to strike a broad, idealistic note, and keep away from 'specialities', such as vegetarianism and agitation against the Jews. See Co-sima Wagner, *Die Tagebücher*, 2 vols. (Munich and Zürich, 1976–77), vol. 2, p. 700; cited by Fischer, p. 118.

5. His article 'Deutsche Kunst und deutsche Politik' (first published anony-mously in a newspaper in 1867, then in book form in 1868) can be 'interpreted, at least in part, as a commentary on *Die Meistersinger*', according to John Deathridge in *The New Grove Wagner* (London, 1984), pp. 52–3. I come back later to the question of whether *Meistersinger* is itself expressly political.

6. There is one significant qualification to be made: that neither in this essay, nor (yet more remarkably) in pieces written during and after the Second World War, did Mann, so far as I know, mention Wagner's anti-Semitism.

7. It was a 'nameless presumptuousness' in wanting to have something to say about everything that Mann particularly had in mind when he said in a letter to Emil Preetorius of 1949 that 'there is a lot of Hitler in Wagner'.

8. For instance: Robert W. Gutman, *Richard Wagner: The Man, His Mind, and His Music* (London, 1968); Hartmut Zelinsky, ' "Die Feuerkur" des Richard Wagner oder die "neue Religion" der "Erlösung" durch "Vernichtung" ', in *Richard Wagner: Wie antisemitisch darf ein Künstler sein?* (Munich, 1978); Barry Millington, *Wag-ner* (London, 1984); Paul Lawrence Rose, *Wagner: Race and Revolution* (London, 1992); Marc A. Weiner, *Richard Wagner and the Anti-Semitic Imagination* (Lincoln, Nebr., and London, 1995). The idea goes back at least to Theodor Adorno, *Versuch über Wagner*, written in 1937–8, first published as a whole in 1952; English transla-tion by Rodney Livingstone, *In Search of Wagner* (London, 1981).

9. Gutman, *Richard Wagner*, pp. xiv, xviii. It is ironical that Gutman drops a condescending sneer towards Wagner's early biographers for their 'Victorian de-light in bringing ethical standards to bear on artistic affairs'.

10. Wagner did very much like the *Parsifal* that he got in 1882, apart from a problem with the moving scenery. See *Wagner on Music and Drama*, selected by Albert Goldman and Evert Sprinchorn from translations by H. Ashton Ellis (Lon-don, 1970), pp. 369–76. It would certainly look very strange now.

11. It is perhaps worth saying that I do not think that this criticism applies to Patrice Chéreau's 1976 Bayreuth production of the *Ring*, which is widely known

on video (issued by Philips). Some of its inventions are gratuitous, but for the most part it embodies extremely sensitive responses to the drama.

12. As Adorno pointed out (*In Search of Wagner*, p. 28), the idea that Wagner was a 'dilettante' goes back to Nietzsche's essay 'Richard Wagner in Bayreuth', written at the time of the first festival in 1876.

13. In the essay 'Über die Benennung "Musikdrama"' (1872).

14. *Nietzsche contra Wagner* (Leipzig, 1889), 'Wo ich Einwände mache'.

15. In Andrew Porter's translation, 'Goodness and truth dwell but in the waters.' See Richard Wagner, *The Ring of the Nibelung* (London, 1977).

16. Trans. Walter D. Morris (New York, 1983).

17. The presence of this among other cultural legacies in Nazi discourse, and above all in Hitler's own speeches, is the subject of J. P. Stern's fascinating book *Hitler: The Führer and the People* (London, 1975).

18. See Lucy Beckett, *Richard Wagner: 'Parsifal'* (Cambridge, 1981), pp. 52–3.

71

Why Philosophy Needs History

'Lack of a historical sense is the hereditary defect of philosophers . . . So what is needed from now on is *historical philosophising*, and with it the virtue of modesty.' Nietzsche wrote this in 1878, but it still very much needs to be said today. Indeed, a lot of philosophy is more blankly non-historical now than it has ever been. In the so-called analytic tradition in particular this takes the form of trying to make philosophy sound like an extension of science. Most scientists, though they may find the history of science interesting, do not think that it is of much use for their science, which they reasonably see as a progressive activity that has lost its past errors and incorporated its past discoveries into textbooks and current theory. The American philosopher who stuck on his office door the notice 'Just say NO to the history of philosophy' was probably riding on the idea that the same could be said of philosophy.

The fact that philosophy is often neglectful of its own history is not, however, the most important point. Many philosophers do have some respect for the history of philosophy: what matters more is their neglect of another history—the history of the concepts which philosophy is trying to understand. The starting point of philosophy is that we do not understand ourselves well enough. We do not understand ourselves well enough ethically (how or why we should be concerned, positively or negatively, with some human dispositions and practices rather than others); we do not fully understand our political ideals; and we do not understand how we come to have ideas and experiences, and seem moreover to know quite a lot about the world. Philosophy's methods of helping us to understand ourselves involve reflecting on the concepts we use, the modes in which we think about these various things; and sometimes it proposes better ways of doing this. So much is (relatively) uncontentious.

In any area of philosophy, the concern that gets reflection going, the failure to understand ourselves, must start from where we are. Who 'we' are, who else is part of 'us', may very well be disputed, above all in ethical and political cases. But reflection must start with us in the narrowest sense—the people who are asking the question and the people to whom we are talking—and it starts from now. The concepts that give rise to the question are ours. But there is a story behind those concepts: a history of how people have come to think like this. In the case of some ideas, such as political equality or democratic legitimacy, or the virtues of sincerity and honesty, the history will be dense and distinctive of our own culture, as contrasted with the cultures of past times and also, perhaps, with those of other existing societies. So much, again, is uncontentious. The standard assumption, however, is that a philosophical inquiry does not need to bother much with that history: the distinctive business of philosophers is reflection, and reflection, roughly speaking, will see them through. The basic point of Nietzsche's remark is that, in ethical and political cases at least, that assumption is wrong.

It is not wrong in every case. A scientific concept—'atom', for instance—can certainly be said to have a history, but typically (for much the same reason that the history of science is not part of science) its history makes little contribution to what may puzzle us about that concept now. Another way of putting it might be to say that the modern idea of an atom, understood in terms of quantum mechanics, is not the same as the one that entered human understanding under (very roughly) that name in the fifth century BC, though it is recognisably a descendant of it. But this is a case where it does not matter much (for our understanding of either the concepts or the history) whether the same or a different concept is employed by different societies or cultures: it is never going to be a highly determinate matter and there are many instances, of which 'atom' is one, where it would be arrant scholasticism to go on about it. There are, however, some very important occasions when we need to say *both* that there is significant historical variation between an idea or concept as used by two different groups, *and* that these are in some sense variant forms of the same concept. We need to say this particularly with value concepts such as freedom and justice, where there can be significant conflicts between interpretations of the value at different times or between different groups: between freedom as a disciplined life within an independent republic, for instance, and freedom on Eighth Avenue. Trying to understand the problems that we have with the idea of freedom, we need to describe and understand these differences, and we need to say that in some sense they represent different interpretations of the same thing: simply giving different names to these conflicting values would significantly miss the point of the conflict.

In such cases, it is helpful to think in terms of a common core shared by the conflicting values, which is developed or expressed by them in different ways. It is this kind of structure, of central core and historical variation, that I try to explain in *Truth and Truthfulness*[1] in the case of what I call the 'virtues of truth': basically, 'accuracy', the qualities involved in getting one's beliefs right, and 'sincerity', which is involved in honestly expressing them to other people. We have various problems with such notions in our culture now. Why are we concerned with the truth? No doubt, in part, because having true beliefs is useful. But having false beliefs is also useful: from the point of view of usefulness, the value of truth, if positive, will be so only on balance. But most of us, at least some of the time, recognise a value of truth which is not just that—for instance, when we recognise that self-deceit is in itself not the best of states.

Again, our ideas of truthfulness are under a great deal of strain at present. On the one hand, we tend to be pervasively suspicious, anxious not to be fooled, eager to see through appearances to the real motives and structures that underlie them. On the other hand, there is an equally powerful suspicion about truth itself—whether there is such a thing (really), and, if there is, whether it can be other than relative or subjective or something of that sort. (Some, such as Richard Rorty, say that 'truth' is not really the object of our inquiries or our concerns at all: what we should aim at is rather something like solidarity.) The first of these impulses of course fuels the second: the demand for honesty and truthfulness turns against truth itself. But the impulses are certainly in conflict. If you do not believe in the existence or significance of truth, what is the passion for truthfulness a passion for? In pursuing truthfulness, what are you being true to? That second question arises, too, in relation to authenticity, itself a variant of truthfulness, and a characteristic modern ideal. If one has an idea of some way of life, or set of ambitions, or allegiance that will be true to or express one's real self, what reality must it answer to, and how?

These questions arise from our present ideas of such qualities or ideals as honesty, truthfulness, sincerity and realism. They are appropriate to philosophy, in that they involve a recognition that we do not adequately understand ourselves. It is obvious that our ways of conceiving these qualities have not been everybody's, and that there is a historical story to be told about the way they came to be ours. Can we understand these concepts and so face the problems that they generate for us without understanding something of that story? How is it, for example, that we have a special ideal of personal authenticity? I think that philosophy can get a real hold on its task only with the help of history; or, rather, as Nietzsche put it, philosophising in such a case must itself be historical.

Philosophy can start on the task without history. Mere reflection on the conditions and demands of communication between human beings can tell us something at the most basic level about the 'virtues of truth'. Every society involves a division of labour in finding things out, if only to the minimal extent that some people observe things at one place or time, and others at another, and they need to inform one another. Merely reflecting on this, one can see that there need to be, in some form, qualities of accuracy and sincerity; people need to be reliable observers, and other people need to be able to trust what they say. These basic functional needs, and some of their consequences, can be laid out in a stripped-down and explicitly fictional account of an elementary society which, in the traditional phrase from political philosophy, I call the 'State of Nature'. But the State of Nature story itself already implies that there must be a further, real and historically dense story to be told. No society could work simply on the basis that its members saw that telling the truth a lot of the time was useful. Individuals and family groups have many reasons for not telling the truth to others (the basis of Voltaire's remark about men having language in order to conceal their thoughts). So, institutions of trust, which every society needs in some form, demand that there should be some dispositions to think that telling the truth (to the right people, on the right occasions) is in itself a good thing. What form those dispositions will take in different societies at different times is a matter of real history. In this sense, real history *fills in* the merely schematic picture offered by the State of Nature story. If you stop at the schematic picture, you may be left with the idea that truthfulness is a merely functional quality, and then be puzzled by the fact that it manifestly is not. Perhaps you will move to the general idea that it is a functional quality that needs to be understood as not merely functional. Philosophy without history will not get you much further than that: you will have little insight into how this might be possible, and none into the various conflicts that surround the virtue of truthfulness—is there, for instance, something specially bad about lying as distinct from other forms of misleading speech? More insight will come from seeing something of how we came to be where we are.

Moreover, real history does more than fill in the schematic story. In the dimension of accuracy, cultural developments can *raise the demands* of what it is to tell particular kinds of truth. The invention of writing made it unavoidable for people to distinguish among stories about the remoter past those that purported to be true (even if it was not known whether they were true), and those that were myths or legends. With that distinction, there came a new notion of historical truth and indeed a new, determinate, concept of historical time. Philosophical analysis without history encourages us to think that these concepts, so central to our thought, must always have existed, and that to the extent that members of oral cultures did not recognise the distinctions, they were in a muddle. They were not. The invention of historical time was an intellectual advance, but it did not consist in refuting error: like many other inventions, it enabled people to do things they could not conceive of doing before it happened. Together with that, we must hold on to the point that it was indeed an advance — as we naturally say, a discovery. A few modern critics, in deconstructive or relativist spirit, have tried to undo this advance, claiming that the whole idea of sequential time in history is a Western hegemonic imposition. Unsurprisingly they have failed, both to undo the advance and to make sense of their own undertaking. As the historian Richard J. Evans has pointed out, the critic who wrote that 'historical time is a thing of the past' needs to consider her position.

There are other dimensions in which real history has gone even further beyond the abstract structural necessities of the State of Nature story. Values of sincerity and accuracy — for example, the demand for truth for its own sake — have taken on a cultural life of their own, and have issued in such self-conscious ideals as intellectual honesty. Like personal authenticity, which emerged as an ideal towards, very roughly, the end of the 18th century, it was the product of a complex history which involved such vast contingencies as Christianity. None of this could be foreseen on the basis of the structural demands of human communication, which is what philosophy in the narrowest sense might work out, but it has formed our world and our problems, and must be taken into account by our philosophy. Without an understanding of history, the connections of some of these values with truthfulness may be overlooked altogether, and our actual concept of truthfulness will seem at best an arbitrary assemblage of ideas.

A method that combines the representation of universal requirements through the fiction of a State of Nature with an account of real historical development, I call 'genealogy'. It is Nietzsche's term, and an inquiry of this kind is supposed to meet some of the demands that Nietzsche associated with it. Where the genealogy of truthfulness is concerned, it was Nietzsche himself who first clearly identified the tensions in our culture which the inquiry aims to confront. However, there is another implication of 'genealogy' in Nietzsche's own use of the term, as also, for the most part, in Foucault's: that it is disobliging, uncovers shameful origins, and shows the phenomenon that is explained in this way in a bad light. This is not necessarily entailed in the method. It is so in some cases, including Nietzsche's own prime example, which is morality in a narrow, pure and law-driven sense, but it does not have to be. There can be a 'vindicatory' genealogy, such as Hume gave of justice. One may not accept Hume's account of the 'origin' of justice, but if one does, it need not make one feel less respect for justice: indeed, the account may make one feel more respect for it, if one comes to see it for the first time as intelligibly related to human needs and sentiments rather than as a moral or metaphysical revelation. I think one can give a vindicatory genealogy in this sense of the virtues of truth in some of the forms that concern us now.

Some philosophers deny that any historical story could vindicate (or fail to vindicate) our values. They see any such idea as an instance of the 'genetic fallacy': it is reasons or justifications that count, not origins. But this overlooks the possibility that the value in question may understand itself and present itself and claim authority for itself in terms which the genealogical story can undermine. The 'morality' that Nietzsche's genealogy damaged claimed to be the expression of a spirit that was higher, purer and more closely associated with reason, as well as transcending negative passions such as resentment, and if Nietzsche's account of it, in its functional and its historical aspects, were true, it would emerge as self-deceived in that respect. Similarly, when it is argued that the values of contemporary liberalism cannot possibly be criticised in terms of their history, this will be so only to the extent that those values can be separated from the claim—one which is often made for them—that they have emerged from the spread of reason and represent a cognitive achievement. There is a real question here: if liberal values represent the true moral order of the world, why should they have revealed themselves only in certain places and only in the past three centuries or so? A similar question can of course be asked about physical theories or molecular biology, but in those cases it gets an answer. Does the history of liberalism share enough with those cases for the claims which are made for it to be true? That is a question of historical interpretation. To the extent that the question gets a negative answer, there is no vindicatory genealogy of liberalism *in that form*. But if it is stripped of its false self-understanding, important parts of what remains may indeed have a vindicatory genealogy, in the sense that we can understand it and at the same time respect it, support it and live within it. We can also urge it against alternative creeds whose own self-understandings (as divine revelations, for instance) are themselves not going to survive a genealogical inquiry.

In *Truth and Truthfulness*, my own genealogical account of the virtues of truth, I systematically argue against 'deniers', as I call them: those who claim that the concept of truth does nothing for us in our inquiries or in our conceptions of freedom and other values, and who hold, consequently, that either truthfulness should not be one of our values, or that it has nothing to do with truth. These sceptics, who have been very influential in the humanities, have a point, or several different points, about the status of history, and of psychological and narrative understandings; and those philosophers and others who have, rightly, argued against the deniers have too often supposed that if one gets rid of their muddles about truth and language, it will be business as usual, a business that sometimes seems to be identified with a stupid positivism, a faith in the power of the unaided truth to make sense of things. Truthfulness is a vital virtue, and it is essentially connected with the truth, but it has many more demanding tasks than simply assembling truths.

Some think that what is needed to supplement abstract philosophical reflection and to show us why we have the ideas we have is not history but science. At the moment there is a clamorous strain of opinion to the effect that questions such as these can be answered by evolutionary psychology. Genealogy itself is not an application of evolutionary theory; the State of Nature is not intended to represent some early hominid environment, and evolutionary theory could not offer what genealogy claims to offer. The State of Nature sets out in a professedly abstract form certain functional demands on human communication, which can be arrived at by reflection. Nobody knows very much at present about early hominid environments, and theories about their selective effects on human cognition cannot be formed without taking these and other such functional requirements for granted. There is nothing wrong with this, and evolutionary theorists will have to go on doing it even if they come to know more than they do about early hominid development. The actual story about early communicative practices will then be another piece of the genealogy, a lot less dense and doubtless a lot more speculative than the one based on more recent developments.

Some evolutionary theorists think that subsequent cultural developments are themselves to be explained in terms of natural selection. They do not mean that cultural changes express genetic mutations: rather, that cultural change is strongly influenced by specific psychological characteristics selected for in *Homo sapiens* in those early environments. It is a platitude that human beings have whatever psychological peculiarities emerged during their evolution; among these peculiarities must be those that underlie the overwhelmingly significant and successful innovation represented by this species: the capacity to live under culture and so to benefit from a vast elaboration of non-genetic learning. All this is true, but there is nothing in it to indicate how far differences between cultures, or their changes over time, are themselves determined by these peculiarities. Manifestly, not all the way: plausibly, not very far. Evolutionary science may eventually show why human beings everywhere make and enjoy music, but it is not going to explain Beethoven's op. III. The basic point is that only interpretation of the historical (and anthropological) record could answer such questions, and show how far traits identified by evolutionary science will explain differences in culture. That interpretation cannot be done by evolutionary science itself.

Genealogy applied to the virtues of truth has reason to be critical of the 'deniers', but, here and more generally, it has even more reason to be opposed to the more reductive ambitions of evolutionary psychology. Deconstructionist deniers may not always read books very well, but at least they may encourage people to read books, and to understand the history from which those books came. Science that takes on reductive ambitions does not encourage anyone to understand history at all. Like the more historically impoverished styles of philosophy, and, still more, in alliance with them, it stands in the way of our understanding who we are, what our concepts are, what we are up to, since there is no way of our understanding these things without a hold on our history.

Notes

1. *Truth and Truthfulness: An Essay in Genealogy* was the last book Bernard Williams wrote. It was published by Princeton University Press in 2002.

ACKNOWLEDGMENTS

I would like to thank Al Bertrand and his colleagues at the Princeton University Press for initiating this project and for all their support; Hannah Paul and Lauren Lepow for working so hard to bring the material together for publication; and Tom Strawson for his editorial assistance.

I am very grateful to Michael Wood, who took on the task of writing the foreword with characteristic generosity and flair.

My thanks also to Barry Stroud and Jonathan Williams, who commented on many more candidates for inclusion than it would have been wise to republish, and greatly helped to shape the final content; and to Geoffrey Hawthorn, John Gray, Thomas Nagel, Adrian Moore, Richard Moran, Samuel Scheffler, and Robert Pippin for their advice and encouragement.

Bernard died exactly ten years ago. I was touched by the enthusiasm of friends and readers for looking back to these reviews which span over forty years. I hope people will continue to enjoy his distinctive voice.

Patricia Williams
June 2013

ACKNOWLEDGMENTS TO COPYRIGHT HOLDERS

The Princeton University Press would like to acknowledge the publishers who have kindly given their permission to reprint material in this book.

The Cambridge University Press for articles 2 and 47; the *London Review of Books* for articles 31, 32, 34, 35, 36, 37, 41, 44, 46, 49, 52, 53, 56, 58, 62, 63, 64, 65, 66, 68, and 71; John Wiley & Sons for article 33; the *New Scientist* for article 28; the *New Statesman* for article 11; the *New York Times Book Review* for articles 51 and 61; the *New York Review of Books* for articles 13, 20, 26, 27, 39, 42, 48, 55, 57, 59, 67, 69, and 70; the *Observer* for articles 16, 19, 22, 43, and 45; the *Spectator* for articles 1, 5, 6, 9, and 18; the *Sunday Times* for article 38; the *Times Educational Supplement* (*TES*) for article 54; and the *Times Literary Supplement* for articles 21, 23, 24, 40, 50, and 60.

INDEX

abortion, 115, 116, 146–52, 312; consequences of, 150–51; and foetal research, 117; and murder, 146–48, 149–50; and Rawls, 330; and religion, 146; and rights, 148–49, 150; and rights of women vs. doctors, 146; and Schelling, 233; and slippery slope, 148; and status of foetus, 147–48, 149, 150; voluntary, 117, 118; as widely accepted, 117
academia, 31–32, 33, 244. *See also* education; universities
academic detachment, 176
Achilles (Homer), 398
action, 172, 203, 207; free and responsible, 14; and Hampshire, 11, 12–17, 15; and philosophy, 364; and religion, 19, 21
Adorno, Theodor, 359, 404n8, 405n12
Aeschylus, 180
aesthetics, 9–10, 11, 52, 143, 179, 180, 381
affirmative action, 312
Agrippa von Nettesheim, Heinrich Cornelius, 352
Alexander the Great, 339
Alfonsín, Raúl Ricardo, 248
algorithms, 90
alienation, 105, 185, 186, 303
Allen, Woody, 170, 240
altruistic behaviour, 141
ambiguity, 92–93, 95
American Committee for Cultural Freedom, 253–54
American Nazi Party, 347
analogue devices, 91
anarchism, 108, 109, 110, 111
animals, 16–17, 96–97, 141, 312, 313
anthropology, 238, 287, 359
anti-Semitism, 389, 391, 392, 394
apartheid, 139
Apollonian, the, 179, 180, 181
Apostles, 216
Aquinas, Thomas, 284, 288, 316
Arab writers, 284
ARA General Belgrano, 249–51

Argentina, 246–51
Aristotle, 232; and Descartes, 31; *Ethics*, 54; explanations of, 188; and Galileo, 31; and Hampshire, 14; and Hegel, 166; and Hume, 285; and MacIntyre, 185, 186, 284, 285, 310, 316; and Nozick, 188; and Nussbaum, 339, 340; *Poetics*, 181; and Rorty, 208; style in, 368–69; and Willey, 54, 55
art, 9–10; and Dworkin, 257; German, 390, 400; and Hampshire, 10, 14; history of, 49, 50, 302; and Johnson, 292–93; Murdoch on, 142–43, 144, 145; and Nietzsche, 180, 182–83; politics of, 400; and pornography, 351; religious imagery in, 145; and Rorty, 298; and rubbish, 158; and Skinner, 89; and Taylor, 305, 307; and Wagner, 390, 400–401
Artificial Intelligence (AI), 91–92, 94, 95, 276, 279
artificial organism, 100
artificial reason, 90–100
ataraxia, 340, 342
Athens, 3, 238–39
Augustine, 284, 302
Auschwitz, 300
Austin, J. L., 46, 76; *Philosophical Papers*, 42, 43, 44; *Sense and Sensibilia*, 40–45
authenticity, 407, 408, 409
authoritarianism, 300
Ayer, A. J., 42; *Bertrand Russell*, 127, 130; "Can there be a Private Language?", 47; *The Concept of a Person*, 45–47; *The Foundations of Empirical Knowledge*, 41; *Language, Truth, and Logic*, 9, 45, 71; *Russell and Moore: The Analytical Heritage*, 75–77
Ayers, M. R., 104

Bach, Johann Sebastian, 388
Bacon, Francis, 33–34, 42, 43
Bakke case. See *University of California v. Bakke*